A·N·N·U·A·L E·D·I·T·I·O·N·S

Juvenile Delinquency and Justice

06/07

Second Edition

EDITOR

David R. Struckhoff, Ph.D.

Loyola University, Chicago

David R. Struckhoff is the Executive Director of the Justice Research Institute—a not-for-profit criminal justice consulting and publishing consortium and an associate professor at Loyola University, Chicago. His early field experience has involved relatively confidential evaluation, report preparation, and consulting for government and private agencies. David received his doctorate in sociology from Southern Illinois University where he was a Justice Department Research Fellow at the Center for the Study of Crime, Delinquency, and Corrections.

He regularly speaks to groups, presents research and evaluation, has written the definitive book on *The American Sheriff*, sits on public and private boards, is identified as a role model, and has been asked by his students to be the University Moderator of the International Golden Key Honor Society.

Contemporary Learning Series

2460 Kerper Blvd., Dubuque, IA 52001

Visit us on the Internet
http://www.mhcls.com

NOV 0 5 2007

Credits

1. **Nature and Extent of Delinquency**
   Unit photo—© Getty Images/Don Tremain
2. **Theoretical Views**
   Unit photo—© Getty Images/PhotoLink
3. **The Criminal Justice System and Juveniles**
   Unit photo—© Photograph courtesy of Jill Peter
4. **Future Prospects**
   Unit photo—© Digital Vision

Copyright

Cataloging in Publication Data
Main entry under title: Annual Editions: Juvenile Delinquency and Justice. 2006/2007.
1. Juvenile delinquency. 2. Juvenile corrections. I. Struckhoff, David, *comp.* II. Title: Juvenile Delinquency and Justice.
ISBN 0–07–351597-3   364.36   ISSN 1525-3619

© 2006 by McGraw-Hill Contemporary Learning Series, Dubuque, IA 52001, A Division of The McGraw-Hill Companies.

Second Edition

Cover image © S. Meltzer/PhotoLink/Getty Images Mel Curtis/Getty Images
Printed in the United States of America   1234567890QPDQPD98765   Printed on Recycled Paper

Editors/Advisory Board

Members of the Advisory Board are instrumental in the final selection of articles for each edition of ANNUAL EDITIONS. Their review of articles for content, level, currentness, and appropriateness provides critical direction to the editor and staff. We think that you will find their careful consideration well reflected in this volume.

Preface

In publishing ANNUAL EDITIONS we recognize the enormous role played by the magazines, newspapers, and journals of the public press in providing current, first-rate educational information in a broad spectrum of interest areas. Many of these articles are appropriate for students, researchers, and professionals seeking accurate, current material to help bridge the gap between principles and theories and the real world. These articles, however, become more useful for study when those of lasting value are carefully collected, organized, indexed, and reproduced in a low-cost format, which provides easy and permanent access when the material is needed. That is the role played by ANNUAL EDITIONS.

One of the problems for students of behavior in our fast-paced society is the compression of information into "sound bites." We sacrifice depth of analysis for quick impressions. Unfortunately, sound bites do not contribute to understanding the complexity of human issues, or almost any issue for that matter. We are beset by the scourge of oversimplification. This series of *Annual Editions: Juvenile Delinquency and Justice* seeks to offer both cutting edge information and some of the classic thinking on the subject. These classics are often forgotten—leading us to repeat the omissions of the past, to reinvent the wheel, and to suffer from lack of necessary perspective.

Annual Editions: Juvenile Delinquency and Justice 06/07 reflects the concerns of educators and the general public with the issues of juvenile delinquency today. It is intended to stimulate discussion and sharpen critical reading ability. We ask you, our students, to look closely at who is writing the texts and the articles that you are reading and to "consider the source." This gives you an edge in understanding the content. It is our conviction that poor theory and knowledge produce poor policy. We encourage the law enforcement efforts at sanitizing the community so that socializers—parents, teachers, clergy, and community activists—can work with children in a safe and secure place that allows children to grow and blossom into fulfilled human beings.

This edition shows a modest change in structure. The readings are presented on the same general outline used by our noted colleagues Robert Regoli and John Hewitt in *Delinquency in Society*. Our reader this year also follows most other standard text outlines more closely. I am deeply indebted to the McGraw-Hill Contemporary Learning Series team members for their professionalism and encouragement in this project. Our advisory board editors are sterling and have opened our eyes to new viewpoints and issues. This group holds a considerable and wonderfully diverse store of knowledge and experience in this field that is evident in the critiques they make and the suggestions for new articles that they have provided.

Special mention must be made of the staff at Justice Research, my wife Patricia and supportive colleagues at various schools, offices and institutions, and the internet network (you know who you all are). Finally, special thanks to Tyler and Christopher Rinchiuso and Zachary Struckhoff for giving cause to hope for the future.

Over its history, the *Annual Editions* series has become a forum as well as a source of information. You help shape the editions by your knowledge and views of the current events that influence our selections. We value and encourage your feedback and opinions. Our inclusion of relevant Web sites adds to the utility and depth of this edition's coverage. On the last pages is a prepaid article rating form. Please complete it and return it to us. Your opinions and suggestions are very important to us.

David R. Struckhoff
Editor

Contents

UNIT 1
Nature and Extent of Delinquency

The concepts in bold italics are developed in the article. For further expansion, please refer to the Topic Guide and the Index.

UNIT 2
Theoretical Views

The concepts in bold italics are developed in the article. For further expansion, please refer to the Topic Guide and the Index.

The concepts in bold italics are developed in the article. For further expansion, please refer to the Topic Guide and the Index.

UNIT 3
The Criminal Justice System and Juveniles

The concepts in bold italics are developed in the article. For further expansion, please refer to the Topic Guide and the Index.

The concepts in bold italics are developed in the article. For further expansion, please refer to the Topic Guide and the Index.

UNIT 4
Future Prospects

The concepts in bold italics are developed in the article. For further expansion, please refer to the Topic Guide and the Index.

Part B.   Ideas for the Future

The concepts in bold italics are developed in the article. For further expansion, please refer to the Topic Guide and the Index.

Topic Guide

This topic guide suggests how the selections in this book relate to the subjects covered in your course. You may want to use the topics listed on these pages to search the Web more easily.

On the following pages a number of Web sites have been gathered specifically for this book. They are arranged to reflect the units of this *Annual Edition*. You can link to these sites by going to the student online support site at *http://www.mhcls.com/online/*.

ALL THE ARTICLES THAT RELATE TO EACH TOPIC ARE LISTED BELOW THE BOLD-FACED TERM.

Internet References

The following internet sites have been carefully researched and selected to support the articles found in this reader. The easiest way to access these selected sites is to go to our student online support site at *http://www.mhcls.com/online/*.

AE: Juvenile Delinquency and Justice 06/07

The following sites were available at the time of publication. Visit our Web site—we update our student online support site regularly to reflect any changes.

General Sources

Center on Juvenile and Criminal Justice
http://www.cjcj.org

The Center provides technical assistance to state and local governments interested in alternatives to incarceration.

Census Bureau (U.S.)
http://www.census.gov/population/www/socdemo/children.html

Census information on children is available on this U.S. Census site.

Children's Advocacy Institute
http://www.acf.dhhs.gov/programs/cb

This site's goal is to address issues affecting children's well-being, health, and safety.

Harvard Family Research Project (HFRP)
http://www.gse.harvard.edu/~hfrp

The Harvard Family Research Project (HFRP) strives to increase the effectiveness of public and private organizations and communities as they promote child development, student achievement, healthy family functioning, and community development.

Juvenile Justice Evaluation Center Online
http://www.jrsa.org/jjec/

This is a tool designed to assist juvenile justice practitioners, policymakers, and state agency administrators with the assessment and evaluation of programs and initiatives. JJEC Online is composed of several sections, including JJEC Information, State Information, Juvenile Justice Evaluation Program Areas, and Evaluation Resources.

Juvenile Justice Sites
http://talkjustice.com/files/page15.htm

Juvenile Justice links include Youth Crime, School Crime, Delinquency Prevention Programs, Juvenile Justice Resources, Juvenile Court, and Correctional and Treatment Programs for Children.

UNIT 1: Nature and Extent of Delinquency

Birth and the Origins of Violence
http://www.birthpsychology.com/violence/index.html

Among the perspectives on violence at this Web site are papers on the prenatal/perinatal roots of personal and social violence.

Brain Development and Learning
http://www.tyc.state.tx.us/prevention/braindev.htm

Judy Briscoe contends that a child's first 3 years are critical to brain development, and that the influence of early environment on brain development is long lasting.

Federal Integracy Forum on Child and Family Statistics
http://www.childstats.gov

This web site offers easy access to federal and state statistics and reports on children and their families, including: population and family characteristics, economic security, health, behavior and social environment, and education. The Forum fosters coordination and collaboration in the collection and reporting of Federal statistics on children and families.

OJJDP: Office of Juvenile Justice and Delinquency Prevention
http://www.ojjdp.ncjrs.org

Click on Facts & Figures for the latest data on juvenile justice, delinquency prevention, and violence and victimization.

UNIT 2: Theoretical Views

America's Children: Key National Indicators of Child Well-Being 1998
http://www.childstats.gov/ac1999/ac99.asp

This in-depth annual report includes sections on Child Poverty, Adolescent Mortality, Alcohol Use and Illicit Drug Use, and Youth Victims and Perpetrators of Crime.

Center for Substance Abuse Research (CESAR)
http://www.cesar.umd.edu/

This CESAR site provides information regarding drugs, AIDS, and prevention and treatment of substance abuse as well as criminal justice data.

Partnerships against Violence Network
http://www.pavnet.org

A virtual library of information about violence and youth-at-risk is available on this PAVNET site. It includes data from seven federal agencies.

Prevention Pathways
http://www.preventionpathways.samhsa.gov

Prevention Pathways, another new development in the web, is our gateway to a large amount of data and direction. It deals with prevention programs, program evaluation, evaluation technical assistance, online courses and a wealth of other prevention resources.

UNIT 3: The Criminal Justice System and Juveniles

Community Policing Consortium
http://www.communitypolicing.org

This is the Web site of the Community Policing Consortium, a partnership of five of the leading police organizations in the United States, each committed to advancing policing philosophy through development of research and training.

Delinquents or Criminals: Policing Options
http://www.urban.org/crime/delinq.html

Published on the Web by the nonpartisan Urban Institute, this paper, by Jeffrey Butts and Adele Harrell, covers the workings of America's juvenile courts and describes the current battle.

Juvenile Delinquents in the Federal Criminal System

http://www.ojp.usdoj.gov/bjs

This special report is printed in full on the Internet. It discusses the nature of the 468 juvenile delinquents who were referred to federal prosecutors for investigation in 1995.

Juvenile Female Offenders

http://www.ojjdp.ncjrs.org/pubs/gender/

The *Juvenile Female Offenders: A Status of the States Report, 1998* contains a history of female offenders, a profile of current adolescent female offenders, treatment options, and national efforts to address the problems.

Juvenile Violence and Gun Markets in Boston

http://www.ncjrs.org/txtfiles/fs000160.txt

This summary of a research presentation explains the importance of the availability of guns to juvenile violence.

National Youth Court Center

http://www.youthcourt.net

The National Youth Court Center (NYCC) at the American Probation and Parole Association (APPA) serves as a central point of contact for youth court programs across the nation. It serves as an information clearinghouse, provide training and technical assistance, and develops resource materials on how to develop and enhance youth court programs in the United States.

Perspectives on Crime and Justice: 1997–1998

http://www.ncjrs.org/txtfiles/172851.txt

Crime patterns and future trends, drug abuse, gun violence, intermediate sanctions, and law enforcement issues, many related to juveniles, are presented in this lecture series.

Police-Corrections Partnerships

http://www.ncjrs.org/txtfiles1/175047.txt

Issues and practices discussed in this series include community policing, police patrol, crime patterns, and future trends.

UNIT 4: Future Prospects

An Examination of Three Model Interventions and Intensive Aftercare Initiatives

http://www.ncjrs.org/txtfiles/effectiv.txt

Included in this teleconference material from the OJJDP program is a description of how the Florida Environmental Institute operates, the Capital Offender Program, the Multi-Systemic Treatment Approach, and the Importance of Intensive Aftercare.

Children's Defense Fund

http://www.childrensdefense.org

Numerous articles, action alerts, and publications on children's issues are provided here.

Combatting Violence and Delinquency: The National Juvenile Justice Action Plan

http://www.ncjrs.org/txtfiles/jjplanfr.txt

The 128-page plan available here presents effective and innovative strategies designed to reduce violence and victimization.

Girl Power!

http://www.health.org/gpower/

This is a Department of Health and Human Services' site to help encourage and empower 9- to 14-year-old girls to make the most of their lives.

Implementing the Balanced and Restorative Justice Model

http://www.ojjdp.ncjrs.org/pubs/implementing/contents.html

OJJDP's site contains a complete description of the philosophy and workings of the Balanced and Restorative Justice Project.

A Legislator's Guide to Comprehensive Juvenile Justice

http://www.ncsl.org/programs/cyf/jjguide.htm

Offered by the National Conference of State Legislatures, this report is a thorough discussion of the reinvention of juvenile justice at the state level.

Long-Term Effects of Early Childhood Programs on Social Outcomes and Delinquency

http://www.futureofchildren.org/information2826/information_show.htm?doc_id=77676

Hirokazu Yoshikawa's report focuses on programs that have demonstrated long-term effects on antisocial behavior or delinquency. These programs have in common a combination of intensive family support and early education services.

No Child Left Behind

http://www.nochildleftbehind.gov

Three days after taking office in January 2001 as the 43rd President of the United States, George W. Bush announced No Child Left Behind, his framework for bipartisan education reform that he described as "the cornerstone of my Administration." The NCLB Act, which reauthorizes the ESEA (Elementary and Secondary Education Act of 1965), incorporates the principles and strategies proposed by President Bush. These include increased accountability for States, school districts, and schools; greater choice for parents and students, particularly those attending low-performing schools; more flexibility for States and local educational agencies (LEAs) in the use of Federal education dollars; and a stronger emphasis on reading, especially for our youngest children.

What Works Clearinghouse

http://www.w-w-c.org

On an ongoing basis, the What Works Clearinghouse (WWC) collects, screens, and identifies studies of the effectiveness of educational interventions (programs, products, practices, and policies). We review the studies that have the strongest design, and report on the strengths and weaknesses of those studies against the WWC Evidence Standards so that you know what the best scientific evidence has to say. The WWC does not endorse any interventions nor does it conduct field studies. The WWC releases study, intervention, and topic reports. A study report rates individual studies and designs to give you a sense of how much you can rely on research findings for that individual study. An intervention report provides all findings that meet WWC Evidence Standards for a particular intervention.

UNIT 1
Nature and Extent of Delinquency

Unit Selections

1. **Too Young to Die**, Claudia Wallis
2. **Juvenile Population Characteristics**, Office of Juvenile Justice and Delinquency Prevention
3. **The Crackdown on Kids: The New Mood of Meanness toward Children—To Be Young Is to Be Suspect**, Annette Fuentes
4. **Juvenile Offenders: Should They Be Tried in Adult Courts?**, Michael P. Brown
5. **Juveniles as Victims**, Office of Juvenile Justice and Delinquency Prevention

Key Points to Consider

- What is delinquency? What is it in your state or nation?

- Why was "delinquency" created as a justice mechanism?

- Do you agree with the parameters on age of delinquency? Why or why not?

- What does the issue of public perception versus factual reality have to do with delinquency? How does it affect the treatment of youth in your community?

- How does the jurisdiction in which you are studying JD measure delinquency?

- Where are the sources of the official documents?

- Do the statistics gathered say too much about juveniles or too little? Are there things they miss?

- How valid and reliable are these statistics?

Student Website
www.mhcls.com/online

Internet References
Further information regarding these websites may be found in this book's preface or online.

Birth and the Origins of Violence
http://www.birthpsychology.com/violence/index.html

Brain Development and Learning
http://www.tyc.state.tx.us/prevention/braindev.htm

Federal Integracy Forum on Child and Family Statistics
http://www.childstats.gov

OJJDP: Office of Juvenile Justice and Delinquency Prevention
http://www.ojjdp.ncjrs.org

Juvenile delinquency is a construct. It didn't exist as a formal concept prior to the late 1800s. When they lamented—and they did—about the misconduct of the youngsters in their societies, the ancient Babylonians, Egyptians, Greeks, Romans, or the Chinese, may have had a term for it. But they didn't call it "juvenile delinquency" nor did they—as far as we know from hieroglyphics, records of the Oriental dynasties, and other sources—create much law about it. But since the coining of the term and the establishment of the first juvenile court in Cook County (Chicago), "juvenile delinquency" has certainly been evolving. Today, different states and nations use different criteria for defining delinquency—it is relative. Moreover, globalization and comparative criminology have opened many doors to broader concepts of juvenile misconduct and societal response. Given the bad years we've recently had in the United States with juvenile violence, including the shooting at Columbine High School in Littleton, Colorado on April 20, 1999 and this year in Red Lake, Minnesota—which came and went amazingly quickly (perhaps it was overshadowed by the Schaivo affair)—it is hard to get an accurate sense either of the extent or the nature of the contemporary problem.

In regard to extent or prevalence, is the fact that crime is decreasing and the vast majority of juveniles emerge generally unscathed from their teenage years. The percentage of youth we define as delinquent is modest. Yet worse than the misperceptions of the extent are the misperceptions of the resiliency of human nature. Many of us seem ready to give up on today's youth. In a recent *Chicago Tribune* editorial celebrating the 100th Anniversary of the Juvenile Court, Bernardine Dohrn of Northwestern University School of Law's Family and Justice Center noted that Babe Ruth, Robert Leroy (Satchel) Paige, and Ella Fitzgerald were all subjected to the juvenile court process. It worked for them; why will it not work today?

Samuel Walker has done us a great service by posing his "wedding cake" model of the crime and delinquency problem. At the bottom are the plethora, the masses, the hoard of "revolving door" crimes and misbehaviors—the drunks, the drunk drivers, the drug users, the disorderly, the petty thieves, the abusers, the general ne'er-do-wells who overpopulate the justice system. In the smaller, middle level are the serious criminals and delinquents that the system routinely deals with—muggers, killers, robbers, major thieves, bigger drug dealers and merchants, and the "dangerous" ones who worry us so much. But we don't see in the public view how well the system deals with them. We do see, and our attention is focused on, the celebrity cases—the statues and shining candles on the top of the cake that in reality are a small fraction of all the disorder. This year it is Martha Stewart, Michael Jackson, and Robert Blake among other media events, it was in the past (and again now) children killing classmates and O. J. Simpson; who knows what will capture the hearts of the media and the public tomorrow?

In this section we try to present a balanced view of the nature and extent of the problem. We deal with numbers, with history, with some of the more celebrated issues, but also with the sizable group of juveniles whose behavior has come to be so worrisome to so many of us. Our databases have been growing exponentially. Be sure to tap into the OJJDP data on the demographics of contemporary youth. This data is generally not "spun" however, many interpretations and competing interpretations of the same data can be made—some not. We hope that we as teachers, and our students who read this unit, can keep our perspective, which may help to bring some sanity to the discussions about delinquency.

Reference
Walker, Samuel, *Sense and Nonsense about Crime and Drugs: A Policy Guide*, Belmont, CA: Wadsworth, 1997.

Too Young to Die

The Supreme Court nixes the juvenile death penalty.
What that says about the Justices' thinking—and ours

Claudia Wallis

In his Norman, Okla., law office, attorney Steven Presson stores two unusual keepsakes. One is a leather pouch that holds the ashes of Sean Sellers, the only person executed for a crime committed as a 16-year-old since the death penalty was reinstated in the U.S. in 1976. Sellers—who murdered his mother, his stepfather and a store clerk—was dispatched by lethal injection in 1999, when he was 29. Presson's other memento is a plastic box containing the ashes of Scott Hain, who, it now seems fair to say, was the last juvenile offender to be executed in the U.S. Hain, sent to his death in 2003 at the age of 32, was 17 when he and a friend committed a grisly double murder.

Presson, who represented both boys, found it "very bittersweet" when the U.S. Supreme Court ruled last week that it was cruel and unusual to sentence anyone to death for crimes committed before the age of 18. "I'm happy for those on death row, but it came six years too late for Sean and two years too late for Scott," says Presson. "We've been arguing for decades that kids don't have the same moral culpability that adults have, and finally, finally, they listened."

It took 16 years for the high court to come around to Presson's point of view, by a narrow 5-to-4 vote. In 1989 the court ruled 5 to 4 the other way. Justice Antonin Scalia, who wrote the 1989 decision, argued that there was neither a "historical nor a modern societal consensus" forbidding capital punishment for 16- or 17-year-olds (though the court had found such a consensus for those under 16 a year earlier). Last week, however, Scalia was on the short side of the decision.

What changed? The views of Justice Anthony Kennedy, for one thing. While Kennedy voted with Scalia in 1989, he wrote a very different majority opinion this time around. Why did Kennedy change his mind? Legal tradition invites him to do so. Since 1958 the court has applied a flexible standard to interpreting the Eighth Amendment's ban on "cruel and unusual punishments." What we mean by the phrase, wrote then Chief Justice Earl Warren in *Trop v. Dulles*, depends on "the evolving standards of decency that mark the progress of a maturing society."

How do you know that society no longer believes in sentencing a 17-year-old killer to death? Kennedy's

argument mirrors his reasoning in a 2002 decision that outlawed death sentences for the mentally retarded. He notes that since 1989 five states have banned capital punishment for juveniles, making the practice illegal in 30 states, including the 12 with an outright ban on executions. Second, Kennedy cites scientific literature showing that, like the retarded, adolescents lack mature judgment and a full appreciation of the consequences of their actions. They are also more vulnerable than adults to peer pressure. Third, Kennedy points out that only seven other countries have executed juvenile offenders since 1990, and all seven have repudiated the practice: "The United States now stands alone in a world that has turned its face against the juvenile death penalty."

"This reference to international practices is a very big deal," says Cass Sunstein, a constitutional scholar at the University of Chicago Law School, and is part of a surprising new trend in Supreme Court thinking. Overseas legal practices were also cited by the court in the 2002 ruling on the mentally retarded and in a 2003 decision overturning a Texas law banning gay sex. For his part, Scalia blasted his brethren for suggesting that "American law should conform to the laws of the rest of the world" and pointed out that the U.S. has unique legal traditions.

In the 12 states where juvenile offenders have been languishing, death sentences will be lifted for 72 offenders. That brought dismay to many victims' families. Martin Soto-Fong was 17 in 1992 when he and two accomplices robbed the El Grande Market in Tucson, Ariz., for $300 and shot three workers. Richard Gee, who lost a brother and an uncle that day, is not happy to see the murderer exit death row. "We had him at the gates of hell," he says, "and he got kicked back."

OJJDP: Juvenile Population Characteristics

"Overview" quoted from the website:

More than 70 million Americans-about 1 in 4-are younger than 18, the age group commonly referred to as juveniles. This age group has increased consistently since the mid-1980s and is projected to continue increasing until at least 2015. However, different segments of the juvenile population will increase at different rates. As the at-risk population changes, the juvenile justice system will likewise change. This section provides basic statistics necessary to understand these population changes.

Changes in population, though, make up only part of the picture. Social changes caused by moving populations, changing economic conditions, and changing social climate (i.e., education, health care, etc.) will also have an impact on delinquency and the juvenile justice system. This section provides additional information on these and other issues to motivate and develop a more complete understanding of delinquency and the problems facing youth. Delinquency, risk behaviors, and desistance take place within a larger social context.

This section provides demographic data on the juvenile population overall, including age, race, and sex, at the national, state, and county levels. It describes important social indicators such as poverty, education, and quality of life. Much of the information comes from Census Bureau efforts. Other data sources include the Bureau of Labor Statistics, Bureau of Justice Statistics, and other federal statistical agencies.

Please see the website below for further information:
http://ojjdp.ncjrs.org/ojstatbb/population/overview.html

From *Office of Juvenile Justice and Delinquency Prevention.*

THE NEW MOOD OF MEANNESS TOWARD CHILDREN—
TO BE YOUNG IS TO BE SUSPECT.

The Crackdown on Kids

ANNETTE FUENTES

When Kipland Kinkel, Mitchell Johnson and Andrew Golden reportedly unloaded mini arsenals of guns at their classmates, they fulfilled the worst fears about young people that now dominate the nation's adult consciousness. Kinkel, 15, of Springfield, Oregon, allegedly is responsible for the deaths of two students as a result of an incident on May 21, as well as for the deaths of his parents. Johnson, 13, and Golden, 11, were charged in connection with the March 24 deaths of four students and a teacher in Jonesboro, Arkansas. All were instantly transformed from average American boys, perhaps a bit on the wild side, into evil incarnate. Forget that Mitchell sobbed next to his mother in court, or that Drew learned to sling a shotgun from Dad and Grandpa the way many boys learn to swing a bat. "Let 'em have it" was the sentiment, with catchy phrases like "adult crime, adult time."

After the Arkansas incident, Attorney General Janet Reno scoured federal laws for some way to prosecute Johnson and Golden so they could be locked up till age 21 if convicted, a stiffer sentence than the state could mete out. One *Washington Post* Op-Ed called for states to adopt a national uniform minimum age for juveniles to be tried as adults for violent crimes.

The three boys are believed to have committed terrible deeds, no question. But twenty years ago, a Greek chorus would have been clamoring to understand why they went bad. The events themselves would have been seen as aberrations. Redemption might have been mentioned, especially since these were not career delinquents. Instead, we have proposals like the one from Texas legislator Jim Pitts, who wants his state to use the death penalty on children as young as 11. And he's got plenty of support, because this is the era of crime and punishment and accountability for all constituencies without wealth or power to shield them. And the young are such a class of people.

In the past two decades, our collective attitude toward children and youth has undergone a profound change that's reflected in the educational and criminal justice sys-

tems as well as in our daily discourse. "Zero tolerance" is the mantra in public schools and juvenile courts, and what it really means is that to be young is to be suspect. Latino and black youth have borne the brunt of this growing criminalization of youth. But the trend has spilled over racial and ethnic boundaries—even class boundaries, to a degree. Youth, with all its innocence and vulnerability, is losing ground in a society that exploits both.

In fact, youth crime has not changed as dramatically as our perceptions of it. Data from the National Center for Juvenile Justice show that between 1987 and 1996, the number of juvenile arrests increased 35 percent. Juvenile violent-crime arrests were up 60 percent, but they represent a sliver of all juvenile arrests—about 5 percent of the 1996 total of 135,100. A 1997 study by the center found that "today's violent youth commits the same number of violent acts as his/her predecessor of 15 years ago." As to whether criminals are getting younger, a 1997 report from the Justice Department answers clearly: "Today's serious and violent juvenile offenders are not significantly younger than those of 10 or 15 years ago."

What's more, from 1994 to 1995 there was a 3 percent decline in juvenile arrests for violent crime, and from 1995 to 1996 there was a 6 percent decline. "I have people call me up and ask, 'Why is juvenile crime down?'" says Robert Shepherd Jr., a law professor at the University of Richmond in Virginia. "I say, 'Why was it up?' It could be just one of history's cycles. Over the thirty years I've been involved in juvenile justice issues, I've seen very little change in the incidence of violent crime by kids."

One thing that *has* changed is the prominence of guns and their role in violence. A 1997 Justice Department report looked at homicides by youths aged 13 and 14 with and without guns. In 1980 there were 74 murders committed with guns and 68 without by that age group. In 1995 gun-related murders totaled 178; there were 67 non-gun murders.

Violent crimes like those in Oregon and Arkansas are a rarity, but they've become the rationale for a crackdown on young people.

Exaggerated claims about juvenile crime would be a hard sell if people weren't ready to believe the worst about young people. A 1997 report from Public Agenda, a nonprofit policy group, called "Kids These Days: What Americans Really Think About the Next Generation," found that 58 percent of those surveyed think children and teens will make the world a worse place or no different when they grow up. Even kids aged 5 to 12 weren't spared, with 53 percent of respondents characterizing them in negative terms. Only 23 percent had positive things to say about children. What America really thinks about its kids, in short, is: not much.

The generation gap is old news, but this sour, almost hateful view of young people is different. Adults aren't merely puzzled by young people; they're terrified of them. It can't be a coincidence that the shift in adult attitudes began roughly a generation after the height of political and social movements created by young people of all colors. Policy-makers now propelling anti-youth agendas remember how effective young people can be as a force for change. Demographics and the shifting nature of U.S. families also foster the anti-youth bias. According to census statistics, the number of people under age 65 has tripled since 1900, while the population aged 65 or over has increased elevenfold. One-quarter of all households are people living alone. And children are no longer integral to family structure: In 51 percent of all families there are no children under 18 living at home. Young people are easily demonized when their worlds don't coincide with ours. The sense of collective responsibility in raising children disappears as the building blocks of community change.

To an older America in a postindustrial world, children have become more of a liability than an asset. Middle-class parents calculate the cost of raising kids, including an overpriced college education, as they would a home mortgage. Low-income parents are bludgeoned by policies designed to discourage having children, from welfare reform to cuts in higher-education assistance. Young people's place in the economic order is uncertain, and a threat to those elders who are scrambling for the same jobs at McDonald's or in Silicon Valley. Says Barry Feld, professor at the University of Minnesota Law School and author of the upcoming *Bad Kids: Race and the Transformation of Juvenile Court*, "Parents raised kids so they could take care of them when they're old. As caring for the old has shifted to the public sector, the elderly no longer have fiscal investment in their kids. They know Social Security will be there for them."

Another reason adults are willing to condemn children is that it saves them from taking responsibility when kids go wrong. Take this statistical nugget: From 1986 to 1993, roughly the same period of the youth crime "explosion," the number of abused and neglected children doubled to 2.8 million, according to the Justice Department. And just three years later, the total of all juvenile arrests was 2.8 million. What goes around comes around.

Historically, U.S. criminal law followed the definitions of adulthood and childhood laid down by William Blackstone in his *Commentaries on the Laws of England* (1765–69). Children up to 7 were considered incapable of criminal responsibility by dint of their immaturity. At 14, they could be held as responsible as adults for their crimes; the years in between were a gray area of subjective judgment on culpability. But by 1900, reformers had created a separate system of juvenile courts and reform schools based on the principles that delinquency had social causes and that youth should not be held to adult standards. Eighteen was generally held as the entryway to adulthood.

The current transformation in juvenile justice is no less radical than the one 100 years ago. This time, though, we are marching backward to a one-size-fits-all system for youth and adults in which punishment, not reform, is the goal. From 1992 to 1995, forty-one states passed laws making it easier to prosecute juveniles in adult criminal court, and today all fifty states have such laws. In more than half the states, children under 14 can be tried in adult court for certain crimes. In thirteen states, there is no minimum age at which a child can be tried in adult court for felonies. New York permits prosecution of a 7-year-old as an adult for certain felonies. The Hatch-Sessions bill now in the U.S. Senate continues the assault on youthful offenders. It would use block grants to encourage states to toughen further their juvenile justice procedures. One provision eliminates the longstanding mandate to separate incarcerated juveniles and adults. "You're going to see more suicides and assaults if that happens," says Robert Shepherd.

Violent crimes like those in Oregon and Arkansas are a rarity, but they've become the rationale for a widespread crackdown on youth at school and on the streets. If Dennis the Menace were around, he'd be shackled hand and foot, with Mr. Wilson chortling as the cops hauled his mischievous butt off to juvenile hall. In Miami recently, a 10-year-old boy was handcuffed, arrested and jailed overnight because he kicked his mother at a Pizza Hut. His mother protested the police action—it was a waitress who turned him in. The boy now faces domestic battery charges in juvenile court.

Last October at the Merton Intermediate School in Merton, Wisconsin, four boys aged 12 and 13 were suspended for three days and slapped with disorderly conduct citations and fines (later dropped) by the local sheriff after they yanked up another boy's underwear "wedgie style." "The boys were playing, wrestling around in the schoolyard, and there was a pile-on," says Kevin Keane, an attorney who represented one of the boys. "One kid was on the ground and the others gave him a wedgie. He wasn't hurt or upset, and they all went back to class." But the principal learned about the incident and termed it a sexual assault.

Anti-youth analysts prefer to think more juvenile arrests means more kids are behaving recklessly. But it's just as plausible to argue that the universe of permissible behavior has shrunk. Look at curfews, which were virtually unknown twenty years ago. Curfews generated 185,000 youth arrests in 1996—a 113 percent increase since 1987. Disorderly conduct arrests of youth soared 93 percent between 1987 and 1996, with 215,000 arrests in 1996 alone.

Public schools are at ground zero in the youth crackdown. A report released in March by the National Center for Education Statistics surveyed 1,234 public schools on crime and security measures. Three-fourths have "zero tolerance" policies on drugs, alcohol and weapons, which means ironclad punishment for any transgression. Six percent of the schools surveyed use police or other law enforcement on campus at least thirty hours a week, while 19 percent of high schools have stationed cops full time. Public schools are even using dogs to search for illegal drugs. The Northern California A.C.L.U. filed suit in March 1997 against the Galt, California, school district on behalf of two students and a teacher who were subjected to dog searches during a course on criminal justice. "It's a real state police-prison element introduced into the schools," says A.C.L.U. lawyer Ann Bick. "It tells kids, 'We don't trust you.' And they'll live down to those expectations."

If the goal is to change behavior, draconian policies aimed at young people have been a dismal failure. Half a dozen studies have shown that transferring juveniles to adult courts not only doesn't deter crime, it's more likely to spur recidivism. But if the goal of the crackdown on youth is to divert attention from the real crimes plaguing the nation—child poverty, failing educational systems, 15 million kids without health insurance—then it's a success. New York City Mayor Rudolph Giuliani uses that strategy brilliantly: In January a child was killed by a brick falling from a badly managed school construction site, and reading scores were once again abysmally low. What were Giuliani's issues? Uniforms for students and deployment of police in the schools.

The criminalization of young people makes no sense, of course. Kids are a national treasure and natural resource, the bearers of our collective dreams and hopes. But logic and humanity don't often determine public policies or opinion. We are sowing the seeds, the dragon's teeth, of our own comeuppance. Erasing the line between youth and adulthood without granting youths the same constitutional protections and rights of citizenship as adults sets up a powerful contradiction. And sooner or later, to paraphrase Malcolm X, the chickens will come home to roost.

Annette Fuentes has just completed a Prudential Fellowship on Children and the News at Columbia University.

LAW & JUSTICE

JUVENILE OFFENDERS:

Should They Be Tried in Adult Courts?

The "get tough" approach to dealing with young law violators seen throughout the criminal justice system is society's reaction to violent, uncaring youths.

by Michael P. Brown

CHILDREN have been described as our future, our greatest resource, and our hope for a better tomorrow. For many Americans, though, children invoke fear. They represent violence, a segment of society lacking in self-control and devoid of ethics and morals, and the failure of the family to instill traditional values—chief among them being the value of human life and respect for others.

Fear of crime, especially random violence perpetrated by young Americans, is among the nation's greatest concerns. It has served as the motivation for countless numbers of people to change their lifestyles, take self-defense classes, install home security systems, and carry handguns for protection. Moreover, fear of crime has influenced politicians and laypersons to adopt the position that a conservative justice system, which seeks to punish and deter, holds the most promise in curtailing juvenile crime. Waiving juveniles to criminal (*i.e.,* adult) court and imposing criminal penalties, according to the conservative position, are effective ways for society to express outrage for the transgressions of "out-of-control" youth and to placate its desire for retri-

bution. Others, however, contend that treating juveniles as adults is going too far. Although many of these juveniles are incarcerated for their crimes, which the law allows, they often are the easy victims of homosexual rape and other forms of violence at the hands of hardened adult criminals.

The criminal sanctioning of juvenile offenders is not a contemporary phenomenon. Juveniles have been punished as adults for centuries. Prior to the 17th century, for instance, children were seen as being different from adults only in their size. Hence, they were held essentially to the same behavioral standards as adults. Youngsters were perceived of as being miniature adults and, therefore, subject to the same punishments as offenders who were decades their senior. Childhood was considered to end at about age five.

It was not until the 17th century that European church and community leaders successfully advanced the notion that children were weak and innocent and in need of the guidance, protection, and socialization of adults. Consequently, childhood was prolonged, education became a priority, and societal norms emerged specify-

ing age-appropriate behavior. Youngsters no longer were viewed as miniature adults. For the first time in recorded history, they were a separate and distinct group.

By the 18th century, English common law characterized those under the age of seven as being incapable of forming criminal intent. For an act to be considered criminal, there must be *actus reus* (the criminal act itself), *mens rea* (the intent to commit the criminal act), and *corpus delecti* (the interaction between the act and the intent to commit it). Therefore, since youths were considered to be incapable of forming *mens rea,* they were legally unable to commit a crime or to be criminally sanctioned. Between the ages of seven and 14, children were presumed to be without criminal intent unless it could be proven that they knew the difference between right and wrong. At age 14, they legally were considered adults, capable of forming criminal intent and therefore justly sentenced to serve time in jail and prison alongside other adults.

By the early 1800s, there was the belief that juvenile and adult offenders should be incarcerated separately. At that time, special correctional institutions for youthful offenders were established in the U.S.

It was not until 1899, though, that the first juvenile court was established. This uniquely American institution was based on the premise that youthful offenders should be treated differently than their adult counterparts. Instead of deciding guilt or innocence, the court would ascertain whether youths were in need of treatment. Under the driving philosophy of the new court, *parens patriae,* it would serve as the benevolent parent—all-knowing and all-loving, wanting only that which is in the best interest of children. Consequently, instead of harsh, punitive sanctions that sought to deter, the court would seek long-term behavioral change by providing the guidance youths so woefully lacked from their natural parents. Sentences were to be customized to meet the needs of each juvenile so as to optimize the rehabilitative effects of court intervention.

For most juveniles, the *parens patriae* doctrine still serves as the foundation upon which their sentences are based. Such an orientation is not deemed appropriate, however, for those juveniles waived to criminal court. Provisions that allow juveniles to be waived are, on the one hand, in contrast with the original intent and purpose of the juvenile justice system. On the other, they are consistent with the manner in which youthful offenders were sanctioned in the past.

The present-day controversy surrounding waivers appears to be a consequence of at least two factors converging. First, the definitions of childhood and age-appropriate behavior are in a state of flux. Young people are said to be more predisposed toward violence today than they were in the past. National crime data sources seem to support this notion. Violent juvenile crime has increased by nearly 70% since 1986. Moreover, the violence perpetrated by juveniles is portrayed by the mass media as being more heinous than at any other time in history. People are fearful of falling victim to a generation that seemingly holds beliefs and values that diverge drastically from those of normative society.

Second, the "get tough" approach to dealing with law violators—as seen throughout the criminal justice system—increasingly is being applied to juvenile offenders as well. Although a conservative approach to juvenile crime is not new, it is in sharp contrast to the predominant way in which the juvenile justice system has responded to youthful offenders in the U.S. for nearly 100 years. While it is true that waivers have been in existence for more than 70 years, they are used more today than in the past. This has drawn attention to how society's response to juvenile offenders is changing from primarily being oriented toward rehabilitation to increasingly becoming prone to subjecting juveniles to conservative criminal court practices.

"Legal adults"

Every state and the District of Columbia have at least one provision (some states have as many as three) to waive certain juveniles to criminal court. Juveniles may become "legal adults" through judicial waiver, prosecutorial discretion, or statutory exclusion. A judicial waiver involves the juvenile court waiving jurisdiction over a case and sending it to criminal court for prosecution. In all but three states, juvenile court judges have been entrusted with the power to waive juveniles to criminal court. Prosecutorial discretion (also known as concurrent jurisdiction) refers to the prosecutor deciding in which court—juvenile or criminal—charges will be filed. Ten states and the District of Columbia give prosecutors this authority. Statutory exclusion involves state legislatures designating certain offenses for which criminal prosecution is required. Thirty-six states and the District of Columbia have enacted legislation that excludes certain offenses from juvenile court jurisdiction.

"... The majority of those juveniles waived to criminal court will re-enter society stigmatized by their criminal label..."

Age and offense seriousness traditionally have been the criteria by which juveniles are waived to criminal court. Twenty-one states and the District of Columbia have no minimum age requirements for transferring juveniles to criminal court. Among the remaining 29 states, minimum age requirements range from seven to 16. The largest proportion of cases waived to criminal court are serious crimes such as murder; offenses involving serious personal injury (such as aggravated assault); property crimes; public order offenses (such as disorderly conduct, obstruction of justice, and weapons offenses); and drug offenses. Additionally, some minor offenses (such as fish and game violations), which do not fall within the jurisdiction of the juvenile court, are tried in criminal court. Moreover, some states permit juveniles to be waived if their current charge is a felony and there is evidence of prior felony convictions. Furthermore, most states have a provision that allows juveniles to be waived to criminal court if there is reason to believe that offenders are not amenable to treatment.

Using the most recent available data, the Office of Juvenile Justice and Delinquency Prevention (JJDP) reports that, from 1985 to 1994, the number of delinquency cases waived to criminal court rose from 7,200 to 12,300, a 71% increase. Despite this growth, the percentage of cases waived to criminal court during this 10-year period remained relatively constant, ranging from a low of 1.2% to a high of 1.5% of all formally handled delinquency cases.

Over this span, the types of offenses waived to criminal court have changed considerably. While 54% of the cases waived in 1985 were for property crimes, the percentage dropped to 37% by 1994. Cases involving murder and personal injury rose from 33 to 44%. The percentage of drug offenses more than doubled, from five to 11%. Public order offenses remained relatively constant—nine percent in 1985 and eight percent in 1994.

The percentage of cases involving youthful offenders under the age of 16 increased from six to 12%. Males consistently have comprised the majority of cases waived to criminal court—95% in 1985 and 96% in 1994. Of the juveniles waived to criminal court in 1985, 57% were white, 42% black, and two percent of other racial and ethnic groups. By 1994, the percentage of white and black juvenile offenders became more similar (49 and 48%, respectively), and youths from other racial and ethnic groups increased to four percent. (Figures have been rounded off to nearest full percentage point.)

Waiving juveniles to criminal court often is justified on the grounds that they are deserving of more punitive criminal court sanctions and that the "get tough" approach to fighting crime will serve to deter future criminal conduct. Decades of research has yielded mixed findings regarding whether juveniles are sentenced more harshly by criminal courts and are less likely to recidivate. Most studies indicate that juveniles waived to criminal court do not receive substantially more punitive sanctions. In fact, many studies have reported that juveniles are more likely to receive probation instead of incarceration. Of those incarcerated, most receive terms of confinement comparable to those imposed in juvenile court. Moreover, research has revealed that juveniles waived to criminal court are no less likely to recidivate than those sanctioned in juvenile court.

The methods by which the justice system responds to unlawful conduct are not determined in a vacuum. They are a reflection of societal attitudes. In the past, waiving juveniles to criminal court was considered an option after all other avenues of treatment in the juvenile court had been explored. Today, the situation is drastically different. The conservative environment that currently exists not only makes it more acceptable, it is an expectation that judges and prosecutors will act decisively by waiving certain juveniles to criminal court. Hence, waivers no longer are viewed as a last resort. In fact, the use of waivers has been expanded to include first-time juvenile offenders. The establishment of exclusionary statutes, requiring certain juveniles to be waived automatically, eliminates the possibility of the exercise of discretion by those who know youngsters best—juvenile court judges and prosecutors. It is estimated that exclusionary statutes have resulted in more juveniles waived to criminal court than judicial waivers and prosecutorial discretion combined.

Waiving juveniles to criminal court is not the answer to the crime situation. At best, waivers are a short-term solution to a complex social condition that will not be simplified by transferring juveniles to the jurisdiction of the criminal court. At best, they merely serve to mollify the public's desire for retribution. After all, the majority of those juveniles waived to criminal court will reenter society stigmatized by their criminal label and, in all likelihood, more dangerous than they were before being sanctioned as adults. This is especially true of youths who have served time in prison alongside adults.

Nevertheless, it is unlikely that waivers will be repealed. Therefore, it is incumbent upon decision-makers to make an informed, socially responsible use of waivers. In so doing, they would be restricted to those who pose the greatest risk to the safety and security of society—violent youth such as murderers, rapists, and robbers who show no apparent promise for reformation.

As for the others, juvenile court intervention holds the most promise for transforming troubled youths into productive, law-abiding adults. The OJJDP, based upon the results of numerous studies, has proposed a multifaceted strategy for dealing with youthful offenders:

Strengthen the family unit. Parents are primarily responsible for instilling in their children socially redeeming morals and values. Parenting classes may be necessary when mothers and/or fathers lack the skills, abilities, and maturity to socialize their offspring properly. When a functional family is nonexistent, a surrogate one should be established to fill that void in a child's upbringing.

Support core social institutions. Capable, productive, and responsible youths are influenced positively by schools, religious institutions, and community-based organizations. Social institutions impart law-abiding beliefs and values and offer youths legitimate opportunities for economic gain.

Promote delinquency prevention. Communities must be proactive by responding to children who are at risk of committing delinquent acts. Although youths have a responsibility to live within the boundaries of the law, social institutions have a similar responsibility to engage youngsters in activities that encourage productive, law-abiding behavior.

Encourage an effective and immediate justice system response to delinquency. When delinquency occurs, the justice system must respond immediately to prevent future such actions and suppress escalation in their seriousness. The justice system should act in concert with conventional social institutions to enlist the influences that the family and religious organizations, for instance, have on the lives of youths.

Identify and control those youths who already are serious offenders. Youths who have not responded to traditional juvenile court intervention efforts or have demonstrated an unwillingness to abide by the rules of nonsecure community-based treatment efforts should be isolated in secure juvenile facilities for the protection of society. Deviating somewhat from the OJJDP's proposal, this intervention effort would be restricted to nonviolent offenders.

The alternative to waiving juveniles to criminal court is a comprehensive community response to juvenile unlawfulness that views juvenile and criminal justice as components of a larger whole—society. Moreover, it sees crime as a community problem with a community solution, instead of viewing it solely as a justice system problem with a justice system solution.

Many people will resist the notion of instituting alternatives to criminal court waivers. A community response to juvenile crime requires the commitment of the entire society. Therefore, it needs more effort than simply waiving juveniles to criminal court. Nevertheless, it holds the promise of returning children to their natural and rightful position as our future, our greatest resource, and our hope for a better tomorrow.

Dr. Brown is professor of criminal justice, Ball State University, Muncie, Ind.

OJJDP: "Juveniles as Victims" and "Juveniles as Offenders"

Overview of "Juveniles as Victims" quoted from the website:

Public perception of juvenile victimization tends to be incomplete, reflecting the latest headlines rather than day-to-day realities. In fact, many youth are subject to victimization through what might be called normal child activities: fights on the playground, pushing and shoving in the halls. However, many children experience serious victimization from many sources including their family (e.g., child abuse and abduction), peers (e.g., assaults), and strangers (e.g., theft and assault). Violence does not leave its young victims unscathed. Society must deal with the results of such violence for some time to come. Often, the child victims themselves do not understand how their experiences affect their behavior, including being the catalyst for potential future delinquency.

This section provides statistics on child abuse, neglect, and maltreatment. It also delves into the often more visible forms of victimization such as murder and sexual assault. It is important to have a consistent and accurate view of such victimization to develop programs and policy that are based on facts rather than a generalized perception of the problem or a response to severe but relatively rare acts of violence.

Please see the website below for more information:

http://ojjdp.ncjrs.org/ojstatbb/victims/index.html

Overview of "Juveniles as Offenders" quoted from the website:

Arrest statistics have been used as the main barometer of juvenile delinquent activity over the past decades. Unfortunately, many juvenile offenses go unreported and thus do not become a part of the national statistical picture. Indeed, many minor offenses committed by juveniles are considered part of growing up and are handled informally rather than by arrest and adjudication. It is critical to get a firm understanding of the range and prevalence of juvenile offending-from minor fights on playgrounds to aggravated assaults involving weapons.

This section draws on a number of national data sources to provide a picture of juvenile offending. Data from the National Longitudinal Survey of Youth 1997 (NLSY), the National Crime Victimization Survey (NCVS), the National Incident-Based Reporting System (NIBRS), and the FBI's Uniform Crime Reports (UCR) and Supplementary Homicide Reports (SHR) all serve to provide important insights into the types of offenses committed by youth and the prevalence of such offenses.

Please see the website below for more information:

http://ojjdp.ncjrs.org/ojstatbb/offenders/index.html

From *Office of Juvenile Justice and Delinquency Prevention.*

UNIT 2
Theoretical Views

Unit Selections

Key Points to Consider

- In view of the 1999 events in Littleton, Colorado, can any rational and comprehensive theory of behavior be applied?

- With a better understanding of the causes of behavior that is defined as delinquent, can we anticipate changes in our juvenile justice system and our correctional philosophy?

- What are the elements of the youth subculture at the beginning of millennium? How do they differ from the youth culture of 1990?

- What other forms of deviance in the community are not being adequately addressed as we focus on guns and drugs?

- Rank, in your opinion, the five variables that are most important in shaping a child, then do the same for the variables affecting an adolescent. What do you observe from this exercise?

Student Website
www.mhcls.com/online

Internet References
Further information regarding these websites may be found in this book's preface or online.

America's Children: Key National Indicators of Child Well-Being 1998
http://www.childstats.gov/ac1999/ac99.asp

Center for Substance Abuse Research (CESAR)
http://www.cesar.umd.edu/

Partnerships against Violence Network
http://www.pavnet.org

Prevention Pathways
http://www.preventionpathways.samhsa.gov

There is a mixture of scientific evidence that points to various factors that influence behavior, all considered to be delinquent. The list is not complete by any means. The popular culture, especially in the visual media and in rap music, has been cited as a corruptor of children and juveniles. Lack of community support has been tendered, along with the existence of genetic predispositions, single-parent families, poverty, racial discrimination, lack of opportunity, the school system, lack of personal responsibility, lack of moral values (especially this past year), a lenient juvenile justice system, and on and on.

One of the major problems of amateur criminologists is seeking the "causes" of crime. But that is a waste of time and energy since—except in the radical view that law causes crime—the only thing that is "caused" is behavior. It is only after *the* fact that any behavior is considered or defined to be delinquent or a crime. This is verified by the fact that sometimes people are excused for doing what would otherwise be called a crime when the behavior is considered in retrospect.

By and large, examination of existing research in juvenile delinquency discloses a tendency to emphasize select approaches or explanations. Many scholars in criminology have written almost identically that proponents of various theories of behavior defined as delinquent still too often insist that the truth is to be found only in their own special fields of study, and that—ex *hypothesis*—research done by those in other disciplines can contribute very little to the understanding and management of the delinquency/crime problem. Like the blind men and the elephant of the fable, each builds the entire subject in the image of that piece which he happens to have touched.

Given the problems described, however, it makes sense that we use a multifactor approach or an integration of theories. It is necessary not merely to account for the statistical factors that are so powerful such as age, gender, and peers, but also to account for the individual traits such as levels of toxicity, life experiences, and learning. In addition, today's children go through many more doorways (new social situations) than their predecessors. They are exposed earlier and more forcefully to the complete culture—for better or worse. They experience the relative impact of family, peers, media, home, neighborhood, school, and other elements of the environment quite early in life. Again, as several of our colleagues have argued in so many different ways, the person at any given time reflects the hammer of the environment pounding incessantly on the anvil of heredity.

The study of delinquency and crime reflects the dominance (since the 1920s and 1930s) of the sociological perspective and the continuing and understandable reluctance of that community to surrender "turf." Unfortunately, this limited sociological perspective has been translated into policies that fail to account for our current knowledge about the causes of behavior. We are not burdened today, however, by the limits which existed on the tools of the past greats of criminological inquiry such as Quetelet, Lombroso, Sheldon, Goring, and the Gluecks. We carry their scientific spirit forward. Modern neurological and biological sciences keep pushing the frontiers of knowledge about the chemical and other physical influences on human behavior. Our tools are much more sophisticated—unimagined by these pioneers. Instead of looking at the shape of skulls from without, we now look within by way of brain scans and MRIs as the brain processes events electrochemically. The articles in this unit are only a small sample of the diverse approaches to delinquency. They were selected because they are in some way pioneering.

This section also deals with drugs, gender, gangs, and other compounding issues.

There is something about contemporary values and culture in the United States that distinguishes us from much of known civilization. That something is violence and we need to understand why this is happening before we can create a good policy. But violence is not the only thing. Affluence, need in the face of affluence, drugs, basic values, attitudes, integrity, and other factors are very important.

Given that in the United States morality and law are intertwined only slightly less than in the world's theocracies, we have to consider seriously how much of our problem is due to our attitudes toward behavior which we regard as criminal, though it might be tolerated elsewhere as immoral or sick. Radical or conflict criminology approaches just that question—how much of it is the law?

We consider much of what are moral vices to be criminal, and on these issues debates rage: marijuana, sexual behavior, gambling, drinking, drugs, abortion, alternative lifestyles, and so on. We enjoy our great rights and freedoms, but we pay for them with the existence of deviations. We endure a constant battle between individual liberty and social accountability. We further compound the lives of juveniles by criminalizing what is acceptable for adults.

Storm Warning
The Coming Crime Wave Is Washed Up

JACQUES STEINBERG

In 1994, when a small but influential group of criminologists and politicians began fixing their gaze on the end of the 20th century, they saw a crime storm on the horizon, one teeming with a new breed of superpredators who would soon be reaching their teens.

According to their forecasts, the storm should have hit by now. Instead, the sky has been clearing.

For example, the rate of homicides committed by 14- to 17-year-olds, which leapt from 10 per 100,000 in 1985 to 30.2 in 1993, has gone down every year since, to 16.5 in 1997, said James Alan Fox, dean of the college of criminal justice at Northeastern University.

Moreover, statistics released by the Justice Department last week indicated that robberies by offenders of all ages fell a staggering 17 percent in 1997, continuing the seven-year drop in violent crime that followed the crime surge of the 1980's. That drop, criminologists say, is being driven by the falloff in the crack market and by concerted efforts by police departments across the country to seize handguns from juveniles, among other causes.

But that's not exactly what Professor Fox—along with James Q. Wilson of U.C.L.A., John J. DiIulio Jr. of Princeton University and Representative Bill McCollum of Florida, the chairman of the House subcommittee on crime—foresaw in their crystal balls several years ago. In November 1995, for example, Mr. DiIulio, a professor of politics and public affairs, suggested that a dip in crime, already perceptible then, was "the lull before the crime storm."

But if that was the case, said Franklin E. Zimring, a professor of law at the University of California at Berkeley, who was skeptical of such forecasts, "We should have our umbrellas open right now."

Professor Wilson of U.C.L.A., who doesn't recall using a weather analogy but did firmly predict rising youth crime, is more blunt than Professor Zimring.

"So far, it clearly hasn't happened," he said. "This is a good indication of what little all of us know about criminology."

At the heart of the pessimistic predictions was a historical fact: teen-agers commit a lot of crimes. Therefore, it seemed to follow, more teen-agers would mean more crime.

While it is not too late for the doomsday prognostications to come true, given that they were projected from now through 2010 and beyond, it's worth examining why they have not held so far.

Perhaps the most exaggerated factor underpinning the anticipated youth crime wave has been demographics. In January 1996, the Council on Crime in America, an organization of prosecutors and law-enforcement experts, issued a report compiled by Professor DiIulio describing violent crime as a "ticking time bomb" that would go off as the number of teen-agers soared in the coming few years.

But Professor Zimring contends that too much has been made of the anticipated boom in the adolescent population. Consider that the number of Americans aged 14 to 24 is expected to grow about one percent a year from 1995 to 2010—from 40.1 million to almost 47 million—a total increase of about 16 percent. By comparison, the growth in adolescents during the baby boom, from 1960 to 1975, was 50 percent, he said.

Though the correlation between increases in the juvenile population and a rise in violent crime has been regarded as conventional wisdom, the link has hardly proven strong in recent years.

During the five years that the homicide rate among teen-age offenders has been falling, the population of adolescents has already begun to rise. And when the homicide rate among adolescents was spiking in the early 1990's, the adolescent population was flat.

Mr. Wilson, a professor emeritus in the school of management at U.C.L.A. who has written extensively about crime, now says that in foreseeing a youth crime wave, he may have focused too much on population increases at the expense of intangibles like "the perception of young people about the costs and benefits of crime."

Though rates of violent crime have been influenced by a host of more quantifiable factors—the availability of guns, the growth in the economy, the expansion of crime-prevention programs—Professor Zimring says he is uncomfortable with trying to predict the criminal potential of someone who may be just a toddler now, if born at all.

"What's been weird has been this single focus: we're only interested in kids four years old now and how many kids they're going to shoot," he said.

Howard Snyder, director of systems research for the National Center for Juvenile Justice in Pittsburgh, a longtime skeptic about the predicted crime wave, thinks many people, especially politicians, have an incentive to be pessimistic.

"People naturally have this pessimism about what's going to happen, especially with kids," he said. "If you predict the future's going to be terrible, you're in a win-win situation. If it does happen, you were right. If it doesn't, your raising the flag of concern helped turn it around."

He said the gloomy oratory has already "changed the nature of juvenile justice," by enabling many states to pass laws that make it easier to try and imprison youthful offenders as adults.

Mr. DiIulio, one of the most vocal prophets of the coming storm, did not return telephone calls last week. But Professor Fox of Northeastern, whose analysis Mr. DiIulio has cited, says that a number of signs remain ominous.

He projects, for example, that growth in the population of black males—those 14 to 17 years old, as well as to 18 to 24—will grow at a steeper rate than their white male counterparts during the first two decades of the 21st century. And if history holds, he said, young blacks will be responsible for a disproportionate share of violent crimes when compared to whites.

He suggests further that the rate of homicides committed by youths 14 to 17 years old—16.5 per 100,000 in 1997—while nearly half of what it was in 1993, remains nearly double the 20-year low of 8.5 in 1984.

Does that mean that Professor Fox continues to see bad weather on the horizon, as he did so clearly three years ago?

"We may indeed see a resurgence in youth violence," Professor Fox said. "I say 'may.' I didn't say 'will.'"

Kids Who Kill

A conversation with John DiIulio

Michael Cromartie

John DiIulio is worried about a new breed of violent young criminal—and he wants you to be worried, too. The answer? Look to the inner-city churches, and get involved.

Though he hasn't yet turned 40, John J. DiIulio, Jr., is one of the nation's leading experts in the field of criminal justice. Professor of politics and public affairs at Princeton University, Douglas Dillon Senior Fellow and director of the Brookings Institution's Center for Public Management, and an adjunct fellow at the Manhattan Institute, DiIulio carries an impressive list of academic credentials, including a number of scholarly publications. He is also a widely quoted public intellectual whose essays appear regularly in the Weekly Standard, The New Republic, National Review, *and other leading journals of opinion.*

DiIulio was one of the first to sound the warning about the now widely acknowledged increase in juvenile crime. In particular, he has drawn attention to the young criminals—mostly male— whom he calls "super-predators," characterized by violent impulsiveness and a chilling lack of empathy or remorse. Because he writes and speaks about crime without employing fashionable evasions, DiIulio has been harshly criticized by some of his scholarly peers, but he does not belong in anybody's political pigeonhole. As James Traub observed in a New Yorker profile (Nov. 4, 1996),

> *Besides being a tenured Ivy League professor, he is a Democrat who has sharply, and publicly, attacked the Contract with America and the new welfare law. He may be the only academic in the country who could say, as he did in a speech earlier this year, "It is no more true that most welfare recipients are lazy, undeserving people than it is true that most prisoners are mere first-time nonviolent criminals."*

Lately DiIulio has been working with a coalition of black ministers who believe that churches, given adequate funds, are the best hope—maybe the only hope—for neglected and abused kids in the inner city. Michael Cromartie of the Ethics and Public Policy Center met with DiIulio in Philadelphia to talk about that ongoing work and about DiIulio's new book, Body Count, *coauthored with William Bennett and John P. Walters.*

You have said America is sitting on a ticking demographic crime bomb. Can you explain that to us?

In 1994 there were 2.7 million arrests of persons under age 18, up from 1.7 million in 1991; 150,000 of those arrests of juveniles were for violent crimes. Juveniles are now responsible for ever-larger shares of both property and violent crime. If you look at the estimates by the U.S. Bureau of the Census, they will tell you that by the year 2010 we'll have about 4,500,000 more boys, males under the age of 18, in the population than we had in 1990. Even if the increase isn't that big, even if fertility rates nationally trend downward as some people suggest they well might, almost everyone believes that there is going to be an increase in the number of at-risk juvenile males: kids who are basically unsupervised, not in homes where they are given the most rudimentary education.

A good proxy for what's going to happen down the road is rates of child abuse and neglect. We know that, all other things being equal, child maltreatment will increase the chances of delinquency by about 40 percent. That sheer demographic effect is going to have an impact. Lots of other things could happen to mitigate the situation: law enforcement changes, social-policy changes—all sorts of other things can make a difference; it's a multi-variant world. But ultimately, I think, the news is not very good.

Is this what you mean when you write about the coming of the "super-predators"?

Among the increasing population of children who are growing up without adequate supervision and care, there is a small fraction of kids who are simply surrounded by deviant, delinquent criminal adults, in fatherless, godless, and jobless settings. That kind of criminogenic environment is the breeding ground for the kids who have been referred to as the super-predators. They are remorseless, radically present-oriented, and radically self-regarding;

they lack empathic impulses; they kill or maim or get involved in other forms of serious crime without much consideration of future penalties or risks to themselves or others. The stigma of arrest means nothing to them.

The important thing about the super-predators concept is that it's at one end of the juvenile crime continuum. At the other end is the old concept of delinquent youth, stealing hubcaps or going for a joyride. Most of the kids who are committing crimes are not at either of these ends. But if only one-tenth of 1 percent of the kids who are out there committing crimes are at the super-predator extreme, that's very bad news, because those kids exercise an influence that is completely out of proportion to their numbers. The most radically impulsive and violent kids tend to be the ones who are leading the more than 200,000 kids who are organized into gangs in this country today.

The super-predators are the kids who will commit and instigate the most serious crimes, but they are also among the most needy kids. Every super-predator I've come up close and personal to is a kid who has suffered unrelenting abuse and neglect. They are desperately in need of spiritual and material help.

Are you encouraged at all, as a counter to this pessimistic forecast, by the recent drop of crime in New York?
I am encouraged by it. I'm encouraged by the fact that New York has had such success. I attribute that largely, but not solely, to the improvements that have been made in policing in New York City. If you look at the data that have been reported (they are essentially the FBI's uniform crime reports), fully a third of the decrease in reported crimes in America over the past several years is concentrated in New York. So if you throw New York out of the mix, we haven't had a national decrease in crime. It's been stable, and some categories have been increasing. New York is the national story as well as the northeastern U.S. story.

I'm not quite as thrilled as a lot of people for at least two reasons, however. One is that reported crimes are not all crimes. We measure all crimes through the National Crime Victimization Survey. To make a long story short, the National Crime Victimization Survey showed that in 1995 there had been a drop in violent crimes nationally, from 10.9 to 9.9 million criminal victimizations, which is real and true and good news. The bad news, however, comes in two parts. Number one, the way in which crimes are counted and measured is different from the way it was done only a few years ago. So, for example, until May of 1995, the same survey instrument had never counted as many as 7 million violent crimes in a single year. So as far as anyone knew, as of May 1995, Americans had never suffered as many as 7 million violent crimes in a single year. Now we're cheering the fact that we've decreased under this new way of measuring victimizations from 10.9 to 9.9 million. We ought to cheer, because I think crime is nationally in that direction, but again, that's more crimes than we knew we had before.

Second, if you compare crime rates today with those in the 1950s or '60s, you'll find that we are living with rates of violent criminal victimization that are four and five times what they were as little as three or four decades ago. I want to cheer the decrease in New York, but we ought not define criminality down, we ought not be happy that New York City may only have a thousand or so murders this year, when in the 1940s with a population as large and with paramedics who weren't as fast, we had 44 gunshot murders in a typical year.

Let me bring this around to a new book you've written with Bill Bennett and John Walters (*Body Count: Moral Poverty ... and How to Win America's War Against Crime and Drugs*), wherein you all suggest that the principal reason for the increase in violent crime is "moral poverty." Can you explain what you mean by that?
Let me take the first word, briefly, because it's often a source of confusion. When we talk about moral poverty, we're thinking about morality as something that doesn't inhere in the individual, but that is learned. So by moral poverty we mean growing up in the absence of parents, coaches, teachers, clergy, and other adults who teach you right from wrong, who nurture you, who show you unconditional love, or something that is close to it, and give you loving discipline as well. More and more kids in this country, not just poor kids or inner-city kids, but kids across the board, are growing up with some degree of moral poverty.

So you don't have to be in an urban neighborhood to grow up in moral poverty?
Absolutely not. In fact, over half of kids in this country, by some estimates, will reach the age of 18 without having experienced consistent adult supervision and guidance. You can be at Princeton University and have grown up in moral poverty and have problems as a result of it. You could be on the streets of Camden. It knows no race, creed, color, or zip code.

You suggest in *Body Count* that the religious dimension of moral poverty is the most important of all. Why do you say that?
For two reasons. First, we're concerned not just about crime and not just about criminals, but about the spiritual condition of the people who are doing the crime. If you told us that there is a gun-control program or strategy that could take every high-tech gun off the streets of North Philadelphia, we would run, not walk, to get that program implemented. We would also, at the end of the day, remain very concerned about the spiritual condition of kids who would use high-tech guns if they could get them. When everything is said and done, we believe that, as Christians, we should feel convicted by the fact that we are dealing with this problem of moral poverty and so-called super-predators. Our response can't be simply to lock these kids up, even though that's something we must do in far too many cases. We're concerned about the child behind the crime.

Second, we talk about religion because, as much effective monitoring as you can do through juvenile justice, as much effective mentoring as you can do through programs like Big Brothers and Big Sisters, there are many, many kids in the most abject moral poverty who will not be reached by these programs. And here the church needs to step in. These are the kids who are the biggest street-level crime problem. They are the most abused, neglected, and underserved. In the inner-city communities where this problem is most acute, the churches have a moral obligation—and many of them are already doing this—to open their doors to these kids.

How is the involvement of the church in these issues viewed by your colleagues in the social science community?
I'm laughing a bit because over the past ten years, first I thought there was nothing less popular in academic and intellectual circles than a pro-family intellectual. Then I concluded, no, it was a pro-incarceration intellectual, but now I nominate pro-religion intellectuals. Not because of out-and-out disregard or dislike of religious institutions, so much as the knee-jerk suspicion among a lot of elite academics, in particular, that if you believe in God you have some form of mental illness, and you need to be treated rather than encouraged.

We believe that, purely as a good social scientist, you need to look at the efficacy of religious commitment, attachment to religious institutions, and so on, as a factor in explaining variants in juvenile crime rates. You simply cannot explain variants in juvenile crime rates without some reference to the religion variable, or the so-called faith factor. It just keeps coming up. As hard as some people have tried to bury it, suppress it, sweep it under the rug, there is more and more research evidence, and there will be more and more scientific research evidence, to suggest that kids who have some attachment to religious institutions do better in terms of staying off drugs, staying out of crime, than other kids who are the same in all other ways we can know, but lack that attachment. We think the spiritual dimension here is real and important. The at-risk kids, like all kids, need adults in their lives who are there because they see in the child not just another statistic or body but a spiritual being who needs to be saved, saved from the horrors of the streets and saved spiritually.

We also think there is a very practical dimension. There may be a church in your neighborhood, as there are in some of the most depressed areas of Philadelphia, for example, where kids can go and get literacy training, and get drug treatment that addresses the whole person—not just credentialed therapy, but a whole-person treatment: what's going on in the home, what's going on in school, what's troubling you, what's driving this, why did you do it, how can we help you; we're here for you, we love you even when the world hates you. That kind of care makes a positive difference. So our position is, if you

want to view religion purely in a secular light, do so. If you want to talk about measuring the performance of competing ways of dealing with substance abuse, that's fine, too. Just give the churches a chance to compete, and give the faith factor its due in explaining the variants in crime rates.

Now you do say something a bit controversial when you say that government officials should enable churches to do more. Is this possible, given the church-state issues?
I have to be clear that in answering this I am speaking for myself, not for my coauthors in *Body Count*. America has somewhere in the vicinity of 23,000 black churches, many of them in inner-city areas where the problems are worst, and they are doing all kinds of good things. I say, let the government fund programs that are targeted to serve kids who have these attributes, with the aim of reducing their frequency of drug use and their recidivism rates, and so on. Don't specify process criteria—how many Ph.D.'s you need to have, and what the treatment modalities need to be—just specify the performance criteria and let the churches compete for those funds, like anyone else. Don't regulate them to death. Don't make it impossible for them to get local zoning waivers. Don't bar them from competition for federal dollars.

I'm hoping to be a part of building a systematic inventory of evaluative research on the churches, and I believe that the black churches are already outperforming many of the secular alternatives in terms of primary and secondary prevention programs. Beyond that, I would simply point out that in many places, a fairly substantial fraction of the social-services dollar is going to religious institutions today. Catholic Charities, for example, gets about 62 percent of its funds through various government entities. Now, as a good Catholic, I will maintain for the sake of the organization that there is no proselytizing going on. It's like Jiffy Lube, only it happens to have a religious orientation. But if we really believe that, I don't think we understand the nature of the Catholic church's mission here on earth, or what Christians are about. I want to do it up front, not through the back door; I want people to know that when we do literacy training, that literacy training is going to occur using the Bible, as it has occurred for generations and generations, and very effectively. I want people to be aware of that up front. I want people not to be afraid of it or scared by it. My own take on the constitutional questions differs radically from what I consider to be the myth of the separation of church and state, but I'll fall silent on that.

That's why your guiding principle is, "Build churches, not jails."
That's right. We will probably build scores more maximum-, medium-, and especially minimum-security prisons, including ones for juveniles, over the next 15 years. This will happen regardless of whether the demographic crime bomb goes off or not. The laws have been passed,

the kids are in the pipeline, the crimes are being committed. So the prisons are going to be built. But I truly believe, not simply as a matter of religious faith, but as a matter of empirical observation, that if we could build 10 or 15 churches with youth-outreach ministries like we have at the Deliverance Evangelist Church in Philadelphia, we could make a real difference.

When you say "if we could build churches," who is the "we"?
I'm part of an effort that is forming a nonprofit organization to raise private funds to identify the churches in major metropolitan areas in America that are actually doing this now—not talking about it, but doing it—who need help in getting the dollars and the personnel and the logistical support. So when I say "build churches," in some cases I mean literally the bricks and mortar of building a facility, which in some cases is the only decent physical dwelling in the entire neighborhood, with open doors and with staffing and with space and activities going on for the kids of the community.

They need help in money. We could fit in every at-risk kid in Philadelphia who doesn't have parental or home support. We could do it in this city. We don't *have* to have a major juvenile crime problem in the city of Philadelphia, we don't *have* to have kids who are growing up without any decent adult care. If we empower the churches, we can change that.

Can you tell us a little bit more about the coalition you put together on this?
I've been working over the past ten months or so with a group of inner-city ministers here in Philadelphia and in Boston. The Boston coalition is headed by Reverend Eugene Rivers, a self-described Christian black nationalist, who has been at it for the better part of a decade in the Four Corners neighborhood of Boston. In Boston, they've been working around a ten-point plan which basically runs the gamut from being ombudsman for juvenile pro-

bationers to one-on-one drug treatment, to literacy training, to Boston Freedom Summer, where they give kids the opportunity to be together in a structured, disciplined, but loving environment. Walking among the poor: that's what they're doing. It's really as simple as that.

The difficulty that I've discovered is, as Reverend Rivers likes to say, there are lots and lots of churches with lots and lots of resources, both public and private resources, that haven't lived their faith commitment on the streets. They haven't gotten the money to where it is needed and haven't gotten the help to where it is needed. That's not an indictment of all the churches, it's merely to say there's an awful lot that needs to be done here, and it's going to take some kind of radical action to get it done.

So you are trying to build a network in something like 35 cities?
We have a goal. We talk about job one being to refine the ten-point plan; job two, shoring up the Boston operation and making it truly citywide; job three, taking that and replicating it here in Philadelphia, a much bigger, tougher, more crime-ridden city; and all the while beginning to develop a network of people all across the country in our 20 biggest cities, with the goal of a thousand churches by the year 2006 that are doing some or all of the key ten points of this holistic youth-outreach ministry. It's a coalition not only among the various black Protestant inner-city churches, but also involving the Catholic church. It is an alliance that transcends a lot of the usual theological, ideological, and denominational divides. I've met and talked to everyone from Ralph Reed to Ron Sider. Again, the problem defines the solution here. I think we've gotten a tremendous amount of support from lots of people. So far, mostly rhetorical support, but I hope soon financial support, and best of all, hands and feet in the neighborhoods and the communities, which is really ultimately what we need.

From *Books & Culture*, January/February 1997, Vol. 3, No. 1. Copyright © 1997 by Ethics & Public Policy Center. Reprinted by permission.

Does Kindergarten Need Cops?

The youngest schoolkids are acting out in really outrageous ways. Why?

Claudia Wallis

Temper tantrums are nothing new in kindergarten and first grade, but the behavior of a 6-year-old girl this fall at a school in Fort Worth, Texas, had even the most experienced staff members wanting to run for cover. Asked to put a toy away, the youngster began to scream. Told to calm down, she knocked over her desk and crawled under the teacher's desk, kicking it and dumping out the contents of the drawers. Then things really began to deteriorate. Still shrieking, the child stood up and began hurling books at her terrified classmates, who had to be ushered from the room to safety.

Just a bad day at school? More like a bad season. The desk-dumping incident followed scores of other outrageous acts by some of the youngest Fort Worth students at schools across the district. Among them: a 6-year-old who told his teacher to "shut up, bitch," a first-grader whose fits of anger ended with his peeling off his clothes and throwing them at the school psychologist, and hysterical kindergartners who bit teachers so hard they left tooth marks.

"I'm clearly seeing an increasing number of kindergartners and first-graders coming to our attention for aggressive behavior," says Michael Parker, program director of psychological services at the Fort Worth Independent School District, which serves 80,000 students. The incidents have occurred not only in low-income urban schools but in middle-class areas as well. Says Parker: "We're talking about serious talking back to teachers, profanity, even biting, kicking and hitting adults, and we're seeing it in 5-year-olds." And these are not the kids who have been formally labeled emotionally disturbed, says Nekedria Clark, who works in Parker's department. "We have our E.D. kids, and then we have our *b-a-d* kids."

The alarming trend has been confirmed by Partnership for Children, a local child-advocacy group that has just completed a survey of child-care centers, elementary schools and pediatricians throughout Tarrant County, which includes Forth Worth and suburban Arlington. The final report is due out in January, but a preliminary version obtained by TIME shows that 93% of the 39 schools that responded to the survey said kindergartners today have "more emotional and behavioral problems" than were seen five years ago. More than half the day-care centers said "incidents of rage and anger" had increased over the past three years. "We're talking about children—a 3-year-old in one instance—who will take a fork and stab another child in the forehead. We're talking about a wide range of explosive behaviors, and it's a growing problem," says John Ross, who oversaw the survey.

> ## "WE'RE TALKING ABOUT PROFANITY, EVEN BITING, KICKING AND HITTING ADULTS."

Is Tarrant County a unique hotbed of precocious delinquency? Not at all, says Ronald Stephens, director of the National School Safety Center in Westlake Village, Calif. Across the country, he says, "violence is getting younger and younger." In the past five years, Stephens says, an increasing number of school districts in the U.S. have instituted special elementary schools for disruptive youngsters. "Initially, it was high schools that created these schools, then middle schools. Now it's elementary. Who would have thought years ago that this would be happening?" he asks.

Despite the proliferation of such programs, few school districts will admit to a violence problem—and certainly not at the kindergarten level. Philadelphia is a rare exception. "We aggressively report serious incidents regardless of the age of the child," says Paul Vallas, CEO of Philadelphia's schools, which serve 214,000 students. This year the largely poor urban district has already had 19 reports of weapons possession and 42 assaults by kids in kindergarten or first grade. Last year at the McDaniel elementary school alone, there were 21 assaults in the first two months of school, including one by a kindergartner who punched a pregnant teacher in the belly. Vallas adopted a get-tough policy and suspended 33 kindergarten students in the first six weeks of last year, up from just one in the same period the year before, earning him local notoriety as a "kindergarten cop." This year he has chosen instead to send the youngest offenders to "accommodation" rooms to cool down and learn to behave.

Not every school district in America is besieged by kamikaze kindergartners, but those who see a problem believe they are witnessing the result of a number of social trends that have come together in a most unfortunate way. Many cite economic stress, which has parents working longer hours than ever before, kids spending more time in day care and everyone coming home too exhausted to engage in the kind of relationships that build social skills. "Kids aren't getting enough lap time," says Karen Bentley, a seasoned elementary school administrator in Miami, who sees increased aggression in young students.

In addition, many educators worry about rising academic pressure in kindergarten and first grade in anticipation of the yearly tests demanded by the No Child Left Behind Act. In Texas, which has led the nation in embracing such tests, most kindergartens now go the full day, yet some have eliminated recess or limited it to 15 minutes a day. "It's a mistake to focus exclusively on academic readiness," says Stephen Hinshaw, chair-elect of the psychology department at University of California, Berkeley. "Even more vital than early reading," he says, "is the learning of play skills, which form the foundation of cognitive skills." Hinshaw points out that in Europe, kids often aren't taught to read until age 7. Insisting that they read at 5, he says, "puts undue pressure on a child."

Hinshaw and other experts on child behavior also point out that aggressive behavior in children has been irrefutably linked to exposure to violence on TV and in movies, video games and other media. "Dozens of studies have shown this link. Probably hundreds," says psychologist Jerome Singer, co-director of the Yale University Family Television Research and Consultation Center. "The size of the effect is almost as strong as the relationship between smoking and cancer."

There is little doubt that very young children are watching loads of TV before they even reach kindergarten. In October the Henry J. Kaiser Family Foundation released the results of a survey of 1,065 parents with children ages 6 months to 6 years. The stunning finding is that 43% of the kids age 2 and younger watched TV on a typical day and that 26% had a TV in their room. The median amount of time spent watching: two hours a day.

And that's two hours a day that are not spent doing what toddlers most need to do: interacting with people who love them and can teach them how to behave. Parker, in Fort Worth, blames this lack of socialization at home more than anything else for the wild behavior he's seeing in his district's youngest students. He recounts, for example, that the mother of an obstreperous 4-year-old told him the child has no formal mealtimes and eats whenever he wants. "If you don't have to sit down at a dinner table and stay there, how are you going to learn to sit in a seat at school and finish an assignment?" Parker wonders. Kids who are chronologically 6 years old are showing up in school with "emotional experience you would expect of a 3-year-old," says Dr. Bruce Perry, a child psychiatrist who works with the nonprofit group ChildTrauma Academy, based in Houston. "Imagine a child with the terrible twos in a 6-year-old body. It's a huge problem in education and mental-health circles." This "relational poverty," he says, affects even the wealthiest kids.

On the front lines in Philadelphia and Fort Worth, schools are trying to teach kids what they have failed to learn at home. Philadelphia has extensive anti-bullying and character-education programs. It has Saturday counseling for troublemakers and truants, and requires parents to attend. This year it has extended the program to kids in kindergarten through fourth grade. For now, the Fort Worth district is working mainly with individual students and their parents. But sadly, it, along with districts throughout Texas, is also training more and more teachers how to physically restrain a furious, flailing 5-year-old.

LOOKING FOR SOLUTIONS

Frustrated Officials Find Standard Answers Don't Suffice

Christi Parsons

A DAY AFTER two black-clad teenagers killed a teacher and a dozen classmates in Colorado, a stunned Illinois lawmaker stood on the House floor to give a long, wandering speech most uncharacteristic of the chamber.

"I look for blame in many areas," state Rep. Lee Daniels (R-Elmhurst) told fellow legislators. "I thought, 'You know, I am going to go back to the House floor and I am going to move to pass every piece of legislation that I can pass so that I can protect my children and your children and the children of the future...'

"I don't care what it is ... This violence must stop. I look for the answers. And I don't have them..."

Accustomed to purposeful addresses and clear calls to action, several listeners privately commented afterward that they had no idea what Daniels had been trying to say.

Nevertheless, in meandering around the topic, Daniels aptly if inadvertently summed up what many of his colleagues say they have been feeling in the wake of the school shooting: confusion fraught with intense frustration.

Such sentiments rarely are acknowledged in political circles. Lawmakers and other elected officials usually respond to incidents of national tragedy as if they know precisely what they are doing. In fact, their response to such instances of violence has become almost predictable: They offer up new gun control measures and talk about increasing penalties for gun violence.

But this time around, the course of public action isn't so clear. The nation already has witnessed four such school shootings, and none of the solutions that ensued has done much to make people feel any safer.

With their quiver of legislative arrows now seeming so useless, public policymakers are beginning to come to some startling—and, for some, dreadful—conclusions.

First, it might be time to try something entirely new. Second—and most frightening—nothing they do can guarantee the safety of schoolchildren or anyone else.

"Look at all we've done to make airports secure. And you still find people on planes with guns," said state Rep. Lou Lang (D-Skokie), a liberal lawmaker and frequent sponsor of gun control legislation. "It's frustrating, but we start [out] with the notion that it might be impossible to rid schools of the violence."

Lawmakers with near-opposite views about the role of government in society echo the thought.

"We have passed legislation creating safe school zones, enhancing penalties for just about anything imaginable that happens within 1,000 feet of a school," said state Sen. Ed Petka (R-Plainfield), a staunch conservative and opponent of gun control. "Certain areas have police officers stationed right in the schools themselves...

"The one thing we really can't control is in the heart of a person."

Of course, the shared belief hasn't stopped lawmakers from trying. The Colorado shooting gave new impetus to bills pending in the Illinois legislature, including several to increase penalties for people who fire guns near schools and to prevent minors from gaining access to firearms.

In Washington, U.S. Sen. Dick Durbin (D-Ill.) and others were promoting passage of stricter gun laws as one way to help prevent such school violence.

And across the nation, other policymakers displayed an urge to keep current tough gun laws in place. In the Colorado, Alabama and Florida legislatures, the shooting prompted lawmakers to withdraw measures expanding the right to carry guns or protecting gunmakers from legal liability for gun violence.

But amid the usual clamor that followed the shooting was the murmur of a quieter conversation, one that suggested small signs of interest in trying something other than the old methods. Surprisingly, it involved some of the people most likely to turn to get-tough measures for answers.

Late in the week, for example, the Clinton administration launched the "Safe Schools/Healthy Students Initiative," a $300 million program to promote school and community mental health treatment and early childhood psycho-social and emotional development programs.

And at a national meeting of state attorneys general held in Chicago in the wake of the shooting, one top prosecutor introduced the idea—novel for prosecutors to ponder—that community leaders start considering how counseling and intervention programs might be used to head off school violence.

Mike Moore of Mississippi, the president of the National Association of Attorneys General, said he thinks that only part of the solution can be found in the law.

"Students (have) said they need real counselors," Moore said. "Not just counselors who also handle money in the Coke machine or handle the band or do something else, but a counselor that talks to them, somebody who understands their problems....

"These kids many times just need someone they can really trust and talk to."

With that in mind, the attorneys general have taken the unusual step of including discussions on early childhood development on the agenda for their national conference on Youth and School Violence in early May.

Do those voices in political leadership indicate a change in thinking on the subject? Some experts who work with high school students hope so.

They suggest that instead of simply toughening laws, politicians might also consider investing more money in programs aimed at helping solve basic problems of youth in crisis and teaching young people to resolve conflict peacefully.

Indeed, some studies indicate that early childhood education for at-risk youth can reduce the likelihood that they will run into trouble with the law later in life.

Poor 3- and 4-year-olds randomly selected for an educational preschool program in Ypsilanti, Mich., were only one-fifth as likely as others to have become chronic lawbreakers by age 27, according to a study published by the not-for-profit High/Scope Educational Research Foundation in 1993.

Studies also show that intervention programs in the teenage years can make a difference, experts say.

"We have a choice on how we expend our resources," said Douglas Breunlin, vice president for programs and academic affairs at the Family Institute at Northwestern University, where experts study relationships among people.

"We could invest resources to prevent violence and we could invest resources to create peace," Breunlin said. "We live in a violent society, and we can't just snap our fingers and make it go away so that people can feel protected.

"I'd rather see an 'advisory program' funded in a school than five more security guards or a metal detector."

Many schools have such advisory programs, in which students get together with a trained adult adviser and other students on a regular basis and talk about such things as their personal development, goals and how to get along with others.

"One day the adviser might say, 'Today we're going to talk about what you do when you get angry,'" said Breunlin. "Or, 'Today we're going to talk about prejudice.'"

Besides teaching all students how to get along better during difficult teenage years, he said, the programs also give adults more chances to spot problems with particular students early on.

But such set-ups aren't cheap. Some schools spend as much as $1 million a year on theirs, Breunlin said.

Officials at all levels of government are often reluctant to talk about spending a lot of money on things like counseling.

To illustrate the point, consider Gov. George Ryan's response this week to a question about whether schools ought to have full-time psychologists on staff.

He shrugged off the suggestion, saying, "You can overdo those kinds of things and kids go the other way.

"When I was in school, there were traumatic things that happened, and nobody sat down and held your hand and said, 'Poor old Joe got killed last night.'"

Still, people may be ready for at least a modest step in that direction, suggests former U.S. Sen. Paul Simon, director of the Institute for Public Policy at Southern Illinois University.

Already, the recent spate of school shootings has made it plain that the consequences of ignoring the psychological root of teenage problems can be deadly.

"When students express extreme views and wear strange clothing, what they're doing is sending a signal, 'I have emotional problems,'" said Simon.

"School superintendents and counselors and teachers are realizing more and more that they ought to pay attention to this and get help for these kids."

But in the end, even those with the most faith in programs and legal mandates must acknowledge the limitations of their power to solve the problem.

Some believe the answer is to be found only in the church, the synagogue or the mosque.

Others look to the home or the prison for solutions.

Many, like Daniels, are simply baffled as to which way to turn.

"God bless our children," he said as he concluded his plaintive speech last week. "And God help us all that we find the right way."

Christi Parsons is a Tribune staff writer based in Springfield.

Early Violence Leaves Its Mark on the Brain

DANIEL GOLEMAN

With rates of violence among teen-agers rising precipitously, the argument over the causes of violent behavior has never been more charged. Nature got a hearing last month at a University of Maryland meeting on possible genetic influences on violence. Last weekend, nurture had its day, at a meeting at the New York Academy of Sciences on the childhood causes of violence.

Several strands of findings presented by researchers at the weekend conference pointed to the same conclusion: brutality and cruelty to children can leave a clear mark on the chemistry of the brain. And those changes in brain chemistry may be the route by which a brutalized child becomes a violent adult. The conference also offered some glimmers of hope for changing an established inclination to violent behavior.

One animal study that was particularly telling showed that normally mild-mannered golden hamsters that were threatened and attacked when they were young, and that grew up to be cowardly bullies, had lasting changes in the brain circuitry for two neurotransmitters that regulate aggression. And parallel data from several long-range studies of large groups of children show that those who were childhood victims of abuse or neglect were the most violent as teen-agers.

The hopeful news came from programs that seek to help these children learn to better control their aggressive impulses.

"Even if a child has a predisposition to aggression, he can learn to override it," said Dr. Karen Bierman, a psychologist at Pennsylvania State University. "The more aggressive kids just need more help from their parents, teachers and friends."

The research on golden hamsters took advantage of that species' habit of living singly, and being fiercely protective of their nesting territory—or, in this case, laboratory cage.

In the wild, adolescent hamsters ordinarily go off on their own and establish a solitary nest. But in the experiment, adolescent hamsters were placed in the cage of a mature one, thus violating its territory, for an hour a day over a week's time—about half a hamster's adolescence. The older hamsters threatened and attacked the younger ones to protect their territory from the interloper.

When those younger hamsters grew up they were given their own territories, and experimenters placed other hamsters in the cages of the traumatized ones. If an interloper was the same size, the traumatized hamster tended to cower or run.

But if the interloper was smaller and weaker, the resident hamster attacked—with a vengeance. "They were far more aggressive than normal," said Dr. Craig Ferris, a neuroscientist in the Behavioral Neuroscience Program in the psychiatry department at the University of Massachusetts Medical Center in Worcester. He conducted the study with Dr. Yvonne Delville.

In a related study, anatomical studies of adult hamsters that had gone through similar experiences showed changes in the neural circuitry for vasopressin, a brain substance involved in the regulation of aggressive impulses in hamsters. The vasopressin circuitry was diminished, with less of the substance being synthesized by the cells. That seems to make the receptors for the scarcer vasopressin more sensitive. Dr. Ferris plans to do similar anatomical studies of the hamsters that were terrorized in adolescence.

For serotonin, which plays a role in restraining aggressive impulses, the traumatized hamsters had circuitry that secreted larger amounts of the neurotransmitter, which seems to make the receptors for serotonin less sensitive. "The serotonin system is just not doing its job," Dr. Ferris said.

Exactly how all this affects the hamsters depends on what they are confronting. "Normally, vasopressin facilitates aggression and serotonin inhibits it, but the system doesn't work very well in these hamsters," Dr. Ferris said. "They either get too timid or you get an explosion of aggression," depending on whether they are with an animal of equal size or one that is a potential victim.

Sluggish serotonin circuitry seems typical of more violent humans, too, according to studies in which people are injected with a dose of fenfluramine, a substance that stimulates receptors for serotonin. The injection leads to the release of prolactin, a stress hormone that can be measured in the blood; higher levels of prolactin indicate greater serotonin activity.

"We find that people who are easily angered and impulsive—prone to shouting and throwing things, for example—release less prolactin than those who are not so irritable and impulsive," said Dr. Emil Coccaro, a psychiatrist in the Clinical Neuroscience Unit at the Medical College of Pennsylvania in Philadelphia. "That implies that the less active or responsive your serotonin system is, the more impulsive and aggressive you'll be."

Several studies presented at the conference showed that children who were abused or otherwise severely stressed in childhood were far more likely than others to be violent as teen-agers or adults. And, again, some of the data implicated changes in serotonin or related neurotransmitter systems.

Dr. Cathy Spatz Widom, a psychologist at the State University of New York in Albany, identified 908 children who had been victims of criminal neglect or physical abuse that led to the filing of criminal charges. Tracking the children's criminal records over the next 20 years, she found that those who had been childhood victims of neglect went on to have 50 percent more arrests for violent crimes than did a comparison group, while for those who suffered physical abuse, the rate of violent crimes was double that of the comparison group.

Similar findings were reported from a study of 66 aggressive boys winnowed from an overall sample of 1,037 inner-city children in Montreal. While the neighborhoods themselves tend to breed children somewhat more prone to aggression, these 66 boys were at the age 6 already the most violent among them.

Adolescent violence is traced to abuse and neglect in childhood.

"These are the boys who are always getting in trouble for fighting all through elementary school," said Dr. Richard Tremblay, a psychologist at the University of Montreal, who reported the main results of a 10-year study that assessed the boys annually. "As adolescents, these are the boys most frequently involved in crimes, especially violent ones." And, he said, they come from families that "tend to be more physically punitive with their children, beating them or using other physical punishment."

A test of pain sensitivity—an indirect measure of serotonin function—in these same boys suggested that they had lower levels of the substance, according to data presented by Dr. Jean Seguin, a colleague of Dr. Tremblay.

Louise Arseneault, a graduate student at the University of Montreal who worked on the study, presented data showing that the aggressive boys had difficulty focusing on activities and were easily distracted. The result is that they are impulsive, she said, and so "unable to inhibit bad behavior—even if they know they'll be punished for it—they don't seem to be able to stop themselves."

Boys who showed this deficiency on neuropsychological tests had the biggest increase from the age of 13 to 14 in picking fights and other aggressive acts—a jump of 50 percent. Their main deficiency, Ms. Arseneault said, "is in self-regulation, the ability to keep yourself from fighting because you know it's bad or inappropriate."

At the weekend conference, Dr. Adrian Raine, a psychologist at the University of Southern California, reported on a study of 4,269 boys, some of whom suffered some form of birth complication and whose mothers were abusive or neglectful in infancy. He found that those boys with birth complications and abuse were three times as likely as the others to be arrested for a violent crime by the age of 18.

Particularly damaging, Dr. Raine said, is early child abuse, like shaking a child vigorously. He said, "We know that can lead to laceration of the white nerve fibers that link the prefrontal cortex to deeper brain structures like the amygdala, which are involved in the generation of aggressive impulses, while the prefrontal lobes inhibit those impulses."

The ability to control aggression is learned during childhood. The crucial importance of such childhood learning was underscored by studies done with rhesus monkeys in which some monkeys were raised by their mothers, and others spent childhood without their mothers but in the company of same-aged peers. The result of the motherless childhood was something like a rhesus version of "Lord of the Flies."

While mother-reared monkeys with low serotonin levels are more aggressive than others as juveniles, "they are also more prosocial," engaging in many friendly acts, too, said Dr. Gary Kraemer, a psychologist at the Harlow Primate Laboratory at the University of Wisconsin.

"But if they have low levels of serotonin and are raised deprived of interaction with their mom, they show inordinate, unpredictable and extreme aggression," Dr. Kraemer said. "The rhesus mother helps the young one learn to organize its responses to other monkeys."

Those results, of course, can be read as hopeful as well—since mothering has such a powerful effect on modifying aggressive impulses. And at the conference, educators presented hopeful reports on special programs to help more aggressive children learn to keep their impulses under better control.

"We see that after a year, children who are prone to aggression can learn to talk about their feelings and think of different ways of solving a difficulty instead of just hitting," said Dr. Karen Bierman, a psychologist at Penn State. "But the interventions can't be just with the child—parents and friends have to help the child find alternatives to aggression and learn a broader array of skills for resolving problems."

Dr. Bierman reported results from a curriculum used in the early grades to teach children better ways to manage their emotional impulses. In one technique, for example, teachers help children recognize the cues in their bodies that signal that they are about to lose control and lash out, and remind them to calm down instead. The children also regularly pair up with a buddy to play games, supervised by a trained neighborhood volunteer, and solve problems that commonly lead to fights at that age, for example, learning about the need to take turns.

"We think doing this repeatedly and consistently helps children build self-regulation skills for handling aggressive impulses," said Dr. Mark Greenberg, a psychologist at the University of Washington who is a colleague of Dr. Bierman. "Presumably, it strengthens connections between the centers for emotional control in the prefrontal lobes and those for emotional impulse in the limbic areas."

Dr. Bierman reported that the program resulted in fewer arguments and fights in the classroom and the playground, and enabled children who were prone to aggression to control their impulses. "This, in turn, helped them to become more popular with their playmates.

"The brain circuits that regulate aggression in humans are malleable through childhood, so there may be some corrective experiences that reverse or otherwise improve any adverse impact from early abuse," Dr. Ferris said. "My hope is that we'll focus resources on these kids so they don't go down the path of social failure and inappropriate, excessive aggression."

What Makes Teens Tick

A flood of hormones, sure. But also a host of structural changes
in the brain. Can those explain the behaviors that make
adolescence so exciting—and so exasperating?

Claudia Wallis

Five young men in sneakers and jeans troop into a wait-ing room at the National Institutes of Health Clinical Cen-ter in Bethesda, Md., and drape themselves all over the chairs in classic collapsed-teenager mode, trailing back-packs, a CD player and a laptop loaded with computer games. It's midafternoon, and they are, of course, tired, but even so their presence adds a jangly, hormonal buzz to the bland, institutional setting. Fair-haired twins Corey and Skyler Mann, 16, and their burlier big brothers An-thony and Brandon, 18, who are also twins, plus eldest brother Christopher, 22, are here to have their heads ex-amined. Literally. The five brothers from Orem, Utah, are the latest recruits to a giant study that's been going on in this building since 1991. Its goal: to determine how the brain develops from childhood into adolescence and on into early adulthood.

It is the project of Dr. Jay Giedd (pronounced *Geed*), chief of brain imaging in the child psychiatry branch at the National Institute of Mental Health. Giedd, 43, has de-voted the past 13 years to peering inside the heads of 1,800 kids and teenagers using high-powered magnetic resonance imaging (MRI). For each volunteer, he creates a unique photo album, taking MRI snapshots every two years and building a record as the brain morphs and grows. Giedd started out investigating the developmen-tal origins of attention-deficit/hyperactivity disorder (ADHD) and autism ("I was going alphabetically," he jokes) but soon discovered that so little was known about how the brain is supposed to develop that it was impos-sible to figure out where things might be going wrong. In a way, the vast project that has become his life's work is nothing more than an attempt to establish a gigantic con-trol group. "It turned out that normal brains were so in-teresting in themselves," he marvels. "And the adolescent studies have been the most surprising of all."

Before the imaging studies by Giedd and his collabo-rators at UCLA, Harvard, the Montreal Neurological In-stitute and a dozen other institutions, most scientists believed the brain was largely a finished product by the time a child reached the age of 12. Not only is it full-grown in size, Giedd explains, but "in a lot of psycholog-ical literature, traced back to [Swiss psychologist Jean] Piaget, the highest rung in the ladder of cognitive devel-opment was about age 12—formal operations." In the past, children entered initiation rites and started learn-ing trades at about the onset of puberty. Some theorists concluded from this that the idea of adolescence was an artificial construct, a phenomenon invented in the post—Industrial Revolution years. Giedd's scanning studies proved what every parent of a teenager knows: not only is the brain of the adolescent far from mature, but both gray and white matter undergo extensive struc-tural changes well past puberty. "When we started," says Giedd, "we thought we'd follow kids until about 18 or 20. If we had to pick a number now, we'd probably go to age 25."

Now that MRI studies have cracked open a window on the developing brain, researchers are looking at how the newly detected physiological changes might account for the adolescent behaviors so familiar to parents: emotional outbursts, reckless risk taking and rule breaking, and the impassioned pursuit of sex, drugs and rock 'n' roll. Some experts believe the structural changes seen at adolescence may explain the timing of such major mental illnesses as schizophrenia and bipolar disorder. These diseases typi-cally begin in adolescence and contribute to the high rate of teen suicide. Increasingly, the wild conduct once blamed on "raging hormones" is being seen as the by-product of two factors: a surfeit of hormones, yes, but also a paucity of the cognitive controls needed for mature be-havior.

In recent years, Giedd has shifted his focus to twins, which is why the Manns are such exciting recruits. Al-though most brain development seems to follow a set plan, with changes following cues that are prepro-grammed into genes, other, subtler changes in gray mat-ter reflect experience and environment. By following twins, who start out with identical—or, in fraternal twins, similar—programming but then diverge as life takes them on different paths, he hopes to tease apart the influences of nature and nurture. Ultimately, he hopes to find, for instance, that Anthony Mann's plan to become a pilot and Brandon's to study law will lead to brain differences that are detectable on future MRIs. The brain, more than any other organ, is where experience becomes flesh.

Throughout the afternoon, the Mann brothers take turns completing tests of intelligence and cognitive function. Between sessions they occasionally needle one another in the waiting room. "If the other person is in a bad mood, you've got to provoke it," Anthony asserts slyly. Their mother Nancy Mann, a sunny paragon of patience who has three daughters in addition to the five boys, smiles and rolls her eyes.

Shortly before 5 p.m., the Manns head downstairs to the imaging floor to meet the magnet. Giedd, a trim, energetic man with a reddish beard, twinkly blue eyes and an impish sense of humor, greets Anthony and tells him what to expect. He asks Anthony to remove his watch, his necklace and a high school ring, labeled KEEPER. Does Anthony have any metal in his body? Any piercings? Not this clean-cut, soccer-playing Mormon. Giedd tapes a vitamin E capsule onto Anthony's left cheek and one in each ear. He explains that the oil-filled capsules are opaque to the scanner and will define a plane on the images, as well as help researchers tell left from right. The scanning will take about 15 minutes, during which Anthony must lie completely still. Dressed in a red sweat shirt, jeans and white K-Swiss sneakers, he stretches out on the examining table and slides his head into the machine's giant magnetic ring.

MRI, Giedd points out, "made studying healthy kids possible" because there's no radiation involved. (Before MRI, brain development was studied mostly by using cadavers.) Each of the Mann boys will be scanned three times. The first scan is a quick survey that lasts one minute. The second lasts two minutes and looks for any damage or abnormality. The third is 10 minutes long and taken at maximum resolution. It's the money shot. Giedd watches as Anthony's brain appears in cross section on a computer screen. The machine scans 124 slices, each as thin as a dime. It will take 20 hours of computer time to process the images, but the analysis is done by humans, says Giedd. "The human brain is still the best at pattern recognition," he marvels.

Some people get nervous as the MRI machine clangs noisily. Claustrophobes panic. Anthony, lying still in the soul of the machine, simply falls asleep.

CONSTRUCTION AHEAD

One reason scientists have been surprised by the ferment in the teenage brain is that the brain grows very little over the course of childhood. By the time a child is 6, it is 90% to 95% of its adult size. As a matter of fact, we are born equipped with most of the neurons our brain will ever have—and that's fewer than we have in utero. Humans achieve their maximum brain-cell density between the third and sixth month of gestation—the culmination of an explosive period of prenatal neural growth. During the final months before birth, our brains undergo a dramatic pruning in which unnecessary brain cells are eliminated. Many neuroscientists now believe that autism is the result of insufficient or abnormal prenatal pruning.

> The last area of the brain to mature is the part capable of deciding, I'll finish my homework, take out the garbage, and then I'll IM my friends.

What Giedd's long-term studies have documented is that there is a second wave of proliferation and pruning that occurs later in childhood and that the final, critical part of this second wave, affecting some of our highest mental functions, occurs in the late teens. Unlike the prenatal changes, this neural waxing and waning alters not the number of nerve cells but the number of connections, or synapses, between them. When a child is between the ages of 6 and 12, the neurons grow bushier, each making dozens of connections to other neurons and creating new pathways for nerve signals. The thickening of all this gray matter—the neurons and their branchlike dendrites—peaks when girls are about 11 and boys 12½, at which point a serious round of pruning is under way. Gray matter is thinned out at a rate of about 0.7% a year, tapering off in the early 20s. At the same time, the brain's white matter thickens. The white matter is composed of fatty myelin sheaths that encase axons and, like insulation on a wire, make nerve-signal transmissions faster and more efficient. With each passing year (maybe even up to age 40) myelin sheaths thicken, much like tree rings. During adolescence, says Giedd, summing up the process, "you get fewer but faster connections in the brain." The brain becomes a more efficient machine, but there is a trade-off: it is probably losing some of its raw potential for learning and its ability to recover from trauma.

Most scientists believe that the pruning is guided both by genetics and by a use-it-or-lose-it principle. Nobel prizewinning neuroscientist Gerald Edelman has described that process as "neural Darwinism"—survival of the fittest (or most used) synapses. How you spend your time may be critical. Research shows, for instance, that practicing piano quickly thickens neurons in the brain regions that control the fingers. Studies of London cab drivers, who must memorize all the city's streets, show that they have an unusually large hippocampus, a structure involved in memory. Giedd's research suggests that the cerebellum, an area that coordinates both physical and mental activities, is particularly responsive to experience, but he warns that it's too soon to know just what drives the buildup and pruning phases. He's hoping his studies of twins will help answer such questions: "We're looking at what they eat, how they spend their time—is it video games or sports? Now the fun begins," he says.

No matter how a particular brain turns out, its development proceeds in stages, generally from back to front. Some of the brain regions that reach maturity earliest—through proliferation and pruning—are those in the back of the brain that mediate direct contact with the environment by controlling such sensory functions as vision, hearing, touch and spatial processing. Next are areas that coordinate those functions: the part of the brain that helps you know where the light switch is in your bathroom even if you can't see it in the middle of the night. The very last part of the brain to be pruned and shaped to its adult dimensions is the prefrontal cortex, home of the so-called executive functions—planning, setting priorities, organizing thoughts, suppressing impulses, weighing the consequences of one's actions. In other words, the final part of the brain to grow up is the part capable of deciding, I'll finish my homework and take out the garbage, and *then* I'll IM my friends about seeing a movie.

"Scientists and the general public had attributed the bad decisions teens make to hormonal changes," says Elizabeth Sowell, a UCLA neuroscientist who has done seminal MRI work on the developing brain. "But once we started mapping where and when the brain changes were happening, we could say, Aha, the part of the brain that makes teenagers more responsible is not finished maturing yet."

RAGING HORMONES

Hormones, however, remain an important part of the teen-brain story. Right about the time the brain switches from proliferating to pruning, the body comes under the hormonal assault of puberty. (Research suggests that the two events are not closely linked because brain development proceeds on schedule even when a child experiences early or late puberty.) For years, psychologists attributed the intense, combustible emotions and unpredictable behavior of teens to this biochemical onslaught. And new research adds fresh support. At puberty, the ovaries and testes begin to pour estrogen and testosterone into the bloodstream, spurring the development of the reproductive system, causing hair to sprout in the armpits and groin, wreaking havoc with the skin, and shaping the body to its adult contours. At the same time, testosterone-like hormones released by the adrenal glands, located near the kidneys, begin to circulate. Recent discoveries show that these adrenal sex hormones are extremely active in the brain, attaching to receptors everywhere and exerting a direct influence on serotonin and other neurochemicals that regulate mood and excitability.

The sex hormones are especially active in the brain's emotional center—the limbic system. This creates a "tinderbox of emotions," says Dr. Ronald Dahl, a psychiatrist at the University of Pittsburgh. Not only do feelings reach a flash point more easily, but adolescents tend to seek out situations where they can allow their emotions and passions to run wild. "Adolescents are actively looking for experiences to create intense feelings," says Dahl. "It's a very important hint that there is some particular hormone-brain relationship contributing to the appetite for thrills, strong sensations and excitement." This thrill seeking may have evolved to promote exploration, an eagerness to leave the nest and seek one's own path and partner. But in a world where fast cars, illicit drugs, gangs and dangerous liaisons beckon, it also puts the teenager at risk.

That is especially so because the brain regions that put the brakes on risky, impulsive behavior are still under construction. "The parts of the brain responsible for things like sensation seeking are getting turned on in big ways around the time of puberty," says Temple University psychologist Laurence Steinberg. "But the parts for exercising judgment are still maturing throughout the course of adolescence. So you've got this time gap between when things impel kids toward taking risks early in adolescence, and when things that allow people to think before they act come online. It's like turning on the engine of a car without a skilled driver at the wheel."

DUMB DECISIONS

Increasingly, psychologists like Steinberg are trying to connect the familiar patterns of adolescents' wacky behavior to the new findings about their evolving brain structure. It's not always easy to do. "In all likelihood, the behavior is changing because the brain is changing," he says. "But that is still a bit of a leap." A critical tool in making that leap is functional magnetic resonance imaging (fMRI). While ordinary MRI reveals brain structure, fMRI actually shows brain activity while subjects are doing assigned tasks.

At McLean Hospital in Belmont, Mass., Harvard neuropsychologist Deborah Yurgelun-Todd did an elegant series of FMRI experiments in which both kids and adults were asked to identity the emotions displayed in photographs of faces. "In doing these tasks," she says, "kids and young adolescents rely heavily on the amygdala, a structure in the temporal lobes associated with emotional and gut reactions. Adults rely less on the amygdala and more on the frontal lobe, a region associated with planning and judgment." While adults make few errors in assessing the photos, kids under 14 tend to make mistakes. In particular, they identify fearful expressions as angry, confused or sad. By following the same kids year after year, Yurgelun-Todd has been able to watch their brain-activity pattern—and their judgment—mature. Fledgling physiology, she believes, may explain why adolescents so frequently misread emotional signals, seeing anger and hostility where none exists. Teenage ranting ("That teacher hates me!") can be better understood in this light.

Hormone surges make them emotional tinderboxes. An immature cortex gives them shaky judgment. Melatonin throws their sleep schedules out of whack.

At Temple University, Steinberg has been studying another kind of judgment: risk assessment. In an experiment using a driving-simulation game, he studies teens and adults as they decide whether to run a yellow light. Both sets of subjects, he found, make safe choices when playing alone. But in group play, teenagers start to take more risks in the presence of their friends, while those over age 20 don't show much change in their behavior. "With this manipulation," says Steinberg, "we've shown that age differences in decision making and judgment may appear under conditions that are emotionally arousing or have high social impact." Most teen crimes, he says, are committed by kids in packs.

Other researchers are exploring how the adolescent propensity for uninhibited risk taking propels teens to experiment with drugs and alcohol. Traditionally, psychologists have attributed this experimentation to peer pressure, teenagers' attraction to novelty and their roaring interest in loosening sexual inhibitions. But researchers have raised the possibility that rapid changes in dopamine-rich areas of the brain may be an additional factor in making teens vulnerable to the stimulating and addictive effects of drugs and alcohol. Dopamine, the brain chemical involved in motivation and in reinforcing behavior, is particularly abundant and active in the teen years.

Why is it so hard to get a teenager off the couch and working on that all important college essay? You might blame it on their immature *nucleus accumbens*, a region in the frontal cortex that directs motivation to seek rewards. James Bjork at the National Institute on Alcohol Abuse and Alcoholism has been using fMRI to study motivation in a challenging gambling game. He found that teenagers have less activity in this region than adults do. "If adolescents have a motivational deficit, it may mean that they are prone to engaging in behaviors that have either a really high excitement factor or a really low effort factor, or a combination of both." Sound familiar? Bjork believes his work may hold valuable lessons for parents and society. "When presenting suggestions, anything parents can do to emphasize more immediate payoffs will be more effective," he says. To persuade a teen to quit drinking, for example, he suggests stressing something immediate and tangible—the danger of getting kicked off the football team, say—rather than a future on skid row.

Persuading a teenager to go to bed and get up on a reasonable schedule is another matter entirely. This kind of decision-making has less to do with the frontal lobe than with the pineal gland at the base of the brain. As nighttime approaches and daylight recedes, the pineal gland produces melatonin, a chemical that signals the body to begin shutting down for sleep. Studies by Mary Carskadon at Brown University have shown that it takes longer for melatonin levels to rise in teenagers than in younger kids or in adults, regardless of exposure to light or stimulating activities. "The brain's program for starting nighttime is later," she explains.

PRUNING PROBLEMS

The new discoveries about teenage brain development have prompted all sorts of questions and theories about the timing of childhood mental illness and cognitive disorders. Some scientists now believe that ADHD and Tourette's syndrome, which typically appear by the time a child reaches age 7, may be related to the brain proliferation period. Though both disorders have genetic roots, the rapid growth of brain tissue in early childhood, especially in regions rich in dopamine, "may set the stage for the increase in motor activities and tics," says Dr. Martin Teicher, director of developmental biopsychiatry research at McLean Hospital. "When it starts to prune in adolescence, you often see symptoms recede."

Schizophrenia, on the other hand, makes its appearance at about the time the prefrontal cortex is getting pruned. "Many people have speculated that schizophrenia may be due to an abnormality in the pruning process," says Teicher. "Another hypothesis is that schizophrenia has a much earlier, prenatal origin, but as the brain prunes, it gets unmasked." MRI studies have shown that while the average teenager loses about 15% of his cortical gray matter, those who develop schizophrenia lose as much as 25%.

WHAT'S A PARENT TO DO?

Brain scientists tend to be reluctant to make the leap from the laboratory to real-life, hard-core teenagers. Some feel a little burned by the way earlier neurological discoveries resulted in *Baby Einstein* tapes and other marketing schemes that misapplied their science. It is clear, however, that there are implications in the new research for parents, educators and lawmakers.

In light of what has been learned, it seems almost arbitrary that our society has decided that a young American is ready to drive a car at 16, to vote and serve in the Army at 18 and to drink alcohol at 21. Giedd says the best estimate for when the brain is truly mature is 25, the age at which you can rent a car. "Avis must have some pretty sophisticated neuroscientists," he jokes. Now that we have scientific evidence that the adolescent brain is not quite up to scratch, some legal scholars and child advocates argue that minors should never be tried as adults and should be spared the death penalty. Last year, in an official statement that summarized current research on the adolescent brain, the American Bar Association urged all state legislatures to ban the death penalty for juveniles. "For social and biological reasons," it read, "teens have increased difficulty making mature decisions and understanding the consequences of their actions."

Most parents, of course, know this instinctively. Still, it's useful to learn that teenage behavior is not just a matter of willful pigheadedness or determination to drive you crazy—though these, too, can be factors. "There's a debate over how much conscious control kids have," says Giedd, who has four "teenagers in training" of his own. "You can tell them to shape up or ship out, but making mistakes is part of how the brain optimally grows." It might be more useful to help them make up for what their brain still lacks by providing structure, organizing their time, guiding them through tough decisions (even when they resist) and applying those time-tested parental virtues: patience and love.

WHY THE YOUNG KILL

Are certain young brains predisposed to violence?
Maybe—but how these kids are raised can either save them
or push them over the brink. The biological roots of
violence.

BY SHARON BEGLEY

THE TEMPTATION, OF COURSE, IS TO SEIZE on one cause, one single explanation for Littleton, and West Paducah, and Jonesboro and all the other towns that have acquired iconic status the way "Dallas" or "Munich" did for earlier generations. Surely the cause is having access to guns. Or being a victim of abuse at the hands of parents or peers. Or being immersed in a culture that glorifies violence and revenge. But there isn't one cause. And while that makes stemming the tide of youth violence a lot harder, it also makes it less of an unfathomable mystery. Science has a new understanding of the roots of violence that promises to explain why not every child with access to guns becomes an Eric Harris or a Dylan Klebold, and why not *every* child who feels ostracized, or who embraces the Goth esthetic, goes on a murderous rampage. The bottom line: you need a particular environment imposed on a particular biology to turn a child into a killer.

It should be said right off that attempts to trace violence to biology have long been tainted by racism, eugenics and plain old poor science. The turbulence of the 1960s led some physicians to advocate psychosurgery to "treat those people with low violence thresholds," as one 1967 letter to a medical journal put it. In other words, lobotomize the civil-rights and antiwar protesters. And if crimes are disproportionately committed by some ethnic groups, then finding genes or other traits common to that group risks tarring millions of innocent people. At the other end of the political spectrum, many conservatives view biological theories of violence as the mother of all insanity defenses, with biology not merely an explanation but an excuse. The conclusions emerging from interdisciplinary research in neuroscience and psychology, however, are not so simple-minded as to argue that violence is in the genes, or murder in the folds of the brain's frontal lobes. Instead, the pic-

ture is more nuanced, based as it is on the discovery that experience rewires the brain. The dawning realization of the constant back-and-forth between nature and nurture has resurrected the search for the biological roots of violence.

Early experiences seem to be especially powerful: a child's brain is more malleable than that of an adult. The dark side of the zero-to-3 movement, which emphasizes the huge potential for learning during this period, is that the young brain also is extra vulnerable to hurt in the first years of life. A child who suffers repeated "hits" of stress—abuse, neglect, terror—experiences physical changes in his brain, finds Dr. Bruce Perry of Baylor College of Medicine. The incessant flood of stress chemicals tends to reset the brain's system of fight-or-flight hormones, putting them on hair-trigger alert. The result is the kid who shows impulsive aggression, the kid who pops the classmate who disses him. For the outcast, hostile confrontations—not necessarily an elbow to the stomach at recess, but merely kids vacating en masse when he sits down in the cafeteria—can increase the level of stress hormones in his brain. And that can have dangerous consequences. "The early environment programs the nervous system to make an individual more or less reactive to stress," says biologist Michael Meaney of McGill University. "If parental care is inadequate or unsupportive, the [brain] may decide that the world stinks—and it better be ready to meet the challenge." This, then, is how having an abusive parent raises the risk of youth violence: it can change a child's brain. Forever after, influences like the mean-spiritedness that schools condone or the humiliation that's standard fare in adolescence pummel the mind of the child whose brain has been made excruciatingly vulnerable to them.

In other children, constant exposure to pain and violence can make their brain's system of stress hormones unresponsive, like a keypad that has been pushed so often it just stops working. These are the kids with antisocial personalities. They typically have low heart rates and impaired emotional sensitivity. Their signature is a lack of empathy, and their sensitivity to the world around them is practically nonexistent. Often they abuse animals: Kip Kinkel, the 15-year-old who killed his parents and shot 24 schoolmates last May, had a history of this; Luke Woodham, who killed three schoolmates and wounded seven at his high school in Pearl, Miss., in 1997, had previously beaten his dog with a club, wrapped it in a bag and set it on fire. These are also the adolescents who do not respond to punishment: nothing hurts. Their ability to feel, to react, has died, and so has their conscience. Hostile, impulsive aggressors usually feel sorry afterward. Antisocial aggressors don't feel at all. Paradoxically, though, they often have a keen sense of injustices aimed at themselves.

Inept parenting encompasses more than outright abuse, however. Parents who are withdrawn and remote, neglectful and passive, are at risk of shaping a child who (absent a compensating source of love and attention) shuts down emotionally. It's important to be clear about this: inadequate parenting short of Dickensian neglect generally has little ill effect on most children. But to a vulnerable baby, the result of neglect can be tragic. Perry finds that neglect impairs the development of the brain's cortex, which controls feelings of belonging and attachment. "When there are experi-

ences in early life that result in an underdeveloped capacity [to form relationships]," says Perry, "kids have a hard time empathizing with people. They tend to be relatively passive and perceive themselves to be stomped on by the outside world."

RISK FACTORS

Having any of the following risk factors doubles a boy's chance of becoming a murderer:

- **Coming from a family with a history of criminal violence**
- **Being abused**
- **Belonging to a gang**
- **Abusing drugs or alcohol**

Having any of these risk factors, in addition to the above, triples the risk of becoming a killer:

- **Using a weapon**
- **Having been arrested**
- **Having a neurological problem that impairs thinking or feeling**
- **Having had problems at school**

These neglected kids are the ones who desperately seek a script, an ideology that fits their sense of being humiliated and ostracized. Today's pop culture offers all too many dangerous ones, from the music of Rammstein to the game of Doom. Historically, most of those scripts have featured males. That may explain, at least in part, why the murderers are Andrews and Dylans rather than Ashleys and Kaitlins, suggests Deborah Prothrow-Smith of the Harvard School of Public Health. "But girls are now 25 percent of the adolescents arrested for violent crime," she notes. "This follows the media portrayal of girl superheroes beating people up," from Power Rangers to Xena. Another reason that the schoolyard murderers are boys is that girls tend to internalize ostracism and shame rather than turning it into anger. And just as girls could be the next wave of killers, so could even younger children. "Increasingly, we're seeing the high-risk population for lethal violence as being the 10- to 14-year-olds," says Richard Lieberman, a school psychologist in Los Angeles. "Developmentally, their concept of death is still magical. They still think it's temporary, like little Kenny in 'South

Park'." Of course, there are loads of empty, emotionally unattached girls and boys. The large majority won't become violent. "But if they're in a violent environment," says Perry, "they're more likely to."

There seems to be a genetic component to the vulnerability that can turn into antisocial-personality disorder. It is only a tiny bend in the twig, but depending on how the child grows up, the bend will be exaggerated or straightened out. Such aspects of temperament as "irritability, impulsivity, hyperactivity and a low sensitivity to emotions in others are all biologically based," says psychologist James Garbarino of Cornell University, author of the upcoming book "Lost Boys: Why Our Sons Turn Violent and How We Can Save Them." A baby who is unreactive to hugs and smiles can be left to go her natural, antisocial way if frustrated parents become exasperated, withdrawn, neglectful or enraged. Or that child can be pushed back toward the land of the feeling by parents who never give up trying to engage and stimulate and form a loving bond with her. The different responses of parents produce different brains, and thus behaviors. "Behavior is the result of a dialogue between your brain and your experiences," concludes Debra Niehoff, author of the recent book "The Biology of Violence." "Although people are born with some biological givens, the brain has many blank pages. From the first moments of childhood the brain acts as a historian, recording our experiences in the language of neurochemistry."

There are some out-and-out brain pathologies that lead to violence. Lesions of the frontal lobe can induce apathy and distort both judgment and emotion. In the brain scans he has done in his Fairfield, Calif., clinic of 50 murderers, psychiatrist Daniel Amen finds several shared patterns. The structure called the cingulate gyrus, curving through the center of the brain, is hyperactive in murderers. The CG acts like the brain's transmission, shifting from one thought to another. When it is impaired, people get stuck on one thought. Also, the prefrontal cortex, which seems to act as the brain's supervisor, is sluggish in the 50 murderers. "If you have violent thoughts that you're stuck on and no supervisor, that's a prescription for trouble," says Amen, author of "Change Your Brain/ Change Your Life." The sort of damage he finds can result from head trauma as well as exposure to toxic substances like alcohol during gestation.

Children who kill are not, with very few exceptions, amoral. But their morality is aberrant. "I killed because people like me are mistreated every day," said pudgy, be-spectacled Luke Woodham, who murdered three students. "My whole life I felt out-casted, alone." So do a lot of adolescents. The difference is that at least some of the recent school killers felt emotionally or physically abandoned by those who should love them. Andrew Golden, who was 11 when he and Mitchell Johnson, 13, went on their killing spree in Jonesboro, Ark., was raised mainly by his grandparents while his parents worked. Mitchell mourned the loss of his father to divorce.

Unless they have another source of un-conditional love, such boys fail to develop, or lose, the neural circuits that control the capacity to feel and to form healthy rela-tionships. That makes them hypersensitive to perceived injustice. A sense of injustice is often accompanied by a feeling of abject powerlessness. An adult can often see his way to restoring a sense of self-worth, says psychiatrist James Gilligan of Harvard Medical School, through success in work

or love. A child usually lacks the emo-tional skills to do that. As one killer told Garbarino's colleague, "I'd rather be wanted for murder than not wanted at all."

THAT THE LITTLETON MASSACRE ENDED in suicide may not be a coincidence. As Michael Carneal was wrestled to the ground after killing three fellow students in Paducah in 1997, he cried out, "Kill me now!" Kip Kinkel pleaded with the school-mates who stopped him, "Shoot me!" With suicide "you get immortality," says Michael Flynn of John Jay College of Criminal Justice. "That is a great feeling of power for an adolescent who has no sense that he matters."

The good news is that understanding the roots of violence offers clues on how to prevent it. The bad news is that ever more children are exposed to the influences that, in the already vulnerable, can produce a bent toward murder. Juvenile homicide is twice as common today as it was in the

mid-1980s. It isn't the brains kids are born with that has changed in half a generation; what has changed is the ubiquity of vio-lence, the easy access to guns and the glo-rification of revenge in real life and in entertainment. To deny the role of these in-fluences is like denying that air pollution triggers childhood asthma. Yes, to develop asthma a child needs a specific, biological vulnerability. But as long as some children have this respiratory vulnerability—and some always will— then allowing pollu-tion to fill our air will make some children wheeze, and cough, and die. And as long as some children have a neurological vulner-ability—and some always will—then turn-ing a blind eye to bad parenting, bullying and the gun culture will make other chil-dren seethe, and withdraw, and kill.

With ADAM ROGERS, PAT WINGERT
and THOMAS HAYDEN

WHERE RAMPAGES BEGIN
A special report.

From Adolescent Angst To Shooting Up Schools

TIMOTHY EGAN

MOSES LAKE, Wash.—Well before the school shootings in Oregon and the South prompted a search to the depths of the national soul, a 14-year-old honors student named Barry Loukaitis walked into his algebra class in this hard little farm town and shot his teacher in the back and two students in the chest.

Guns and violent videos were always around the boy's house. He learned how to fire weapons from his father. And he picked up a pose from the Oliver Stone movie "Natural Born Killers," telling a friend it would be "pretty cool" to go on a killing spree just like the two lead characters in the film.

Dressed in black and armed with three of the family firearms, Barry entered Frontier Middle School in this desert town 180 miles east of Seattle on Feb. 2, 1996, and turned his guns loose on fellow ninth graders.

"This sure beats algebra, doesn't it," Barry said, according to court records, as he stood over a dying boy who was choking on his own blood. He was tackled by a teacher and hauled off to jail, where he promptly took a nap.

A sign soon appeared on a nearby school, bearing a single word: Why? Of late, that question has been asked around the nation, following a spate of multiple-victim school shootings over the last nine months that have left 15 people dead and 42 wounded. People wonder whether something aberrant and terrifying—like a lethal virus, some have called it—is in the bloodstream.

While precise answers may be elusive, the recent killing sprees share a remarkable number of common traits. The first of the rural, multiple-victim student shootings, here in Moses Lake, looks in many respects like a road map of what was to come. From this case and interviews with police officers, prosecutors, psychologists and parents of the attackers—as well as the boys' own words—several patterns emerge:

- Each case involved a child who felt inferior or picked on, with a grudge against some student or teacher. The attackers complained of being fat or nearsighted, short or unloved—the ordinary problems of adolescence, at first glance. But in fact, most of the assailants were suicidal, and of above-average intelligence, according to mental health experts who have examined most of the children arrested for the shootings. Their killings are now viewed by some criminologists and other experts as a way to end a tortured life with a blaze of terror.

- The killers were able to easily acquire high-powered guns, and in many cases, their parents helped the children get them, either directly or through negligence. Guns with rapid-fire capability, usually semiautomatic rifles that can spray a burst of bullets in a matter of seconds, were used in the incidents with the most victims. Single-fire, bolt-action guns or revolvers would not have caused near the damage in human life, the police say.

- To varying degrees, each of the attackers seemed to have been obsessed by violent pop culture. A 14-year-old in West Paducah, Ky., was influenced by a movie in which a character's classmates are shot during a dream sequence, according to detectives. Violent rap lyrics may have influenced one of the boys in the Jonesboro, Ark., case, his mother says. In particular, a song about a stealth killing eerily matches what occurred. The killer who has confessed in Pearl, Miss., says he was a fan of violent fantasy video games and the nihilistic rock-and-roll lyrics of Marilyn Manson, as was the boy charged in the Springfield, Ore., shootings last month. The Springfield youth was so enmeshed in violent television and Internet sites that his parents recently unplugged the cable television and took away his computer, a close family friend said.

- The student killers gave ample warning signs, often in detailed writings at school, of dramatic, violent outbursts to come. The boy in Moses Lake wrote a poem about murder, saying, "I'm at my point of no return." Similar jottings were left by the boys in the South, and in Springfield. In virtually all of the cases, adults never took the threats and warning signs seriously. Or they simply overlooked them.

"When you look at the overall pattern, it's a pretty serious wake-up call," said Dr. Ronald D. Stephens, executive director of the National School Safety Center, which monitors school violence from its headquarters in Westlake Village, Calif. "We are seeing an increasing number of violent, callous, remorseless juveniles.

"What's behind it," Dr. Stephens said, "seems to be a combination of issues that range from the availability of weapons to the culture our kids immerse themselves in to the fact that many youngsters simply have no sense of the finality of death."

People argue, in the age-old debate, either that the killers are simply bad human beings or that their actions can be linked to a corrosive family environment—nature versus nurture. Certainly, the recent shootings give plenty of new material for both sides.

Parents of the young killers place blame on the surfeit of guns, the influence of junk culture and children stressed to a snapping point. But they also look at themselves, their broken marriages, their lives of stress and hurry, and wonder how all that affected their children.

"I didn't think about Barry at all," said JoAnn Phillips, the mother of Barry Loukaitis in Moses Lake, in court testimony last year in her son's case. A few weeks before the shooting, she had told her son that she planned to divorce her husband and that she herself was suicidal, but she was oblivious to how this would affect her son.

"We are responsible for our kids, but you tell me, where did I go wrong?" Gretchen Woodward said in an interview recently in which she discussed her son, Mitchell Johnson, the seventh grader accused, along with Andrew Golden, of killing 5 and wounding 10 in Jonesboro last

March. "I think there's a lot more pressure on our kids today than there was when we were growing up."

The Killings

Urban Trend Takes Rural Turn

Children have long killed children in the United States. The peak was the 1992-93 school year, when nearly 50 people were killed in school-related violence, according to the School Safety Center. Most of those killings were in urban schools, and prompted a Federal law banning guns from schools, security measures like metal detectors, and efforts to control the influence of gangs. What is different now is that the shootings are largely rural, have multiple victims and, within the warped logic of homicide, seem to make no sense; many of the victims have been shot at random.

In looking at the 221 deaths at American schoolyards over the last six years, what leaps out is how the shootings changed dramatically in the last two years—not the number, but the type.

Most earlier deaths were gang-related, or they were stabbings, or they involved money or a fight over a girlfriend. (Boys are almost always the killers.) Then came the Moses Lake shooting in 1996. Barry Loukaitis, who confessed to the shootings and was found guilty as an adult in trial last fall, did have a target in mind when he walked into the afternoon algebra class—a popular boy who had teased him. He shot the boy to death.

But then he fired away at two other students, people against whom he said he had no grudge. He shot the teacher, Leona Caires, in the back. She died with an eraser still in her hand.

When asked in a tape-recorded session with police why he shot the others, Barry said, "I don't know, I guess reflex took over."

After Moses Lake, shootings of a somewhat similar nature followed. In February 1997 in Bethel, Alaska, a boy armed with a 12-gauge shotgun

that had been kept unlocked around the home killed a popular athlete, fired shots at random and then tracked and killed the principal. Like Barry, the 16-year-old Alaskan killer thought it would be "cool," prosecutors said, to shoot up the school.

"He loved what he did," said Renee Erb, who prosecuted the youth, Evan Ramsey. "This was his moment of glory."

By the end of last year, the killings seemed to come with numbing sameness. All but one of the victims apparently were chosen at random in the shootings outside a high school in Pearl, Miss.

"I wasn't aiming at anyone else," said Luke Woodham, convicted this week in the shootings, in a tape-recorded confession played at his trial in Hattiesburg, Miss. "It was like I was there, and I wasn't there."

In West Paducah, Ky., three girls were killed and five other students wounded in a shooting with no apparent motive. "It was kind of like I was in a dream," the accused attacker, 14-year-old Michael Carneal, told his principal.

In March, an 11-year-old steeped in gun culture and a 13-year-old with a troubled past opened fire, in what seemed like a military assault, at students who filed out of Westside Middle School in Jonesboro, Ark.

And finally in Springfield last month—where a boy with a love of guns is accused of mowing down as many students as possible in the crowded school cafeteria, using a semiautomatic rifle taken from his father—the victims were anyone who happened to be in the way, the police said.

People ask why this is happening now in white, rural areas, said Dr. Alan Unis, a University of Washington psychiatrist who did an examination of the Moses Lake assailant for the court. "It's happening everywhere," he said. "One of the things we're seeing in the population at large is that all the mood disorders are happening earlier and earlier. The incidence of depression and

MOSES LAKE, WASH., FEB. 2, 1996

Three killed and one wounded when Barry Loukaitis, 14, fired on an algebra class at Frontier Middle School. He was convicted [in 1997] of murder and assault, and sentenced to two consecutive life terms without parole, plus 205 years.

BETHEL, ALASKA, FEB. 19, 1997

Two people killed, a student and the principal, when Evan Ramsey, 16, went on a shooting rampage at Bethel High School. He was convicted in February [1998] of two counts of first-degree murder and 15 counts of assault.

PEARL, MISS., OCT. 1, 1997

Three people killed and seven wounded when a boy fired on students at Pearl High School after stabbing his mother. Luke Woodham was found guilty of killing his mother, and convicted of two other murders.

WEST PADUCAH, KY., DEC. 1, 1997

Three people killed and five wounded when a student opened fire on a prayer circle inside Heath High School. Michael Carneal, 14, has been charged with the killings.

JONESBORO, ARK., MARCH 24, 1998

Five people killed and 10 wounded when two students who lay in wait in the grass opened fire on teachers and students who had filed out of Westside Middle School after an alarm had been pulled. Andrew Golden, 11 and Mitchell Johnson, 13, have been charged with the killings, though they cannot be tried as adults and could be released, under Arkansas law, after they reach their 18th birthdays.

SPRINGFIELD, ORE., MAY 21, 1998

Four people killed (including the parents of the alleged assailant) and 22 injured in a shooting rampage that started at home and moved to Thurston High School. Kipland Kinkel, 15, has been formally accused of the killings.

suicide has gone way up among young people."

Suicide rates for the young have increased over the last four decades and have leveled off near their all-time highs. More than 1.5 million Americans under age 15 are seriously depressed, the National Institute of Mental Health says. The number may be twice that high, in the view of the American Academy of Child and Adolescent Psychiatry.

Most of the attackers in the recent cases had shown signs of clinical depression or other psychological problems. But schools, strapped for mental health counselors, are less likely to pick up on such behavior or to have the available help, principals at the schools where the shootings happened said.

The Guns

Troubled Children And Easy Access

A depressed, insecure child is one thing, and quite common. But that same boy with a gun can be a lethal threat. In all of the recent shootings, acquiring guns was easier than buying beer, or even gas. And these children armed themselves with small arsenals, as if preparing for battle.

The Moses Lake assailant used to play at home with his family guns as if they were toys, friends testified in court. In his confession, Barry Loukaitis said he took two of his father's guns from an unlocked cabinet, and a third one—a .25-caliber semiautomatic pistol—from a family car.

The gun used in the Alaska school shootings was kept unlocked at the foot of the stairs in a foster home where Evan Ramsey was living, according to police.

The shootings in West Paducah, Jonesboro and Springfield were similar in that semiautomatic weapons—capable of firing off dozens of rounds in less than a minute—were used to kill children. Weapons of less rapid-fire capability would likely have reduced the death tolls, the police said.

In Jonesboro and Springfield, the parents of the accused assailants taught their children, at an early age, how to use guns properly, which is the general advice of the National Rifle Association. The story of how Andrew Golden, accused in the Jonesboro shooting, was given a gun by Santa Claus at age 6, and was an expert marksman in the Practical Pistol Shooters Club a few years later has been widely reported.

But less well-known is how the other accused Jonesboro killer came by his knowledge of guns. Mitchell Johnson's mother, Mrs. Woodward, said in an interview that she taught her boy how to shoot a shotgun, and then he took a three-week course.

When the boys were arrested after hitting 15 human targets at Westside Middle School, police found nine guns in their possession. Most of them had been taken from the home of Andrew's grandfather, Doug Golden, a conservation officer who says he usually kept his guns unlocked in the house.

The parents of Kipland Kinkel, the boy accused of the Springfield shootings, were not gun enthusiasts, but their son was, according to interviews with family friends. The parents agonized over the boy's gun obsession, finally giving in and buying him a weapon. The father and son took courses in marksmanship and safety, and the guns were kept under lock and key.

But given Kip Kinkel's moods and temper, the parents had debated over whether to get him a single-loading bolt-action weapon or something with more rapid-fire capability. They settled on the more powerful gun, a .22-caliber semiautomatic Ruger rifle. It was a fatal mistake, said some people who are studying the recent shootings. It was that rifle that Kip used to fire off 50 rounds at Thurston High School.

"The kid had them by the throat," said Dr. Bill Reisman, who does profiling of deviant youth behavior for law-enforcement officials and recently gave a closed-door briefing to community leaders from cities where the school shootings occurred. "They were terrified of his interest in guns, but they went out and bought him guns."

A Kinkel family friend, Tom Jacobson, who played tennis every other week with the boy's father, said the parents were looking for a way to control and connect with their volatile child. The parents, Bill and Faith Kinkel, were both killed by their son, prosecutors in Oregon said.

"These were devoted parents in a tight-knit family," Jacobson said in an interview. "Bill had tried everything with Kip. I think he just ran out of ideas."

The Culture

Too Influenced By Music and Film?

Just as easy to get as guns were videos or cassettes in which murder is a central theme, and often glorified. Jurors in the trial of Barry Loukaitis were shown a Pearl Jam video, "Jeremy," about a youth who fantasizes about using violence against classmates who taunt him. That video, along with "Natural Born Killers," a movie about a pair who kill their parents and then go on nationwide shooting spree, were among Barry's favorites, his friends testified.

At least one of the boys accused in the Jonesboro attack, Mitchell Johnson, was a big fan of gangsta rap. Friends and family members say a favorite song was one by Bone Thugs-n-Harmony, called, "Crept and We Came," about killings in a massacre-like way.

The boy also played Mortal Kombat, a popular video game that involves graphic killing of opponents, his mother said.

"There are many cultural forces predisposing kids to violent behavior," said the Rev. Chris Perry, a youth minister for Mitchell Johnson

at Central Baptist Church, who has talked to the boy three times since the shootings. "There is a profound cultural influence, like gravity, pulling kids into a world where violence is a perfectly normal way to handle our emotions."

But Mitchell also loved gospel music, the preacher said, and he sang at nursing homes. Millions of children listen to violent-themed rap music, play Mortal Kombat and witness thousands of killings on television by age 10, and do not become murderers.

"Barry Loukaitis was obviously influenced by 'Natural Born Killers,'" said John Knodell, who prosecuted the Moses Lake assailant. "But there are hundreds of thousands of kids who watch these things and don't blow away their schoolmates."

The psychiatrist in the Loukaitis case, Dr. Unis, also is reluctant to blame violent cultural influences. But he and other experts say there is a syndrome at work, in which a child who sees one shootout on the news may be inspired to try something similar.

"The media or violent videos do not by themselves make the event happen," said Ms. Erb, the prosecutor in Alaska. "But it shows them a way."

The Signs

Cries for Help Often Overlooked

The boys accused of shooting classmates are portrayed as average children. But a look inside their bedrooms or journals, or a discussion with their friends shows they left ample clues of trouble to come.

Michael Carneal was known as a slight boy who played baritone sax in the school band in West Paducah. After the killings, his principal, Bill Bond, looked at some of his writing and found a child who felt weak and powerless, with an angry desire to lash out.

A week before the shooting, Michael warned classmates that

"something big was going to happen" and they should get out of the way, detectives said. At least three boys accused in other cases did the same thing.

The Alaskan assailant warned specific students the night before the killings to go up on a second-floor balcony. "These kids didn't tell anyone," said the prosecutor, Ms. Erb. "Instead, they got right up there the next day to get their view of the killings."

In his ninth-grade English class, Barry Loukaitis wrote a poem about murder that ended this way:

I look at his body on the floor,
Killing a bastard that deserves to die,
Ain't nothing like it in the world,
But he sure did bleed a lot

Kip Kinkel read a journal entry aloud in English class about killing fellow students.

Most of the attackers were also suicidal, writing notes before the killings that assumed they would die.

Luke Woodham's journal writings were particularly graphic. He left a last will and testament, leaving music cassettes to the older boy who is said by police to have influenced him. "I do this to show society, 'Push us and we will push back,'" he wrote. "I suffered all my life. No one ever truly loved me. No one ever truly cared about me."

Dr. Reisman said parents and teachers should be alarmed by such writings. Animal abuse, arson and a sudden interest in death and darkness are red flags, he said.

Often the assailants live in the shadow of successful older siblings, Dr. Reisman added. But the most common element is deep depression, he said.

"They'll all have depression, in the state in which they do these things," Dr. Reisman said. "When they're cornered, the first thing they say is, 'Kill me.' It's suicide by cop."

From *The New York Times,* June 14, 1998, pp. 1, 22. © 1998 by the The New York Times Company. Reprinted by permission.

THE CULTURE OF YOUTH*

Marvin E. Wolfgang

THE SUBCULTURE OF YOUTH

The first issue confronted in discussing youth is whether social analysts may validly refer to a given age group as constituting a culture or a subculture. The term "culture" has gone through many definitional forms since E. B. Tylor's famous statement in 1871 defining it as "... that complex whole which includes knowledge, belief, art, morals, law, custom, and any other capabilities and habits acquired by man as a member of society."[1]

By 1962, A. L. Kroeber and Clyde Kluckhohn had analyzed 160 definitions in English by anthropologists, sociologists, and others, and offered a synthesis that embodied the elements accepted by most contemporary social scientists: "Culture consists of patterns, explicit and implicit, by symbols, constituting the distinctive achievements of human groups, including their embodiment in artifacts; the essential core of culture consists of traditional (i.e., historically derived and selected) ideas and especially their attached values; culture systems may, on the one hand, be considered as products of action, on the other as conditioning elements of further action."[2]

In discussing the elements of culture, social scientists usually refer to life style, prescribed ways of behaving, norms of conduct, beliefs, values, behavior patterns and uniformities, as well as the artifacts which these "nonmaterial" aspects create. The writings of Franz Boas, Ralph Linton, Otto Klineberg, Pitirim Sorokin, Robert MacIver and Leslie White are only a few examples among the many important contributions to the embellishment of the meaning of culture.[3]

More recently, A. L. Kroeber and Talcott Parsons have provided a meaningful distinction between "society" and "culture" in the following way: "We suggest that it is useful to define the concept culture for most usages more narrowly than has been generally the case in American anthropological tradition, restricting its reference to transmitted and created content and patterns of values, ideas and other symbolic-meaningful systems as factors in the shaping of human behavior and the artifacts produced through behavior. On the other hand, we suggest that the term society or, more generally, social system be used to designate the specifically relational system of interaction among individuals and collectivities."[4]

The term subculture, although not the concept, did not become common in social science literature until after World War II. Alfred McClung Lee[5] made use of the term in 1945; Milton Gordon in 1947 defined subculture as "... a subdivision of the national culture, composed of a combination of factorable social situations such as class status, ethnic background, regional and rural or urban residence, and religious affiliation, but forming in their combination a functional unity which has an integrated impact on the participating individual.[6]

In sociological criminology, Albert Cohen,[7] in his "Delinquent Boys," describes the term by referring to the following items: The cultural patterns of subgroups; the emergence of subcultures "only by interaction with those (persons) who already share and embody, in their belief and action, the culture pattern"; the psychogenic situation of physical limitations in problems requiring solution; the fact that human problems are not randomly distributed among the roles that make up the social system; reference groups for interaction, for the sharing of values, and as the means of achieving status, recognition, and response.

Even before the publication of Richard Cloward and Lloyd Ohlin's "Delinquency and Opportunity,"[8] its significant breakdown into criminal, conflict, and retreatist subcultures, Milton Yinger[9] noted over 100 books and articles that made some use of the idea of subculture. After a comprehensive review of such terms as "situation," "anomie," and "role," which should not, he says, be confused with the meaning of subculture, Yinger introduced the concept of contraculture to refer to those subcultural groups that are at considerable variance with the larger culture.

*A publication of the Office of Juvenile Delinquency, Welfare Administration, U.S. Department of Health, Education, and Welfare, 1967. Reproduced by permission.

It is not our purpose to try to add new clarity, precision, or quantifiable parameters to the meaning of subcultures.[10] We are drawing attention to the generally communicative meaning of subculture in order to indicate that youth represent a separate subculture in society. We do assume, however, that not all values, beliefs, or norms in a society have equal status, that some priority allocation of them is made which the persons in a subculture partially accept and partially deny. The representatives of a subculture may even construct antitheses to elements of the central or dominant values while still remaining within the larger cultural system.

These assumptions lead us to assert that a subculture implies that there is a cluster of value judgments, or a social value system, which is both apart from and a part of the central value system. From the viewpoint of the larger, dominant culture, the values of the subculture set the latter apart and prevent total integration, occasionally causing open or covert conflicts. The dominant culture may directly or indirectly promote this apartness, and the degree of reciprocal integration may vary, but whatever the reason for the difference, some normative isolation and solidarity of the subculture result. There are, thus, shared values that are learned, adopted, and even exhibited by participants in the subculture, and these values differ in quantity and quality from the dominant culture.

A subculture is, then, only partly different from the parent culture, the larger culture from which subcultural elements have stemmed as different offshoots of its own value system. But there must be a sufficient number and variety of significant values commonly shared between "parent" and "child" if the latter is to retain its theoretical attribution of subculture. Some of the values of a subculture may, however, be more than different from the larger culture; they may be in conflict or at wide variance with the latter. Thus, a delinquent subculture represents a contractual system that is more than merely different from the parent culture, for in its dysfunctional character it is also antithetical to the broader social system. To be part of the larger culture implies that some values related to the ends and means of the whole are shared by the part. The subculture that is only different is a tolerated deviation; what we generally refer to as the youth subculture is in fact a tolerated form of variation from the parent culture. Values shared in the subculture are often made evident in terms of conduct that is expected, ranging from permissible to required expectations in certain kinds of life situations. These conduct norms generated by the value content of the subculture (indeed, of any subculture) have not yet been subjected to much quantified measurement.

It is difficult to discuss subcultures and conduct norms without reference to social groups, for values are shared by individuals, and individuals sharing values make up groups. In most cases, when we refer to subcultures we are thinking of individuals who share common values and who socially interact in some limited geographical or residential isolation. However, value sharing does not necessarily require direct or primary social interaction. Consequently, a subculture may exist widely distributed spatially and without interpersonal contact among individuals or whole groups of individuals. Several delinquent gangs, for example, may be spread throughout a city and rarely, if ever, have contacts; yet they are referred to collectively as the "delinquent subculture," and properly so, for otherwise each gang would have be considered as a separate subculture.

If a subculture, like a culture, is composed of values, conduct norms, social situations, role definitions and performances, sharing, transmission, and learning of values, then there is sufficient reason to speak of the subculture of youth in American society. We have said that the degree of concordant and tolerated, as well as discordant and untolerated, values of various segments of youth are related to the dominant culture themes of American society. A detailed analysis of the establishment and measurement of the parameters of the youth subculture would seem to be necessary in order to establish exactly where the values vary, to measure the intensity or strength of these values among youth, and to determine the degree of commitment or allegiance that youth has to certain values that when clustered together, may be called the value system of youth. It may be contended that an age group roughly embracing 12 to 20 years represents a subcultural system, although there are, of course, other subcultures, or other transmittable value systems, within which youth functions.

Without appropriate measurements of values and value systems, it is difficult to indicate exactly where subcultures blend into one another. However, the subculture of the lower class poor, of a Negro subsociety, delinquent subcultures, and other varieties of subcultural affiliations may be assumed to have groups of individuals who represent not only separate subcultures, but also conclaves where these various subcultures overlap. The descriptive characteristics of the generic term "youth" are often of little help to the social analysts or the consumers of social observations who wish to understand the variety of youth problems. Our attention, therefore, should be drawn not merely to the ways in which an age group called youth fits functionally into the larger culture system created and maintained by adults; what is needed beyond these age-graded and age-linked descriptive features is some notion of how several subcultures combine with youth. In a more elaborate treatise, the linkages should contain an interwoven tread of theory and be embraced by meaningful sociological conceptualisms. One of the main conceptual propositions to be employed later in this paper includes protest against the lack of, and request or even demand for more power and for participation in the larger culture system and its processes.

An interesting feature in the present generation that contributes to this age-graded subculture we call youth is the massive network of communication. Instant awareness of news and the rapid spread of innovations in dress, dancing, and dating habits quickly unify people and make rapid the sharing of values and norms across the entire country. The structure of our mass communication functions to make elements in the youth subculture quickly reinforced by supportive acts and attitudes on a numerically larger scale and spatially wider arena than ever before. For example, a university sit-in protest is known abroad even while it happens, and repetitive reinforcement readily appears in other universities. The transistor radio carried by a West Berlin teenager reports same musical styles heard in Boise, Idaho. Thus, the contraction of time and the extension of space for spreading the elements attractive to and shared by youth combine to create a firm subculture of their own.

It should be remembered, however, that more new things lasting shorter periods of time create only an illusion of diversity. The young listeners to television and transistors, more sensitive than their elders to innovation, fads, and fashion, do not have alternatives of action that correspondingly increase with the number of changes they witness. Their repertoire of response may even be reduced as the youth culture grows stronger. Deviance adult models may be more evident now, but the more committed the youth become to their own subculture, the more captive they become to their conformity. The more they strive to be recognized, loved, wanted, and feared within their own group culture, the more they contribute to their own captivity. The shared mass media of magazines and electronics probably produce greater homogenization among the young than among adults, and within the youth subculture of today more than during any previous period. This generalization is applicable to the considerable variability that exists in the youth subculture, ranging from Saturday afternoon dance clubs to Florida and Bermuda springtime frolics, the free university students, the Berkeley free speech movement, and the local drugstore crowd of the "Street Corner Society."[11]

EXTENDED SOCIALIZATION AND DEPENDENCY STATUS

Gertrude Stein is alleged to have said that the United States is the oldest country in the world because it has had the most experience with modem industrial society and its complex consequences. With similar perception, Dwight Macdonald[12] has said that the United States was the first to develop the concept of the teenager, a concept which is still not well accepted in Europe, and that we have had the longest experience with the subculture of youth. The way we handle a nearly "overdeveloped" society with transportation, bureaucratization, impersonal, automated living, and the way we learn to understand the new problems of youth and the existence of poverty to remind us of our social imperfection, will be lessons of value to underdeveloped or newly developed countries. Despite our longer experience with modernity and the teenage subculture, we still have lessons to learn about the problems created by both, and the particular interrelation of modern youth and modern poverty is especially important and striking in many ways.

Our youth in general are richer today than they have ever been and have more alternatives of action and more privileges. The list of privileges usurped by youth has not only increased but has shifted downward in age. The high school student of today has the accoutrements of the college student of yesteryear—cars, long pants, money, and more access to girls. This downward shift in privileges, precocious to younger ages, is a phenomenon well known to every parent whose own youth subculture was devoid of them.

Not only are our youth more privileged and richer, but they have for some time constituted an increasingly significant portion of American purchasing power. The statistics of consumption of lipsticks and brassieres, even by 12- and 13-year-olds, are well known, as are those of records, used cars, popular magazines, and transistor radios. The magnified purchasing power of young teenagers is one of the factors that tends to make them want to grow up faster or not at all, which is suggestive of Reuel Denney's credit-card viewpoint of "grow up now and pay later."[13]

The ambivalence of the analyzers regarding whether our youth become aduitlike too early or behave as adolescent children too long is a scholastic debate that has not yet been resolved by empirical data. Moreover, a valid appraisal of the "youth problem" is also made difficult by the existence of conflicting cultural prescriptions for youth. We appear to want teenagers to act like young adults in our society, yet we are increasingly stretching the whole socialization process from childhood to adulthood. And the number of people involved in the subculture stretch is increasingly large. There are nearly 70 million persons in the United States under 18 years of age, or nearly one-third of the Nation's population.[14]

The number reaching age 18 each year has, however, doubled within a decade. There were 2 million in 1956 and 4 million in 1965, the result of the "baby boom" of the late forties. Of the more than 1.5 million who graduate from high school, about half will register for college, and the 25 percent of the 16–24 age group now in college will increase. One could say with Denney[15] that the age of extended socialization is already in full swing.

It is of correlative interest that the public has become disturbed by the announced figure of 7.5 million school dropouts during the 1960's, despite some queries about whether we really want to or can prevent all school dropouts. The middle-class and middle-aged producers of prescriptions for youth want to keep them in, or return them to school for reasons that extend from a genuine belief that all youth should benefit from more formal education to fears that dropout youths inundate the labor market and thereby contribute to delinquency and crime. Our society would apparently like more children to go to college, often without commensurate concern for how the extended period of dependency, socialization, and an indiscriminate density of college population may contribute to producing mediocrity of educational standards. Yet, without continued education, the dropouts are commonly dependent in other ways. As Lucius Cervantes has very recently pointed out, although the dropout group cuts across social class, ethnic, and geographic lines, most come from the blue- and lower white-collar economic classes. In summarizing, he says: "The dropout rate nationally is between 30 and 40 percent. The rate is higher in the South than in the North; higher among boys than girls (53 percent versus 47 percent); higher in the slums than in the suburbs. Most dropouts withdraw from school during or before their 16th year. There is 10 times the incidence of delinquency among the dropouts as there is among the stayins. In view of society's educational expectations for modern youth and dropout youth's inability to get a job while 'just waiting around for something to happen,' the very state of being a dropout has all but become by definition a condition of semidelinquency."[16]

On the one hand, then, the privileges and age roles are being extended by being lowered, and young teenagers are as sophisticated or cynical, as fantasy-filled and joyriding as our older teenagers used to be. On the other hand, and at the other end of the range of the youth age, the period of their not moving into adult roles is also being extended.

This extended socialization is accompanied by the problem of poor adult models. Throughout the social classes, it appears that the search for the adult to be emulated is often a desperate and futile quest. Part of the reason for this futility is due to the very rapid social and technological changes occurring in our society which make it more difficult for the adult to perform his traditional role of model and mentor to youth. Social change is so rapid, says Kenneth Keniston,[17] that growing up no longer means learning how to fit into society because the society into which young people will someday fit has not yet been developed or even, perhaps, cannot properly be imagined. Many youth feel forced into detachment and premature cynicism because society seems to offer youth today so little that is stable, relevant, and meaningful. They often look in vain for values, goals, means, and institutions to which they can be committed because their thrust for commitment is strong. Youth can be a period of fruitful idealism, but there are few of what Erik Erikson[18] would call "objects of fidelity" for our youth; so that "playing it cool," is more than an ephemeral expression— it becomes a way of avoiding damaging commitments to goals and life styles of the parent generation which may be outmoded tomorrow. Times and viewpoints shift rapidly, and many of our children resemble world-weary and jaded adults at age 14. The social isolation, social distance, alienation, and retreat from the adult world are increased by many social and technological mechanisms operating to encourage a youth subculture. As the numbers and intensity of value sharing in the youth subculture increase, the process of intergenerational alienation also escalates. Parents have almost always been accused of not understanding their children. What may be new is that more parents either do not care that they do not understand, or that it is increasingly impossible for them to understand. Perhaps, then, it is not that parents are poor models for the kinds of lives that the youths will lead in their own mature years; parents may simply be increasingly irrelevant models for their children. So rapid is current social change that the youth of today have difficulty projecting a concept of themselves as adults.

This double stretch in that band of the life cycle we call youth has systemic effects on definitions and dependency. As the period of socialization extends further for more people, the concept of youth embraces later ages. When to this conceptual change is added the fact of greater life expectancy and a larger proportion of our population living longer, the social and perhaps physical meaning of middle age has changed, likewise moving upward. Our society has created linguistic support for this notion by its references to young adults, older youth, young or junior executives when referring to men who are in their midthirties or early forties.

The conceptual extension of what being young means is also reflected in the perpetration of a dependency status started in youth (that is, during late adolescence and early adulthood). The child from an economically deprived family, the dropout who becomes, like his parents, economically dependent on welfare benefits, remains in his dependency condition throughout much or most of his life. Others, mostly from the middle class, shift their extended dependency from being supported by parents or educational grants to being dependent on bureaucratic systems which continue the socialization process that often leads to the pathos of the organization man.

THE MASCULINE PROTEST AND ITS TRANSFORMATION

Social scientists have long stressed the importance of the theme of masculinity in American culture and the effect that this image of the strong masculine role has had on child rearing and the general socialization process. The inability of the middle-class child to match himself to this masculine model and the neuroticism that is the consequence of this increasingly futile struggle was vividly brought to our attention years ago by Arnold Green.[19] The continuity of this masculine role in the lower classes has often been asserted and was made one of the "focal concerns" in Walter B. Miller's[20] profile of the lower class milieu. There is reason to believe, however, that this once dominating culture theme is dissipating, especially in the central or middle-class culture, and that this dissipation is diffusing downwards through the lower classes via the youth subculture. It may be argued that in the United States, while the status of the sexes in many social spheres of activity has been approaching equality, there has been an increasing feminization of the general culture. Instead of females becoming more like males, males have increasingly taken on some of the roles and attributes formerly assigned to females. It is not so much that maleness is reduced as a goal motivating young boys; rather, physical aggressiveness, once the manifest feature of maleness, is being reduced and the meaning of masculinity is thereby being changed to more symbolic forms. The continued diminution of the earlier frontier mores which placed a premium on male aggressiveness has been replaced by other attributes of masculinity. The gun and fist have been substantially replaced by financial ability, by the capacity to manipulate others in complex organizations, and by intellectual talents. The thoughtful wit, the easy verbalizer, even the striving musician and artist are, in the dominant culture, equivalents of male assertiveness where broad shoulders and fighting fists were once the major symbols. The young culture heroes may range from Van Cliburn to the Beattles, but Bill the Kid is a fantasy figure from an earlier history.

It may well be true that in many lower class communities violence is associated with masculinity and may not only be acceptable but admired behavior. That the rates of violent crimes are high among lower class males suggests that this group still strongly continues to equate maleness with overt physical aggression. In the Italian slum of the Boston West End, Herbert Gans[21] describes families dominated by the men and where mothers encourage male dominance. On the other hand, lower class boys who lack father or other strong male figures, as is the case with many boys in Negro families, have a problem of finding models to imitate. Rejecting female dominance at home and at school, and the morality which they associate with women, may be the means such boys use to assert their masculinity, and such assertion must be performed with a strong antithesis of feminity, namely by being physically aggressive. Being a bad boy, Parsons[22] has said, can become a positive goal if goodness is too closely identified with feminity.

Whatever the reasons for this stronger masculine role among lower class youth, its retention will continue to result in violence, because the young male is better equipped physically to manifest this form of masculinity than the very young, the middle-aged, or the very old. Because he needs no special education to employ the agents of physical aggression (fists, feet, agility), and because he seeks, as we all do, reinforcement from others for his ego and commitment, in this case to the values of violence, a youth often plays violent games of conflict within his own age-graded violent subcultural system. So do others play games, of course; the artist when he competes for a prize, the young scholar for tenure, the financier for a new subsidiary, and a nation for propaganda advantage. But the prescribed rules for street fighting produce more deadly quarrels with weapons of guns and knives than do competitions among males who use a brush, a dissertation, or a contract.

Jackson Toby[23] recently suggested that if the compulsive masculinity hypothesis has merit, it ought to generate testable predictions about the occurrence of violence. He lists the following: "(1) Boys who grow up in households headed by women are more likely to behave violently than boys who grow up in households headed by a man.... (2) Boys who grow up in households where it is relatively easy to identify with the father figure are less likely to behave violently than boys in households where identification with the father figure is difficult.... (3) Boys whose development toward adult masculinity is slower than their peers are more likely to behave violently than boys who find it easy to think of themselves as 'men'.... (4) Masculine ideals emphasize physical roughness and toughness in those populations where symbolic masculine power is difficult to understand. Thus, middle-class boys ought to be less likely than working class youngsters to idealize strength and its expression in action and to be more likely to appreciate the authority over other people exercised by a physician or a business executive."[24] As Toby indicates, it is unfortunate that evidence at present is so fragmentary that these predictions are not subject to rigorous evaluation.

The male self-conception is both important and interesting. Recently Leon Fannin and Marshall Clinard[25] tested for differences between lower class and middle class boys through informal depth interviewing and by forced-choice scales. While self-conceptions were quite similar, lower class boys felt themselves to be tougher, more powerful, fierce, fearless, and dangerous than middle class boys. "It was unexpected," claim the authors, "that they (the lower class boys) did not feel themselves to be significantly more violent, hard, and pugilistic." The middle class boys conceived themselves as being more clever, smart, smooth, bad, and loyal. The self-conceptions were also related to specific types of behavior, for the "tough guys" significantly more often "committed violent offenses, fought more often and with harsher means, carried weapons, had lower occupational aspirations, and stressed toughness and related traits in the reputation they desired and in sexual behavior."[26]

Should the lower classes become more like the middle class in value orientation, family structure, and stability, there is reason to believe the emphasis on masculine identification through physical prowess and aggression will decline. The need to prove male identity may not disappear, but even being "bad" in order to sever the linkage of morality and femininity may become increasingly difficult to perform in a purely masculine way. And if there are available, as some believe, new and alternative models for demonstrating masculinity, ways that may be neither "bad" nor physically aggressive, then we should expect masculine identity to be manifested differently, that is symbolically, even by lower class boys. As the larger culture becomes more cerebral, the refined symbolic forms of masculinity should be more fully adopted. And as the disparity in life style, values, and norms between the lower and middle classes is reduced, so too will be reduced the subculture of violence that readily resorts to violence as an expected form of masculine response to certain situations.

If this social prognosis proves correct, there may not always be functional and virtuous expertise in the masculine symbolism. We could witness, for example, a shift from direct physical violence to detached and impersonalized violence or to corruption. The dominant, middle class culture has a considerable tolerance for distant and detached violence expressed in ways that range from dropping heavy bombs on barely visible targets, to the stylized, bloodless violence of film and television heroes, and to the annual slaughter of 50,000 persons on our highways. This same culture, for reasons too complex to detail here, not only tolerates but sometimes creates structural features in its social system that seem to encourage corruption, from tax evasion to corporate crime.[27] To transform the theme of male aggressiveness may mean assimilation with the larger culture, but this may merely increase the distance between the user and consumer of violence, and increase the volume of contributors to corruption. It may be hoped, of course, that changes in the current direction of the dominant culture may later produce a more sanguine description of this whole process.

YOUTH AND VIOLENT CRIME

There is little more than faulty and inadequate official delinquency statistics to answer basic questions about the current extent and character of youth crime. Recording techniques have changed, more juvenile police officers are engaged in handling young offenders, more methods are used for registering such minor juvenile status offenses as running away from home, being incorrigible, or truant. For over a decade most city police departments have used a dichotomy of "official-nonofficial arrest" or "remedial-arrest" or "warned-arrest" for apprehending juveniles, but not for adults. Yet both forms of juvenile disposition are recorded and rates of delinquency are computed in the total. Separate treatises have been written on these matters[28] which we cannot pursue here in detail.

The public image of a vicious, violent juvenile population producing a seemingly steady increase in violent crime is not substantiated by the evidence available. There may be more juvenile delinquency recorded today, but even that is predominantly property offenses. Rather consistently we are informed by the Uniform Crime Reports, published by the Federal Bureau of Investigation, that two-thirds of automobile thefts and about one-half of all burglaries and robberies are committed by persons under 18 years of age. Among crimes of personal violence, arrested offenders under age 18 are generally low; for criminal homicide they are about 8 percent; for forcible rape and aggravated assault, about 18 percent.

What this actually means is not that these proportions of these crimes are committed by juveniles, but that among persons who are taken into custody for these offenses, these proportions hold. Most police officers agree that it is easier to effect an arrest in cases involving juveniles than in cases involving adults. Most crimes known to the police, that is, complaints made to them or offenses discovered by them, are not "cleared by arrest," meaning cleared from their records by taking one or more persons into custody and making them available for prosecution. The general clearance rate is roughly 30 percent. Thus, the adult-juvenile distribution among 70 percent of so-called major crimes (criminal homicide, forcible rape, robbery, aggravated assault, burglary, larceny over $50, auto theft) is not known and cannot safely be projected from the offenses cleared or the age distribution of offenders arrested.

In addition, very often the crude legal labels attached to many acts committed by juveniles give a false impression of the seriousness of their acts. For example, a "highway robbery" may be a $100-theft at the point of a gun and may result in the victim's being hospitalized from severe wounds. But commonly, juvenile acts that carry this label and are used for statistical compilation are more minor. Typical in the files of a recent study were cases involving two 9-year-old boys, one of whom twisted the arm of the other on the school yard to obtain 25 cents of the latter's lunch money. This act was recorded and counted as "highway robbery." In another case, a 9-year-old boy engaged in exploratory sexual activity with an 8-year-old girl on a playlot. The girl's mother later complained to the police, who recorded the offense as "assault with intent to ravish."

Nothing now exists in the official published collection of crime statistics to yield better information about the qualitative variations of seriousness. Weighted scores of seriousness are possible and available for producing a weighted rate of crime and delinquency, much like the operating refinements in fertility and mortality rates or in econometric analyses.[29] Without a weighted system, it is the incautious observer who is willing to assert that youth crime is worse today than a generation or even a decade ago.

Moreover, computing rates of crime or delinquency per 100,000 is an extremely unsatisfactory and crude technique. Even a rate for all persons under 18 years of age fails to account for the bulges in specific ages like 14, 15, 16, 17, 18 that have occurred because of high fertility rates shortly after World War II. Without age-specific rates, most criminologists are reluctant to make assertions about trends or even the current amount of juvenile crime and violence. Research is now underway that hopefully will provide new and more meaningful age specific rates. It would not be expected if, when these rates are computed, much of any recorded increase in violent juvenile crime for the past 8 years or so could be attributed to standard statistical error.

By making certain gross assumptions about the proportion of juvenile population between the meaningful ages of 10 and 17 for the population in cities of 2,500 and over included in the survey areas of the Uniform Crime Reports from 1958 to 1964,[30] it has been possible to provide some juvenile rates for violent or assaultive crimes against the person. Computations were performed in the following way: the population of all cities of 2,500 inhabitants and more, included in the Uniform Crime Reporting area, was summed for each of the 7 years from 1958 through 1964. (1958 was a year of important revisions in the UCR classification system, hence a safe year with which to begin the analysis.) The total populations of the United States and of the children from ages 10 through 17 were obtained for each of the 7 years from reports of the Bureau of the Census. The respective proportions of the 10- to 17-year-old population for each year were readily obtained from these census reports and then applied to the UCR survey population. The number of juveniles under 18 years of age arrested for specific offenses, divided by the population of persons aged 10 to 17, multiplied by 100,000, yielded a rate for each of the years. The table below shows these rates:[31]

Urban Rates of Crimes of Violence for Persons Arrested, Ages 10-17

	1958	1959	1960	1961	1962	1963	1964
Criminal homicide: murder and nonnegligent manslaughter	1.9	2.3	3.0	3.2	2.9	2.9	3.1
Negligent manslaughter	1.15	0.98	1.10	0.96	0.79	1.00	0.87
Forcible rape	10.0	9.8	10.9	11.4	11.2	10.3	10.0
Aggravated assault	34.4	35.8	53.2	60.1	61.6	63.0	74.5
Other assaults	95.9	118.0	118.7	126.0	139.2	153.7	163.6

Caution must be applied to these figures because of two major assumptions that had to be made: That the UCR survey population contained roughly the same proportion of persons aged 10–17 as the general population of the United States; that the overwhelming bulk of arrests of juveniles under 18 years of age, for offenses against the person, involved offenders no younger than age 10. It is assumed that little error is involved in this latter assumption because most juvenile court statutes with a lower age limit do not go below ages 6 or 7, and very few of these offenses are ever recorded for ages below 10. Moreover, computing a rate based on the entire population under 18 years would continue the unsatisfactory practice of including in the denominator preschool and infant children.

With this caution and these assumptions, the table can nevertheless be said to show substantially the same rates in 1964 as in 1960 for murder and nonnegligent manslaughter and for rape. Murder and nonnegligent manslaughter reached a peak rate in 1961 of 3.2, was under a rate of 3.0 per 100,000 in 1962 and 1963, and was 3.1 in 1964. These slight variations are of no statistical consequence, considering the operation of chance errors.

Negligent manslaughter was highest in 1958 (1.15), had no statistically significant increase in the years since then, and in 1964 was down to 0.87. This offense mostly refers to automobile deaths, and despite the fact that more teenagers are driving today, the rate has not increased. Forcible rape has not significantly changed over the 7 years: the high was 11.4 in 1961 and has dropped to 10.3 in 1963 and 10.0 in 1964. Aggravated assault jumped from 34.4 in 1958 to 53.2 in 1960, had a relatively stable rate of 60.1 to 63.0 between 1961 and 1963 and then rose to 74.5 in 1964. Other assaults (not part of the UGR index offenses) climbed steadily from 95.9 in 1958 to 163.6 in 1964.

There is little in these figures of criminal homicide or rape that should cause alarm. Assaults appear to be the main area of violence that should cause concern. But not until better data are available from some of the studies previously mentioned can we make proper conclusions and interpretations.

Among city gangs selected for their reputation for toughness and studied in detail by detached workers, the amount of violent crime, reports Walter B. Miller, is surprisingly low. Twenty-one groups, numbering about 700 members, yielded cumulative figures of 228 known offenses committed by 155 boys during a 2-year period and 138 court charges for 293 boys during a 12-year span. Miller remarks that "… violence appears neither as a dominant preoccupation of city gangs nor as a dominant form of criminal activity,"[32] even among these toughest of gang members, the yearly rate of assault charges per 100 individuals per year of age was only 4.8 at age 15, 7.2 at 16, 7.2 at 17, and 7.8 at 18, after which the rates dropped through the early twenties. Violent crimes were committed by only a small minority of these gang members, represented a transient phenomenon, were mostly unarmed physical encounters between combatting males, did not victimize adult females, and were not ideological forms of behavior.[33]

It should be mentioned also that the increasingly methodologically refined studies of hidden delinquency have not clearly and consistently reported a significant reduction in the disparity of social classes for crimes of violence.[34] The incidence and frequency of crimes of violence appear to remain considerably higher among boys from lower social classes when the appropriate questions are asked about these offenses over specific periods of time. In their recent study of delinquents, Fannin and Clinard reported: "One of the more important of the tests was a comparison of the frequency with which reported and unreported robberies and assaults were committed by members of the two class levels (middle and lower). The vast majority of all lower class delinquents, 84 percent, had committed at least one such offense compared to 28 percent of the middle class (probability less than 0.01); 28 percent of the lower and 8 percent of the middle class had committed 10 or more violent offenses. Class level was also related to the frequency of fighting with other boys. Lower class delinquents fought singly and in groups significantly more often (probability less than 0.05) than middle class delinquents, with 20 percent of them averaging five or more fights per month compared to 4.0 percent."[35]

It should also be kept in mind that the proportion of the entire juvenile population under 18 years of age that, in any calendar year, is processed by the police and juvenile court is generally no higher than 3 to 5 percent. There are, however, several factors denied clarity by this kind of commonly reported statistic: (1) Arrest or juvenile-court-appearance statistics include duplicate counting of the same juveniles who have run away, been truant, or committed malicious mischief more than once during the year, and for some types of offenses this amount of duplication can be sizable; (2) the figure ignores the fact that children have been delinquent during preceding years, and that in many census tracts throughout large cities as many as 70 percent or more of all juveniles under 18 years, at one time or another during their juvenile-court statute ages, may have been delinquent. Solomon Kobrin[36] and others have drawn attention to this perspective; Nils Christie[37] in Norway has done the most elaborate study on the topic by analyzing a birth cohort; and Thorsten Sellin and Marvin Wolfgang[38] are presently engaged in a large-scale research of a birth cohort of approximately 10,000 males in Philadelphia in order to compute a cohort rate of delinquency, examine their cumulative seriousness scores by age and over time, and to provide a prediction model that might aid in decisions about the most propitious time in juvenile life cycles for maximizing the effectiveness of social intervention.

The data needed to describe the volume of youth crime are inadequate at present, but an alarmist attitude does not appear justified. Age-specific and weighted rates are required before trends can be validly presented and analyzed, but because of the known rise in the present adolescent population due to high fertility rates of the late forties, there is reason to suspect that any overall increase in juvenile delinquency can be largely attributed to the population increase in the ages from 14 to 18. The absolute amount of delinquency can be expected to increase for some time, for this same reason, but there is no basis for assuming that rates of juvenile violence will increase.

Moreover, as the suburban population increases, the amount of juvenile delinquency can be expected to rise in these areas even without a rate increase. In addition, as the social class composition of suburbs changes, as it has been, from being predominantly upper class to containing more middle and lower middle class families, the rates of delinquency of the last migrating class will travel with them. And as Robert Bohlke[39] has suggested, what is often viewed as middle class delinquency is not middle class in the sense of the traditional middle class value system or life style but only in terms of the middle income group. There is considerable theoretical merit in this suggestion which should be further explored through empirical research.

Finally, with respect to delinquency, it might be said that a certain amount of this form of deviancy has always existed, will continue to exist, and perhaps should exist. In the sense discussed by Emile Durkheim,[40] crime is normal, and perhaps even, in some quantity, desirable. Not only does the existence of delinquency provide the collective conscience an opportunity to reinforce its norms by applying sanctions, but the presence of deviancy reflects the existence of something less than a total system of control over individuals. Moreover, there appear to be personality traits among many delinquents that could be viewed as virtues if behavior were rechanneled. For instance, Sheldon and Eleanor Glueck noted, in "Unraveling Juvenile Delinquency,"[41] that among 500 delinquents compared to 500 nondelinquents, the delinquent boys were characterized as hedonistic, distrustful, aggressive, hostile and, as boys who felt they could manage their own lives, were socially assertive, and defied authority. The nondelinquents were more banal, conformistic, neurotic, felt unloved, insecure, and anxiety-ridden. The attributes associated with the delinquents sound similar to descriptions of the Renaissance Man who defied the authority and static orthodoxy of the middle ages, who was also aggressive, richly assertive, this-world rather than other-world centered, and was less banal, more innovative, than his medieval predecessors. The Glueck delinquents also sound much like our 19th century captains in industry, our 20th century political leaders and corporation executives. The freedom to be assertive, to defy authority and orthodoxy may sometimes have such consequences as crime and delinquency, but it is well to remember that many aspects of American ethos, our freedom, our benevolent attitude toward rapid social change, our heritage of revolution, our encouragement of massive migrations, our desire to be in or near large urban centers, and many other values that we cherish, may produce the delinquency we deplore as well as many things we desire.

THE SEARCH FOR POWER AND PARTICIPATION: YOUTH, NEGROES, AND THE POOR

We have said that to speak generically of youth overlooks variability in a pluralistic society, and we have drawn attention to some notable variations between middle class and lower class youth. There are, however, many more versions of the concatenation of variables that differentiate youth. Being young, middle class, white, and from an economically secure family generates a quite different image from being young, lower class, poor, and Negro. In sheer absolute numbers, more young people are located in the former group that in the latter and probably suffer fewer strains from culture contradictions, anomie, and psychological deprivation that do the latter. There is likely to be greater conformity to parental prescriptions in the former, more familial transmission of group values, more cohesiveness of the family. The Negro, lower class of youth drop out of school and drift into delinquency in greater proportions than do white middle class youth. Class is probably a stronger factor contributing to value allegiance and normative conduct than is race, which is to say that Negro and white middle class youth are more alike than are Negro middle and lower class or white middle and lower class youngsters.

Yet, with all the variabilities that might be catalogued in an empirically descriptive study of youth, there are characteristics of the life stage, status, and style of youth in general which are shared by the status of poverty and the status of being Negro in American society. All may be described as possessing a kind of structural marginality[42] that places them on the periphery of power in our society. When the multiple probabilities of being young, Negro, and poor exist, the shared attributes are more than a summation. The force of whatever problems they represent is more of multiplicative than an additive function.

Youth, Negroes, and the poor have subcultural value systems different from, yet subsidiary to the larger culture. They often share many features, such as being deprived of certain civil rights and liberties, barred from voting, and denied adequate defense counsel and equality of justice. Their current statuses are frequently subject to manipulation by an enthroned elite and their power to effect change in their futures may be minimal. They tend to have common conflicts with authority and to be dominated by females in the matriarchial structure of their own social microcosms.

All three groups know the meaning of spatial segregation, whether voluntary or compulsory. For youth, it is in schools, clubs, seating arrangements, occupations, forms of entertainment, and leisure pursuits. For the poor and for Negroes, it may be all of these as well as place of residence and other alternatives of work, play, and mobility opportunities. There are similarities in their subordinate and dependency status, and in having poor, inadequate, or irrelevant role models. The values and behavior of the dominant culture and class in American society, as adopted by Negroes, often reveal a pathetically compulsive quality; the poor have been denied access to the ends to which they subscribe, and youth is, at best, a power-muted microculture. For all three, norms seem to shift and change with more than common frequency or are not clearly designated. All three groups tend to be more romantic, nonrational, impulsive, physically aggressive, more motivated toward immediacy and directness than their counterparts in the dominant culture. There is among youth, Negroes, and the poor more deviant and criminal behavior, and a greater disparity between aspiration and achievement. At times their revolt against authority erupts into violence for which they feel little guilt or responsibility.

Increasingly they are self-conscious, aware of their own collectivities as subcultural systems, partly because their revolt is today a greater threat to the systems which have been established to control, govern, or manipulate them. The poor are being asked for the first time what they want and what they would like to do to help themselves or have done for them. Negroes are acting as advisers and consultants on Federal policy, and young people are being heard when they speak about Vietnam, restrictions on passports, college curricula, faculty appointments, and new notions of freedom and sexual morality.

With more clarity and conscience, the three groups are searching for meaningfulness, identity, and social justice. They are articulating their protest against powerlessness, are seeking participation in decision making processes that affect their own life conditions. That some retreat into drugs, alcohol, and other symptoms of alienation is now viewed as dysfunctional by their own majorities as well as by the establishment. That some resort to violence, whether in Watts or in Hampton Beach,[43] episodic, meant to display boredom with their condition, blatant protest, and latent power. As achievement, as a danger signal, and as a catalyst, violence for them may serve the social functions outlined by Lewis Coser.[44] But their use of violence is end-oriented and cannot be viewed as a cultural psychopathology. They desire to be recognized, not to be forgotten, because they now see themselves for the first time. They are seeking what Edmund Williamson,[45] dean at the University of Minnesota, calls the most important freedom of all—to be taken seriously, to be listened to.

One of the interesting things about American youth today, especially the older student segment, is its activistic character and increasing identification with the poor and with the civil rights movement. There is an intense morality and a demand for clear commitments. In many cases young people are directly involved in working in neighborhoods of poverty or in the Negro struggle in the South, whether in song, march, or litigation. Moreover, the idealism of youth and this identification with the process toward participation in power is being fostered by Federal support of the Peace Corps program, both foreign and domestic, and by much governmental concern and protection of young civil rights workers in the South. But the reference here to identification is not to these overlapping involvements; it is to the means for communicating their lack of participation in formulating the rules of life's games. Impatience, discontent, and dissatisfaction with the state of American society[46] become healthy reflections of a new commitment, a commitment to the desire for change and for participating in the direction of change.

Obviously, there are also differences among the three groups, the most striking of which is the fact that youth is a temporary stage in a life cycle and that ultimately the structural marginality and status deprivation are overcome for many by the passage of time. The representatives of the subculture of youth are mobile, eventually leave the subculture, and with age, birth cohorts socially fold into one another. But the status designation of Negro is, except for race crossings, permanent, and the poor commonly have oppressive generational continuity. That youth in its temporariness shares with the major minority groups certain attributes of being and of the struggle for becoming is itself noteworthy, even if the youth were less affected by and conscious of their mutual interests, means, and goals. Perhaps the short sample of time represented by youth will one day be viewed in the long perspective as symbolic of the longer, but also temporary, state of deprivation and disenfranchisement of being poor or of having the status of Negro in American society.

The identity of youth with the protestation process, whether similar to or in common with the poor and the Negro, is, of course, not universal and may not even be a cultural modality. Its expression is, nonetheless, vigorous and viable. It has entered the arena of public attention and functions as a prodder for its concepts of progress. With this identity, the youth of today are unlike the "flaming youth" in the frenetic milieu of the twenties, the youth associated with the political left and the proletarian cult of the thirties, the uninformed youth of the forties, or the passive youth of the fifties. And yet, even with this identity they are without a systematic ideology. Despite the fact that they have come to realize the advantages of collective drives that prick the giants of massive and lethargic organization into action, they have developed no political affiliation. Perhaps the closest these young groups come to a focal concern is in their alerting their peers and adults to the ethical conflicts and issues embraced by society's increasing ability to reduce individual anonymity and to manipulate lives. In one sense it could be said that they jealously guard the constraints a democratic society ideologically imposes on overcontrol, invasion of privacy, and overreaction to deviancy.

There are fringes to most movements, and there are parasites attached to the youth we have been describing as healthier segments of society. Frequently the fringe looms larger than the core in the public image of youth and an excessive degree of rebelliousness is conveyed. The bulk of our youth are not engaged in a rebellion against adults, and the degree of dissimilarity between the generations has often been overstressed, as some authors have recently asserted.[47] Rather than rejecting most parental norms, the majority of those in the youth subculture are eager to participate in the larger society. Individuals resisting specific authority patterns do not constitute group rejection of dominant social norms.

Moreover, except for those suppressed beyond youth by their status of being poor or being Negro, achievement comes with aging and that convergence often leads to the collapse of a once fiery, romantic drive. And, as Peter Berger[48] has eloquently remarked, with success, prophets become priests and revolutionaries become administrators.

The gravity of time pulls hard on our muscles and ideals and too often the earlier triumph of principle gives way to the triumph of expedience. The once lambent minds of youth are frequently corroded by conformity in adulthood, and a new flow of youth into the culture is needed to invoke their own standards of judgment on our adult norms.

FOOTNOTES

1. E. B. Tylor, Primitive Culture, London: John Murray, 1871, p.

2. A. L. Kroeber and Clyde Kluckhohn, A Critical Review of Concepts and Definitions, Papers of the Peabody Museum of American Archeology and Ethnology, vol. 47, No. 1, 1952.

3. Typical statements of these authors may be found in Franz Boas, "Anthropology," in E. R. A. Seligman (ed.), Encyclopedia of the Social Sciences, New York: Macmillan Co., 1930, vol. II, p. 79; Ralph Linton, The Study of Man, New York: D. Appleton-Century, 1936, p. 78; Otto Kleinberg, Race Differnces, New York: Harper & Brothers, 1935, p. 255; Pitirim Sorokin, Society, Culture and Personality, New York: Harper & Brothers, 1947, p. 313; Robert M. MacIver, Social Causation, Boston: Ginn & Co., 1942, pp. 269–290; Robert M. MacIver and Charles H. Page, Society: An Introductory Analysis, New York: Rinehart & Co., 1949, pp. 498 ff; Leslie White, The Science of Culture, New York: Farrar and Strauss, 1949, p. 25.

4. A. L. Kroeber and Talcott Parsons, "The Concepts of Culture and of Social Systems," American Sociological Review (October 1958), 23: 582–583. See also the seminal article by Gertrude Jaeger and Philip Selznick, "A Normative Theory of Culture," American Sociological Review (October 1964).

5. Alfred McClung Lee, "Levels of Culture as Levels of Social Generalization," American Sociological Review (August 1945), 10:485–495; "Social Determinants of Public Opinion," International Journal of Opinion and Attitude Research (March 1947), 1:12–29; "A Sociological Discussion of Consistency and Inconsistency in Inter-Group Relations," Journal of Social Issues (1949) 5:12–18.

6. Milton M. Gordon, "The Concept of the Sub-Culture and Its Application," Social Forces (October 1947), 26: 40. For additional discussions by Gordon, using the term "subculture," see also "A System of Social Class Analysis," Drew University Studies, No. 2 (August 1951), pp. 15–18. Social Class in American Sociology, Durham, N.C.: Duke University Press, 1958, pp. 252–256; "Social Structure and Goals in Group Relations," Morre Berger, Theodore Abel, and Charles H. Page (eds.), Freedom and Control in Modern Society, New York: D. Van Norstrand Co., 1954. In these references, Gordon uses the term to refer to subsociety as well.

Gordon has recently gone further and proposes a new term, ethclass, to refer to "the subsociety created by the intersection of the vertical stratifications of ethnicity with the horizontal stratifications of social class...." (Assimilation in American Life. New York: Oxford University Press, 1964, p. 51.)

7. Albert K. Cohen, Delinquent Boys, Glencoe, Ill.; Free Press, 1955.

8. Richard Cloward and Lloyd Ohlin, Delinquency and Opportunity, New York: Free Press of Glencoe, 1960.

9. Milton Yinger, "Contraculture and Subculture," American Sociological Review (October 1960), 25:625–635.

10. An effort to show how parameters of subcultures might be designed appears in Marvin E. Wolfgang and Franco Ferracuti, Subculture of Violence, London: Tavistock Publications, 1967. Some of the notions expressed in this section of the paper are contained in more detail in the Wolfgang-Ferracuti book. See also Thorsten Sellin, Culture Conflict and Crime, New York: Social Science Research Council, Bulletin 41, 1938, for some of the provocative theoretical antecedents to current ideas about subcultures; and Leslie T. Wilkins, Social Deviance, London: Tavistock Publications, 1964.

11. William Foote Whyte, Street Corner Society, Chicago: University of Chicago Press, 1943 and 1955.

12. Dwight Macdonald, "Profile," The New Yorker, Nov. 22, 1957. Both this reference and the remark by Gertrude Stein are cited in Reuel Denney, "American Youth Today: A Bigger Case, A Wider Screen," in Erik H. Erickson (ed.), The Challenge of Youth, Garden City, N.Y.: Anchor Books Edition, Doubleday, 1965, pp. 155–179.

13. Reuel Denney, op.cit.

14. We might parenthetically remind ourselves that at the time of the signing of the Declaration of Independence, about one-half of the Nation was under 18 years of age.

15. Denney, op. cit.

   For other detailed descriptions of adolescents, teenagers, the youth subculture, etc., see the following useful examples:

   F. Elkin and W. Westley, "The Myth of Adolescent Culture," American Sociological Review (1955), 20:680–684.

   Hermann H. Remmers and D. H. Radler, The American Teenager, Indianapolis: Bobbs-Merrill, 1957.

   Edgar Z. Friedenberg, The Vanishing Adolescent, Boston: Beacon Press, 1959.

   Paul Goodman, Growing Up Absurd, New York: Random House, 1960. Jessie Bernard (ed.), "Teen-Age Culture," Annals of the American Academy of Political and Social Science (November 1961), 338. J. S. Coleman, The Adolescent Society, New York: Free Press of Glencoe, 1961.

   Lee G. Burchinal (ed.), Rural Youth in Crisis: Facts, Myths, and Social Change, Proceedings of A National Conference on Rural Youth in a Changing Environment, Stillwater, Okla., 1963. Washington, D.C.: U.S. Government Printing Office, 1965.

   David Gottlieb and J. Reeves, Adolescent Behavior in Urban Areas, New York: Macmillan and Co. 1963.

   Orville G. Brin, Jr., "Adolescent Personality as Self-Other Systems," Journal of Marriage and the Family (May 1965), 27:156–162.

   Erik H. Erikson (ed.), The Challenge of Youth, Garden City, N.Y.: Anchor Books Editor, Doubleday, 1965.

   David Gottlieb, "Youth Subculture: Variations on a General Theme," in Muzafer W. Sherif and Carolyn Sherif (eds.), Problems of Youth: Transition to Adulthood in a Changing World, Chicago, Aldine Publishing Co., 1965, pp. 28–45.

   Kenneth Keniston, The Uncommitted: Alienated Youth in American Society, New York: Harcourt Brace and World, 1965. John Barron Mays, The Young Pretenders: A Study of Teenage Culture in Contemporary Society, London: Michael Joseph, 1965.

   Blaine R. Porter, "American Teen-Agers of the 1960's—Our Despair or Hope?" Journal of Marriage and the Family (May 1965), 27:139–147.

   Graham B. Blaine, Jr., Youth and the Hazards of Affluence, New York: Harper and Row, 1966.

16. Lucius F. Cervantes, "The Dropout," Ann Arbor: University of Michigan Press, 1965, p. 197.

17. Kenneth Keniston, "Social Change and Youth in America," in Erik H. Erikson (ed.), The Challenge of Youth, 1965, pp. 191–222.

18. Erik H. Erikson, "Youth: Fidelity and Diversity," in Erik H. Erikson, ibid., pp. 1–28.

19. Arnold W. Green, "The Middle Class Male Child and Neurosis," American Sociological Review (February 1946), 11:31–41.

20. Walter B. Miller, "Lower Class Culture as a Generating Milieu of Gang Delinquency," Journey of Social Issues (1958), 14:5–19.

21. Herbert J. Gans, The Urban Villages, New York: Free Press of Glencoe, 1962.

22. Talcott Parsons, "Certain Primary Sources and Patterns of Aggression in the Social Structure of the Western World," Psychiatry (May 1947), 10:167–181.

23. Jackson Toby, "Violence and the Masculine Ideal: Some Qualitative Data," in Marvin E. Wolfgang (ed.) "Patterns of Violence," The Annals of the American Academy of Political and Social Science (March 1966), 364:19–27.

24. Ibid., pp. 21–22.

25. Leon F. Fannin and Marshall B. Clinard, "Differences in the Conception of Self as a Male Among Lower and Middle Class Delinquents," Social Problems (fall 1965), 13:205–214.

26. Ibid., p. 214.

27. We have borrowed from a quite different context in which Georges Sorel expressed similar ideas about

the shift from force to fraud, from violence to corruption as the path to success and privilege. The first edition of Reflextions sur la violence appeared in 1906; also, Paris: M. Riviere, 1936. For additional reference to this work, see Marvin E. Wolfgang, "A Preface to Violence," in "Patterns of Violence," The Annals of the American Academy of Political and Social Science (March 1966), 364:1–7.

28. See for example, Thorsten Sellin and Marvin E. Wolfgang, The Measurement of Delinquency, New York: John Wiley and Sons, Inc. 1964. A new summary of these problems from around the world may be found in T. C. N. Gibbens and R. A. Ahrenfeldt (eds.), Cultural Factors in Delinquency, London: Tavistock Publications, 1966.

29. For details of one such weighting system, see Sellin and Wolfgang, The Measurement of Delinquency, op cit.

30. Uniform Crime Reports, Washington, D.C.: Federal Bureau of Investigation, Department of Justice, 1958 to 1964. See also the report of the New York Division of Youth on this period, "Youth Crime—A Leveling Off?", Youth Services News (spring 1966), 17:3–5, and the succinct analysis of UCR and California data, found in Ronald H. Beattie and John P. Kenney, The Annals of the American Academy of Political and Social Science (March 1966), 364:73–85.

31. The following data were used for computing the rates:

The UCR survey population of cities of 2,500 and more inhabitants, for the years 1958 through 1964, was: for 1958—52,329,497; 1959—56,187,181; 1960—81,660,735; 1961—85,158,360; 1962—94,014,000; 1963—94,085,000; 1964—99,326,000. (Source: UCR Reports, Tables 18, 17, 18, 21, 21, 28, 27 for the respective years.) The U.S. population for the years 1959–64 was: 171,822,000; 177,830,000; 180,684,000; 183,756,000; 186,591,000; 189,417,000; 192,119,000. (Source: Estimates of the Bureau of the Census, Department of Commerce, Current Population Reports, Series P-25, No. 314, August 1965.)

The percentages which the UCR survey population represented of the total U.S. population were: 29, 31, 45, 46, 50, 50, and 52 percent. (Computed.)

The U.S. child population aged 10–17 for the years 1958–64 was: 23,433,000; 24,607,000; 25,364,000; 26,023,000; 27,983,000; 29,119,000. (Source: Estimates of Bureau of Census, Department of Commerce, Current Population Reports, Series P-25.) The UCR child population aged 10–17 for the years 1958–64 was 6,798,470; 7,628,170; 11,423,800; 13,468,000; 13,999,150; 15,141,880. (Assumed and computed.)

The number of persons under 18 years of age arrested for each of the five offenses over each of the 7 years may be found on the specific tables in the UCR annual reports. In gathering and computing these data, the author had the assistance of Bernard Cohen, Research Assistant, Center of Criminological Research, University of Pennsylvania.

32. Walter B. Miller, "Violent Crimes in City Gangs," in Marvin E. Wolfgang (ed.), "Patterns of Violence," The Annals of the American Academy of Political and Social Science (March 1966), 364:96–112.

33. Ibid.

For a new, detailed listing of research and theory in this area, see Dorothy Campbell Tompkins, Juvenile Gangs and Street Gangs—A Bibliography, Berkeley, Calif.: Institute of Governmental Studies at the University of California, Berkeley, 1966.

34. See Robert Hardt and George F. Bodine, Development of Self-Report Instruments in Delinquency Research, Syracuse, N.Y.: Youth Development Center, Syracuse University, 1965. This item is a conference report on methods of doing research on hidden delinquency and includes a good bibliography of major items in that area. See also Nils Christie, Johs. Andenacs, and Sigurd Skirbekk, "A Study of Self-Reporting Crime," in Karl O. Christiansen (ed.), Scandinavian Studies in Criminology, vol I, London: Tavistock Publications, 1965; Kerstin Elmhorn, "Study in Self-Reported Delinquency among School-Children in Stockholm," in Karl O. Christiansen (ed.), Scandanavian Studies in Criminology, vol. I, London: Tavistock Publications, 1965.

35. Fannin and Clinard, op. cit. p. 211.

36. Solomon Kobrin, "The Conflict of Values in Delinquency Areas," American Sociological Review (October 1951), 16:653–661.

37. Nils Christie, Unge norske lovovertrebere, Oslo, Norway: Institute Criminology, Oslo University, 1960.

38. Thorsten Sellin and Marvin E. Wolfgang, The Extent and Character of Delinquency in an Age Cohort, research project of the Center of Criminological Research, University of Pennsylvania, sponsored by the National Institute of Mental Health.

39. Robert H. Bohlke, "Social Mobility, Stratification Inconsistency in Middle Class Delinquency," Social Problems (spring 1961), 8:351–363. See also, Ralph W. England, Jr., "A Theory of Middle Class Delinquency," Journal of Criminal Law, Criminology and Police Science (April 1960) 50:535–540.

40. Emile Durkheim, Rules of Sociological Method, 8th Edition, translated by Sarah A. Solvay and John H. Mueller and edited by George E. G. Catlin, Glencoe, Illinois: Free Press, 1950, pp. 65–73.

41. Sheldon and Eleanor Glueck, Unraveling Juvenile Delinquency, Cambridge, Mass.: Harvard University Press for the Commonwealth Fund, 1950.

42. Tamme Wittermans and Irving Kraus, "Structural Marginality and Social Worth," Sociology and Social Research (April 1964), 48:348–360. For an excellent summary of theory and research on lower class

family life, see the recent work of Suzanne Keller, *The American Lower Class Family,* Albany: New York State Division for Youth, 1965.

43. See the Hampton Beach Project, Paul Estaver, Director, Project Director's Report, Hampton Beach, N.H.: Hampton Beach Chamber of Commerce, n.d.

44. Lewis A. Coser, "Some Social Functions of Violence," in Marvin E. Wolfgang (ed.), "Patterns of Violence," The Annals of the American Academy of Political and Social Science (March 1966) 364:8–18.

45. The New York Times, Nov. 21, 1965, p. 72.

46. On this point, see Talcott Parsons, "Youth in the Context of American Society," in Erik H. Erikson, The Challenge of Youth, 1965, pp. 110–141.

47. Robert C. Bealer, Fern K. Willits, and Peter R. Maida, "The Myth of a Rebellious Adolescent Subculture: Its Detrimental Effects for Understanding Rural Youth," in Lee G. Burchinal (ed.), Rural Youth in Crisis, Proceedings of a National Conference on Rural Youth in a Changing Environment, Stillwater, Okla., 1963, Washington, D.C.: U.S. Government Printing Office, 1965.

48. Peter Berger, An Invitation to Sociology: A Humanistic Perspective, New York: Doubleday & Co., Anchor Book, 1963.

MARVIN E. WOLFGANG

A.B., 1948, Dickinson College; M.A., 1950, Ph.D., 1955, University of Pennsylvania

Marvin E. Wolfgang is the Graduate Chairman of the Department of Sociology of the University of Pennsylvania and Criminology Director of the University's Center for Studies in Criminology and Criminal Law. He is also codirector of the Study of Violence Project at the University of Puerto Rico; Criminology Editor of the Journal of Criminal Law, Criminology and Police Science; Associate Editor of The Annals of the American Academy of Political Science; President of the American Society of Criminology; and President of the Pennsylvania Prison Society.

Among the books he has written are: THE SOCIOLOGY OF CRIME AND DELINQUENCY (coauthor, 1962); THE SOCIOLOGY OF PUNISHMENT AND CORRECTION (coauthor, 1962); THE MEASUREMENT OF DELINQUENCY (coauthor, 1964); CRIME AND RACE: CONCEPTIONS AND MISCONCEPTIONS (1964). In addition he has contributed many articles to professional journals.

From *Task Force Report:* Juvenile Delinquency and Youth Crime, 1967, pp. 145-154. Reprinted by permission of the National Institute of Justice, National Criminal Justice Reference Service.

Preventing Crime, Saving Children:
Sticking To The Basics

By John J. DiIulio, Jr.

"Post-Crack," Not Post-Problem

Like media coverage of most complicated social problems, press attention to the problems of youth crime and substance abuse ebbs and flows. But make no mistake: the passing of the much publicized inner-city crack-cocaine-and-crime epidemic of the late 1980s and early 1990s is *not* synonymous with the passing of the challenges of youth crime and substance abuse, least of all in urban America. The news spotlight on juvenile crime and delinquency flickers, but the practical and moral challenges posed by millions of juveniles who murder, rape, rob, assault, burglarize, vandalize, join street gangs, deal illegal drugs or consume illegal drugs does not thereby fade.

To the contrary, an intellectually and ideologically diverse range of expert voices has been proclaiming that the challenges of youth crime and substance abuse are more pressing today than they were at the height of the crack plague. Consider, for example, reports released over the last several years by the National Research Council, the International Association of Chiefs of Police, and the Council on Crime in America.

A few years ago, the National Research Council's Panel on High-Risk Youth reported that at least seven million young Americans—roughly a quarter of adolescents aged 10 to 170—are at risk of failing to achieve productive adult lives.[1] The United States, the panel warned, is in danger of "losing generations" of low-income children who abuse illegal drugs, engage in unprotected premarital sex, drop out of school, prove unable to get and keep jobs, succumb to the blandishments of illegal drugs, commit serious crimes or become victims of serious crimes.

In 1996, the International Association of Chiefs of Police (IACP) held a major summit on youth violence. The IACP noted that the number of juvenile offenders had risen rapidly in recent years, and warned that juvenile crime "will get considerably worse as a big new group of youngsters reach their teenage years." Looking over the horizon of the next few years, the IACP envisioned more kids, more drugs, more guns and more murders.[2] According to the IACP, in 1996 crack cocaine use was down, but crack was hardly invisible on East Coast inner-city streets, heroin was making a roaring comeback (especially on the West Coast), and LSD, amphetamine, stimulant and inhalant use was rising among teenagers nationwide. Thus, in several big cities, the percentage of juveniles in custody who tested positive for illegal drug use has more than tripled since 1990.

In 1997, the bipartisan Council on Crime in America stated flatly that "America's crime prevention challenge—at core a challenge of at-risk youth in need of adults—must be met, and soon." According to the Council, in 1994 there were over 2.7 million arrests of persons under age 18 (a third of them under age 15), up from 1.7 million juvenile arrests in 1991. Some 150,000 of these 2.7 million arrests were for violent crimes. In all, juveniles were responsible for an estimated 14 percent of all violent crimes and a quarter of all property crimes known to the police. Nationally, juveniles perpetrated 137,000 more violent crimes in 1994 than in 1985, and were responsible for 26 percent of the growth in violent crime over that period, including 50 percent of the increase in robberies, 48 percent of the increase in rapes, and 35 percent of the increase in murders. Juvenile violent crime arrest

rates rose 5.2 percent in 1987–88, 18.8 percent in 1988–89, 12.1 percent in 1989–90, 7.6 percent in 1990–91, and by at least 4.4 percent in every year thereafter until 1994–95, when arrests for violent crime among juveniles aged 10 to 17 fell by 2.9 percent. While such recent drops in juvenile arrest rates are obviously welcome, the Council urged all Americans to place them against the backdrop of a decade's worth of steep annual increases in youth crime and violence.

Moreover, the Council warned, America is now home to about 57 million children under age 15, some 20 million of them aged four to eight. The teenage population will top 30 million by the year 2006, the highest number since 1975. Thus, "no one," the Council concluded, "should feel certain that recent declines in crime will continue into the next century.

Indeed, the nation's two most widely respected criminologists, Professor James Q. Wilson of UCLA and Professor Marvin E. Wolfgang of the University of Pennsylvania, have both expressed deep concerns about present and impending youth crime and delinquency patterns and trends. According to Wilson, average Americans of every race, creed and region are right to "believe that something fundamental has changed in our patterns of crime," namely, the tangible threat of unprecedented levels of youth crime and substance abuse, including acts of violence committed by youngsters who "afterwards show us the blank, unremorseful stare of a feral, pre-social being."[4] Likewise, Wolfgang has observed that today's juvenile offenders probably do about three times as much serious crime as did the crime-prone boys born in the 1940s and 1950s, and could represent a new and especially challenging "subculture of violence."[5]

The expert understandings, statistics and warnings about youth crime and substance abuse seem broadly consistent with the well-founded worries of young Americans themselves. Any juvenile between ages 12 and 17 is more likely to be the victim of violent crime than are persons past their mid-twenties, and about half of all crimes of violence committed by juveniles are committed against juveniles.[6] A 1994 survey asked teenagers "How much of the time do you worry about being the victim of a crime?" In response, about 36 percent of white teenagers and 54 percent of black teenagers said "A lot of some or some of the time."[7] Apparently, the number of youngsters who are growing up scared in America—scared of other juveniles, that is—has been increasing for some time now. A 1995 Gallup Youth Survey found that between 1977 and 1994 the fraction of teenagers who regularly fear for their physical safety at school increased by 38 percent to one in four. And one teen in four said there was at least one time in the past year when they feared for their physical safety while in school classrooms or hallways, on playgrounds, or walking to and from school.[8]

Sticking to the Basics, Acting Now

The good news is that we do know a lot about youth crime and substance abuse that is relevant to saving at-risk youth—and acting now. Strategically, the key to preventing youth crime and substance abuse among our country's expanding juvenile population is to improve the real, live, day-to-day connections between responsible adults and young people—period. Whether it emanates from the juvenile justice system or from the community, from government agencies or from civil institutions, from faith-based programs or secular ones, from nonprofits or for-profits or public/private partnerships, from structural theorists or cultural theorists, from veteran probation officers or applied econometricians, no policy, program or intervention that fails to build meaningful connections between responsible adults and at-risk young people has worked, or can.

It is all well and good to acknowledge both the multivariate character of social problems, and the myriad legal, political, administrative, financial and other difficulties of replicating what works. But it is also all too easy to let such intellectually

de rigueur acknowledgments of social complexity become convenient covers for academic excuse-mongering, inaction and, of course, calls for more grants for more basic research, more research symposia, more conferences—more of everything save more human and financial support of people and existing programs that actually put responsible adults into the daily lives of the at-risk kids of inner-city Detroit, Philadelphia, and other major metropolitan regions.

Of all the factors we have found as contributing to delinquency, the clearest and most exhaustive evidence concerns the adequacy of parenting. Parents who are incompetent, abusive, or rejecting parents who fail to maintain adequate supervision over their children, and parents who, indeed, are little more than children themselves, have direct effects on anti-social behavior of their children.

James Q. Wilson has argued that uncovering "the subtle interaction between individual characteristics and social circumstances requires policy-related research of a sort and on a scale that has not been attempted before."[9] I agree. But there is already a voluminous private foundation-funded literature on understanding and reducing violence.[10] There is also a huge and still-growing government-funded literature on the literally dozens of "contexts and factors" that determine crime patterns.[11]

Besides, easily the most persistent, policy-relevant and common-sensical finding of the literature is that most disadvantaged youth who commit crimes and abuse drugs begin as neglected or maltreated children in need of responsible adults. In the words of a 1996 draft report of an American Society of Criminology task force on juvenile delinquency:

Of all the factors we have found as contributing to delinquency, the clearest and most exhaustive evidence concerns the adequacy of parenting. Parents who are incompetent, abusive, or rejecting, parents

who fail to maintain adequate supervision over their children, and parents who, indeed, are little more than children themselves, have direct effects on anti-social behavior of their children. Inadequacy of parenting cannot be viewed in isolation as the sole cause of delinquency. However, its association with other factors is critical in predicting future delinquency.[12]

Likewise, in a magisterial, still unsurpassed and only slightly dated 500-plus-page summary of the scientific literatures on criminal behavior, Wilson and the late Richard J. Hernstein concluded that "after all is said and done, the most serious offenders are boys who begin their careers at a very early age."[13] Numerous empirical studies have indeed found that most juveniles who engage "in frequent criminal acts against persons and property... come from family settings characterized by high levels of violence, chaos, and dysfunction."[14] For example, a study that compared the family experiences of more violent and less violent incarcerated juveniles found that 75 percent of the former group had suffered serious abuse by a family member, while "only" 33 percent of the latter group had been so abused; and 78 percent of the more violent group had been witnesses to extreme violence, while 20 percent of the less violent group had been witnesses.[15]

Similarly, a recent ethnography of nearly 200 young West Coast street gangsters and felons found that, almost without exception, the kids' families "were a social fabric of fragile and undependable social ties that weakly bound children to their parents and other socializers." Nearly all parents abused alcohol and illegal drugs or both. Most young street criminals and drug abusers had no father in the home; many had fathers who were in prison or jail. Parents who were present in the home often "beat their sons and daughters—whipped them with belts, punched them with fists, slapped them, and kicked them."[16] Much the same was found in a 1996 study that reconstructed the entire juvenile and adult criminal histories of a randomly selected sample of 170 Wisconsin prisoners from Milwaukee: "Most inmates were raised in dysfunctional families.... Drug and alcohol abuse was common among inmates, their parents, and siblings."[17]

Of course, today's at-risk child in need of meaningful connections with responsible adults is also tomorrow's young adult in need of a meaningful, living-wage job. At least with respect to the crime- and drug-abuse-reduction value of legitimate work opportunities, "liberal and conservative criminologists do not differ all that much about the causes of street crime."[18] There is almost universal agreement among crime analysts that "jobs matter," and that in the big-city neighborhoods that so many at-risk youth and the adults in their lives call home, jobs have virtually disappeared.[19] And there is also almost complete agreement among employment and training experts that, regardless of how bright or bleak general economic conditions may be, the most effective way—and perhaps the only way—to help no- and low-skill urban youth get and keep jobs is to "stick to basics: adult caring and guidance, plenty of legitimate things to do in a youth's spare time, and real help in connecting to employers. This is the stuff of successful human, citizen and worker development."[20]

Unfortunately, on youth crime, substance abuse and related social problems, sticking to the basics is anything but common, and anything but easy. The very conceptual and moral simplicity of the hard work that needs to be done—that is, the hard person-, place-, and institution-specific work of building meaningful connections between responsible adults and at-risk young people—makes getting it done very hard indeed. One little-acknowledged reason is that in the elite social policy, foundation and research communities, most financial, reputational and other rewards have been, and continue to be, skewed in favor of peddling "original" and esoteric (if often emptily erudite) ideas and "comprehensive" (if hardly feasible) top-down program strategies and designs.

But if we really care about getting a handle on our present and impending youth crime and substance abuse problems, then the time has come to proceed inductively, building meaningful connections between at-risk youth and responsible adults via existing community-based programs; focusing on the highly particular and often banal barriers to helping at-risk youth in particular places with particular people at particular times; having the money to fix a broken pipe that flooded the inner-city church basement where a "latch-key" ministry operates; finding a way to transport a young job-seeker from a public housing site to a private job site; get-

ting police and probation officers in a particular neighborhood to work together on a daily basis; funding an incremental expansion of a well-established national or local mentoring program; and so on.

In fact, the youth crime and delinquency problem is highly concentrated where America's most severely at-risk youth are concentrated, namely, on the predominantly minority inner-city streets of places like Newark, New Jersey, not on the predominantly white tree-lined streets of places like Princeton, New Jersey. This is hardly a new social fact. For example, in 1969, a presidential commission on violent crime broadcast it far and wide.[21] Still, the concentration of at-risk youth and associated social ills in America's big cities easily ranks among the most often ignored, distorted or forgotten of all policy-relevant social realities.

The concentration of crime and delinquency among low-income urban minority youth is especially striking for crimes of violence, including murder. In 1995, a nationwide total of 21,597 murders were reported to police, a total 7 percent lower than the 1994 total, and representing a national murder rate of 8 per 100,000 inhabitants. But 77 percent of murder victims in 1995 were males, 48 percent were black, and 12 percent were under age 18. Moreover, recent studies find that males ages 14 to 24 are roughly 8 percent of the country's total population, but they constitute over a quarter of all homicide victims and nearly half of all murderers. Between 1985 and 1992, for example, black males ages 14–24 remained just above 1 percent of the population but increased from 9 to 17 percent of the murder victims and from 17 to 30 percent of the assailants.[22]

One thing is tragically clear: "Homicide for young black males is very concentrated geographically," and remained so throughout the epidemic increases of the last decade.[23] As a 1994 study of youth violence concluded: "The violence now occurring within our cities is a national scourge. The fact that minority youth are disproportionately its victims makes it a tragedy as well as a disgrace."[24]

There is growing evidence of a substantial overlap between the highly concentrated populations of young crime victims and the highly concentrated populations of young offenders. For example, in an ongoing analysis of youth homicides in Boston, Professor Anne Morrison Piehl of Harvard Uni-

versity has found that about 75 percent of both offenders and victims of youth homicides (victim age 25 or younger) have criminal histories consisting of at least one arraignment. "In fact," Piehl observes, "among those with criminal histories, the victims and offenders were virtually indistinguishable in terms of criminal records. This finding suggests several things: the distribution of victimization may be even more concentrated than commonly believed, and strategic innovations based on law enforcement may be able to diffuse violent situations because there is leverage over both potential victims and potential offenders."[25]

Few "Guppies," Few "Great Whites"

But, as you well know, most juvenile offenders with whom the justice system deals are neither violent nor incorrigible.[26] Metaphorically speaking, today the system must handle relatively more young "Great White Sharks" (serious, violent, and predatory juvenile criminals) and relatively fewer "Guppies" (mere first-time midemeanants or delinquents) than it did in previous decades. Still, most juvenile offenders are neither Great Whites nor Guppies, and, for that reason, and even with the passage of so-called get-tough laws in many states, the system still rightly responds by putting the vast majority of juvenile offenders on probation, not behind bars.

For example, in 1993 public juvenile detention, correctional and shelter facilities held a total of over 60,000 juveniles (89 percent of them male, 43 percent of them black)—the largest number of juveniles in such public facilities on any given day since these data on juveniles in public facilities were first compiled in 1974. There were 1,025 facilities with a median population capacity of 24 and a mean capacity of 57—clearly not the huge, 500-plus bed juvenile reformatories of old. From 1991 to 1993, the one-day population of juveniles in publicly operated facilities increased by 5 percent. And note: the one-day population figures grossly minimize the actual amount of traffic in and out of these facilities each year. In 1993, for example, about 674,000 juveniles were admitted to these facilities, and 669,000 were released from their custody.[27]

Still, even today, it is probation authorities, not custodial institutions, that remain the true "workhorses" of the juvenile justice system. In 1993, 520,600 cases disposed by juvenile courts resulted in probation—a

21 percent increase over the 428,500 cases handled via probation in 1989. Probation has long been, and continues to be, the most severe disposition in over half (56 percent) of adjudicated delinquency cases. Between 1989 and 1993, the number of adjudicated juvenile cases placed on formal probation rose by 17 percent to 254,800. Over the same period, the number of juvenile probation cases involving a "person offense" such as homicide, rape, robbery, assault or kidnapping, soared by 45 percent to 53,900.[28]

As you also are well aware, alcohol, illegal drugs and substance abuse are clearly implicated in youth crime. The trouble almost always begins—both for the at-risk children and often for their parents as well—with child maltreatment in the home or a severe lack of positive adult-child relationships. Recently, a number of popular books have spoken to this harsh social reality in the vivid way that only first-rate journalism can.[29] In one such account, we are treated to the following summary of the research on at-risk youth, juvenile crime and related social ills:

Boiled down to its core (the research teaches) that most adolescents who become delinquent, and the overwhelming majority who commit violent crimes, started very young…. They were the impulsive, aggressive, irritable children…. If children know someone is watching them and that they may get caught, they are less likely to get into trouble.[30]

Even some older children who have gone badly astray and gotten "caught" (even incarcerated) can be saved if they are not only watched or monitored in the future, but mentored or ministered to as needed by responsible adults. Weigh the following synopses of a representative armful of relevant research monographs published over the last decade or so:

• Since 1986, the National Institute of Justice and the National Institute of Alcohol Abuse and Alcoholism have been conducting an ongoing examination of 1,575 child victims identified in court cases of abuse and neglect from 1967 to 1971. By 1994, almost half the victims (most of whom were then in their late twenties or early thirties) had been arrested for some type of nontraffic offense. About 18 percent had been arrested for a violent crime. Substance abuse rates were elevated, especially among women who were maltreated as children. Blacks who had been abused or neglected as children had higher crime rates than whites with the same background: 82 percent of black males had been arrested for some type of nontraffic offense; half of black males had at least one arrest for violence. For all child victims, in terms of future criminality, neglect appeared to be as damaging as physical abuse. The rate of arrest for violent crimes of those who had been neglected as children was almost as high as the rate for those who had been physically abused. Overall, maltreatment of children increased their chances of delinquency and crime by about 40 percent.[31]

• A 1985 study based on a representative national sample of 7,514 adolescents aged 12 to 17 compared delinquency rates of children in single-parent (mother-only) households to rates of children in two-parent households. Delinquency was measured in terms of number of arrests, school disciplinary problems (truancy, for example), and similar indicators. By all measures, the children in single-parent households were more likely to be delinquent.[32]

• A major re-analysis of data from a classic study of crime and delinquency confirmed the primacy of family factors: "Despite controlling for these individual difference constructs, all family effects retained their significant predictive power. And once again mother's supervision had the largest of all effects on delinquency, whether official or unofficial. A major finding of our analysis is that the family process variables are strongly and directly related to delinquency… family processes of informal social control still explain the largest share of variance in adolescent delinquency."[33]

• A study of the relationship between adolescent motherhood and the criminality of her offspring revealed a birds-of-a-feather phenomenon. About "25 percent of boys with criminal fathers also have a criminal mother, compared to 4 percent in the case of non-criminal fathers. Similarly, 67 percent of boys with criminal mothers also have a criminal father, compared to just 19 percent when the mother is not convicted…. Our results suggest that the children latest in the birth order of women who begin childbearing early are at greatest risk of criminality. This finding appears to reflect the coming together of the deleterious impacts of poor parenting and role modeling and diminished resources per child."[34]

A study of urban street criminals concluded: "An abundance of scholarly research shows that anti-social and delinquent tendencies emerge early in the lives of neglected, abused, and unloved youngsters, often by age nine. My ethnographic data support these findings and show that, once these youngsters leave home and go on the street, they are at best difficult to extricate from street culture…."[35]

• A study of "resilient youth"—the half of all high-risk children who do not engage in delinquency or drug use—indicated that child "maltreatment itself has for a long time been associated with problematic outcomes for children…. Considerable research in both criminology and child development suggests that family deviance, including criminality and substance abuse of family members, affects developing children because such parents are likely to tolerate and model deviance for children."[36]

Four decades ago, child psychologist Emmy Werner began studying the offspring of desperately poor, alcoholic and abusive Kauai, Hawaii parents. She was hoping to discover how these dysfunctions were passed from one generation to the next. Instead, she found that about a third of the children reached adulthood virtually unscathed—healthy, happy, employed, without substance abuse problems, and so on. So she shifted her attention to these abuse-and-neglect survivors, hoping to discover what made them so resilient and capable of beating the social odds. In 1992, a major storm flattened Kauai, leaving over 15 percent of its residents homeless and many others scrambling to find money for repairs, avoid bankruptcy, and fend off deep depression. But most of the study's resilient youth, then in their thirties, were not among the homeless, the foreclosed, or the depressed. They had heeded storm warnings, prepared their properties, saved for a stormy day, and bought insurance. For them, successfully riding out the storm was, as it were, an old habit. During the social hurricanes of their early lives, Kauai's resilient youth had responsible nonparental adults enter their lives, and through relationships with these adults the children had developed not only a sense of self-worth and respect for others, but, in Werner's words, personalities as "planners and problem solvers and picker-uppers." As she argued in her book, the crux of the Kauai story is consistent with the bottom line of the basic research on resilient youth: caring adults are the bedrock of a young person's behavior toward self and others, as well as the primary avenue for securing those skills, services, and opportunities (such as jobs) that are key to a civil and self-sufficient life.[37]

Thus, our brisk walk through the literatures on the concentrations and causes of youth crime and substance abuse returns us to the core strategic principle: no approach that does not build connections between responsible adults and at-risk youth has worked, or should rationally be expected to work. Again, no one can reasonably deny that, whatever the state of adult-child relationships, growing up in neighborhoods with few opportunities for healthy play and employment is a breeding ground for youth crime and substance abuse. But improving those opportunities, without first ensuring that there is adequate parental or nonparental adult caring, supervision, guidance and support, is unlikely to prevent or reduce youth crime and substance abuse, and hence unlikely to forestall the adult dysfunctions and criminal activities that fuel the "cycle of violence."

The single most consistent and powerful finding in the evaluation literature on youth development interventions is that positive effects accrue while at-risk children are in the programs, and sometimes for a few years thereafter, but diminish or dwindle to nothing by the time the child reaches adulthood. Many have met this finding as a counsel of despair. Logically, however, all the finding says is that the young generally do better when they are being helped by adults than when that help has stopped—better with and while in Head Start than without and after it; better when they stay in structured drug treatment than when they drop out of it; better during a summer education and training program than two summers later when they are older, more challenged, and unhelped by responsible adults; and so on. Many social programs do not so much "fail" as "stop." The obvious need, therefore, is to translate a series of short-term, non-stop positive adult-child connections into that long-term developmental success known as responsible, self-sufficient adulthood. To employ a football metaphor, winning at at-risk youth development is impossible when your most ill-equipped players have coaches or quarterbacks but only on alternate game days, are only occasionally given playbooks or schedules, and, should they even bother to keep playing, get invited to take the field as a team only during the first and third quarters of a four-quarter game. Or, shift the context from at-risk youth in need of responsible

adults to children living with both parents in the best of all possible emotional, material and cognitive early life circumstances. Even for well-loved, advantaged children in their teens, we know that when their circumstances change for the worse—when, for example, their family breaks up or falls suddenly on economic hard times—the youth are more likely to experience a wide variety of life troubles than are comparable youth who remained, as it were, in the 'advantaged childrens' program. In short, the plural of short-term is long-term.

Likewise, many well-intentioned persons have concluded that unless interventions into the lives of at-risk youth are quite early, intensive and expensive, not much good can come of them. To some, "early" means while still in dirty diapers, and certainly no later than ages seven or eight. This perspective is, to be sure, a useful corrective to unfettered optimism about social programs, especially, perhaps, where our country's most severely at-risk youth are concerned. But there are, alas, few unfettered optimists still walking the social planet, and the "dirty diapers or doom" perspective is grossly inconsistent with recent findings on the efficacy of mentoring programs like Big Brothers Big Sisters. Moreover, it is largely beside the point: whether or not we think we can help at-risk youth who are out of dirty diapers, the fact is that there are millions of them out there and on the way. In particular, intellectual confidence that these children are beyond help, even if it were justified (and I think it is most certainly not justified), would constitute no real answer to challenges posed by youth criminals and substance abusers—our youngest, most needy, and potentially our most dangerous fellow citizens.

The 3 M's of Youth Crime and Substance Abuse Prevention

The nation's at-risk youth population, including the segment of it that is involved in illegal activities, is not an undifferentiated mass. The best way, I believe, to think about and relate to present and potential juvenile offenders is with respect to their varying needs for adult supervision and guidance.

Specifically, I believe that some at-risk juveniles—for example, truants, petty thieves or kids who have had non-violent run-ins with their peers, neighbors and the law—need little more than a dedicated probation officer or a caring adult volunteer looking over their shoul-

der. They need monitoring. Other at-risk juveniles need responsible adults in their lives on a deeper, more intensive level, helping them with their personal problems, offering a sympathetic ear and a guiding hand. They need mentoring. Still other juveniles are among the nation's most severely at-risk children—abused and neglected as infants and toddlers, exploited for sex, drugs and money as adolescents, and already involved in (or quite likely to become involved in) serious, organized or predatory street crime as teenagers and young adults. Their badly broken lives and spirits cry out for a type and a degree of adult help that is holistic, personal and challenging. They need some type of ministering.

Over the last two years, I have spent most of my time working on the "3rd M"—ministering. I believe that local churches represent the single best hope for reaching some of our most severely at-risk youth, and I have witnessed, if you will, the capacity of "super-preachers" to stop potential "super-predators" before it's too late. But preachers and church volunteers need the support of prosecutors, probation and police to succeed.

In conclusion, a recent report from the Bureau of Justice Statistics indicates that, at present, the lifetime risks of a black male going to prison or jail in America are 1 in 3 versus 1 in 20 for the population as a whole.[38] Strategies that put responsible adults into the lives of at-risk youth can change both odds for the better. But how much have monitoring, mentoring and ministering-type efforts proliferated to date? These programs are far from being taken to scale and need lots of human and financial help if they are to make a real difference. Precious little is now being done by private foundations to bolster this strategic, street-level approach to youth crime and substance abuse.

Endnotes

1. National Research Council, Panel on High-Risk Youth, Losing Generations (National Academy Press, 1993).

2. Youth Violence in America: Recommendations from the IACP Summit (International Association of Chiefs of Police, 1996), section III, tables 11 and 12.

3. Council on Crime in America, Preventing Crime, Saving Children (Center for Civic Innovation, Manhattan Institute, 1997), pp. 1–3.

4. James Q. Wilson, "Crime and Public Policy," in Wilson and Joan R. Pertersilia, Crime

(Institute for Contemporary Studies, 1995), p. 20.

5. Marvin E. Wolfgang, "From Boy to Man, From Delinquency to Crime," University of Pennsylvania, Wharton School, Public Policy and Management Crime Policy Seminar Series, October 17, 1996, and personal correspondence of February 11, 1997; also see Wolfgang and Franco Ferracuti, The Subculture of Violence (Tavistock, 1967), esp. pp. 158–161.

6. Juvenile Offenders and Victims (U.S. Office of Juvenile Justice and Delinquency Prevention, June 1996), pp. 20, 47. Note: These estimates of youth crime and youth victimization in America are based on data gathered via the U.S. Bureau of Justice Statistics (BJS) and the National Crime Victimization Survey (NCVS). Unfortunately, the NCVS undercounts youth crime and youth victimization because it does not survey persons age 12 or younger; see John J. DiIulio, Jr. and Anne Morrison Piehl, "What the Crime Statistics Don't Tell You," Wall Street Journal, January 8, 1997, p. A22. Experts disagree about how severe the NCVS undercount is, but for some crimes it is clearly substantial. For example, other BJS data indicate that as many as 1 in 6 rape victims are age 12 or younger, but the NCVS does not capture these rapes; see Child Rape Victims 1992 (Bureau of Justice Statistics), June 1994. Likewise, it has been estimated that the NCVS undercounts the number of gun-shot victims by a factor of three; see Philip J. Cook, "The Case of the Missing Victims," Journal of Quantitative Criminology, 1985, pp. 91–102.

7. New York Times/CBS News Poll, as reported in The New York Times, July 10, 1994, p. 16.

8. George H. Gallup with Wendy Plump, Growing Up Scared in America (George H. Gallup International Institute, 1995), p. 2.

9. James Q. Wilson, On Character (American Enterprise Institute), p. 179 also see Wilson et al., Understanding and Controlling Crime (Springer-Verlag, 1986), and Wilson and Joan R. Petersilia, eds., Crime, op. cit.

10. For example, see 1993 Report of the Harry Frank Guggenheim Foundation: Research for Understanding and Reducing Violence, Aggression and Dominance (The Harry Frank Guggenheim Foundation, 1993).

11. For example, see "Understanding the Roots of Crime," National Institute of Justice Journal (National Institute of Justice, November 1994), p. 14.

12. "Critical Criminal Justice Issues," Task Force Reports from the American Society of Criminology, compiled by National Institute of Justice, draft, 1996, p. 2. I am grateful to Ross D. London for supplying a copy of this draft document.

13. James Q. Wilson and Richard J. Hernstein, Crime and Human Nature (Simon and Shuster, 1985), p. 509.

14. David M. Altschuler and Troy L. Armstrong, "Intensive Aftercare," in Armstrong, ed., In-

tensive Interventions with High-Risk Youths (Criminal Justice Press, 1991), p. 48.

15. Ellen Schall, "Principles for Juvenile Detention," in Francis X. Hartmann, ed., From Children to Citizens, vol. 2 (Springer-Verlag, 1987), p. 350.

16. Mark S. Fleisher, Beggars and Thieves (University of Wisconsin Press, 1995).

17. John J. DiIulio, Jr. and George Mitchell, Who Really Goes to Prison in Wisconsin? (Wisconsin Policy Research Institute, April 1996), pp. 2, 3.

18. Jerome H. Skolnick, "Passions of Crime," The American Prospect, March–April 1996, p. 92.

19. For example, see the following: Richard Freeman, "Crime and the Economic Status of Disadvantaged Young Men," in George Peterson and Wayne Vroman, eds., Urban Labor Markets and Job Opportunity (Urban Institute Press, 1992); Freeman, "Why Do So Many Young Men Commit Crimes and What Might We Do About It?," Journal of Economic Perspectives, Winter 1996, pp. 25–42; Jeffrey Grogger, "The Effect of Arrests on Employment and Earnings of Young Men," Quarterly Journal of Economics, February 1995, pp. 51–71; Joel Waldfogel, "The Effect of Criminal Conviction on Income and the Trust 'Reposed in the Workmen'," Journal of Human Resources, 1994, pp. 62–81; William Julius Wilson, When Work Disappears (Knopf, 1996).

20. Gary Walker, "Back to Basics: A New/Old Direction for Youth Policy," Public/Private Ventures News, Spring 1996, p. 3 and Gary Walker, testimony before the U.S. Subcommittee on Employment and Training, March 11, 1997.

21. Violent Crime: The Challenge to Our Cities (George Braziller, 1969). The commission's central findings were reinforced a few years later by the results of a major longitudinal study; see Marvin E. Wolfgang et al., Delinquency in a Birth Cohort (University of Chicago, 1972).

22. Trends in Juvenile Violence (Bureau of Justice Statistics, March 1996), p. 2.

23. Ibid, p. 30.

24. Violence in America: Mobilizing a Response (National Academy Press, 1994), p. ix.

25. Anne Morrison Piehl, personal correspondence of March 1997; also see Piehl et al., "Youth Gun Violence in Boston," in Law and Contemporary Problems, forthcoming 1997. I am grateful to Professor Piehl for Supplying us with a copy of this draft essay, and for her additional insights.

26. For example, see James Alan Fox, "The Calm Before the Juvenile Crime Storm?," Population Today, September 1996, pp. 4, 5, and "Yes, the Federal Government Should Have a Major Role in Reducing Juvenile Crime," Congressional Digest, August–September 1996, pp. 206, 208, 210, and 212 and see DiIulio, "Our Children and Crime," Keynote Address, International Association of Chiefs of Police, April 25, 1996 testimony before the U.S. Senate Subcommittee on Children and Families, "Ju-

venile Crime: An Alarming Indicator of America's Moral Poverty," July 18, 1996 and "Stop Crime Before It Starts," The New York Times, July 25, 1996.

27. Juveniles in Public Facilities, 1993 (Office of Juvenile Justice and Delinquency Prevention, May 1995), p. 1, and Juveniles in Public Facilities, 1991 (Office of Juvenile Justice and Delinquency Prevention, September 1993), p. 1.

28. Juvenile Probation: Workhorse of the Juvenile Justice System (Office of Juvenile Justice and Delinquency Prevention, March 1996).

29. For example, see Fox Butterfield, All God's Children (Knopf, 1995), and Leon Dash, Rosa Lee: A Mother and Her Family In Urban America (Basic Books, 1996).

30. Butterfield, ibid., p. 327–328.

31. The cycle of Violence (National Institute of Justice, 1992), and The Cycle of Violence Revisited (National Institute of Justice, 1996).

32. Sanford M. Dornbusch et al., "Single Parents, Extended Households, and the Control of Adolescents," Child Development, 1985, pp. . Also see the following: Anthony Pillay, "Psychological Disturbances in Children of Single Parents," Psychological Reports, 1987, pp. 803–806 Laurence Steinberg, "Single Parents, Stepparents, and Susceptibility of Adolescents to Antisocial Peer Pressure," Child Development, 1987, pp. 201–220 and Brigitte Mednick et al., "Patterns of Family Instability and Crime," Journal of Youth and Adolescence, 1990, pp. 95–96. I am grateful to Boston probation officer Milton Britton for directing our attention to these additional studies.

33. Robert J. Sampson and John H. Laub, Crime in the Making (Harvard University Press, 1993), pp. 95-96.

34. Daniel S. Nagin et al., "Adolescent Mothers and the Criminal Justice System," unpublished paper, Carnegie Mellon University, December 15, 1995, pp. 28, 30.

35. Fleisher, Beggars and Thieves, op. cit., pp. 262–263.

36. Carolyn Smith et al., "Resilient Youth: Identifying Factors That Prevent High-Risk Youth from Engaging in Delinquency and Drug Use," Current Perspectives on Aging and the Life Cycle, 1995, p. 221.

37. Emmy Werner and Ruth Smith, Overcoming the Odds: High-Risk Children from Birth to Adulthood (Cornell University Press, 1992), and Joseph P. Shapiro, "Invincible Kids," U.S. News & World Report, November 11, 1996.

38. I am grateful to Dr. Allen Beck of the Bureau for supplying a draft copy of this document.

This article was based on an address given to the National District Attorneys Association on July 14, 1997.

John J. DiIulio, Jr. is a Professor of Politics and Public Affairs at Princeton University and a Douglas Dillon Senior Fellow at the Brookings Institute.

From *Perspectives*, Spring 1998, pp. 24-29. © 1998 by The Council of State Governments. Reprinted by permission of the American Probation and Parole Association.

Boys will be Boys

Developmental research has been focused on girls; now it's their brothers' turn. Boys need help, too, but first they need to be understood.

BY BARBARA KANTROWITZ AND CLAUDIA KALB

It WAS A CLASSIC MARS-VENUS EN-COUNTER. Only in this case, the woman was from Harvard and the man well, boy—was a 4-year-old at a suburban Boston nursery school. Graduate student Judy Chu was in his classroom last fall to gather observations for her doctoral dissertation on human development. His greeting was startling: he held up his finger as if it were a gun and pretended to shoot her. "I felt bad," Chu recalls. "I felt as if he didn't like me." Months later and much more boy-savvy, Chu has a different interpretation: the gunplay wasn't hostile—it was just a way for him to say hello. "They don't mean it to have harsh consequences. It's a way for them to connect."

The Wonder (and Worry) Years

There may be no such thing as *child* development anymore. Instead, researchers are now studying each gender's development separately and discovering that boys and girls face very different sorts of challenges. Here is a rough guide to the major phases in their development.

Boys
0–3 years At birth, boys have brains that are 5% larger than girls' (size doesn't affect intelligence) and proportionately larger bodies—disparities that increase with age.

4–6 years The start of school is a tough time as boys must curb aggressive impulses. They lag behind girls in reading skills, and hyperactivity may be a problem.

Age 1	2	3	4	5	6	7

Girls
0–3 years Girls are born with a higher proportion of nerve cells to process information. More brain regions are involved in language production and recognition.

4–6 years Girls are well suited to school. They are calm, get along with others, pick up on social cues, and reading and writing come easily to them.

7–10 years While good at gross motor skills, boys trail girls in finer control. Many of the best students but also nearly all of the poorest ones are boys.

11–13 years A mixed bag. Dropout rates begin to climb, but good students start pulling ahead of girls in math skills and catching up some in verbal ones.

14–16 years Entering adolescence, boys hit another rough patch. Indulging in drugs, alcohol and aggressive behavior are common forms of rebellion.

8	9	10	11	12	13	14	15	16

7–10 years Very good years for girls. On average, they outperform boys at school, excelling in verbal skills while holding their own in math.

11–13 years The start of puberty and girls' most vulnerable time. Many experience depression; as many as 15% may try to kill themselves.

14–16 years Eating disorders are a major concern. Although anorexia can manifest itself as early as 8, it typically afflicts girls starting at 11 or 12; bulimia at 15.

SOURCES: DR. MICHAEL THOMPSON, BARNEY BRAWER. RESEARCH BY BILL VOURVOULIAS—NEWSWEEK

Trouble Spots: Where Boys Run Into Problems

Not all boys are the same, of course, but most rebel in predictable patterns and with predictable weapons: underachievement, aggression and drug and alcohol use. While taking chances is an important aspect of the growth process, it can lead to real trouble.

When Johnny Can't Read

Girls have reading disorders nearly as often as boys, but are able to overcome them. Disability rates, as identified by:

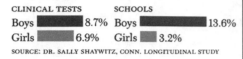

CLINICAL TESTS		SCHOOLS	
Boys	8.7%	Boys	13.6%
Girls	6.9%	Girls	3.2%

SOURCE: DR. SALLY SHAYWITZ, CONN. LONGITUDINAL STUDY

Suicidal Impulses

While girls are much more likely to try to kill themselves, boys are likelier to die from their attempts.

SUICIDE ATTEMPTS*		SUICIDE FATALITIES	
Boys	3,000	Boys	260
Girls	23,000	Girls	77

1995, AGES 5–14. *NEWSWEEK ESTIMATE. SOURCES: NCHS, CDC

Binge Drinking

Boys binge more on alcohol. Those who had five or more drinks in a row in the last two weeks:

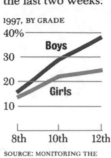

1997, BY GRADE

SOURCE: MONITORING THE FUTURE STUDY

Aggression That Turns to Violence

Boys get arrested three times as often as girls, but for some nonviolent crimes the numbers are surprisingly even.

Arrests of 10- to 17-year-olds: ■ Boys ■ Girls

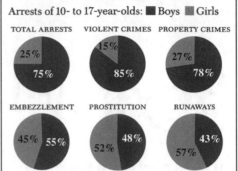

ESTIMATES, 1996. SOURCE: NAT'L CENTER FOR JUVENILE JUSTICE

Eating Disorders

Boys can also have eating disorders. Kids who used laxatives or vomited to lose weight:

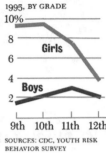

1995, BY GRADE

SOURCES: CDC, YOUTH RISK BEHAVIOR SURVEY

Researchers like Chu are discovering new meaning in lots of things boys have done for ages. In fact, they're dissecting just about every aspect of the developing male psyche and creating a hot new field of inquiry: the study of boys. They're also producing a slew of books with titles like "Real Boys: Rescuing Our Sons From the Myths of Boyhood" and "Raising Cain: Protecting the Emotional Life of Boys" that will hit the stores in the next few months.

What some researchers are finding is that boys and girls really are from two different planets. But since the two sexes have to live together here on Earth, they should be raised with special consideration for their distinct needs. Boys and girls have different "crisis points," experts say, stages in their emotional and social development where things can go very wrong. Until recently, girls got all the attention. But boys need help, too. They're much more likely than girls to have discipline problems at school and to be diagnosed with attention deficit disorder (ADD). Boys far outnumber girls in special-education classes. They're also more likely to commit violent crimes and end up in jail. Consider the headlines: Jonesboro, Ark.; Paducah, Ky.; Pearl, Miss. In all these school shootings, the perpetrators were young adolescent boys.

Even normal boy behavior has come to be considered pathological in the wake of the feminist movement. An abundance of physical energy and the urge to conquer— these are normal male characteristics, and in an earlier age they were good things,

even essential to survival. "If Huck Finn or Tom Sawyer were alive today," says Michael Gurian, author of "The Wonder of Boys," "we'd say they had ADD or a conduct disorder." He says one of the new insights we're gaining about boys is a very old one: boys will be boys. "They are who they are," says Gurian, "and we need to love them for who they are. Let's not try to rewire them."

Indirectly, boys are benefiting from all the research done on girls, especially the landmark work by Harvard University's Carol Gilligan. Her 1982 book, "In a Different Voice: Psychological Theory and Women's Development," inspired Take Our Daughters to Work Day, along with best-selling spinoffs like Mary Pipher's "Reviving Ophelia." The traditional, unisex way of looking at child development was profoundly flawed, Gilligan says: "It was like having a one-dimensional perspective on a two-dimensional scene." At Harvard, where she chairs the gender-studies department, Gilligan is now supervising work on males, including Chu's project. Other researchers are studying mental illness and violence in boys.

While girls' horizons have been expanding, boys' have narrowed, confined to rigid ideas of acceptable male behavior no matter how hard their parents tried to avoid stereotypes. The macho ideal still rules. "We gave boys dolls and they used them as guns," says Gurian. "For 15 years, all we heard was that [gender differences] were all about socialization. Parents who raised their kids through that period said in the end, 'That's not true. Boys and girls can be

awfully different.' I think we're awakening to the biological realities and the sociological realities."

But what exactly is the essential nature of boys? Even as infants, boys and girls behave differently. A recent study at Children's Hospital in Boston found that boy babies are more emotionally expressive; girls are more reflective. (That means boy babies tend to cry when they're unhappy; girl babies suck their thumbs.) This could indicate that girls are innately more able to control their emotions. Boys have higher levels of testosterone and lower levels of the neurotransmitter serotonin, which inhibits aggression and impulsivity. That may help explain why more males than females carry through with suicide, become alcoholics and are diagnosed with ADD.

The developmental research on the impact of these physiological differences is still in the embryonic stage, but psychologists are drawing some interesting comparisons between girls and boys (chart). For girls, the first crisis point often comes in early adolescence. Until then, Gilligan and others found, girls have an enormous capacity for establishing relationships and interpreting emotions. But in their early teens, girls clamp down, squash their emotions, blunt their insight. Their self-esteem plummets. The first crisis point for boys comes much earlier, researchers now say. "There's an outbreak of symptoms at age 5, 6, 7, just like you see in girls at 11, 12, 13," says Gilligan. Problems at this age include bed-wetting and separation anxiety. "They don't have the language or experience" to articulate it fully, she says, "but the feelings are no less intense." That's why Gilligan's student Chu is studying preschoolers. For girls at this age, Chu says, hugging a parent goodbye "is almost a nonissue." But little boys, who display a great deal of tenderness, soon begin to bury it with "big boy" behavior to avoid being called sissies. "When their parents drop them off, they want to be close and want to be held, but not in front of other people," says Chu. "Even as early as 4, they're already aware of those masculine stereotypes and are negotiating their way around them."

It's a phenomenon that parents, especially mothers, know well. One morning last month, Lori Dube, a 37-year-old mother of three from Evanston, Ill., visited her oldest son, Abe, almost 5, at his nursery school, where he was having lunch with his friends. She kissed him, prompting another boy to comment scornfully: "Do you know what your mom just did? She kissed you!" Dube acknowledges, with some sadness, that she'll have to be more sensitive to Abe's new reactions to future public displays of affection. "Even if he loves it, he's getting these messages that it's not good."

There's a struggle—a desire and need for warmth on the one hand and a pull toward independence on the other. Boys like Abe are going through what psychologists long ago declared an integral part of growing up: individualization and disconnection from parents, especially mothers. But now some researchers think that process is too abrupt. When boys repress normal feelings like love because of social pressure, says William Pollack, head of the Center for Men at Boston's McLean Hospital and author of the forthcoming "Real Boys," "they've lost contact with the genuine nature of who they are and what they feel. Boys are in a silent crisis. The only time we notice it is when they pull the trigger."

No one is saying that acting like Rambo in nursery school leads directly to tragedies like Jonesboro. But researchers do think that boys who are forced to shut down positive emotions are left with only one socially acceptable outlet: anger. The cultural ideals boys are exposed to in movies and on TV still emphasize traditional masculine roles—warrior, rogue, adventurer—with heavy doses of violence. For every Mr. Mom, there are a dozen Terminators. "The feminist movement has done a great job of convincing people that a woman can be nurturing and a mother and a tough trial lawyer at the same time," says Dan Kindlon, an assistant professor of psy-

chiatry at Harvard Medical School. "But we haven't done that as much with men. We're afraid that if they're too soft, that's all they can be."

And the demands placed on boys in the early years of elementary school can increase their overall stress levels. Scientists have known for years that boys and girls develop physically and intellectually at very different rates (time-line). Boys' fine motor skills—the ability to hold a pencil, for example—are usually considerably behind girls. They often learn to read later. At the same time, they're much more active— not the best combination for academic advancement. "Boys feel like school is a game rigged against them," says Michael Thompson, coauthor with Kindlon of "Raising Cain." "The things at which they excel—gross motor skills, visual and spatial skills, their exuberance—do not find as good a reception in school" as the things girls excel at. Boys (and girls) are also in academic programs at much younger ages than they used to be, increasing the chances that males will be forced to sit still before they are ready. The result, for many boys, is frustration, says Thompson: "By fourth grade, they're saying the teachers like girls better."

A second crisis point for boys occurs around the same time their sisters are stumbling, in early adolescence. By then, say Thompson and Kindlon, boys go one step further in their drive to be "real guys." They partake in a "culture of cruelty," enforcing male stereotypes on one another. "Anything tender, anything compassionate or too artistic is labeled gay," says Thompson. "The homophobia of boys in the 11, 12, 13 range is a stronger force than gravity."

Boys who refuse to fit the mold suffer. Glo Wellman of the California Parenting Institute in Santa Rosa has three sons, 22, 19 and 12. One of her boys, she says, is a "nontypical boy: he's very sensitive and caring and creative and artistic." Not surprisingly, he had the most difficulty growing up, she says. "We've got a long way to go to help boys… to have a sense that they can be anything they want to be."

In later adolescence, the once affectionate toddler has been replaced by a sulky stranger who often acts as though torture would be preferable to a brief exchange of words with Mom or Dad. Parents have to try even harder to keep in touch. Boys want and need the attention, but often just don't know how to ask for it. In a recent national poll, teenagers named their parents as their No. 1 heroes. Researchers say a strong parental bond is the most important protec-

tion against everything from smoking to suicide.

For San Francisco Chronicle columnist Adnir Lara, that message sank in when she was traveling to New York a few years ago with her son, then 15. She sat next to a woman who told her that until recently she would have had to change seats because she would not have been able to bear the pain of seeing a teenage son and mother together. The woman's son was 17 when his girlfriend dumped him; he went into the garage and killed himself. "This story made me aware that with a boy especially, you have to keep talking because they don't come and talk to you," she says. Lara's son is now 17; she also has a 19-year-old daughter. "My daughter stalked me. She followed me from room to room. She was yelling, but she was in touch. Boys don't do that. They leave the room and you don't know what they're feeling." Her son is now 6 feet 3. "He's a man. There are barriers. You have to reach through that and remember to ruffle his hair."

With the high rate of divorce, many boys are growing up without any adult men in their lives at all. Don Elium, coauthor of the best-selling 1992 book "Raising a Son," says that with troubled boys, there's often a common theme: distant, uninvolved fathers, and mothers who have taken on more responsibility to fill the gap. That was the case with Raymundo Infante Jr., a 16-year-old high-school junior, who lives with his mother, Mildred, 38, a hospital administrative assistant in Chicago, and his sister, Vanessa, 19. His parents divorced when he was a baby and he had little contact with his father until a year ago. The hurt built up—in sixth grade, Raymundo was so depressed that he told a classmate he wanted to kill himself. The classmate told the teacher, who told a counselor, and Raymundo saw a psychiatrist for a year. "I felt that I just wasn't good enough, or he just didn't want me," Raymundo says. Last year Raymundo finally confronted his dad, who works two jobs—in an office and on a construction crew—and accused him of caring more about work than about his son. Now the two spend time together on weekends and sometimes go shopping, but there is still a huge gap of lost years.

Black boys are especially vulnerable, since they are more likely than whites to grow up in homes without fathers. They're often on their own much sooner than whites. Black leaders are looking for alternatives. In Atlanta, the Rev. Tim McDonald's First Iconium Baptist Church just chartered a Boy Scout troop. "Gangs are so prevalent because guys want to belong to something," says McDonald. "We've got to give them something positive to belong to." Black educators like Chicagoan Jawanza Kunjufu think mentoring programs will overcome the bias against academic success as "too white." Some cities are also experimenting with all-boy classrooms in predominantly black schools.

Researchers hope that in the next few years, they'll come up with strategies that will help boys the way the work of Gilligan and others helped girls. In the meantime, experts say, there are some guidelines. Parents can channel their sons' energy into constructive activities, like team sports. They should also look for "teachable moments" to encourage qualities such as empathy. When Diane Fisher, a Cincinnati-area psychologist, hears her 8- and 10-year-old boys talking about "finishing somebody," she knows she has mistakenly rented a violent videogame. She pulls the plug and tells them: "In our house, killing people is not entertainment, even if it's just pretend."

Parents can also teach by example. New Yorkers Dana and Frank Minaya say they've never disciplined their 16-year-old son Walter in anger. They insist on resolving all disputes calmly and reasonably, without yelling. If there is a problem, they call an official family meeting "and we never leave without a big hug," says Frank. Walter tries to be open with his parents. "I don't want to miss out on any advice," he says.

Most of all, wise parents of boys should go with the flow. Cindy Lang, 36, a full-time mother in Woodside, Calif., is continually amazed by the relentless energy of her sons, Roger Lloyd, 12, and Chris, 9. "You accept the fact that they're going to involve themselves in risky behavior, like skateboarding down a flight of stairs. As a girl, I certainly wasn't skateboarding down a flight of stairs." Just last week, she got a phone call from school telling her that Roger Lloyd was in the emergency room because he had fallen backward while playing basketball and school officials thought he might have a concussion. He's fine now, but she's prepared for the next emergency: "I have a cell phone so I can be on alert." Boys will be boys. And we have to let them.

With KAREN SPRINGEN *in Chicago,* PATRICIA KING *in San Francisco,* PAT WINGERT *in Washington,* VERN E. SMITH *in Atlanta and* ELIZABETH ANGELL *in New York*

Young and Violent

Crimes by girls flying off the charts

In the last decade, the FBI recorded a 114 pct. increase in arrests of girls for violent offenses.

Maureen Graham
Rita Giordano
and Christine Bahls
FOR THE INQUIRER

By the time Adelle Steele was 14, the Kennett Square girl had been arrested 10 times for theft and assault. Once, while in a treatment facility, she kicked, punched and helped tie up a teacher, then tried to run away.

Steele, now 15, was arrested for stealing a car and for numerous assaults, including beating up her sister, after which she pushed over a full-sized refrigerator. The reason: "I just wanted to fight. I'd hit, and they'd fall."

Steele, a teenager who is alternately sweet and strong-willed, is at the forefront of a national surge in violent crimes committed by girls and young women. Today's female teenagers are fighting more, forming their own gangs, using weapons regularly, and robbing with greater frequency than at any time in recent American history, according to FBI statistics.

Between 1986 and 1996, the number of girls younger than 18 arrested nationwide for violent crimes—murder, rape, robbery, aggravated assault—increased 114 percent, according to FBI statistics. In the same period, the number of boys ar-

rested for violent crime increased 39 percent.

In interviews, teenage girls who have been arrested for crimes say there is little difference between boys and girls when it comes to breaking the law.

"Girls are just as aggressive as guys, sometimes more," said Brenda Hall, a suburban New Jersey 19-year-old now serving time for armed robbery. "Whatever guys are doing, girls are doin—holding a gun, fighting, joining a gang."

Some law enforcement authorities say they are beginning to see a pattern of "macho" attitudes and behavior among girls.

In interviews, teenage girls in Pennsylvania and New Jersey described running illegal drug operations and carrying weapon—either for protection or to commit crimes. They said they engage in violent fights either to stake claim to a boyfriend or because someone has shown them disrespect. If they need money, they rob or burglarize. Some said they are not afraid to carry a gun.

Crime statistics show that in 1996, nearly one of every four juveniles arrested was a girl. In 1985, one in ev-

ery nine juveniles arrested for a violent crime was female. Between 1992 and 1996, there was a 20 percent increase in the number of girls arrested for robbery, while the number of boys arrested for robbery rose 6 percent. Theft arrests for girls were 25 percent higher, while the increase among boys was 2 percent.

According to police, prosecutors and juvenile counselors, the same forces at work among boys who commit crimes are now affecting girls: A lack of parental guidance; a notion that they will not be held accountable for their actions; overindulgence by parents; an increase in drug use; greater access to guns; and a desire for excitement.

Case workers also see a parallel between greater freedom in the workplace for women and the growing number of female juvenile offenders. In the same way that women in recent years have stepped into roles traditionally held by men, girls now feel freer to commit crimes.

"When women began to take nontraditional jobs and became more independent, it crossed over into the world of juvenile crime," said Cleet Davis, who directs the Florence Crittendon girls detention center in Trenton. "Girls began to feel they could be their own bosses. They didn't need the boys to sell the drugs, they could have their own gangs. I hear it all the time."

Twenty years ago roles were different, said Don Haldeman, a probation officer in Delaware County. "Girls weren't allowed to be violent. Society wouldn't accept it at all. They were brought up on that, and they bought into that. Now they don't. All the walls have crashed and they're free to do whatever the boys do."

Philip W. Harris, a criminal justice professor at Temple University who is working with the city to keep track of some juvenile offenders, said female delinquents are shedding traditional roles.

"Girls sense they don't have to play these charming little-girl roles anymore," Harris said.

Heather Corbett, 16, of Pennsauken, served time for assault. She said girls in school get into serious fights every week.

"Some of them feel like they have to fight," she said. "They don't want people to think they're punks. They fight because some girls think they're being disrepected. They're losing their pride. If somebody calls you a bitch, you will fight."

Kaveen Dudley, 16, of Mizpah, N.J., is serving time for assaulting a girl in the Oak Crest High School cafeteria. She said the girl had been telling other girls she was contacting Kaveen's boyfriend with a pager. As a result of the assault, the victim lost her peripheral vision.

"I lunged," Dudley said. "I was out of it. I don't know what happened. I was kicking her and stuff. I didn't have to react, but I wanted to. I wasn't angry. I was just fighting."

Leah Miller, 18, of Atlantic County, is serving time for drug possession. She said she has cut school, taken drugs, and participated in robberies. She said she has gone to a local park with a group of boys to steal. She said she held all the guns, because there was no female officer on

the local police force, and she could not be frisked.

"I was having fun," Miller said. "Once I got into the fast life, they wasn't stopping me."

Authorities say dealing with girls is more difficult than dealing with boys.

"The girls are the toughest, they are more incorrigible," said Anthony Guarna, chief juvenile probation officer in Montgomery County.

"The girls are more bullheaded," said Lisa Douple, a Bucks County public defender.

Law enforcement officials and case workers say that each year, the crimes by some girls have become more violent.

"Girls are using razors and baseball bats as weapons now," said Ellen Cohill, who runs Valentine, a facility for delinquent girls in Bordentown, N.J. "They are very angry, and they are very aggressive. It's vicious."

Police, who once took a benign approach with delinquent girls, now arrest them.

"The guys hesitate to arrest girls. It goes back to the mentality of their being female," said Detective Jim Waltrop of Lansdale. "The younger officers are starting to realize that the girls are as violent as the boys, but the older officers still have this thought that this is somebody's daughter, will be somebody's mother."

Another contributor to crimes by girls is childhood abuse.

Adelle Steele's mother, Roxanne, said her daughter was routinely and severely beaten by her father, who died in 1994.

"The abuse issues and the subsequent anger were always there," said William Ford, chief juvenile probation officer of Bucks County.

But in recent years, case workers say, girls have expressed their anger in more violent and criminal ways.

"If there are 20 girls in a detention room, 18 of those have been raped or sexually abused," said Davis, of the girls' center. Davis, who has supervised the detention center since 1991,

said girls come to her angry and frustrated.

"If she's raped at 12, by 13 she's out on the street raising hell," Davis said.

"They've just lost their way," said Alisa Brown of Big Sisters of Philadelphia. "You can't help them with the delinquency issues until you deal with the other things."

The 1995 lavender Dodge Neon was a teenager's dream.

Brenda Hall was given the car by her parents as a reward for good grades, for volunteer church work, and for tending to her three younger brothers and sisters. She was the "good daughter," with not a hint of problems in her background.

In 1997, Hall used the Dodge as a getaway car in a series of armed robberies in Gloucester County, she said. She took part in cuffing and terrorizing a gas station attendant with a sawed-off shotgun. She said she also planned the burglary of a bagel store, where she and two other youths stole more than $10,000.

In a three-month period, the high school senior whom everyone considered level-headed committed violent crimes. She pleaded guilty to three robberies, and in May was sentenced to 10 years, facing a minimum of three years and three months.

There are few answers to why and how Hall started her life of crime. Her parents, Carol and Harry Hall of Franklin Township, say they are still searching. They think part of the problem is that they spoiled her and gave her too much freedom too soon.

"It was so much of everything," Brenda Hall said. "It was fitting in. It was being accepted." And at first, she said, "It was so exciting."

A somewhat overweight young woman with curly red hair, Hall never really liked herself, she said. As a child, her classmates would tease her about her weight and call her ugly. She did "everything right," trying to please everyone, she said.

By her senior year her friends were dating, but she had no one. She desperately sought out friends, she said, and met a 16-year-old boy and an 18-year-old girl, both of whom had juvenile criminal records.

They told her of exploits that seemed glamorous. Before long, she joined them.

"I didn't want to be the one person to say no," she recalled.

Her purple Neon gave Hall instant acceptance. Neither of her new friends, Jason Nigro and Sharin Stallings, had a car. Whenever the three went out, Hall drove. One night in March 1997, the three planned to rob a Heritage store in Franklin Township, Hall and Nigro said in separate interviews. (Stallings declined to be interviewed.) Hall drove. They stole more than $200.

Within two weeks, they had planned a second robbery.

Hall was working part time at Don's Bagels in Glassboro. Don Brasco, the owner, had deducted $35 from her pay because money was missing from the cash register, she said. Denying that she took the money and angered that Brasco had charged her for it, she suggested to Stallings and Nigro that they rob the bagel store, Hall said. She sketched the inside of the bakery and gave them her key.

They were expecting to get a couple hundred dollars. Instead, they said, beneath the floorboards they found thousands of dollars. Amazed, they grabbed what they could—$10,000—and left.

In celebration, they rented a limousine and went to South Street in Philadelphia.

Realizing how much trouble she could get into, she told Nigro and Stallings she wanted out. Stallings objected, she said, telling Hall she would tell Hall's parents everything if she didn't continue to help.

Several weeks later, the three decided to rob a Franklin Township gas station.

Tom Severance was working that night when Hall and Nigro drove to the back of the station. Severance said a young woman, later identified as Stallings, approached him and told him that she and her friend were having car trouble.

"I went in the back, and the hood of the car was up," Severance said. "When I saw two girls in trouble, I just started to help."

He recalled seeing movement out of the corner of his eye. Then, a masked person appeared holding a shotgun. It was Nigro.

"You know what I want," Nigro said, according to Severance.

Forced to lie on the ground, Nigro and Stallings searched him, he said. Then Nigro told him to get up. "We're going for a walk."

"I was scared," Severance said in an interview. "I wondered whether I was going to get shot. It was scary looking down the barrel of that shotgun and not knowing what they were going to do."

Hall stayed in her car, waiting to provide the getaway, she said. They ordered him to take money out of the cash register, and give it to them. It was about $100. They then tied Severance to a tree and drove away.

Nigro and Stallings pleaded guilty on three robbery charges and are in jail.

F or Barbara Washington, fighting was a way of life.

Once, she went after a man with a knife and a brick. Fighting was a regular occurrence at school. But when Washington committed an assault so brutal that the victim was hospitalized, the Darby girl, who had just turned 15, found herself in court.

Despite the seriousness of the charge, she stood before the judge alone.

"Where are the parents?" demanded Juvenile Court Judge A. Leo Sereni.

Informed that they had been subpoenaed, the usually gentlemanly jurist exploded.

"This court will not tolerate noncompliance of parents!" Sereni said. He ordered bench warrants for the parents, called for child welfare to investigate the home, and kept Washington in detention.

Everyone in the courtroom snapped to attention. Except Barbara Washington.

It was not the first time she had stood alone.

Washington remembers the time her mother left her and her half-brother, Danny. She was 5, he was 10.

"She left us at some lady's house and she never came back," Washington said. "The lady kicked us out." She ended up on the street, she said. "My brother was carrying me on his back. I had no shoes on."

At 12, Washington struck a small boy who wouldn't play her way, she said. When the boy's father objected and hit Barbara on the back, she said she went after the father with a knife. Then she hit the father over the head with a brick.

She said she even fought when in detention. She remembers fighting because a girl was "talking trash." She punched the girl, knocking her onto a couch.

Washington said she often hit her mother. She learned to fight from her brother, who taught her at an early age to fight back.

"I was taught that nobody hits me," she said.

Washington's first arrest occurred in 1997. She said she was "helping" a 13-year-old friend, who was arguing with a woman. Washington said she bashed the woman's head seven times with a hard object.

"It just happened," she said, adding that she "went blank" when she assaulted the woman. At the time, Washington said she felt "nothing." Later, she said, she felt sorry.

The woman, badly bruised and terrified, was hospitalized. Washington and her friend were found guilty in juvenile court of aggravated assault.

Throughout Washington's short life, her parents have been often too mired in their own criminal entanglements, imprisonments and bouts of substance abuse to allow for a decent childhood, they said.

At one point, Washington lived with Shirley Carmichael, a school cleaning woman who was her half-brother's maternal grandmother. Carmichael said of Washington: "I don't blame little Barbara. I blame her mother, I blame her father."

At Quakertown High School, Joanna Seifert had a tough time making friends, she said. She did not belong to any clubs but maintained good grades. "I felt a little different," she said. "I had low self-esteem."

Then, in the summer of 1996, when she was 16, her grandfather bought her a black 1985 Porsche 944. The car quickly became her pride and joy, she said. Every week, she would vacuum and shine it in her grandparents' driveway.

At school, the car stood out as a singular attraction, she said. And Seifert, a quiet, hard-to-read, reticent girl, was becoming noticed by fellow classmates.

"I liked to show it off," she said.

She also liked to drive fast. Within months after she got the car, she got a ticket for tailgating; soon after that, she got a speeding ticket. And after that, she hit a van and was cited for reckless driving. A stop-sign violation followed. She said her grandparents paid most of the fines.

On the evening of Aug. 1, 1997, she left her part-time job at a Quakertown movie theater to visit a friend, she said. Traveling 50 m.p.h. in a 10 m.p.h. zone, she struck and killed a pedestrian.

Afraid of facing the consequences, she said, she sped away. But a witness gave state police her license number.

By midnight, she had been arrested at her grandparents' house, the place she had called home for most of her life. She was charged with involuntary manslaughter, homicide by vehicle and related offenses.

On Nov. 14, Bucks County Common Pleas Court President Judge Isaac Garb ordered her to a residential treatment facility near Harrisburg.

Her probation officer, Mark Maryott, told the court that Seifert's "family situation has caused very serious problems, and her drug usage has compounded the situation.

"She truly lacks any insight into her problems. Anything short of this [placement] won't be effective with her," Maryott said.

When Seifert was 8, and her sister 11, their parents separated after a stormy marriage. The children chose to move in with their maternal grandparents.

Seifert said that she did not feel abandoned, and was not angry at her parents. "I love them, I just don't feel close," she said.

In late 1996, Seifert said, she became friends with some kids she considered to be "cool."

"The popular kids were the bad kids, and I wanted the recognition," she said. "Once I had that, I didn't have low self-esteem."

By April last year, after experimenting with a host of drugs, including heroin, she decided to push her popularity one step further by selling drugs, she said.

"Basically, I had a variety store going on," she said.

Supplying friends, she would travel to Philadelphia for cocaine and marijuana. She bought acid in the Quakertown area, she said.

Using the cellular phone her grandfather bought her for her birthday, Seifert conducted business from her car and in friends' houses. She was rarely home.

"I would go home to sleep and shower, and sometimes I would stay out all night," Seifert said. "Sometimes I would go from the crack house to work. I would call my grandmother and tell her I was all right. She would be on the phone crying."

She recalled the night she killed a man with her car:

Driving fast through a development, she headed toward a woman in the street who was yelling, "Slow the H down!"

"I put my brakes on, to swerve around her," Seifert said. A man, Harold Winkler, was in the street. "All I seen was the middle portion of his body," Seifert said. Winkler was struck by the side of the car; the impact dented the door. Flying in the air, he landed, head first, on the curb.

"To me, it was like, I pushed him away," Seifert said. "I was scared of what happened; I was scared of the woman in the street. I knew I would get in a lot of trouble. I was trying to get away from it."

She said she sped home, then went to a pizzeria to meet her friend. They headed for Allentown and bought crack cocaine.

From the treatment facility, she said the only thing she regretted about the accident was that Winkler died.

"I'm basically a thrill seeker," she said. "I was just living it up."

The *Inquirer* interviewed and received consent from the parents or legal guardians of all subjects under 18 to be named and fully quoted in this series..

Girls' Study Group Launches Web Site

The emergence of the **feminist perspective** and the recognition that **delinquency is a reality among girls as well as boys** in the **modern world has occasioned an interdisciplinary effort to organize existing data** and **foster** new research into the phenomenon. The site has a wealth of information. The lead investigator for this group, RTI International in North Carolina, is Dr. Margaret Zahn and all the investigators are identified in the site.

Please access this website at:
http//girlsstudygroup.rti.org

Go first to the link "About the Study" to orient yourself to this work. Then, go to the to the link About Girls. There, go to the sublink "Brief Literature Review" for one of the best written summaries of the literature on female delinquency.

Quote from the website section "About the Study"

"The ultimate goal of the Girls Study Group project is to develop the research foundation that communities need to make sound decisions about how best to prevent and reduce delinquency and violence by girls. The Girls Study Group will be responsible for developing and providing scientifically sound, useful guidance on program development and implementation to policymakers, practitioners, and the research community. RTI's plans for carrying out the Girls Study Group project are summarized in its proposal abstract.

The work of the Girls Study Group is guided by several overarching research questions. In order to answer the research questions identified by the Girls Study Group, research activities include a comprehensive literature review, statistical analysis of secondary datasets, a review of Federal programs targeting female delinquency, a review of screening and assessment instruments, and the development of model programs. More information about the Girls Study Group is available by viewing presentations given at recent meetings and conferences."

From *Office of Juvenile Justice and Delinquency Prevention*, January/February 2005.

The Real Root Cause of Violent Crime

THE BREAKDOWN OF THE FAMILY

Social scientists, criminologists, and many other observers at long last are coming to recognize the connection between the breakdown of families and various social problems that have plagued American society. In the debate over welfare reform, for instance, it is now a widely accepted premise that children born into single-parent families are much more likely than children born into intact families to fall into poverty and welfare dependency.

While the link between the family and chronic welfare dependency is much better understood these days, there is another link—between the family and crime—that deserves more attention. Why? Because whole communities, particularly in urban areas, are being torn apart by crime. We desperately need to uncover the real root cause of criminal behavior and learn how criminals are formed if we are to fight this growing threat.

There is a wealth of evidence in the professional literature of criminology and sociology to suggest that the breakdown of family is the real root cause of crime in America. But the orthodox thinking in official Washington assumes that crime is caused by material conditions, such as poor employment opportunities and a shortage of adequately funded state and federal social programs.

The Violent Crime Control and Law Enforcement Act of 1994, supported by the Clinton administration and enacted last year, perfectly embodies official Washington's view of crime. It provides for billions of dollars in new spending, adding 15 new social programs on top of a welfare system that has cost taxpayers $5 trillion since the "War on Poverty" was declared in 1965. But there is no reason to suppose that increased spending and new programs will have any significant positive impact. Since 1965, welfare spending has increased 800 percent in real terms, while the number of major felonies per capita today is roughly three times the rate prior to 1960. As Republican Senator Phil Gramm rightly observes, "If social spending stopped crime, America would be the safest country in the world."

Still, federal bureaucrats and lawmakers persist in arguing that poverty is the primary cause of crime. In its simplest form, this contention is absurd; if it were true, there would have been more crime in the past, when more people were poorer. And in poorer nations, the crime rates would be higher than in the United States. History defies the assumption that deteriorating economic circumstances breed crime and improving conditions reduce it. America's crime rate actually rose during the long period of real economic growth in the early 20th century. As the Great Depression set in and incomes dropped, the crime rate also dropped. It rose again between 1965 and 1974, when incomes rose. Most recently, during the recession of 1982, there was a slight dip in crime, not an increase.

Official Washington also believes that race is the second most important cause of crime. The large disparity in crime rates between whites and blacks often is cited as proof. However, a closer look at the data shows that the real variable is not race but family structure and all that it implies in terms of commitment and love between adults and between adults and children.

A major 1988 study of 11,000 individuals found that "the percentage of single-parent households with children between the ages of 12 and 20 is significantly associated with rates of violent crime and burglary." The same study makes it clear that the popular assumption that there is an association between race and crime is false. Illegitimacy, not race, is the key factor. It is the absence of marriage and the failure to form and maintain intact families that explains the incidence of crime among whites as well as blacks.

From *Vital Speeches of the Day*, February 5, 1995. © 1995 by Patrick Fagan, Fitzgerald Fellow of the Heritage Foundation. Reprinted with permission of *Imprimis*, the monthly journal of Hillsdale College.

When Our Children Commit VIOLENCE

BY ANN F. CARON

WHEN I RECENTLY ASKED A GROUP OF PARENTS how many felt responsible for their children's behavior, only a few raised their hands. Their response was not surprising. After all, most of us assume that children are responsible for their own behavior.

But family research consistently shows that parents who feel responsible for their children's behavior are more effective parents. Likewise, the children of these parents are more likely to behave responsibly.

The tragic schoolyard slaughters in Arkansas and Oregon have escalated concerns about violence and responsibility. We cannot exonerate the boys who killed and injured classmates on the basis of their ages. Eleven, 13- and 15-year-olds know that killing people is wrong. They also know that cheating, lying, stealing and meanness to others are wrong.

What many children do not know, however, is that when they do something wrong, they harm themselves as well as others. Further, few of them know that their actions have consequences.

That is where responsible parents come in. They are the primary teachers of right and wrong to the 2-year-old and to the 18-year-old. Their children know that bad actions have bad consequences. But not all parents set those limits or follow through with those consequences. The schools cannot do the job. The church cannot do the job. Only parents can. And now many states are deciding to fill the responsibility gap left by parents and adults.

According to a report in the *New York Times*, legislators around the country are "rushing" to enact laws that make parents responsible for their children's misdeeds. Under Arkansas law, parents of shooting victims can bring civil lawsuits against the killers' parents. Also in Arkansas, the parents of a truant child who is deemed a delinquent must perform court-ordered public service with their child. In Virginia, parents whose children are caught defacing or vandalizing property (even mailboxes) can face $2,500 in fines.

Why does government feel obligated to perform a basic parental role? When school violence was confined to inner-city schools, many blamed poverty, single-parent families and drug-infested streets. But now rural and suburban communities with two-parent families feel the re-

percussions of youth violence. The nation is, at last, waking up to the issue of responsibility.

Are Americans failing to raise civilized children? Are we trying so hard to be non-judgmental that we hesitate to tell our children that some issues are black and white— that some behavior is clearly wrong?

I don't agree with the popular radio psychologist Dr. Laura Schlesinger, who said in a television interview after the Arkansas shootings that children possess an "innate sense of cruelty." But I do believe that we must teach our children how to behave in a civil manner. Some children intimidate their parents, teachers and schoolmates and never feel the sting of a reprimand, a "time out" or an appropriate consequence. When as adults we don't teach our children right from wrong, they learn from an early age that anything goes. They learn that their will is primary.

"But," parents protest, "aren't children, particularly adolescents, responsible for their own behavior?" Yes and no is the answer.

By the time children are adolescents, they must assume responsibility for living up to their parents' and society's rules. But if we don't articulate or demonstrate those ideals, we leave our children with no direction or moral compass. A psychologically or physically absent parent basically abandons his or her children, and, unfortunately, no one is picking up the slack. Neither the community nor the schools can assume parental obligations. Therefore, all citizens must face the adolescent angst that arises when a child feels that no one cares. Every child who grows into a responsible adult believes that he or she really matters to someone.

When two high-school boys in my suburban community agreed to kill each other using one of their parent's guns (a murder-suicide), no adult could explain it, but their friends could. No adult had reached out to them as they struggled with anger and sexual confusion. When I interviewed students for a book I was writing, most children whose parents had divorced told me that no adult ever talked to them about the worst event in their young lives. No one showed sympathy or understanding. In other words, adults ignored the topic. Where were the so-called "godparents" or even their parents' friends? Responsible adults seem to have disappeared from the lives of adolescents. Same-age friends fill the void.

Sometimes even adults can send a child the wrong message about responsibility. A teacher at a local school, for instance, told me a student's father threatened him with a lawsuit. The teacher had given the man's son a failing grade on an essay because he had copied someone's work. The father was indignant. His wrath came not because his son cheated, but because the teacher had given him an "F." By threatening a lawsuit, the father clearly absolved his son from any responsibility. If he had doubts about the teacher's decision, he should have asked his son to write another essay in the presence of the teacher and prove his ability. But now the boy realizes that his father will do anything, even threaten a lawsuit, to cover for him.

A mother told me that she has written her daughter's essays and term papers since her daughter was in the fifth grade. Her reason? When she is assigned a research paper, the daughter "gets a headache," and the mother can't stand to watch her daughter's discomfort. At first I thought her story was unique, but now I think attempts to cover up children's failures, mistakes or misdeeds are becoming more commonplace.

Who is teaching responsibility?

Rationalizing children's misbehavior feeds into their sense of invulnerability. Nothing bad will ever happen, no matter what they do. When a 5-year-old sneaks other children's toys into his pockets to claim as his own, he should return those items with an apology. His parents should not ignore or laugh at the incident. If 12-year-old girls maliciously tease an acquaintance, parents and teachers should not consider their taunts "just part of growing up." The parents and teachers should tell the girls that harassing classmates is unacceptable behavior.

What can caring parents and adults do to encourage their children to honestly face life, accept responsibility and live in civilized harmony? First, parents must be the authorities in parenting. In short, even if their children are 18, parents know more than their children.

These confident adults possess two major characteristics. They demand a lot of children, yet they are highly responsive to children's needs. Whether a child is a preschooler or a high-schooler, a responsible parent offers the stability of firmness and the warmth of caring love.

Some parents are there but "not there"" I have talked to many children who feel like appendages to their families. They feel insignificant because no one has shown them that they are needed.

Yet, healthy children come from families that stress the interdependence of all family members. A man told me that his parents owned a restaurant, and he worked with them from the time he was nine. He knew they could not run the restaurant without him. He recalls those experiences as forming his own sense of responsibility. Now he runs a major company and is trying to figure out how to give his 12-year-old son that same sense of being essential to the family.

How can parents and adults articulate the values that lead to responsible behavior? Television and films offer many opportunities to discuss moral issues. An 8-year-old asked her mother if girls had to have sex when they went to senior prom. She had watched a popular show in which the main character was trying to decide whether she and her boyfriend should sleep together the night of her senior prom. This was an important parental moment to teach sexual values.

Violence as well as sex is endemic to film and television, and the most popular computer games feature combat action geared for young males. Parents don't have to buy those games, allow their children to attend those movies or permit guns in the house. Children who know that their homes are dedicated to non-violence learn how to solve disputes without fighting. Harvard University research confirms that children who discuss moral issues, such as sex and violence, with adults tend to make better moral and responsible decisions when they are in their late teens.

Responsible parents don't fear their children's outcry when they enforce limits. Whether the offense is shoplifting by a 9-year-old or breaking curfew expectations by a 17-year-old, these children know that if they get into trouble, their parents will not approve or cover up for them.

A boy said it well when he told me: "Let him know the rules before he goes out so he knows what he has to fulfill before he gets in trouble. If he doesn't know the rules, you can't get mad at him."

In contrast, the father of the 15-year-old Oregon boy who killed his parents and classmates confided in a stranger he met at an airport that he was "terrified" of his son. Yet, in order to win his son over, he bought him the automatic rifle that his son eventually turned on him and his wife. We will never know why this father bought his son a weapon of destruction, but the purchase itself reflected complete irresponsibility.

Part of teaching responsibility is teaching self-regulation. For instance, a mother said that during her son's senior year, she asked him daily whether he had filled out his college application. At last, frustrated by his easy-going attitude, she resolved never to ask about college again. Consequently, when his friends went off to college her son stayed home and worked. But by October, without his parents saying anything, he finished his applications and joined his classmates in college a year late. His mother reported that the best thing she ever did for him was to stop nagging him about his application. He learned that he—not his mother or his father—had the responsibility for getting into college.

But who taught him that? His parents.

A fear many adults secretly harbor is that adolescents will not like them or turn on them. When adults realize that adolescents are children who need and want guidance, this unfounded fear will abate. Their bravado, their seeming indifference and their anger do not have to break out in violence. Wise parents and adults who teach them, love them, commit to them and take responsibility for them can direct those adolescent traits.

These children know their voices are heard and, in turn, will grow up feeling responsible to themselves, to their parents and to society.

A 1954 Mundelein graduate, Ann F. Caron is a developmental psychologist, lecturer and author of Strong Mothers, Strong Sons: Raising the Next Generation of Men (Harper Collins); Don't Stop Loving Me: A Reassuring Guide for Mothers of Adolescent Daughters (Harper Collins); and Mothers and Daughters: Searching for New Connections (Henry Holt and Co.). *She and her husband, John, are parents of six adult children and live in Connecticut.*

THE CHILDREN'S CRUSADE

A '60s-style campaign aims to put kids first in this year's budget battles and the presidential race

By ELIZABETH GLEICK

For Marian Wright Edelman, the youngest daughter of a Baptist preacher, from adversity springs strength. From defeat comes inspiration. If her courage ever fails her, she is not about to say so. Life as she lives it day by day is a series of battles fought along starkly moral lines. That, is why Edelman—who helped register black voters in the segregated South, who stood on the steps of the Lincoln Memorial during Martin Luther King Jr.'s "I Have a Dream" speech and who gave Robert Kennedy a personal tour to see the malnourished children in the Mississippi Delta—is manning the barricades once more.

As the president of the Children's Defense Fund, she has for nearly 25 years been the single loudest voice on behalf of those too young to speak for themselves. But to hear her tell it, the test of her mettle is now. "I knew it would take 20 years, 25 years to seed a movement," she says. "You just have to keep planting and watering and fertilizing. And then, when it is time, you do what you have to do. But you have to stand up—win, lose or draw. And it's time."

Edelman has summoned Americans to a rally at the Lincoln Memorial this Saturday to Stand for Children. Like the Million Man March, the event is less about defining an agenda than it is about evoking a spirit—and filling what organizers see as a terrifying vacuum of leadership and resolve at a time when every premise about what this country owes its children is being challenged. "Children are never going to get what they need until there is a fundamental change in the ethos that says it is not acceptable to cut children first," says Edelman of the current budget battles in Washington. She hopes to use this period of fiscal conflict to mobilize the troops. "God really did put rainbows in the clouds," she says. "Without Newt Gingrich and the incredible threat to everything, we would never have been able to bring folks together in this way. So, in many ways this is the thing that will launch the children's movement."

Unlike the civil rights movement, however—or for that matter the seatbelt, drunk-driving and environmental movements, all of which

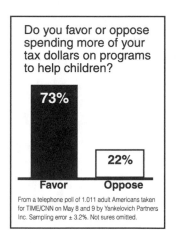

Do you favor or oppose spending more of your tax dollars on programs to help children?

73% Favor
22% Oppose

From a telephone poll of 1,011 adult Americans taken for TIME/CNN on May 8 and 9 by Yankelovich Partners Inc. Sampling error ± 3.2%. Not sures omitted.

have changed the way Americans live—the children's movement is more like a series of spasms than a focused, well-coordinated effort. True, when a Polly Klaas or Megan Kanka is abducted and murdered, or when Elisa Izquierdo falls through the gaping holes in New York City's social-services system, outraged parents and community leaders can rear up, roar and carry the day for "three strikes" or Megan's Law. And in the endless wrangle over welfare reform, which hit the headlines again last week, children have proved to be a deal breaker. "I can win any argument by saying we need reform of welfare, but not at the cost of kids," says Senator Edward Kennedy, who derailed Bob Dole's welfare proposal by branding it the "home alone" bill because there was no money specifically targeted for child care.

Even so, despite activism by Edelman and her allies, most political leaders still don't do what she wants them to do: ask, every time they cast a vote or cut a dollar, "How will this affect kids?" And even if they did, they would not necessarily answer the question Edelman's way because of the growing sense, embraced by both major presidential candidates, that government has its limitations. "Read between the lines of everything Marian Wright Edelman says, and what you get is this," says Robert Rector of the conservative Heritage Foundation. "The problem affecting kids is material poverty, so if we give the family more money for housing and food, things will turn out better for the kids. The reality is that despite 30 years of this effort, there is no evidence whatsoever that [this] has a positive effect on kids at all, except for cases of gross malnutrition."

In the broadest sense, Edelman's positions are extremely popular. Who, after all, would ever stand against children? In a recent TIME CNN poll, 73% of those surveyed favor having more of their tax dollars go to programs that benefit the young. For the most part, that sentiment has proved beneficial. Since Edelman launched the Children's Defense Fund in 1973, American children are doing better in such areas as math and science proficiency, immunizations and infant survival rates, thanks in part to government action.

BUT AS AMERICA POLARIZES into a land of rich and poor, the number of children on the losing side is growing at an alarming rate. According to a report released last month by the Department of Health and Human Services, the percentage of children in "extreme poverty"

(with a family income less than half the official poverty level) has doubled since 1975: it now stands at 10%, or 6.3 million children. The ranks of the merely poor include 1 in every 5 children in the U.S. In 1992 there were 850,000 substantiated cases of child abuse or neglect, while the homicide rate for teens more than doubled between 1970 and 1992.

Such numbers are not just a snapshot of how we live today. To experts who understand the trajectory of childhood development, the statistics predict a grim future for American society. As Douglas Nelson, executive director of the Annie E. Casey Foundation, puts it, "It may well be that the nation cannot survive—as a decent place to live, as a world-class power or even as a democracy—with such high rates of children growing into adulthood unprepared to parent, unprepared to be productively employed and unprepared to share in mainstream aspirations."

The Children's Defense Fund works to fix this disconnect between what Americans say they want for children and what they actually do for them. With offices just a few blocks from Capitol Hill, the Defense Fund stands out among youth advocacy groups for its Washington-based organization and strategic coalitions, its many alliances with state and local groups, and its many service oriented programs. In the District of Columbia, the Defense Fund has established City Lights, which works with severely troubled adolescents. At what was once the Tennessee farm of *Roots* author Alex Haley, the Fund conducts leadership training sessions. And, often in partnership with Junior Leagues, it runs public-education programs throughout the country, exposing business and community leaders to the problems of the young. In the mid-1980s, the Children's Defense Fund helped focus national attention on the problem of teen pregnancy. In the late '80s, it put together a coalition that was instrumental in the 1990 passage of a multibillion-dollar child-care bill for low-income working parents.

Edelman learned early that you have to play politics to change lives. When Head Start funds were made available to the states in 1965, for example, Mississippi did not sign up. But a group of public, private and church organizations, with Edelman on its board, applied for the money and saw Head Start become a powerful catalyst in the state's black community. When then Senator John Stennis tried to get Congress to cut off its funding, Edelman, at that point 25, went to Washington to fight back—and won. "This was my first big lesson about government," she says. "There was no one in Washington for these folks, like General Motors had. That was seed No. 1 for the Children's Defense Fund." In the 1970s, Edelman helped defeat a proposal to turn Head Start funding over to the states. Today, with devolution again the coin of the realm, Edelman, a child of the segregated South, remains deeply skeptical that all states will voluntarily care for their neediest citizens. "Where you can see a general need everywhere," she contends, you try to have a national solution."

As she travels around the country stirring up support for the march in Washington, Edelman talks about "the silence of good people about the injustice of it all." By this she means, in large part, her old friend the President. Marian and her husband, Peter Edelman, a lawyer whom she met when he was an adviser to Bobby Kennedy, have known the Clintons for many years. Mrs. Clinton worked as a lawyer for the Children's Defense Fund, resigning from the board when she became First Lady. In August 1995, the President almost nominated Peter, who currently works for the Department of Health and Human Services, to the federal district court in Washington, changing his mind at the last minute, fearing he was too liberal. Last fall, as Edelman watched the welfare battle take shape, she privately implored the President not to compromise federal standards. When Clinton nevertheless signaled his support for a

Should each of the following programs for children be among the hightest priorities for government, an important priority or a low/no priority?

	Highest		Low/No
Free immunization shots against disease	67%	26%	5%
Nutrition programs for children who need them	61%	32%	6%
Health insurance for all children	54%	29%	15%
Day-care programs for poor children so their parents can work	52%	33%	12%
Providing information and assistance to teens on preventing unwanted pregnancies	51%	30%	17%
Prenatal health-care programs for pregnant mothers who need them	49%	36%	13%
Preschool education programs	45%	34%	20%

Senate bill that would transform federal welfare spending into a system of smaller, block grants to the states—thereby eliminating the safety net of protections that children have, regardless of which state they live in—Edelman spoke out.

In "An Open Letter to the President," which ran last Nov. 3 in the Washington *Post,* Edelman urged Clinton to oppose welfare and Medicaid block grants. She wrote, "Do you think the Old Testament prophets, Isaiah, Micah and Amos—or Jesus Christ—would support such policies?" If he were to let federal protections go, she warned, "we may not get them back in our lifetime or our children's." She concluded: "What a tragic irony it would be for this regressive attack on children and the poor to occur on your watch. For me, this is a defining moral litmus test for your presidency." In the end, Clinton withdrew his support for the bill, perhaps in part because he was shamed by his old friend, but also because it was good politics to do so. Senator Daniel Patrick Moynihan had forced the White House to disclose its estimate that more than 1 million additional children would be thrown into poverty by the Senate measure. (The Clintons and the Edelmans remained friends. Peter rode Air Force One to Yitzhak Rabin's funeral last fall and stayed up most of

the night playing hearts with the President on the trip home.)

The word moral appears seven times in Edelman's letter, and the certitude with which she plunges ahead is both her greatest strength and her greatest flaw. What looks like "morality" to her is merely discredited 1960s liberalism to others. Her opponents believe that all of Edelman's big talk about children masks her true goal: to solve the problems of poverty—for people of all ages—through the expenditure of federal money. While most Americans agree children deserve extra help, when policymakers start talking about solutions they speak completely different languages. "As long as liberals talk about economics and government and conservatives talk about culture and values, there will never be a political debate that reaches a successful conclusion," says William Galston, a former domestic-policy adviser in the Clinton White House.

The unshakable conviction that they have God on their side may also help explain why advocates for children are not more effective lobbyists. A 1995 report on how state legislative leaders view children's issues and the people who come to lobby on their behalf discovered a vast chasm of misunderstanding and miscommunication. Few of the 177 legislative leaders who were interviewed could identify by

name the children's-advocacy organizations in their states. Many complained that those who ask them to act on behalf of children do not understand the legislative process and tend to arrive too late in the budget cycle. Says Michael Iskowitz, Senator Kennedy's aide on children's issues: "Just expecting people to do the right thing is often not enough. You have to give them a range of arguments about why it is in their interest."

Chief among those arguments are votes and money, yet the study found that children's advocates rarely work in political campaigns or contribute to candidates. Worse still, they have little organized, grassroots support. "[The legislators] are not getting calls in their office asking, 'What are you doing for kids?'" says Margaret Blood, who ran the study. Even some of Edelman's supporters acknowledge this has been a problem with her work. CDF has been enormously effective on a national level," says Eve Brooks, president of the National Association of Child Advocates. "It has been less effective in building a constituency that stays in place."

It is a truism that children can't vote, but Sylvia Ann Hewlett, author of *When the Bough Breaks: The Costs of Neglecting Our Children,* has discovered that their parents don't vote either. In the last national election, only 39% of adults with children at

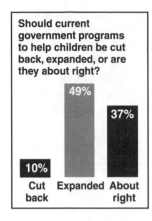

Should current government programs to help children be cut back, expanded, or are they about right?

49% Expanded
37% About right
10% Cut back

home cast a ballot, as compared with 61% of the elderly. During the 1950s, says Hewlett, who runs a nonprofit organization aimed at getting parents to the polls, 65% of parents voted.

In their interviews, the legislators indicated that if children's advocates are to be effective, they will need to organize themselves more like the National Rifle Association and the American Association for Retired Persons—with well-defined goals, politically active members, and lobbyists who work throughout the entire legislative session. (The Children's Defense Fund operates on an annual budget of $13 million, compared with $66 million for the N.R.A.; AARP has annual revenues of $300 million.)

The latter comparison is particularly apt since the elderly may have strengthened their own safety net at the expense of the young. "Is there a disproportionate amount of money being spent on people over the age of 65 versus under the age of three?" asks one legislative leader. "Yes, unquestionably. Is it in part a function of their lobbying efforts? Yes, unquestionably. Is it largely a function of their need? No, it is not." Yet as Ira Schwartz, dean of the School of Social Work at the University of Pennsylvania, notes, "Seniors and those in the work force don't understand that the survival of the Social Security system is really dependent on the future of our children." Or perhaps they do: AARP has endorsed the Stand, in part, says spokesman Peter

Ashkenaz, because so many grandparents are rearing children.

In the end, the most pressing question for children's advocates is the one that Saturday's march intentionally sidesteps: setting a common agenda. It is a daunting task, not just because children's issues are so numerous and so fragmented, but because no one is certain what solutions, if any, will work. Even people committed to reducing teen pregnancy may disagree vehemently about the means to that end. Some feel that social trends like no-fault divorce pose the greatest threat to children.

"One of the biggest problems we have is that it's so hard to show results," says Frank Sanchez Jr., who runs delinquency-prevention programs for the Boys & Girls Clubs of America. The child who doesn't get into trouble is the dog that doesn't bark. "We don't have a lot of studies to build a broad, knowledgeable base," agrees Kristin Moore, executive director of the research firm Child Trends Inc., because most of the efforts to help kids are "too late, too shallow, too brief and too cheap."

Among some children's advocates, enthusiasm has faded for homegrown, experimental approaches. In 1988 Lisbeth Schorr and her husband, National Public Radio's Daniel Schorr, wrote *Within Our Reach: Breaking the Cycle of Disadvantage*, which enthusiastically described 24 new programs for children. Today half of them are gone, and Schorr has had a change of heart about what such initiatives can accomplish. "Foundations fund innovative programs for several years with the idea that when they work, public funds will pick up the cost and continue the program," she says. "But that hasn't happened for years. It's an illusion. Anything you want to do in an organized way, a big way, needs government funding." Adds Vivien Stewart of the Carnegie Foundation: "In this country we are very good at pilot programs, but we are very bad at

scaling up to a point where we can actually turn some of these things around. It can't be done with the resources of small organizations."

Senator Dan Coats, an Indiana Republican, could not disagree more. Originator of the "charity tax credit" endorsed by Bob Dole last week, Coats believes "federal programs have almost become an excuse for people not to become personally involved." A tax credit that allows people to support local social initiatives, he contends, would keep both donor and recipient accountable. "If you want to know that your money is really going to make a difference," he asks, "would you rather give $1,000 to Habitat for Humanity or to HUD?" Yet one study that Catholic Charities cited in Senate testimony earlier this year estimates that private giving in the year 2000 would have to be 50 times greater than it has been to replace government support for social services.

The Coats thesis notwithstanding, many of the nonprofit groups that work with children have rallied to Edelman's call. Her Stand for Children has been endorsed by almost 3,000 organizations. Thousands of Girl Scouts are expected to attend, as well as thousands more teachers and members of the YWCA and the YMCA. The latter group, which serves 17 million children and families, and whose leadership is generally conservative, has gone out of its way to avoid the politics associated with the rally. "We hope not to be sidetracked by who is calling this event," says Y public-policy senior associate John Brooks. "Supporting kids shouldn't be a partisan issue."

Nor, in the final analysis, should it be limited to children in poverty or in crisis. "Any broad-based politics about family issues is going to have to engage parents as citizens and as actors, not simply as objects of attention," says Theda Skocpol, a professor of government and sociology at Harvard, who believes Edelman must inspire "the missing middle," the working parents stressed out by juggling work and family. One reason why children's issues are likely to become a prominent campaign issue is that both parties are working hard to attract blue-collar mothers. "Women are more likely to vote the family issues and want to be sure children get the right start," says Stanley Greenberg, pollster for the Democratic National Committee.

Politicians are not invited on Saturday, though. They would only obscure what Edelman, a veteran of many marches, sees as this event's main goal: to inspire the heady awareness—found in the civil rights campaigns and the antiwar movement—that individuals can change the world.—*Reported by Melissa Ludtke with Marian Wright Edelman, Ann Blackman and Ann M. Simmons/Washington, and Tammerlin Drummond/Miami*

The Victims of Victims

Anthony Wilson killed 19-month-old Semaj Rice, and he'll pay for it in prison.
But who do you punish for generations of abuse and bureaucratic neglect?

Steve Bogira

Assistant state's attorney Marie Taraska: *Anthony, I talked to you earlier, and you told me about the death of Semaj Rice. … In the last week or two, on several occasions you struck Semaj Rice while disciplining him. A few days ago you saw Semaj sticking his hand in his diaper and you felt he needed to be disciplined, so you struck him several times in his legs and back. … Is that correct?*
Anthony Wilson: *Correct.*
Taraska: *I'm going to read you your rights again.*
—from the videotaped statement of Anthony Wilson, taken on March 15, 2002, and played at his trial on March 15, 2004

Semaj Rice died on March 14, 2002, when he was 19 months old. The people entrusted with his care, 17-year-old Anthony Wilson and 16-year-old Vanessa (not her real name), were wards of the state who'd run away from their group home two months earlier.

The group home was the Maryville Farm Campus in Durand, a small town northwest of Rockford. Most of the residential programs for troubled youth run by the Maryville City of Youth are in or near Chicago. According to the agency's Web site, the farm campus is for youth who "require distance from city life."

Anthony was placed there in September 1999, when he was 14. "I wasn't used to seeing no cornfields and deers," he says. His mother had abandoned him when he was five, after which he'd bounced between relatives and foster homes in Chicago and west-suburban Maywood. Anthony liked the farm campus's gym and outdoor basketball court, but not the "distance from city life."

The farm campus had four dormitories, two for boys and two for girls, each housing eight to ten youths. Vanessa arrived a year after Anthony, in July 2000. She was 15 and had been turned out of a foster home. "It was a friend of mine that hooked us up," Anthony says. Some nights he climbed out of his bedroom window and sneaked into her room.

Late in December 2001 Anthony and Vanessa left the farm campus on holiday passes and didn't return. A DCFS investigation would later determine that their caseworkers made little attempt to find them.

The couple moved in with Vanessa's 50-year-old grandmother, Thomasa Brown. She lived in Cabrini-Green in a four-bedroom apartment in a 16-floor building at 534 W. Division. It was there that Anthony first met Semaj, Vanessa's toddler brother. A couple of Brown's daughters lived there as well, along with their boyfriends. Another daughter, Natalia, the mother of Vanessa and Semaj, also stayed in the apartment, but only sporadically. "She'd leave, don't come back," Anthony says. "Go out, do her thing—do drugs."

Natalia, who was 34, had been using drugs for years. "She'd smoke rock, toot blow," says Brown, who wound up caring for Semaj as a result.

Semaj was a happy, engaging child, Brown says. "If you was mad at him he would charm you by looking at you with his big ol' eyes."

But raising Semaj wasn't a responsibility Brown had sought or wanted. She had 30 grandchildren and had helped care for many of them. By the time Semaj was born she was worn down by chronic ailments—congestive heart failure, hypertension, asthma. "It's hard to take care of those little ones," she says. One-year-olds "can get into a lot of stuff. People talk about the terrible twos, I talk about the terrible ones." Semaj liked to sleep with Brown, and Brown let him because then she could be sure he wasn't wandering around the apartment getting into trouble.

Brown took to Anthony when he and Vanessa started staying in her apartment. "He was easy to get along with," she says. "He was mannerable. If I asked him to do something he would do it, no questions asked. He called me grandma just like everyone else did." And, she says, "He was crazy about Semaj."

According to Anthony, after he and Vanessa moved in, Brown quickly delegated Semaj's care to them. Brown denies this, though she allows that she sometimes asked the two teens to watch him during the day and she had him sleep with Vanessa at night instead of with her. Brown says that one night Vanessa and Semaj were sleeping in a top bunk in one of the bedrooms when Semaj rolled over Vanessa and "fell out the bed." She says she'd put pillows on the floor "because this concrete don't give" and that one of them broke his fall, so that he had only a swollen lip.

Anthony says that soon after he arrived Brown became unhappy with the situation in her apartment. "Mama ain't there taking care of her kid, aunties arguing, everything getting crazy," he says. "Too many people in the house."

It seemed clear to him that Brown wanted him and Vanessa to move, and when they heard there were abandoned apartments in the Cabrini-Green high-rise at 1230 N. Larrabee they moved into one. Semaj went with them.

Taraska: *A week or two ago, were you living at an apartment that you call 1230 apartment, which is at about 1230 Burling? [Actually it was Larrabee.]*

Anthony Wilson: *Yes.*

T: And while you were living in that vacant apartment at 1230 Burling, was there a time when you felt it was necessary to discipline Semaj?

AW: *Yes.*

Anthony's videotaped statement was taken at Area Three headquarters, at Belmont and Western. He was hunched over in a molded plastic chair at the far end of a table, smoking a cigarette, when assistant state's attorney Taraska began questioning him on camera. An ashtray and a can of Coke sat on the table to his left, a Raggedy Ann doll to his right. Anthony is a short, stocky, medium-complected African-American. His hair was braided, and he was wearing a black athletic jersey. The left sleeve of the jersey hid a tattoo: "Vanessa—I Love You—Tony." Taraska sat at the side of the table to his right,

a pen in her hand and papers in front of her. A gray-haired Chicago police detective sat at his left, hands folded on the table.

In her opening questions Taraska asked Anthony how far he'd gone in school. He told her he'd gone to Proviso East, in Maywood, until his junior year. Actually he'd never been there, but he didn't want the police to know he'd been living at the farm campus and had run away—he was afraid they'd send him back.

Anthony told Taraska that one afternoon he and Vanessa were in the bathroom of the 1230 apartment "busting little bumps in our face"—squeezing pimples, he explained. Semaj "was standing by the sink with us, then he just wandered off by the toilet. It was some bread in the toilet. … Then I turned around, seen him trying to eat the bread out the toilet, and I stopped—and I popped—and I whupped him."

"And why was there bread in the toilet?" Taraska asked.

"'Cause in the vacant apartment there was no garbage cans," he said.

"When you say you whupped him, specifically tell me what you did."

"I whupped him on his leg, on the back area."

Taraska lifted the Raggedy Ann doll off the table and offered it to Anthony, asking him to demonstrate. He took the doll. "I told him to stop and he didn't," he said. "So I walked over there, and he was still digging in the toilet trying to reach for the bread and eat the bread. So I went over there, and I [said], 'Don't dig in there—that's nasty.'" He thumped the doll's butt, hard, three times with his palm.

"OK," Taraska said. "Can you hold the doll up, 'cause you're holding it under the table."

Anthony lifted the doll up. "Don't dig in there—it's nasty," he repeated, smacking the doll again.

Anthony had made his first trip to a police station 12 years earlier, in 1990, when he was five. His mother

had left him and his four siblings with her sister and then disappeared. The children ranged in age from two to eight. Five days later their maternal grandmother dropped them off at a west-side police station. Anthony recalls sitting on a bench there with his brother and three sisters, wondering what was going on and what would happen next. The police called DCFS.

Anthony had been born to an 18-year-old high school dropout named Veronica, who in the late 80s began smoking crack. He was her fourth child. Their father did little to help raise them.

After police called DCFS, the kids were placed with their paternal grandmother. "From there, everything was going haywire," Anthony says. The kids were shuttled between various relatives and foster homes. In 1994 DCFS returned the kids to Veronica less than a week after she tested positive for cocaine. According to DCFS records, two months later, after she failed to get additional drug tests, the children were placed with their maternal grandmother—the same grandmother who'd left them at the police station four years earlier. Anthony says he never got the feeling she was pleased to have her grandchildren in her Maywood home or that they were there for good.

Yet for three and a half years they didn't have to move. Anthony says he enjoyed this period even though his grandmother had a temper and beat the children with hangers and extension cords. When he was 12 or 13 he got suspended from school for "telling the teachers something outrageous—you know, something sexual. Went home, faced the consequences—a beat down."

As Anthony and his siblings moved into adolescence they became more than his grandmother could handle. Anthony picked fights at school and was repeatedly suspended. When his oldest sister was 16 she was briefly confined to a mental hospital after she tried to stab the grandmother. By the following year

the girl was pregnant. Anthony says the grandmother continued to beat the children, but now they resisted. "We would tell her, 'Naw, you ain't fittin' to hit me,'" Anthony says. "I think that was some of the reason she said, 'I don't want y'all no more.'" Early in 1998 the grandmother called DCFS and insisted the children be taken away.

Anthony, then 13, and two sisters were placed in a Maryville group home in Des Plaines. He didn't do well there. He tried to hit a staff member with a golf club and tried to stab another kid with a knife. He ran away repeatedly. Early in 1999 he was moved to a Maryville psychiatric facility for teen boys in Streamwood, where he was diagnosed as having major depression, an impulse-control disorder, and post-traumatic stress disorder. Tests indicated he had an IQ of 69. That fall he was sent to the farm campus in Durand.

"Kids always feel that it's their fault, that they're being moved because they were bad," says a caseworker who was once assigned to Anthony. The caseworker, who asked not to be named, added, "If you grow up from the time you were five thinking you keep getting moved because you did something wrong, that's a heavy load. And it's worse when your own relatives put you out."

Cook County public guardian Patrick Murphy, whose agency represents wards of the state in court, thinks children who are moved from one family to the next often end up more damaged emotionally than children who are physically abused by a steady caregiver. "Whoever beat you might on some level be saying, 'I love you,'" he says. "But when you're kicked out of a home it's like saying, 'We don't even like you.'"

"In and out these placements—man, I got tired of that," Anthony says. "You get comfortable here, then you gotta leave and go back here. You keep getting older, and it keep going on."

T: *Didn't you move in with a woman named Trina?*

AW: *Yes.*

T: *And who is Trina?*

AW: *Natalia friend.*

T: *Now, when you moved in with Trina, were there two times when you felt it was necessary to discipline Semaj?*

AW: *Yes.*

The police chased the numerous squatters out of the 1230 building after Anthony, Vanessa, and Semaj had been there about a week.

They moved into another Cabrini-Green apartment, in a high-rise at 624 W. Division. Trina, a friend of Vanessa's and Semaj's mother, lived there with her three-year-old and four-year-old. Anthony told Taraska that the two children said Semaj woke them up one morning by smacking them in the face, and so he "whupped" Semaj.

Taraska asked him to demonstrate with the Raggedy Ann doll. He said he first hit Semaj on his leg. "I told him, 'Don't do that while they sleeping—that's bad,'" he said, swatting the doll. "Then he turned over, and I hit him in his back. And then he started crying." He said Semaj quieted down when he and Vanessa gave him his bottle.

Anthony told Taraska that another time in the apartment Semaj tried to open the oven door while food was cooking on the stove. He hit him five or six times on his legs and hands.

Before long, Anthony, Vanessa, and Semaj moved back in with Brown. This time they got a bedroom and a bunk bed to themselves. Anthony and Vanessa slept on the top bunk, Semaj on the bottom.

Anthony told Taraska that one day he and Vanessa were in the bunk bed and Semaj was alone in the front room. They called Semaj to the bedroom, and he came to the door. But then he "started running and laughing like it was fun and games." Vanessa told Anthony to go get him. Anthony jumped down from the top bunk, went to the front room,

grabbed Semaj "in his stomach area," and took him back to the bedroom.

Taraska asked Anthony to show how he'd grabbed Semaj. The Raggedy Ann was still resting in his cupped hands, facing up. He lifted the doll with one hand and with the other smacked its stomach and clutched its shirt. Semaj "just started crying," he said, cradling the doll again. Vanessa "asked me what did I do. I told her I grabbed his shirt. ... And then we didn't see no bruises once we looked or nothing." He idly flapped the doll's arms with his thumbs as he described how Semaj stopped crying when Vanessa held him. "She was rocking him, and he seemed fine."

Taraska asked Anthony why they checked for bruises. "'Cause normally once you hit somebody it leaves whips and marks and stuff," he said. "And I ain't—wasn't trying to hurt him."

Born on the west side in 1985, Vanessa was Natalia's first child. Natalia was 18. Vanessa's father didn't help care for her.

Natalia had a second child in 1989 and a third in '91. At birth both tested positive for cocaine exposure. The hospital notified DCFS both times. Both times, according to its records, the agency merely offered her services, which Natalia rejected.

The baby born in '91 lived seven weeks. The medical examiner's report attributed his death to dehydration. Natalia was investigated for "medical neglect and inadequate care," but was allowed to keep Vanessa and her second child.

In 1994 Natalia had another cocaine-exposed baby. Again DCFS was alerted; again Natalia refused services. A few weeks after this baby was born, Natalia left her three children with their 12-year-old aunt and was gone for four days. The infant got no formula for several days.

In 1995 Natalia, seven months pregnant, was jailed for armed robbery after she brandished a knife

while stealing underwear from a store. When she went into labor two months later, she was taken from Cook County Jail to Cook County Hospital. According to DCFS records, while she was in the triage room she begged a caseworker to help her get a tubal ligation so she'd stop having children. The baby she delivered tested positive for exposure to barbituates.

During this time Natalia's other three children, Vanessa included, were staying with Brown in Cabrini-Green. DCFS placed the newborn with Brown, and Natalia went back to jail.

The four children lived with Brown for three years. Brown's own mother had been an alcoholic who'd beaten her and her siblings. "I swore I would never do that to my child," she says. Yet she also says, "These kids nowadays couldn't stand the whuppings we got, but it made a better person out of us. Some of the little kids around here [Cabrini-Green] need beat downs." She says Natalia sometimes was physically abusive to her children, but not in front of her. "She knew I would crack her head if she messed with them kids."

According to DCFS records, the children were taken from Brown in 1998 because of her "extensive drug use and failure to complete a drug program." She admits that she smoked crack until the late 90s and that she still drinks regularly. But she didn't think the children should have been taken from her, because, she says, "I was a functioning addict. I paid my bills. If I had money left over, it's mine to do what I want to do with it."

The kids were placed with a foster mother who wasn't a relative. Vanessa was 13.

A year later Vanessa accused her foster mother's boyfriend of molesting her, and the foster mother made the boyfriend move out. Later Vanessa was placed on house arrest for pulling a knife on a classmate's parent at her grammar school. She was rarely in school and failed all of her

classes. In 2000 the foster mother adopted Vanessa's three siblings. DCFS records state that Vanessa wasn't adopted because of her "behavior in the home and the community." In July 2000 DCFS sent her to the Maryville Farm Campus. The foster mother moved to Virginia with Vanessa's three siblings.

A Maryville treatment plan listed Vanessa's problems as "oppositionality, explosive behavior, [and] low frustration tolerance." She needed to "learn to understand her family's problems ... and work on resolving her anger in this area."

Natalia spent two years in prison for the 1995 armed robbery. Nine months after her release she was imprisoned again, for retail theft. The second prison term ended in October 1999. She hadn't gotten the tubal ligation she'd begged for in 1995 and got pregnant almost immediately after her release. The baby was born at Mount Sinai Hospital on the west side in July 2000—the same month 15-year-old Vanessa was sent to the farm campus. Court records show that the baby's father, James Rice, had three felony convictions and was in jail on drug charges. Natalia named the boy Semaj, which is James backward.

Semaj didn't become a ward of the state after his birth even though his father was in jail and his mother had had her parental rights terminated. No system exists to alert DCFS when a baby is born in such circumstances. The agency learns of the birth only if its child-abuse hotline gets a call. "DCFS does not have the resources to monitor everybody we've had contact with, nor should we be doing so," says Jill Manuel, DCFS deputy director of communications. "There are civil liberty issues at stake."

Hotline calls about newborns often come from hospitals when tests show a baby has been exposed to illegal drugs. Brown says that Natalia was still addicted when she had Semaj and that tests at the hospital showed he'd been exposed to drugs.

"But she left the hospital with him before they found out."

One night soon after Semaj's birth, Brown says, police came to Cabrini-Green looking for Natalia and Semaj, but the two were in another high-rise and managed to elude the police. Natalia gave Semaj to a relative, who brought him to Brown. Brown didn't want Semaj to become a ward of the state and wind up in a foster home: "I didn't feel he should be punished for something she did." So she kept him.

The authorities never came looking for Semaj again. "As I look back on it, it might have been a blessing if they'd taken him," Brown says. "He'd probably still be alive today."

As for Natalia's desire for a tubal ligation, the DCFS's Manuel says, "That would not fall under our area of responsibility. Our mission is to investigate child abuse and neglect."

T: *And then was there another incident ... just a few days ago at 534 W. Division [Brown's apartment] that you felt that you needed to discipline Semaj?*

AW: *Yes.*

T: *And tell me what happened with that incident.*

AW: *Semaj, he was playing in his Pampers. And we told him, me and [Vanessa] told him two times, stop playing in his diaper. I told him. Then she told him. Then I told him. Then she told him. He kept on playing in his diaper. And then she was like, "Go stop him from playing in his diaper," 'cause that was nasty. ... So I'm like, "I'm fittin' to whup him." She's like, "Why are you telling me?" And then so I jumped down from the top bunk. ... Whupped him on his right leg. And he turned around, and I hit him on his back.*

Semaj then started crying, Anthony told Taraska. But Vanessa gave him a bottle, "and he was just fine after that."

Taraska again asked Anthony to demonstrate, and he again obliged, thumping the Raggedy Ann three times with his open hand.

"You said that [when] you hit him on his leg he turned around," Taraska said. "Why did he turn around?"

"'Cause ... it must have been hurting him."

"And after you hit him on his back a few times, a short time later did he start throwing up?" Taraska asked.

"Yes."

This was about an hour and a half later, Anthony said. He and Vanessa jumped down from the top bunk when they heard Semaj throwing up below them. He said Vanessa first hit Semaj's hand and told him to stop, because Brown had said he would sometimes throw up "on purpose for attention." But Semaj kept throwing up. Vanessa grabbed a towel and put it on Semaj's mouth "'cause he already ... got the sheets all wet and stuff." Vanessa told Anthony to grab another towel. The vomit was leaking through the first towel and getting on Vanessa's hand.

Anthony told Taraska he started "panicking," because "when I see somebody throwing up like that it make me want to throw up." But then the vomiting stopped. It was unclear from the statement whether this incident occurred on the day Semaj died or earlier.

Taraska began asking about the night Semaj died. That evening, Anthony said, he and Vanessa changed Semaj's diaper, gave him his bottle, and put him to bed around eight or nine. He and Vanessa watched *Moesha* and *The Jamie Foxx Show* in the living room, then sat in the gallery outside the apartment. Shortly after midnight they returned to the bedroom. Anthony switched on a light and told Vanessa that it didn't sound like Semaj was breathing right. Vanessa "checked his stomach. She was like, 'He breathing right. He breathing.'" Then Anthony saw "blood and little spit bubbles" on Semaj's mouth. "And then Vanessa picked him up and ran to his grandma."

Brown remembers seeing blood around Semaj's mouth and nose and

thinking he was having an asthma attack. "Talk to grandma," she says she pleaded. "Say something to grandma."

Shortly before 2 AM on March 14, 2002, a friend of hers carried Semaj downstairs and to the fire station next to the building. Paramedics there detected a faint pulse and rushed him to Children's Memorial Hospital. He was pronounced dead at 2:20 AM.

Doctors noted bruises on Semaj's forehead, chest, and abdomen. After an autopsy at the county morgue later that morning, a medical examiner told detectives Semaj's death was the result of "multiple blunt trauma."

Detectives went to Brown's apartment and started questioning the occupants. In interviews there, and later that day at Area Three headquarters at Belmont and Western, they all said they hadn't seen anyone strike Semaj.

According to police reports, Vanessa said she'd put Semaj to bed at about 9 PM the previous evening. She said she'd changed his diaper and rubbed his back until he'd fallen asleep. He hadn't shown any signs of illness. Then she'd watched TV with Anthony in the living room. Around midnight she heard Semaj crying, and she went to the bedroom and gave him a bottle, after which he seemed to go back to sleep. She and Anthony sat in the gallery outside the apartment from midnight until about 1:20 AM. When she and Anthony went to bed later that night, Anthony told her Semaj was having trouble breathing. They saw the blood and foam on his lips. In a second interview Vanessa added that during the time she and Anthony were sitting in the gallery, he'd gone into the apartment once to use the bathroom and had been inside about 15 minutes.

Vanessa told police that at the time when they realized something was wrong with Semaj, five other adults were home—Brown, Vanessa's two aunts, and their boyfriends.

Anthony was first interviewed at 10:30 PM on the day Semaj died. His story was similar to Vanessa's. He told the detectives he hadn't laid a hand on Semaj, and he agreed to take a polygraph the following day.

Late in December 2001 Anthony and Vanessa left the Maryville Farm Campus on holiday passes and didn't return. A DCFS investigation would later determine that their caseworkers made little attempt to find them.

Anthony slept overnight in an interview room at the station. Detectives questioned him again the next morning. This time, he said he'd struck Semaj a couple of times during the previous week to discipline him but had never intended to seriously hurt him.

He was taken to another police station for the polygraph. After the examiner explained the testing procedures, Anthony admitted striking Semaj to discipline him several other times during the week before his death. Detectives decided the polygraph was no longer necessary and took him back to Area Three headquarters. He agreed to make a videotaped statement, which he gave beginning at 10 PM.

Anthony says detectives told him he'd be charged only with involuntary manslaughter, implying that he'd be freed after he spoke on camera. "They tricked me," he says.

Still, he says his videotaped account was mostly true. He had hit Semaj repeatedly. He never thought he hit him too hard, and he believed hitting was called for. "Some of the things he was doing?" he says. "You would've whupped him too."

Detectives wanted to reinterview Vanessa after Anthony made his statement, since he'd said she was there when he hit Semaj. But Vanessa apparently had told police when they'd interviewed her the day before that she was a DCFS ward, and her caseworker had been contacted. A lawyer retained by DCFS soon called the detectives and told them she wouldn't be answering any questions—she was invoking her Fifth Amendment right not to incriminate herself. Because Anthony had concealed that he was a runaway, DCFS wasn't alerted. Besides, at 17 he was considered an adult under Illinois criminal law.

On March 16, the day after Anthony gave his videotaped statement, detectives went to the county morgue to talk with Dr. Tae Lyong An, the medical examiner who'd performed Semaj's autopsy. Dr. An said Semaj had broken ribs, a bruised lung, and lacerations of the heart, liver, and pancreas. According to one of the detectives, Tony Jin, Dr. An also indicated that the fatal injuries were the result of one or more beatings not long before Semaj died.

Anthony was in an Area Three lockup. The detectives reinterviewed him on March 17, asking him specifically if he'd had any physical contact with Semaj on the night he died. According to a police report, this time Anthony said that when he and Vanessa put Semaj to bed that night, Semaj started to gag as if he were going to throw up. Vanessa patted the toddler on his back several times, then handed him to Anthony and told him to pat Semaj. "Anthony Wilson stated that he took the baby in his left arm and began patting him on the chest," the police report says. "Anthony then demonstrated a striking motion during which he struck approximately 10 firm, hard blows to the chest area with his right hand." Anthony said he then put Semaj back in bed with his bottle. His account of what followed was the same as he'd given before: When he and Vanessa returned to the bedroom several hours later they noticed that Semaj was having trouble breathing and that he had blood and froth around his mouth. Anthony repeated this account to assistant state's attorney Michael Yoon.

The state's attorney's office approved first-degree murder charges. Anthony was taken to the Cook County Criminal Courthouse at 26th and California. A judge set his bond at $800,000, and he was jailed.

T: *Now, Anthony, when did you realize that your hitting Semaj actually caused Semaj's death?*

AW: *After the news reporter came to the house to interview [Vanessa] grandma and said whupping him caused his death. And then we all found out, started feeling bad, started crying.*

Anthony's trial began on March 15, 2004—two years and one day after Semaj's death. No relatives of either Anthony or Semaj attended.

On the advice of his public defender, Woody Jordan, Anthony waived his right to a jury and opted to be tried by the judge, James Egan. Jordan, a public defender for 20 years, believes the beating death of a child is so disturbing that jurors are apt to convict regardless of the evidence. Judges are also susceptible to that bias, Jordan says, but less so, because they've heard so many accounts of shocking crimes.

In his opening statement prosecutor James Murphy said Anthony's admission that he'd hit Semaj repeatedly, coupled with the severity of the toddler's injuries, would prove he was guilty of murder. Jordan responded that Anthony had never used a fist when he demonstrated on the videotape how he hit Semaj and that nothing he said on the tape indicated an intent to kill.

Murphy presented three detectives who recounted their interviews with Anthony. Their testimony showed a progression in Anthony's answers, from the initial denial of any physical contact to the acknowledgment of repeated beatings. The first day of the trial concluded with the playing of the videotape for Judge Egan.

When the trial resumed a week later assistant state's attorney Yoon testified about the statement An-

thony made after the one he gave on camera. "He told me that the baby, Semaj Rice, was coughing like [he] was going to throw up again," Yoon told the judge. "He said that [Vanessa] was patting the baby on the back. And he indicated to me that [Vanessa] told him to pat the baby on the baby's back. He told me that he took the baby in his left arm and with his right hand with an open hand … he hit the baby on his chest ten times."

Jordan called no witnesses on Anthony's behalf. He'd interviewed the other occupants of Brown's apartment and concluded that their testimony wasn't going to help. "Their line was, 'He did it—we just didn't see him do it,'" he says. He also figured that Anthony's own testimony wouldn't help his case.

In his closing argument Jordan reminded the judge of the numerous other people who were in the apartment on the night in question, suggesting that any of them could have administered the fatal beating and that therefore Anthony hadn't been proved guilty beyond a reasonable doubt. But most of his argument was aimed at winning a conviction on the lesser charge of involuntary manslaughter. He contended that when Anthony hit Semaj in the chest several hours before he died, it was because he thought the toddler was choking on something or because he thought it might prevent him from throwing up.

Jordan said, "His actions may not be up to the standards that you would want of your babysitter—but he's a kid. I mean, what knowledge, what experience, what training has he had in child care? … There's no criminal intent, judge. You don't find a person guilty of first-degree murder because they are ignorant, inexperienced, and stupid."

In his closing argument Murphy maintained that Anthony clearly hadn't been fully honest in his videotaped statement "about how many times he hit this little boy, and where in the body he hit this little boy, and with what—meaning a fist—he hit this little boy." He went on, "We will never know how many times he hit this kid. Thank God we have the body of Semaj Rice. … That's what tells us how many times he hit this kid and with what force." He reminded Egan that Anthony had used the word *popped* at one point in the statement when describing how he'd disciplined Semaj. "We all know that *popped* means punched," Murphy said. "He never uses popped again, probably because he realizes that's a dangerous word. … But that indicates his true colors, judge. He popped that kid."

Early in 1999 Anthony was moved to a Maryville psychiatric facility for teen boys in Streamwood, where he was diagnosed as having major depression, an impulse-control disorder, and post-traumatic stress disorder. Tests indicated he had an IQ of 69.

Egan began his ruling by saying, "No 17-year-old should be left in charge of a 19-month-old, but Mr. Wilson less than your average 17-year-old." Anthony had been charged on two subtly different counts. One was that he had "intentionally or knowingly" killed Semaj. The other was that he knew when he struck Semaj that his actions "created a strong probability" that he would kill him. Egan said he didn't believe Anthony had intended to kill Semaj, and he therefore acquitted him of the first count. But he said that given the difference in size between Anthony and Semaj and the extent of the injuries, Anthony must have known when he hit Semaj the way he did that there was a strong probability he'd kill the child. On that count he convicted Anthony of first-degree murder.

Anthony was stunned. Later he said he'd expected to be acquitted, though he'd prepared himself for the possibility of an involuntary manslaughter conviction. He'd barely considered the possibility of being convicted of murder.

Jordan was fuming as he left the courtroom. "That was no fucking murder," he said in the hallway, adding, "My old man spanked me worse" than what Anthony had admitted doing on the videotape. He said that if Egan had convicted Anthony of involuntary manslaughter, he probably would have gotten two years. Now he faced a minimum of 20 and a maximum of 60. Jordan said Egan likely would give Anthony something near the minimum because of his age, but that hardly mattered. "His life is over," he said. "Not that he ever had a chance in the first place."

Anthony's sentencing hearing on April 28 took five minutes. In murder cases prosecutors usually present a statement from the victim's survivors about the crime's impact on them. Semaj's survivors had opted not to provide such a statement. Defense attorneys can lobby the judge for a lighter sentence by presenting mitigation witnesses, who testify about the defendant's achievements or about the hardship his imprisonment will cause them. Jordan presented no such witnesses.

The presentence report submitted to Judge Egan by a probation officer noted that Anthony's mother, Veronica, was then in prison. Anthony had last seen her when she visited him in jail while his case was pending—before she got arrested for drug offenses. "She told me she ain't coming to see me no more, that I'm headed to the penitentiary," he recalls. "She said it like she was sad, like she didn't want to see me behind the glass. I could honor that. But then again, I'm like, 'What? You don't wanna come see me?' I thought it was funny that she ended up in the penitentiary before me."

Anthony and the lawyers stood in front of the bench for the sentencing. Murphy told Egan that a long sentence was necessary to dissuade others from such a crime. If just one person in the gallery today was deterred by Anthony's sentence, he

said, it will have served its purpose. In the gallery was the usual sleepy assortment of defendants on bond and relatives of defendants in custody waiting for other cases to be called. Even from the first row of the gallery it was hard to hear what was being said at the bench, so a deterrent effect seemed unlikely.

Jordan pointed out that Anthony had no criminal record before this case, and asked Egan to give him the minimum 20 years.

Egan told Anthony he'd been "placed in charge of a child that I don't think you were capable of handling at all." He blamed Semaj's relatives for putting the toddler in Anthony's and Vanessa's care. Then he sentenced Anthony to 23 years.

"I thought that was kind of a long sentence," Detective Tony Jin said later. "I told the prosecutor—they always ask—that it wouldn't bother me if the kid [Anthony] took a light hit, because it wasn't a malicious thing. I don't think he meant to kill the baby. He thought he was disciplining him, and he just carried it too far." Jin said that when Anthony had described how he hit Semaj he didn't seem to be trying to conceal what he'd done. "It was just like he was telling me how he made a dinner."

Jin has been a homicide detective for 22 years. "In all my years handling these baby beatings—and I was in Area Four [on the west side], where people in the projects threw their babies out the window—I'd always ask, 'Why'd you do this?' And they'd say, 'Well, you know how it is when they won't stop crying.' I never had any kids, so I never knew how it was." Jin, who just turned 50, now has a two-month-old child. "You walk around with your baby, and his diaper's clean and he's been fed, but he won't stop crying," he says. He knows not to hit his child, but he says, "Now I see what they mean."

An investigation after Semaj's death by Denise Kane, inspector general for DCFS, faulted Anthony's and Vanessa's caseworkers for not working harder to locate the teens when they didn't return to the farm campus. Caseworkers are supposed to contact relatives and previous caregivers when a ward is missing. By the time Kane's investigation was completed, in December 2002, Anthony's caseworker had retired. Kane recommended that the agency discipline Vanessa's caseworker, and he was suspended for three days.

After Semaj's death DCFS placed Vanessa in a group home in Elgin. An "unusual incident" report that year described her cursing and threatening staff members in the home. Another unusual-incident report the following month said she was a month pregnant.

Semaj didn't become a ward of the state after his birth even though his father was in jail and his mother had had her parental rights terminated.

The father wasn't Anthony, who'd been locked up for five months by then. But like Anthony, the father was in jail.

A parenting-skills assessment done while Vanessa was pregnant noted that she said she wanted to use corporal punishment in raising her child but had agreed to comply with the rules prohibiting it in the group home she'd be living in.

In May 2003 Vanessa, then 18, gave birth to a healthy daughter. They were placed in a "transition to motherhood" home in the south suburbs for state wards and their children. A month after the baby was born Vanessa was arrested for shoplifting from a Wal-Mart.

Semaj's grandmother, Thomasa Brown, has mixed feelings about Anthony's sentence. "I think he should have gotten more time because he took a life," she says. But she'd heard from Vanessa about Anthony's own troubled childhood. "So I can't hate him for what he did. All he'd known was abuse. I feel like he's not responsible."

Anthony, who'd been uneasy living 95 miles from Chicago on the farm campus, is now 350 miles away, in the Menard Correctional Center on the banks of the Mississippi River in southwestern Illinois. "I'm trying not to think about the past," he says. "Want to look forward to the future." He hopes he'll win an appeal. He insists he didn't hit Semaj out of anger when he struck his chest ten times the night he died. "I thought it was gonna stop his coughing and all that," he says. "I thought he'd be all right. He did stop."

When he was in Cook County Jail awaiting trial he exchanged letters with Vanessa and had photos of her taped to his cell wall. He'd gaze at the photos frequently and "think of the good times." But he hasn't heard from her since he's been in Menard, and he no longer looks at the photos. He's heard about her child, but says the news didn't upset him. "She got a life of her own. She got hormones just like we do—that's the way I'm looking at it. I can't get mad at her. I can't do nothing. I'm in here."

Anthony's cell mate has told him he talks about Semaj in his sleep. Anthony says he doesn't believe it, then says he wouldn't be surprised, because he thinks about Semaj constantly—about happy moments he and Vanessa shared with the toddler, like the trip to a park they took the day before he died. He says he can still picture Semaj running around the park and having fun. When he thinks of such occasions, he says, "I sit back and just smile, just *laugh*." Other inmates ask him what he's laughing about. "They think I'm crazy."

He wishes he were in a prison closer to Chicago so that his relatives might come visit him. "If I could run from here I'd do it," he says with a laugh. But escapes from this maximum-security prison are unheard of. Barring a successful appeal, he'll be locked up until he's 40. Fourteen years after his mother abandoned him, Anthony finally has a stable placement.

An epoch of cheating

In 1995, a group of students at Steinmetz High School amazed the city by winning the state academic decathlon for the first time. For a few days, the students were celebrated as academic all-stars, underdogs who outperformed the traditional powerhouse schools. Then, the truth spilled. The students had cheated.

Later, one of them explained how and why they had done it. "The coach gave us the answer key last year. He told us everybody cheats, that's the way the world worked and we were fools to just play by the rules."

This would be the place where any upstanding editorial page would harrumph about how cynical and wrongheaded that view is, affirming its belief that most people really are honest. We still believe that, but it would be nice if the world would prove us right, once in a while.

Since the Steinmetz scandal, this country has witnessed an epoch of cheating on a grand scale, conjuring images of the unfettered era of the robber barons. Sammy Sosa's corked bat and Martha Stewart's indictment for obstruction of justice and lying to void some $45,000 in stock losses are the latest entries into the cheating (and lying) scandals of the rich and famous.

They've got plenty of company: the Enron implosion, the WorldCom debacle, the Merrill Lynch and Salomon Smith Barney analysts who regulators said misled investors with stock picks designed to win more business from the companies issuing the stock. All of that caused real, painful damage to millions of Americans, some of whom lost their life savings in the resulting financial bloodbath.

What is most fascinating about the latest crop of cheaters and alleged cheaters is why some are apparently willing to risk so much for what seems so little. How to explain to your kids why someone like Stewart, who is worth hundreds of millions, would risk it all to avoid a few thousand in stock losses, as the indictment alleges? Why would Sosa, revered by many fans, bring an illegal bat to the plate?

Maybe, having reached a pinnacle of American life that few others experience, these superachievers believe that somehow the rules don't apply to them. That is, through a combination of talent, moxie and hard work, they're now untouchable. Or at least infallible. Or maybe they just can't bear the thought of losing their touch—money, prestige, homeruns. Possibly, it's just because

there's no one around to tell them they can't—or shouldn't.

Character, as they say, is destiny.

Could it be that John D. Rockefeller revealed the secret when, as legend has it, he was asked something like, "How much money is enough?" and he replied, "Just a little bit more."

But let's dispense with the usual tut-tutting. We all agree—at least publicly—that cheating is wrong. (Don't we?) But who among us has never cheated?

Riiiiiight.

People cheat all the time, be they baseball players or scientists faking data and writing fraudulent research papers. Some have even convinced themselves that it really isn't cheating if, say, the target is a much-despised institution like the Internal Revenue Service. But it is.

Then there are the people who knowingly get in the 10-items-or-less line with 12 items. (Yes, you have.)

So let's face it, America is a nation of corner-cutters and angle-calculators. We tell our kids cheating is wrong but there's a deep strain of ambivalence in the culture about cheating.

Our values tell us cheating is wrong, period. But popular culture often celebrates the charming rogue or the clever thief. (Remember D.B. Cooper, who took a $200,000 ransom in 1971 and parachuted into the Washington forests, apparently never to be seen again?) Who didn't root for the lovable con artists of "Ocean's Eleven" or "The Sting"? And wasn't there something to secretly cheer in the colorful confession of former major league pitcher Bill Lee, who wrote recently about stitching an emery board into his glove to scuff the ball, which he credits for extending his baseball career for five years?

It's undeniable that Americans often admire those who cleverly bend the rules. And they're often fascinated by those who take the most Shakespearean falls from grace. Why else would former New York Times reporter Jayson Blair be talking to book publishers? Why else would we care what Hillary has to say about Bill?

Even in a nation clearly conflicted about cheating, however, it is impressive, even refreshing, that Americans continue to be surprised, disappointed, and on occasion outraged about cheating, particularly in the power suites. Maybe that's because they're supposed to be role models, on some level. There's a certain amount of satisfaction when a white-collar criminal like former ImClone Systems founder Sam Waksal gets more than seven years in prison for securities fraud.

Some will surely see justice in Sosa's seven-game suspension. But most fans are probably just glad to have him back.

It's easy to work up a lather over high-profile miscreants. Scolding others also carries the added benefit of distracting us from our own transgressions. Yes, this is a forgiving nation, particularly for those who confess their sins. It has to be. There are so many of us who need to be forgiven.

The Trouble With Ecstasy

In a Few Years It's Gone From Obscurity to an Illegal Drug Bought and Sold by Kids. Has Government Done More Harm Than Good?

Greg Raver-Lampman

IT WAS A PARENT'S NIGHTMARE.

In a middle-class town in Prince William County, a killer gunned down 21-year-old Daniel Petrole Jr., a player for top travel soccer teams, a popular graduate of Centreville High School and the son of a one time Secret Service agent.

Danny Petrole was killed by an associate in a drug ring that sold millions of dollars' worth of marijuana and MDMA—or Ecstasy.

There have been many stories about drug killings in urban areas, where often victims are poor and usually African-American—murders that rate a paragraph or two in the *Washington Post's* inside pages. But these kids weren't like that.

The members of the drug ring were from affulent Virginia suburbs, former Little Leaguers who built their empire peddling drugs to suburban high-school students. They hung out in the VIP room of the DC nightclub Bohemian Caverns, vacationed in Hawaii, and spent thousands on weekend parties.

The murder was over a $65,000 drug debt.

After the March 2001 killing, police announced investigations into the group's Ecstasy suppliers. They're still following leads.

When Law-Enforcement Officials Talk About breaking up drug networks, people feel comforted, presuming that the goal is to keep drugs away from kids. Almost all parents see that as laudable—I'm among them. But I'm increasingly skeptical.

As the son of a sometimes-violent, self-destructive alcoholic, I'm aware of the effects of addiction. As the parent of a 14-year-old daughter, I know the temptation teens face to smoke, drink, and use drugs. Whatever people say about various controlled substances, I consider my job as a parent to do whatever I can to lessen the chances my daughter will think she needs illegal drugs to cope with life.

Although virtually all surveys show that cocaine, heroin, and crack are as widely used by whites as by minorities, Ecstasy is portrayed as the hot drug among suburban teens. Politicians have responded to parents' fears by enacting harsh laws with the goal of jailing traffickers.

In May 2000, senators Joseph Biden, Bob Graham, and Chuck Grassley introduced the Ecstasy Anti-Proliferation Act of 2000 "to combat Ecstasy trafficking, distribution, and abuse in the United States." Such measures are popular with many voters.

But the more I watch these events unfold, the more I sense I've heard it before—the announcement of a crisis, a policy to stifle it, followed months later by reports that the crisis has grown worse and tougher measures are in order.

Where does it end? Former US drug czar William Bennett once said he would support beheading drug dealers.

Questioning current drug laws is like throwing a blood-soaked rag into a shark tank. For members of Congress, uttering a phrase suggesting any weakening of drug laws is a ticket to political oblivion.

Increasingly, though, police, judges, and conservative politicians and citizens have begun to weigh in, sometimes comparing drug-enforcement laws to the nation's experiment with alcohol prohibition.

"The myth that people have is that punitive laws will keep kids from being exposed to these drugs," says Joseph D. McNamara, a veteran of the New York City Police Department and now a research fellow at Stanford University's Hoover Institution. "They do the opposite."

David Boaz, of the libertarian Cato Institute in DC, agrees: "I don't think there's any question as to whether it increases the marketing to kids." In an illegal market, drug suppliers will go wherever they can find buyers—often to middle and high schools.

Boaz, McNamara, and other critics usually cite our experience with drugs that have been around a long time—heroin, cocaine, marijuana. Despite decades of well-publicized arrests and drug seizures, these substances are as available as ever.

Almost nine out of ten high-school seniors say marijuana is "fairly easy" or "very easy" to get, according to Monitoring the Future, a government-funded research organization. About half of high-school students will use illicit drugs before graduating.

Economist Milton Friedman argues that current drug policies actually increase addiction and crime by relegating the manufacture and distribution of drugs to hardened criminals, in the same way Prohibition led to the likes of Al Capone.

Debate often bogs down in arguments over the results of drug policies enacted almost a century ago.

In many ways, Ecstasy offers a window into how our drug laws affect the market for illegal substances. The drug was banned relatively recently—in 1985—so it's possible to trace its trajectory from "discovery" through legal use to popularity to crackdowns.

The world of Ecstasy is a microcosm from which to look at the basic questions debated by drug-law advocates and critics: How have laws governing one drug changed its manufacture, use, and distribution?

Although abuse of ecstasy is relatively recent, the drug was discovered almost a century ago.

In 1912, chemists in Darmstadt, Germany, created the drug from the extract of sassafras root, a flavoring once used in root beer. Sassafras oil, or safrole, was treated with hydrobromic acid to create a compound with a name only a chemist could dream up—3,4-methylenedioxymethamphetamine. Known by the acronym MDMA, this is what we now call Ecstasy.

MDMA would have been forgotten if it hadn't been rediscovered in the 1970s by Alexander "Sasha" Shulgin, a California chemist regarded as a pharmacological folk hero. To drug-enforcement officials, he's a nightmare.

Since leaving a career with Dow Chemical, Shulgin has been immersed in a decades-long project to explore the psychoactive effects of chemicals, especially hallucinogens. He brews up concoctions, "tastes" them, often with friends, and publishes his work, including recipes. The late LSD booster Timothy Leary dubbed Shulgin and his wife, Ann, "the two most important scientists of the 20th century." Shulgin has been credited with discovering several common street drugs, including STP.

In the 1970s, a friend suggested Shulgin taste Merck's long-abandoned compound MDMA. Shulgin tried it and claimed it had "magical" qualities. Shulgin gave a sample to a friend, part of a cadre of New Age psychotherapists who used substances such as mescaline and LSD in their practices.

Shulgin's friend was impressed. MDMA, he believed, could help patients deal with problems that otherwise would be too traumatic to discuss. "The Secret Chief," as he was identified in a book about his exploits, abandoned plans to retire and became a psychotropic Johnny Appleseed, traveling around the country introducing other psychotherapists to MDMA. Many early adherents considered themselves "psychedelic guides" leading patients to enlightenment. Many took MDMA with their patients.

MDMA, recent studies have shown, stimulates the release of serotonin, a neurotransmitter that controls mood, pain perception, sleep, appetite, and emotions. Modern psychiatric drugs like Prozac and Zoloft also boost serotonin by blocking its absorption. At one point, MDMA was dubbed "Empathy" because of its ability to break down barriers between strangers.

Therapeutic MDMA use occurred primarily in a handful of cities with large alternative communities, says Jerome Beck, a California public-health researcher whose dissertation documented the demographics of MDMA use.

Such use never caught on in Washington, according to Richard Mikesell, former president of the District of Columbia Psychological Association. In 1985, when he was president, MDMA was largely manufactured by medical chemists, many of them graduate students at universities around Boston; they became known as the Boston Group. MDMA was usually distributed as a powder, and efforts were made to limit its use, out of fear that publicity would prompt the government to crack down.

"The myth that people have is that punitive laws will keep kids from being exposed to these drugs," says a former police officer. "They do the opposite."

"There was this kind of silent conspiracy," says Bruce Eisner, author of *Ecstasy: The MDMA Story.* "The boomer generation wanted to keep it quiet."

In the 1980s, New Age communities began holding MDMA parties. Yogi Bhagwan Rajneesh declared that Ecstasy could aid spiritual development.

The epicenter of recreational Ecstasy use was Dallas. A professional couple, identified in news accounts as the Smiths, was said to have spread its use. They began holding parties in their condo, where they distributed a paper declaring that MDMA "creates in the taker experience of God, ultimate Reality, the ground of Being, Absolute Truth, at-one-ment."

The Smiths "were sort of into the Ram Dass 'be here now' scene," recalls Brian Comerford, 32, at the time a Dallas teenager who went to parties at their condo. "There was a collection of people there who were theater performers, artists, intellectuals, then also a lot of young people who were aspiring to be in that crowd."

In Washington, recreational use was less common. "Roger," a congressional staffer who still works on Capitol Hill, first read about Ecstasy in 1981. But Roger, who was in his forties, didn't try the drug—then called Essence—until late 1984, when he met a group of New Age types at a conference in Manhattan. He loved it: "I could feel my heart chakra spinning."

Roger returned to DC, occasionally gathering friends at his home for "little ceremonies" where people took Ecstasy. His parties were contemplative and spiritual. To get MDMA, he had to ask New York friends because nobody knew any local suppliers.

In DALLAS, A MAN WHO ONCE HAD STUDIED FOR THE PRIESTHOOD recognized that Ecstasy could be a gold mine. Michael Clegg began to manufacture mass quantities, stamping Ecstasy out in pill presses. Clegg's network of distributors became known as the Texas Group.

Clegg was evangelistic. He believed the world would be a better place if everyone used Ecstasy. He pushed it, but with his eye on the bottom line. The Texas Group evolved into a pharmacological Amway, a pyramid scheme that allowed distributors to get a cut of sales from distributors they recruited.

"People were getting rich off it," author Eisner says.

Ecstasy now was promoted as a party drug rather than for therapy or introspection. Distributors printed "flight manuals" describing where and how to take it.

As often happens with "miracle" drugs, MDMA's downsides weren't established right away. The substance produces its euphoric effect by causing a flood of serotonin, Sustained use, research has shown, can damage the neuron that store serotonin.

Using Ecstasy as a party drug poses its own dangers. Because MDMA makes it hard for the body to regulate heat, people taking too much and dancing all night can die from hyperthermia, which essentially cooks their brains.

In 1984, mdma enthusiasm WAS approaching its pre-prohibition zenith, especially in Texas. That year, a group of investors renovated a Dallas brewery and dubbed it the Starck Club. Rock and sports stars, musicians, stockbrokers, artists, and gay people flocked there. Ecstasy was doled out at the door or sold at the bar.

Business students at Dallas's conservative Southern Methodist University promoted Ecstasy as a safe alternative to booze.

"We just applied basic principles that we learned last year in our SMU marketing course, and things took off," one SMU "entrepreneur" told *Life* magazine.

Before long, Ecstasy was available at Dallas bars and convenience stores and from toll-free numbers. You could charge it to American Express. The drug's popularity caught the attention of then-US Senator Lloyd Bentsen Jr. of Texas. He asked the Drug Enforcement Administration to "schedule" the drug, essentially banning it.

The DEA's scheduling procedure, adopted under President Nixon in the 1970s, places drugs in five categories, depending on abuse potential, medicinal value, and harmfulness. Schedule V includes drugs, such as Robitussin with codeine, that can be obtained only from a pharmacist with a prescription.

As drugs climb the scheduling ladder, there are more restrictions. Schedule I drugs include marijuana, LSD, and heroin. They're deemed to have a high potential for abuse and no legitimate medical use. No Schedule I drug can be legally possessed or used for any purpose aside from government-sanctioned research.

In JULY 1984, THE DEA PUBLISHED ITS INTENTION TO PLACE MDMA in Schedule I. A contingent of psychotherapists pro-

tested, contending that they had used MDMA in their practices. A four-year legal battle ensued.

As the controversy went on, Ecstasy got lots of airplay. *The Phil Donahue Show* featured women with breast cancer talking about how MDMA helped them cope. In June 1985, the *Washington Post* weighed in with a 3,000-word story in the Style section: ECSTASY: THE LURE AND THE PERIL.

As often happens with drugs, Ecstasy's downsides weren't established right away. Sustained use can damage neurons that store serotonin.

"They sound like born-agains who have glimpsed a better world, evangelicals of the latest psychoactive reality," Jane Leavy wrote. She quoted a rabbi saying Ecstasy was "like the Sabbath at the end of a long week."

The federal government continued to publish reports about the drug's potentially toxic effects. The warnings drew more attention to the compound.

"It increased use immensely," says Sasha Shulgin. "There's no greater promoter of a drug than making it illegal and telling why it's bad. All these teens say, 'Hey, they wouldn't be getting after this thing unless it's valuable.'"

Publicity—even horror stories—can increase the use of dangerous drugs. A 1972 report by the Consumers Union cited a spate of newspaper articles warning that model-airplane-glue fumes could cause brain damage, even death. A nationwide glue-sniffing epidemic followed.

Ecstasy's publicity generated demand. As the DEA's scheduling process continued to get airplay, pill manufacturer Clegg launched what amounted to a going-out-of-business sale.

"In the month before MDMA became illegal, they made 2 million tablets," says Rick Doblin, founder and president of the Multidisciplinary Association for Psychedelic Studies. The DEA invoked emergency powers to ban MDMA to "avoid imminent hazard to the public safety." The emergency ban went into effect on July 1, 1985. It would remain in effect during litigation, which continued for three years.

On Capitol Hill, Roger read about the ban. "On the last day of its legality," he recalls, "I had a party at my house for everybody who wanted to have this experience."

By outward measures, the ban was a success. Only therapists willing to risk their licenses continued to use MDMA. Chemists at universities shuttered their operations. The selling of Ecstasy by SMU business students ended. Bars and convenience stores stopped advertising it. Young professionals who had a lot to lose quit—or became discreet. Ecstasy use had, by all appearances, been stopped.

But had it?

Brian Comerford, the Dallas high-school student who had attended parties with the Smiths, says Ecstasy started to show up where he'd never seen it—in his school.

"It's almost like as soon as everyone was aware that 'Oh, this is something that the government is trying to suppress,' everyone was interested in it and everyone had their own version of it," he says.

Heather Watts, who attended nearby Lake Highlands High School in the late '80s, says Ecstasy was everywhere: "You didn't have to go out and try to find it."

Did the fact that it was banned have any impact?

"Absolutely," she says. The attitude was, "Why would you buy something that's legal? That's no fun."

The relationship between banning a drug and its use among kids has never been studied.

"That is a big gap," says Jerome Beck, the California public-health researcher.

Virtually all media accounts say Ecstasy didn't start showing up in high schools and middle schools until the rave scene hit in the early 1990s. Comerford and Watts say Ecstasy showed up in their high schools years before.

Soon after the DEA issued its emergency ban, Texas authorities launched crackdowns where Ecstasy use had been most obvious. In July 1985, police impounded a twin-engine charter plane at the Del Rio airport containing "the first Ecstasy lab seized in the United States since the new law making the drug illegal went into effect." The disassembled lab was being shipped to Belize, evidence that manufacturing operations were moving abroad.

Texas police began arresting Ecstasy dealers. They raided the Starck Club. With "legitimate" Ecstasy distribution shut down, underground distributors popped up like Prohibition bootleggers.

"People flock to these dealers, snapping up everything they can get," a narcotics investigator told the *Dallas Morning News* in 1989. "These are well-off college students and high-school kids buying $100 worth a night."

Few of the pills sold as ecstasy IN schools actually contained MDMA. Because Ecstasy is expensive to manufacture, dealers often substituted cheaper, more dangerous compounds like PCP.

"You were getting all these different shapes of pills," Comerford says. "You were getting really big wafers, or these horse capsules, or this brown stuff, and everybody saying, 'Yeah, this is Ecstasy.' All of a sudden you were puking your guts out."

Such product substitution is similar to what happened when bootleggers began peddling bad liquor: The youngest users are at the greatest risk.

"The younger the age group, the more likely it isn't Ecstasy, because they just can't afford the real thing," Beck says. "They're the ones preyed upon by dealers who want to make a quick buck."

With the advent of raves, Ecstasy got more visibility. Raves evolved from spontaneous gatherings of techno-music enthusiasts in England and Spain into worldwide all-night dance and drug fests. Ecstasy was the drug of choice.

"The younger the age group, the more likely it isn't Ecstasy, because they just can't afford the real thing. They're the ones preyed upon by dealers."

Raves are circuslike extravaganzas populated by young, mostly white kids, often clad in tie-dye, waving glow sticks, and dancing all night to trancelike music. Because MDMA can cause teeth clenching, pacifiers became part of the raver's uniform.

In 1994, an organization called Buzzlife Productions launched a series of weekly raves at Nation, a warehouse-style nightclub in Southeast DC. Five years later, Fox5 broadcast a series on the Nation gatherings. Reporter Elisabeth Leamy took a hidden camera and recorded thousands of kids—many from the suburbs—writhing, groping, sucking pacifiers, and taking Ecstasy.

Stories about raves resulted in a crackdown. By then, the drug's manufacture and distribution were following established economic theories about illegal markets.

In the early days, the Ecstasy trade was largely nonviolent, run by the likes of Clegg—blissed-out neo-hippies. In illegal markets, the theory goes, ruthlessness offers a competitive advantage. Al Capone didn't bootleg because he was a drunk but because he stood to get rich. Lucky Luciano wasn't a drug addict; he was a businessman using muscle to control an illegal market.

By the mid-1990s, this dynamic showed up in Ecstasy distribution. Virtually all MDMA production had moved abroad, often to labs in the Netherlands. Israeli and Russian organized-crime syndicates began to take over much of the smuggling, according to federal prosecutors. At the beginning, they recruited Hasidic Jews from New York, paying them $1,500 and airline tickets to Europe to smuggle Ecstasy to the United States from Brussels, Paris, and Montreal.

MDMA also lured old-school organized-crime figures. Among them was Sammy (The Bull) Gravano, a confessed Mafia hit man, who launched an Ecstasy network while in the federal witness-protection program.

In 1985, a UCLA psychopharmacologist, a witness for the DEA, estimated that recreational Ecstasy use amounted to 30,000 tablets a month. Fourteen years later, the ring controlled by Gravano's supplier—one small segment of the global enterprise—shipped 200,000 pills a month to Long Island's Hamptons.

If the former Mafia hit man thought Ecstasy dealing was less violent than the Cosa Nostra, he was wrong. Gravano's supplier—Israel-born Ilan Zarger—testified that he was planning to "whack" Gravano over a price dispute.

In 1997, customs agents seized 350,000 Ecstasy tablets. In 1999, they seized more than 3 million; in 2000, 8 million.

"What accounts for this explosion?" former US Customs Commissioner Raymond Kelly asked before the Senate Caucus on International Narcotics Control in July 2000. "For one thing, greed. Criminal gangs are lining up to reap the irresistible profit margins offered by Ecstasy sales."

The dealers, Kelly elaborated in a conference with law-enforcement officials, "are hardened, violent, and willing to go to any means to get their product through. We expect that drug lords in Colombia and Mexico will soon try to carve out part of the market for themselves."

Former Baltimore mayor Kurt Schmoke, now dean of Howard University's law school, remembers his frustration dealing with Baltimore's drug dealers. Arrests were as effective as scooping buckets of water from the ocean.

"You could keep wiping folks out," Schmoke says, "but as long as there was a market out there, somebody was going to fill it." Schmoke stunned a 1988 US Conference of Mayors by announcing his support of drug-policy reform.

In DC and its suburbs, Ecstasy is most popular in upper-income high schools and private universities, according to Mark Stone, a DC detective who often testifies as an expert in drug cases.

"The majority of Ecstasy users are suburban," Stone says. "It's in the upper-middle class."

Twenty year old Jenny Rosloff, who attended Bethesda's Walter Johnson High School, agrees. Students at Walter Johnson include sons and daughters of scientists at the National Institutes of Health. Those using Ecstasy, Rosloff says, tend to be "well-off students who enjoy spending a lot of money in clubs." Rosloff is now a University of Maryland junior and a chapter president for Students for Sensible Drug Policy.

> In drug-policy debates, "pro-reform" advocates are painted as people who would like to see heroin and crack dispensed in vending machines.

Recently, Ecstasy use has begun to filter into the inner city, sold by drug gangs also peddling PCP, marijuana, and cocaine. Three years ago, DC Ecstasy busts were rare; now detectives make several a week.

"The affinity for this substance by users is going to cause traffickers to fight for turf," Stone says, "like they did with crack cocaine."

In a 2001 Monitoring the Future survey, 61 percent of high-school seniors reported that Ecstasy was easy to get.

In March 2001, the Senate Caucus on International Narcotics Control held a hearing titled "America at Risk: The Ecstasy Threat."

"You can hardly read a newspaper or magazine these days without reading about the use and abuse of the drug Ecstsy," Senator Grassley said. "The use of this drug is growing faster than any other in the nation."

In less than two decades, Ecstasy has gone from a drug used for therapy to a club drug to one that children can buy in school.

Last year, the government announced a marginal decline in Ecstasy use—a first—but there was also a marked decline in the use of alcohol and tobacco. The September 11 attacks may have spurred these declines because "young Americans may be taking their lives and communities more seriously by saying no to drugs," drug czar John Walters said in a press release.

But Stone hasn't seen evidence of these declines on the street.

It would be hard to argue that drug laws created Ecstasy abuse, but there's a growing sentiment that today's laws don't accomplish their objectives.

"I think that among the public there's pretty strong recognition that what we're doing isn't working," says the Cato Institute's Boaz. Today there are police chiefs, former judges, prosecutors, and mayors who believe change is needed. In 1996, William F. Buckley Jr. dedicated an issue of the conservative *National Review* to a symposium entitled "The War on Drugs Is Lost."

In politics, debates over drug policy tend to become polarized, with "pro-reform" advocates painted as people who would like to see heroin and crack dispensed in vending machines. When Gary Johnson, then New Mexico governor, blasted US drug policies as a "mind-boggling failure" in 1999, former drug czar Barry McCaffrey dubbed him Puff Daddy Johnson. Fellow Republicans called him "an idiot" and "an embarrassment."

Few drug-reform advocates endorse outright legalization. "I like to use the terms 'controlled' or 'regulated,'" says Kevin Zeese of Common Sense for Drug Policy. "I don't see the prohibited drugs as controlled at all. The people who control the illegal drugs are the cartels, the drug dealers, the kid selling it in the high school—who is probably the biggest drug user of all."

Many conservatives such as Buckley propose something along the lines of a medical model for various drugs. Dealing to anyone underage would remain a felony, with severe punishment.

Such reform is unlikely to emerge from inside the Beltway. In national campaigns, politicians stick with drug-reform policy that sounds good. Talking about reform can be ammunition for an opponent. Recommending tougher sentences, more prisons, or more money for interdiction is political inoculation.

Reform efforts are increasingly focused on states—often in the face of strenuous opposition from federal officials. Several states have decriminalized marijuana so that users of a small amount receive a lighter punishment than a felony charge. There's no evidence that marijuana use has increased in those states.

Rhode Island recently modified a long-standing policy, touted by federal drug enforcers, that was designed to regulate the sale of hypodermic syringes. In the face of the AIDS epidemic, the state recently permitted pharmacists to sell syringes over the counter to intravenous-drug users. There was an unintended result: Heroin addicts began to seek treatment, in part because they were in contact with medical professionals.

As far as Boaz is concerned, the best "reform" the federal government could make would be to get out of the way: "If you repealed the federal laws tomorrow, no state would legalize drugs. But 50 debates would break out in this laboratory of democracy."

In the case of Ecstasy, those opposing the government's ban were ridiculed, painted as "radical" reformers. Yet none of them suggested that MDMA should be legalized. They wanted MDMA approved, under existing laws, for therapeutic use or research, available only by prescription.

After contentious hearings, Administrative Law Judge Francis Young agreed with the doctors. The DEA rejected the judge's findings, lost its appeals in federal court, then unilaterally announced the drug's permanent ban in 1988, all this time generating more publicity and, many believe, making problems worse.

"I'd rather the government make these drugs sound boring, make it sound like the most uncool thing to do," Kurt Schmoke says. "That to me would be more effective than making it seem like forbidden fruit."

Without protracted legal wrangling, the *Washington Post* would have had a tough time justifying its 3,000-word, pre-ban story. Phil Donahue's show about cancer patients deprived of MDMA never would have hit the airwaves. There would have been far fewer day-before-the-ban Ecstasy parties, which introduced new people to the drug.

"We've been fighting drugs since the Harrison [Narcotic] Act in 1914," Schmoke says. "If we had been fighting any other war this long with these results, we would demand a different strategy."

If the federal government hadn't waged its four-year battle, where would we be? MDMA would be available by prescription, manufactured by medical chemists, under stringent regulations, making it harder for illegal manufacturers to get a foothold. Less money would flow to bootleggers like Sammy Gravano or gangs like the one that set up Danny Petrole's murder. Underground sales might have continued, fueled by diverted prescriptions, but bootleg Ecstasy—containing dangerous compounds like PCP—would be less common.

If psychiatrists had won the right to use MDMA as a prescription drug, would my 14-year-old daughter be in greater danger?

Drug-law supporters often ask reformers to prove the unprovable, that the results of reform would be better. I'd pose a different question: Could the results be any worse?

Norfolk writer Greg Raver-Lampman is a two-time Pulitzer Prize nominee. His memoir, *Magic and Loss*, was translated into 17 languages. *Lost at Sea*, a novel, will be published this year. He can be reached at raver-lampman@signedcopy.com

A Sad Fact of Life

Gangs and their activities are spreading into small-town America

ARTHUR G. SHARP

Gang activity is regularly a hot item for the media. Does it deserve such prominence, or does it receive such attention merely to boost audience interest?

Magali Kupfer, a leader in the Meriden, CT, Hispanic community stated at a conference in 1994 that the way gang violence is portrayed by police and politicians and then reported in the news media has made the problem a racial issue. Kupfer told a reporter for the Hartford Courant that the "politicians and the police departments are really overreacting."

Regardless of who is right in the debate over how the news is reported, gangs do exist—but in how many communities?

In a recent poll, 26% of law enforcement administrators said that gangs are more a topic for the media to dwell on rather than a real problem, at least in their communities. Another 13% were not sure. The remaining 61% stated that gangs are real problems.

That percentage agrees closely with the number of respondents (52%) who said they have gang problems in their communities. Gangs are becoming more widespread, according to 74% of those polled, and are also spreading into rural areas.

While 55% think that gangs are more a problem of bigger cities than small communities, 41% said they are not. Significantly, 59% of the respondents believe that vigorous anti-gang programs by large city departments will have a spillover effect into smaller communities. Only 4% said they were not. That is not good news for administrators in small communities, some of whom are feeling the pressure from gangs already.

Ronald Glidden, Chief of Police in Lee, MA, noted that his small community is a stopping-off point for transient gang members traveling from Hartford, CT, and Springfield, MA, to Pittsfield and North Adams, two small cities in the Berkshire Mountains of western Massachusetts. North Adams' population is only 16,800; Pittsfield's is 48,600. Lee has a population of 6,500 served by an 11-member police force. Springfield, on the other hand, has a population of 160,000 and a 527-member police department. Hartford is home to 130,000 citizens; its police force comprises 460 members.

Why is Lee seeing more gang members? The answer is simple. Both Springfield and Hartford are placing a lot of pressure on gangs operating in their cities. The gangs have been forced to seek new territory and smaller communities seem likely places to go. That explains in part why smaller communities are becoming way stations for gang activity.

A September 10, 1994, article in the Salisbury, MD, Daily Times highlighted the problem of gangs uprooting themselves and expanding their activities. The writer said that gang activity was on the increase in Maryland, in large part due to enforcement actions in cities like Chicago and Los Angeles. There were reports circulating in Maryland that organized gangs in out-of-state locations were seeking to expand their activities in the state because it was basically "virgin territory."

Shortly before the report appeared, police in Torrington, CT, heard rumors involving gang activity in their city of 33,000 people. A newspaper in a nearby city, the Waterbury Republican-American, printed a story about the rumors that fueled the situation. The Torrington department called in officers specifically to augment evening shifts but the rumors never came to fruition.

Were there gang members in Torrington? No one knows for sure. What exactly is a "gang member" anyway?

There is some difference of opinion over exactly what constitutes a "gang." The definition does have some bearing on how large a problem communities have with groups of youths. For example, Police Chief Jim Uhde, North Lauderdale, FL. said that the world "gang" is "overused and hysterically taken out of context."

He stressed that "Most of our problems involve groups, not nearly 'gangs,' as we know them, of young 'wanna-be' punks just trying to act bad." Similarly, Chief Tad Leach, Lincolnwood, IL, questions the use—or overuse—of the word "gang."

Lincolnwood, with 11,300 people and a 34-member police force, is a suburb bordering the north side of Chicago, which is one of the major gang centers in the United States. Chicago's infamous Gangster Disciples, with a murderous history dating to the 1970s, has extended its territory over much of the city's south side and beyond, including several suburbs. It is not surprising, then, that gangs operate in communities like Lincolnwood. That is where the definition of gangs becomes important.

Leach explained gang activity as "street gang members claiming neighborhoods as 'turf' and doing activities which promote the gang's ends." He added that "We do have some crime committed by individuals who are gang members but do not reside in our village."

Perhaps police administrators can differentiate between real gang members and "wanna-be's." Media representatives, however, may not.

In some reporters' minds, all crimes committed by youths can be attributed to what they define as "gangs." As they report on "gang activities," real or imagined, the problem becomes magnified in the public's mind. That puts more pressure on law enforcement.

Administrators agree that gangs in general and crimes perpetrated by young people are problems. There is, after all, a clear connection between gang activities and overall crime rates. (It is important to note, though, that many gang members are well out of their teens. Therefore, they hardly qualify for "youthful offender" status.)

While 48% of the poll respondents theorized that eliminating gang problems in their jurisdictions would significantly reduce their overall crime rates, 35% said it would not. Unfortunately, many administrators believe that a total solution to the gang problem is out of their hands. There are simply too many forces at play in the total picture.

Chief Rudolf Rossmy, Vernon, CT, observed, "Gangs and their activities are a sad fact of life and know no boundaries, whether local or state. Local media dwelling on the subject accomplishes two things: it gives credence to gangs causing real problems and feeds on gang members, and the articles create havoc for the community, resulting in fears that are mostly unfounded."

He concluded that "Police need the community in a partnership to control gangs and their activity and should not have to face community paranoia and/or lack of cooperation." That is exactly the approach many police agencies are using to combat gangs and media involvement in their activities.

Chief Dave Scates of Couer D'Alene, ID, emphasized the need for partnerships between law enforcement and the community. "Police alone cannot deal with the problem of gangs," he said. "It takes a concerted community effort. Unfortunately, in too many cases the problem has been dumped into our lap."

He suggested that people often refuse to recognize the insidious emergence of gangs as influences in their communities. "In some cases," he noted, "community members feel law enforcement is crying wolf. By the time they awake, the problem is deeply rooted."

Police Agent Matthew D. Reed, Administrative Services, South Windsor, CT, concurs with Scates. "We are fortunate—or unfortunate, depending on how you look at it— that a number of upper-level gang members reside in our town," he said. "They tend to keep their activity out of their 'back yard' and we do not have a significant gang activity as a result. The potential, however, is significant."

He does not look forward to that potential being realized. "Communities all around us are constantly battling the activity and it is most likely only a matter of time before we become overwhelmed. Unfortunately, it's a topic no one locally discusses."

If the media publicizes an unpopular topic such as gangs and their activities and nobody wants to listen, when the problem finally erupts the community may be unprepared. "When and if a problem occurs in the future, the police agency will be playing 'catch up,'" Reed said.

Of the agencies contacted, 51% sponsor or participate in special programs aimed at deterring young people's involvement in gang activity. About the same percentage (52%) operate anti-gang forces or their equivalents. They support massive education programs to warn young people about the dangers of involving themselves in gang activities. But, they do question the efficiency of such programs.

Only 18% of the respondents said they feel intensive education programs are effective. Granted, 66% acknowledged they are to some extent, but the question lingers as to whether police agencies should concern themselves more with enforcing laws and apprehending criminals rather than involving themselves in sociological activities. As 82% of the respondents emphasized, the basic underlying sociological reasons contributing to gang activities, e.g., high unemployment and too many single-parent families, are beyond law enforcement's control.

At the same time, 41% said that the gang problem can be eliminated—or at least limited—if young people are given more job and activity opportunities. In their absence, however, sociological problems prevail across all economic strata in contemporary society. These problems affect virtually everyone, as Chief Thomas L. Hennies of Rapid City, SD, suggested.

In his city of 60,000 people, the 100 department members have to deal with Native-American gang activity. "Most gang activity is perceived to involve Blacks, Hispanics, or Asians—at least from a national perspective. Gangs are not just a 'big city' problem," he stressed. "The factors that contribute to the emergence of the gang subculture are everywhere in American society."

In Hennies' opinion, "Gangs are simply a manifestation of many of the social ills that plague our country. The problem must be addressed from a community standpoint, not solely from within the criminal justice system."

One part of the puzzle which administrators are looking closely at is strengthening juvenile offender laws and applying more stringent punishments. In most cases, they do not want more laws. They want stricter enforcement of those that exist.

Chief Emery E. Brejle, Glasgow, MT, pointed out, "Typically, laws increasing punishments for a particular offense are passed by politicians who are more interested in appearing to do something about crime than they are in actually dealing with the complex problems surrounding criminal behavior." He admitted that "There are isolated examples where increasing punishments for a particular offense are effective, but they are the exception." Nevertheless, 89% of the respondents said that juvenile offender laws have to be toughened as one step toward curbing gang problems.

The respondents indicated that current enforcement of youth-related crimes is too lenient and they are frustrated by the courts' treatment of youthful offenders. For instance, 57% reported it is common in their jurisdictions for officers to apprehend gang members only to find them back on the streets within a matter of hours. In many administrators' opinions, there is simply not enough of a deterrent for youthful offenders.

To underline that viewpoint, Assistant Chief Ron Ward, Lawton, OK, related a story that happened in his jurisdiction. Two gang members were caught in a stolen car but only the driver was arrested. The passenger asked the arresting officer if he would tell the driver to call him later that afternoon after he was released. "They know they are not going to spend much time being held, and nothing is going to happen to them," Ward said. "Until this changes, the justice system is doomed to failure."

Perhaps part of the answer, then, is to reach young people before they get involved in gang activities. The town of Hurlock, MD, applied for a $50,000 state grant to improve the seven-member police department's image among local youths. Mayor Don Bradley emphasized that the grant was not made to change any negative images of the police department. Instead, he noted, youths without respect for police is a national problem.

If the mayor and police chief of a town of 1,700 people are concerned with the lack of respect youths have for officers in their community, then the problem must be real! It is no wonder, then, that law enforcement agencies are looking for help in their attempts to combat gangs.

The federal government can be a source of help, and 43% of the respondents said they would like to see more federal involvement in trying to eliminate the gang problem. Newly-appointed Chief Paul Meara of Springfield, MA, said "Since gangs are a problem to every city and town, federal involvement is very important for networking, information, and money."

There is no doubt that the federal government can have a major impact on gang operations. The results, which receive ample exposure in the press, are encouraging.

In March, the federal government convicted eight members and associates of a Chicago gang of drug conspiracy. The convictions could mean life sentences for the defendants. A Hartford gang member who hid the gun used in a fatal drive-by shooting received a 135-month prison sentence for his participation. These sentences are significant, since federal prisoners must serve at least 85% of their sentences. That, according to one State of Connecticut probation officer, is a definite wake-up call to gang members.

The probation officer stated that gang members who visit her change their attitudes considerably when they learn that they may be charged with federal crimes. "They do not have a lot of respect for state laws," she said. "They know that state-mandated prison sentences are short—if they are levied at all. However, federal sentencing policies do make them sit up and take notice."

Is stricter enforcement the answer? Some administrators believe so. A resounding 80% of the poll respondents said they would like to see harsher prison sentences meted out to convicted gang members, regardless of their ages. Only 2% would not.

Sergeant Dave Horton of the San Francisco Police Department stressed that "Our agency believes in strict enforcement of laws—especially gang-related laws (186.22 of the California Penal Code)—and prosecution of incidents involving violence." He tempered his statement somewhat by saying, "The San Francisco Police Department also believes that we must work with community groups to help prevent violent gang activity."

Perhaps the San Francisco approach to dealing with gang activity epitomizes law enforcement's strategy in combating youth crime. It blends strict police activity with community involvement. After all, gang activity is real. Based on law enforcement administrators' opinions, it is not a creation of the media. The combination of strategies being employed today against gang crime by law enforcement agencies is probably the best approach, although the administrators are always open to new weapons in the battle.

It would be a real benefit if the media reported profusely on law enforcement's successes in combating gang-related crime, rather than concentrating on the negative activities of gangs and their mystique.

Arthur Sharp, a professional writer and educator, writes regularly for LAW and ORDER. His surveys have been conducted among agency executives on topics of current concern to law enforcement.

Criminal Behavior of Gang Members and At-Risk Youths

Summary of a presentation by C. Ronald Huff, Ohio State University

During the past decade, the problem of gang-related crime has become a significant policy issue in the United States. According to recent estimates, more than 16,000 gangs are active in this country, with at least half a million members who commit more than 600,000 crimes each year. Two recent studies conducted by researchers at Ohio State University were designed to address three critical questions:

- What is the nature and magnitude of self-reported criminal behavior among youth gang members?
- What is the nature and magnitude of such behavior among at-risk youths—those who are not yet gang members?
- What is the effect of gang membership on criminal behavior?

To answer these questions, the National Institute of Justice funded research in three communities—Aurora, Colorado; Denver, Colorado; and Broward County, Florida—and the Office of Juvenile Justice and Delinquency Prevention (OJJDP) funded research in Cleveland, Ohio. Also, as part of the OJJDP grant, researchers in Columbus, Ohio, tracked leaders of youth gangs to determine what happens to gang leaders over time.

Gang membership leads to criminal behavior

The Colorado-Florida and Cleveland studies obtained self-reported data through one-time confidential interviews. In each community, researchers interviewed 50 gang members and 50 youths who were at risk of becoming gang members, developing as close a demographic match between the two groups as possible. They selected interviewees through referrals from local youth-serving organizations, rather than from police databases of arrestees. Questions focused on criminal and noncriminal activities of the youths and their peers.

The data on criminal activity showed differences between the behavior of gang members and at-risk youths. For example, individual gang members in both studies reported that they had stolen cars (Colorado-Florida, 58.3 percent; Cleveland, 44.7 percent); aggregate rates for auto theft—reflecting statements that members of their gang had stolen cars—were much higher (Colorado-Florida, 93.6 percent; Cleveland, 82.6). Auto theft

rates among at-risk youths were markedly lower (Colorado-Florida, 12.5 percent; Cleveland, 4.1 percent). The researchers found similar contrasts when looking at violent crimes. About 40 percent of gang members in the Cleveland sample said they had participated in a drive-by shooting, compared with 2 percent of at-risk youths. In the Colorado-Florida study, 64.2 percent of gang members said that members of their gang had committed homicide, whereas 6.5 percent of at-risk youths said that their friends had done so.

Although both gang members and at-risk youths admitted significant involvement with guns, gang members were far likelier to own guns, and the guns they owned were larger caliber. More than 90 percent of gang members in both studies reported that their peers had carried concealed weapons; more than 80 percent reported that members of their gang had carried guns to school. In contrast, about one-half of at-risk youths in both studies had friends who had carried a concealed weapon; about one-third of at-risk youths said their friends had carried guns to school.

In both studies, gang members were more involved with selling drugs (Colorado-Florida, 76.9 percent; Cleveland, 72.3 percent) than were at-risk youths (Colorado-Florida, 6.4 percent; Cleveland, 9.1 percent). When asked what level of legitimate wages would induce them to stop selling drugs, about one-quarter of the young people in both studies cited an amount little higher than that earned in fast-food restaurants; approximately half of the interviewees, both gang members and at-risk youths, said they had held jobs in the past year.

Gang leaders engage in more serious criminal behavior

The second component of the Ohio study focused on the criminal activity of identified gang leaders in Columbus. The researchers analyzed the arrest records of 83 gang leaders in the years 1980 to 1994. Membership of 78 of these leaders was distributed among five gangs; the rest belonged to other gangs.

During these 15 years, the 83 gang leaders accumulated 834 arrests, 37 percent of which were for violent crimes (ranging from domestic violence to murder). Property crimes and drug-related offenses also figured prominently. The researchers identified a clear pattern of arrest charges in each of the five prominent gangs. A gang's peak arrest rate for property crimes occurred about 1.5 years before its peak arrest rate for violent crimes; the peak arrest rate for drug crimes followed about 3 months later. The researchers theorized that violent crimes increased as the gangs began engaging in drug activity and may have been connected to the establishment of the drug trade. The increasingly violent activities took their toll on the gangs: By the end of the period studied, a disproportionate number of the gang leaders had died.

Steps to prevention and control

These studies identified a close relationship between gang membership and criminal behavior. Gang membership exposed youths to an increased risk of physical violence and death—often including an assaultive initiation ritual—even though most gang members joined for a sense of belonging and security. In contrast, many young people told the researchers that they suffered no physical reprisal for refusing to join a gang. The research demonstrated that the benefits of resisting a gang far outweigh those of joining. Creative prevention that fosters feelings of belonging in the community as a whole might dissuade many of these youths from joining gangs. Also, since half the young people interviewed had held a job, programs that expand job opportunities in the legitimate economy could induce some to stop selling drugs.

Finally, the Columbus study noted a decline in the arrest rate of gang leaders, which the researchers attributed in part to a reallocation of police resources away from gang activities toward specifically drug-related activities: Drugs and gangs are not synonymous, and the assignment of personnel to drug teams reduced the ability of the police to monitor gang activity.

From *Research Preview, National Institute of Justice,* October 1998, pp. 1-9. Reprinted by permission of the National Institute of Justice, National Criminal Justice Reference Service.

Gang world

Street gangs are proliferating around the world. The United States has unwittingly spurred this phenomenon by deporting tens of thousands of immigrants with criminal records each year. But that only partly explains how gangs went global. Credit also goes to the Internet, where gangs are staking out turf and spreading their culture online. Gang members may have never heard of globalization, but it is making them stronger.

Andrew V. Papachristos

It's a cold winter day in Chicago, and Hector is doing what he does almost every day, standing on his drug spot "serving" customers. Hector, a 19-year-old member of the Latin Kings street gang, is the son of Mexican immigrants. He speaks Spanglish skillfully, mixed with urban slang, and wears a uniform typical of the youth in his neighborhood—puffy coat, baggy jeans, and meticulously clean, white athletic shoes (in a city where snow salt decimates entire wardrobes). Hector has never traveled outside of Chicago and only rarely ventures beyond a three-mile radius of his apartment.

Hector stands at the end of a long and familiar global commodity chain. The little plastic bags in his palm contain $10 chunks of crack cocaine that look like jagged, disfigured sugar cubes. By the time the crack hits the streets of Chicago, it has been touched by more than a dozen people in three countries. Hector has no interest in its global supply chain. His daily concerns and activities center on a few city blocks, his aspirations reaching just as far. The majority of Hector's day is spent doing what other 19-year-olds do—sleeping, hanging out with friends, trying to talk to teenage girls, playing video games, and standing on the street corner laughing. He sells drugs for only a few hours a day, going home with around $50 profit, little more than he'd make working at McDonald's.

Hector's image—that of a young, minority, "inner-city," male gang member—is transmitted, exploited, and glamorized across the world. The increasing mobility of information via cyberspace, films, and music makes it easy for gangs, gang members, and gang wannabes to get information, adapt personalities, and distort gang behaviors. Most often, these images of gang life are not simply exaggerated; they're flat-out wrong. Flashy cars, diamond rings (real ones, at least), and wads of cash are not the gang world norm. Hustling to make ends meet, trying to put food on the table while staying out of jail, wearing the same T-shirt and blue jeans until they have holes in them, and dealing with the humdrum of school, unemployment, and child support are more typical.

Nonetheless, two images of street gangs dominate the popular consciousness—gangs as posses of drug-dealing thugs and, more recently, gangs as terrorist organizations. Although the media like to link gangs and drugs, only a small portion of all gangs actually deal in them. Fewer do so in an organized fashion. The National Youth Gang Center (NYGC) estimates that 34 percent of all U.S. gangs are actively involved in organized drug dealing. Gangs that do sell drugs essentially fill a void in the postindustrial urban economy, replacing the manufacturing and unskilled labor jobs that traditionally served as a means for social mobility.

Similarly, the name Jose Padilla is inevitably followed by two epithets—al Qaeda terror suspect and street gang member. The link between the two is extremely misleading. Padilla was arrested at Chicago's O'Hare International Airport in June 2002, reportedly en route to detonate a "dirty bomb" in a U.S. city. But, as with drug dealing, most gangs lack the organizational wherewithal to operate transnational clandestine networks. Instead, most gangs engage in what one criminologist calls "cafeteria-style" crime—a little bit of drug use, a smattering of larceny, a dab of truancy, a dollop of fighting, and so on. Padilla's attempted terrorist act had little to do with his gang affiliation.

That said, there have been a handful of extreme examples that suggest that some gangs do in fact have the

When gangs go bad

The El Rukns represent the worst of what gangs can become. Originally known as the Blackstone Rangers, the gang emerged in the late 1950s on Chicago's South Side. Their leader, Jeff Fort, eventually consolidated the Blackstone Rangers with 21 smaller gangs, creating a powerful organization. In 1968, Fort was convicted in federal court of embezzling $1.4 million dollars in anti-poverty grants from churches and community organizations. Rather than create jobs, as the grants were intended, Fort used the funds to purchase guns, cars, and drugs. Released from Leavenworth prison in 1976, Fort joined the Moorish Science Temple of America and converted to Islam. The Blackstone Rangers then assumed the new identity of the El Rukns (Arabic for "the foundation of knowledge").

Three high-ranking members of the El Rukns traveled to Libya in March 1986 to broker a deal with military officials in which the gang would commit "terrorist acts on U.S. soil" in exchange for $2.5 million. Again, the gang was apparently motivated by a desire for cash and notoriety. In May, a second meeting between the El Rukns and Libyan officials occurred in Panama. But upon their return, customs officials searched the luggage of two of the gang members and turned up documents that contained the vague outlines to several terrorist plots. Their plans, concocted in Chicago, included destroying federal buildings, blowing up an airplane, assassinating a Milwaukee alderman, and simply committing a "killing here or there."

Two months later, the El Rukns purchased a light anti-tank weapon for $1,800—from an undercover FBI agent. The purchase, as well as the testimony of informants and conversations recorded on wiretaps, convinced a federal judge to issue search warrants. Authorities ultimately uncovered the anti-tank weapon, as well as 32 firearms, including a MAC-10 machine gun, a fully automatic .45-caliber pistol, and several rounds of armor-piercing bullets. Five senior members of the gang, including Jeff Fort, were convicted of conspiracy to commit terrorist acts and remain in prison today. Still, their story shows how a small, seemingly ordinary street gang can turn into something far more dangerous.—AVP

global reach necessary to commit terrorist acts. In 1986, the Chicago-based El Rukns conspired to commit terrorist acts on U.S. soil on behalf of the Libyan government, in exchange for $2.5 million. In the 1990s, the Latin Kings funneled money to the FALN, a militant group based in Puerto Rico, through ties that were cultivated inside the U.S. prison system. And, most recently, leaders of the Mara Salvatrucha (MS-13) gang, which operates in at least 31 states and three countries, met in Honduras with Adnan el Shukrijumah, a key al Qaeda leader, to discuss smuggling immigrants into the United States via Mexico.

One of the most urgent challenges for policymakers is distinguishing between the average street gang and groups that operate as criminal networks. Until recently, gang membership was a common part of city boyhood and not terribly detrimental. Members left as they got married, got a job, enlisted in the military, or simply grew out of gang behaviors. But, as cities have changed, so have gangs. The globalization of the world economy, and the resulting exodus of manufacturing jobs from developed urban centers to the developing world, has left poor neighborhoods geographically and socially isolated. Not surprisingly, street gangs and gang violence have increased dramatically with globalization. Today, gangs serve as de facto protectors, families, and employers. Members are staying in gangs longer, young women are increasingly involved, and gangs are now reported in all 50 U.S. states and in countless countries.

Globalization and street gangs exist in a paradox: Gangs are a global phenomenon not because the groups themselves have become transnational organizations (although a few have), but because of the recent hypermobility of gang members and their culture. At the same time that globalization isolates neighborhoods heavily populated by gangs, it also helps spread gang activity and culture. Gangs have, in a sense, gone global.

GANGSTERS WITHOUT BORDERS

Gangs exist in 3,300 cities across the United States—essentially, any municipality with a population of more than 250,000 people—and in a growing number of small towns and rural areas. This figure is about a 433 percent increase from estimates in the 1970s, when gangs were reported in roughly 200 cities. The NYGC estimates that today there are more than 731,500 gang members in 21,500 different gangs in the United States. Such proliferation is not confined geographically. Gangs and other violent "youth groups" have been reported in France, Greece, South Africa, Brazil, the Netherlands, Spain, Germany, Belgium, Britain, Jamaica, Mexico, Canada, Japan, China, Australia, and elsewhere.

A common myth used to explain such proliferation is that gangs "migrate" in search of new members, turf, or criminal opportunities. Although that is true in the rare cases of groups like the Latin Kings and MS-13, very little evidence suggests that gang proliferation is associated with calculated entrepreneurial ambitions. A more plausible explanation is that when people move, they take their culture with them. For example, Trey, a member of Chicago's massive Gangster Disciples, moved to a small town in Arkansas where his brother, who is not a gang member, had found a job. Although Trey tried to "go legit," he soon found that his status as a Gangster Disciple from the housing projects of Chicago gave him a formidable reputation in small-town Arkansas. Within nine months, he started a new Gangster Disciples "chapter" with 15 members. But this new gang had no formal connection with the group in Chicago.

The same trend is occurring internationally, particularly in Latin America and Asia. In a recent survey of more than 1,000 gang members, the National Gang Crime Research Center found that about 50 percent of gang members believed that their gang had international connections. Analysis conducted by this author suggests the rate is considerably higher for Hispanic (66 percent) and Asian (58 percent) gang members, who are more likely to be immigrants.

The movement of gang members overseas not only spreads gang culture but also helps to establish links between gang members in different countries. When Lito, a member of Hector's Latin Kings gang, ran into trouble with the law in Chicago, his family sent him to live with an aunt in Mexico. There, he quickly became a go-between for gang members in the United States looking to avoid detection and for Mexican immigrants searching for jobs in the United States. The Latin Kings, in fact, turned these connections into a lucrative business by manufacturing fake ID cards. A 1999 investigation of several Latin Kings recovered 31,000 fraudulent IDs and travel documents.

Of course, gang members do not always travel overseas as a matter of free will. Since the mid-1990s, U.S. immigration policy has dramatically boosted the proliferation of gangs throughout Latin America and Asia by deporting tens of thousands of immigrants with criminal records back to their home countries each year, including a growing number of gang members. In 1996, around 38,000 immigrants were deported after committing a crime; by 2003, the number had jumped to almost 80,000. Often, gang members have spent nearly their entire lives in the United States. But once they run afoul of the law, their immigrant status leaves them vulnerable to deportation.

The countries that receive the flood of deportees are usually ill-equipped to deal with so many returning gang members. Although estimates vary, experts believe that there are now nearly 100,000 gang members spread across Central America and Mexico. In 2003, the United States deported more than 2,100 immigrants with criminal records to the Dominican Republic. The same year, nearly 2,000 were deported to El Salvador. The U.S. government does not keep track of how many of these criminal deportees are gang members, but many Latin American states see a connection and say gangs are now one of their biggest threats to national security. In 2003, Honduras, El Salvador, Guatemala, Panama, and Mexico agreed to work together to find new ways to beat the challenges gangs pose.

It's not as though many gang members wish to remain in the countries of their birth. With little or no connection to their new homes, deported gang members typically face a simple choice: either find a way to return to the United States or seek protection from local gang members. In the case of MS-13, the U.S. government has deported hundreds of members, many of whom continue to illegally migrate back and forth, often carrying goods or people with them. Those that remain in their home countries are almost sure to connect with other deported gang members, and authorities in these countries say they are responsible for a large upswing in crime and violence. In a sense, U.S. immigration policy has amounted to unintentional state-sponsored gang migration. Rather than solving the gang problem, the United States may have only spread it.

THE VIRTUAL STREET CORNER

A search for particular gang slogans or phrases on any major search engine uncovers Web sites with gang manifestos, bylaws, pictures, symbols, and, yes, even turf. The Internet provides a new platform for gang warfare, and cyberspace is serving as an outlet for activities that could lead to violence if attempted on the street, such as "disrespecting" rival gangs, making claims of superiority, or disclosing gang secrets. Reputations are developed through verbal combat with vague, often anonymous, rivals. Individual gangs flaunt their Internet savvy by posting complex Web sites, including some with password protection. Entire Web sites are dedicated to celebrating the history and cultural icons of individual gangs, including internal documents, prayers, and photos. But, unlike exchanges in the real world, virtual spats rarely lead to actual violence.

> **U.S. immigration policy has amounted to unintentional state-sponsored gang migration. Rather than solving the gang problem, the United States may have only spread it.**

Still, few gang members ever discuss or mention the Internet. Many don't possess the hardware, software, or technical skills (not to mention the necessary telephone lines) to manage the Web. Most gang-related Web activity appears to come from gang members who have moved beyond their neighborhood, perhaps to attend college, or gang members and wannabes in suburbs or smaller towns. On the Internet, it's easy to co-opt the identity of well-known, mythic gangs.

A now defunct Web site of a gang calling itself "The Black Gangster Disciples," after the notorious Chicago gang, contained several pages of gang prayers, oaths, and other sensitive organizational materials. The Web page's guest book was a virtual street corner where surfers gave shout-outs (salutations or greetings) or disses (slanderous remarks) toward the group. Ironically, the site also contained a picture of the gang—a group of white, adolescent males flashing gang signs (the wrong ones, I might add), in someone's well-furnished basement.

Such digital proliferation has unlimited global potential. Police in the Netherlands have identified groups using the names of California-based gangs, such as the "Eight Tray Crips." But these exported gangs miss the hyperlocal point of their namesakes—the "Black" in the Black Gangster Disciples was added during the 1960s as the gang identified with civil rights activity on Chicago's South Side; "Eight Tray" refers to specific streets in California. Neither of these copycat gangs is able to, geographically or historically, live the local meaning found in the names of their gangs.

This proliferation of gangs on the Net might give the false impression that they are now soliciting members across the globe. The anonymity of cyberspace might build up the egos or reputations of people pretending to be something they are not, giving psychological reasons to seek other gang outlets or create them where none exist. Of course, it is possible that some of the more sophisticated gangs may already be exploiting cyberspace for illicit purposes, such as arranging drug deals or transferring illegal funds. Although it is impossible to stop gangs and gang members from posting Web pages, differentiating between the banal and the potentially dangerous virtual gang activity will be an important task in the years ahead. Gangs will no doubt take advantage of technological advances. The difficult part is figuring out what is real and what is not.

IS GLOBALIZATION JUST A WORD?

Street gangs are proliferating. What comes next depends in part on how globalization continues to affect our cities and how we deal with its consequences. As the global economy creates a growing number of disenfranchised groups, some will inevitably meet their needs in a gang.

Criminal organizations such as the Gangster Disciples, Crips, Bloods, MS-13, and Latin Kings are dangerous entities. But these groups are an anomaly in the gang world; they represent the worst of what gangs can become, not what most gangs are. Treating all gang members like mafia kingpins or terrorist masterminds is overestimating people who, more often than not, are petty delinquents. At their core, gangs are not just a criminal justice problem; they are a social problem. One of the biggest challenges is reintroducing an offender into a community. Labels such as "ex-offender" and "gang member" follow people throughout their lives, making it next to impossible for someone to make a fresh start. Scores of gang members go through the revolving criminal justice door and return to communities that offer no viable employment opportunities. In some prisons, gang members are trained for jobs that are not available when they are released.

No amount of law enforcement will rid the world of gangs. Strategies at all levels must move beyond simple arrest and incarceration to consider the economic structures of the cities and neighborhoods that breed street gangs. Otherwise, there will be nothing there to greet them but the waiting and supportive arms of the gang.

For Hector, globalization is just a word. It means nothing to him. It's possible that he has never even heard it. And it's certain he never sees globalization's benefits or associates its forces with his everyday life. On this cold winter day, I ask Hector where he thinks the drugs he sells come from. He laughs. "Man, what do I care? All I care is that the shit gets here," he says, stomping his feet to stay warm. A block away, I hear another gang member shouting, "Rocks and blow." The Latin Kings are open for business.

Andrew V. Papachristos, a Ph.D. student in sociology at the University of Chicago, has worked with gangs for more than 12 years.

UNIT 3

The Criminal Justice System and Juveniles

Unit Selections

Key Points to Consider

- What are our expectations of community policing with regard to juveniles? Should we change our expectations and thus change police policy?
- Is our understanding of gangs adequate to allow formation of public policy about them? Discuss.
- If the juvenile court does not protect juveniles, who will?
- What juvenile programs exist in your jurisdiction? Are there any alternatives? Are they all doing their job?
- What can the "restorative justice" movement do for the juvenile court and for influencing juvenile behavior?
- Who should set the agenda for juvenile corrections? What should their qualifications be?

Student Website

www.mhcls.com/online

Internet References

Further information regarding these websites may be found in this book's preface or online.

Community Policing Consortium
http://www.communitypolicing.org

Delinquents or Criminals: Policing Options
http://www.urban.org/crime/delinq.html

Juvenile Delinquents in the Federal Criminal System
http://www.ojp.usdoj.gov/bjs

Juvenile Female Offenders
http://www.ojjdp.ncjrs.org/pubs/gender/

Juvenile Violence and Gun Markets in Boston
http://www.ncjrs.org/txtfiles/fs000160.txt

National Youth Court Center
http://www.youthcourt.net

Perspectives on Crime and Justice: 1997–1998
http://www.ncjrs.org/txtfiles/172851.txt

Police-Corrections Partnerships
http://www.ncjrs.org/txtfiles1/175047.txt

The Criminal Justice System and Juveniles

In this section, we deal with the application of policy to our issues of delinquency in the country. Remember, "poor theory provides poor policy." We lead the section off with a firm grounding in fact. Here is the great value of the OJJDP data. The facts will temper all the discussion that follows. I will comment on each major subsection in three separate small essays to introduce you to the material.

The Police and Juveniles

It was determined more than 30 years ago in benchmark research by Piliavin and Briar that police discretion in dealing with juveniles was strongly influenced by a few "readily observable criteria," including the juvenile's prior offense record, ethnicity, grooming, and demeanor. Today, police still have great latitude in encounters with juveniles, which may be enhanced by community policing philosophies.

It was observed back then that police discretion was an extension of the juvenile court philosophy that held that when mak-

ing decisions about youth, more weight should be placed on their character than on the immediate offense. Of course, with the rise of the justice model, this view was modified to a stance that dictates, even for juveniles, that if you do the crime you will do the time.

Still, who becomes an officially recognized delinquent is usually decided by a police officer's judgment. So police define juveniles' behavior in terms of existing laws—laws that are today becoming harsher and harsher as panic develops.

Criminology has studied this phenomenon under the theoretical approach of "labeling," in which it is recognized that the official agents of society—the courts and the police especially—are the main labelers. It must be recognized, in defense of police, that this labeling is not taking place in a vacuum. Bad labels (stigmas) are contingent also on social attitudes, legislatures, media, and interest groups such as community leadership, activist organizations, and lobbying and support groups.

If there is a war on crime, then the police are the front line of the war. Indeed, the introduction of community policing has enhanced the importance of the police officer, who, while not at war in this model, is the main line of community control.

Reference
Piliavin, Irving, and Briar, Scott, "Police Encounters with Juveniles," *American Journal of Sociology*, 70, 2, September 1964, 206-214.

Juvenile Courts

Juvenile delinquency statutes have traditionally assumed that there are qualitative differences (for example, differences in the thought processes, experience, and knowledge base) between the behavior of children, teens, young adults, and adults. Today, to put it mildly, this assumption is under scrutiny, or to put it more vigorously, this assumption is in the process of being obliterated. Note, for example, the willingness of legislatures, the media, and the public to "hang 'em high," "lock 'em up and throw-away the key," or otherwise relegate our troublesome—and especially our threatening—youth to adult penal institutions and similar levels and types of penal sanctions, including the death penalty and life in prison. As Sellin and Wolfgang indicated more than 30 years ago, "the general public does not see the differences in the seriousness of crimes based on the age of the offender" (1964).

These issues are implicit in almost every contemporary discussion of our "delinquency problem." We are torn between trying to save our youth and trying to protect ourselves from the most malicious and destructive among them. We examine and reexamine the fine lines that enable us to make the calls when they need to be made. The juvenile court is the place where, like it or not, those calls are made. Most of us do not have the courage or knowledge to do so; we leave it to our juvenile judges. This might be a great argument for more citizen participation in the decision-making process, for community boards, neighborhood panels, and so on. That is not, however, a comfortable solution, given the inertia that many citizens have about actually doing something constructive about our problems.

As we read the articles in this unit, we ask several questions (Hershey and Gottfredson, 1993) about juveniles. We think here in terms of most juveniles, not *all* juveniles:

1. Is the criminal behavior of juveniles less serious?

2. Are juveniles as responsible as adults?

3. Are juveniles more amenable to treatment than adults?

4. Is there a class of undesirable behaviors (status offenses) that only juveniles can commit?

5. Is it possible to implement penal sanctions against juvenile misbehaviors without jeopardizing their entire life chances and therefore creating our own worst nightmare?

6. Who is ultimately responsible for youth who are misguided (parents, state, community, religion, etc.)?

7. Can juveniles be isolated from the corrupting influences of the world around them and especially of the institutions in which they might be placed with severely disturbed youth or adults?

References
Hershey, Travis, and Gottfredson, Michael, in T. Booth, (Ed.), *Juvenile Justice in the New Europe*, University of Sheffield, 1993.
Sellin, Thorsten, and Wolfgang, Marvin, Measurement of *Delinquency*, New York: Wiley, 1964.

Juvenile Corrections

Today more than ever, we face a dual set of problems when discussing juvenile corrections: (a) the problems of all corrections—overcrowding, violence, and apathy; and (b) the perpetual problems of growing up. There is a danger that we will do with our youth what we are doing with adults—spending ourselves into the poorhouse without getting any bang for our correctional policy bucks.

In regard to overcrowding, there is no question that our juvenile correctional facilities are being overwhelmed by vast numbers of young, violent offenders. Whether this is a policy problem or a young people problem is a separate issue. The corrections community has a number of good ideas and observations to make here, but, unfortunately, the knowledge that the correctional community has is rarely translated into realistic public policy. The very issue of overcrowding, because so many decisions by police, prosecutors, and judges are based on population capacity, dictates that corrections is the "tail of the system that wags the dog." The players in the system—the legislators, police, courts, and media—have more public voice and thus more power to influence the fate of those juveniles who are swamping correctional institutions. But, as has been the case for years, there persists general apathy about the corrections component of the justice system—until something goes wrong or one of the state's adult or juvenile charges "acts out." Then, all these other voices are heard and they usually result in some politically popular legislation that drives corrections further into the hole. Apparently, the critics have forgotten that corrections gets its juvenile clients after all the other social institutions—from family through school and church and the community—have failed the youths.

The strongest element of stability and cohesion that corrections has, the most organized voice, is the American Correctional Association. A lot of good thinking has come out of the ACA historically and more lately as it has networked, embraced, and incorporated a wider variety of concerned professionals.

We agree with the ACA that managing programs and services for juvenile delinquents and aggressive adolescents is complex and demanding (Glick, 1998). Indeed, this is due both to the nature of the client, the turbulent juvenile, and to the inherent complexity of the juvenile justice system itself. This system continues to evolve and modify as times change—much more than does the adult system. And it continues to grow as more clients are sent out of mainstream society. It has become a multi-billion dollar industry.

The Office of Juvenile Justice and Delinquency Prevention's (OJJDP) *Comprehensive Strategy for Serious, Violent and Chronic Juvenile Offenders,* (Wilson and Howell, 1993) has been often cited in ACA publications. It suggests for juvenile corrections that: costs of juvenile corrections must be reduced; conditions of confinement improved; detention and training school populations decreased; risk assessments used more extensively; identification of treatment needs to be improved; and detention visualized as a treatment opportunity. Isn't this the purpose in the first place—and have we moved this far away? We need a continuum of programs in which our use of alternatives could increase. Inequality needs to be eliminated, due process enhanced, the community involved, effective rehabilitation programs developed, prevention deemed a top priority, and aftercare brought into the mainstream.

The challenge is to create or develop a system of juvenile corrections that balances the safety of the public with the safety of the juvenile, that ensures the progress of society while ensuring the growth of the juvenile. All the while, these seemingly contradictory missions have to be carried out in a facility that meets the constitutional requirements of decency and humanity under the protection of the right against cruel and unusual punishment.

As the articles in this unit point out, good theory leads to good policy. Our students need to develop interpersonal skills to be good change agents and we all need patience for correctional programs to work—patience that apparently was not available from family, school, or other community organizations. Our students need exposure to the critical and constructive role that corrections must play in our plans for juvenile justice.

OJJDP Statistical Summaries

These are the **official data** about:
"Juvenile Justice System Structure and Process"
"Law Enforcement and Juvenile Justice"
"Juveniles in Court"
"Juveniles on Probation"
"Juveniles in Corrections" and
"Juvenile Reentry and Aftercare"

These data sets are very easy to manipulate and access, as were the earlier OJJDP datasets. Again, these are the facts with minimal opinion. We will try to point you to the most comprehensive documents for class discussion. You, the **reader** will be able to make policy and **value judgments** from the data.

"Juvenile Justice System Structure and Process"

This website (http://ojjdp.ncjrs.org/ojstatbb/structure_process/index.html) is a lead-in to the whole system of juvenile justice. Some observers, partially correctly, note that because of differing state and federal codes, there is no real system. However, most of us agree that enough can be **abstracted** or **synthesized** from all the systems to make straightforward observations. In this website, look first at the "related publication," *Juvenile Justice: A Century of Change*

Overview quoted from the website

"The first juvenile court in the United States was established in Chicago in 1899, more than 100 years ago. During the last 30 years, the juvenile justice system has weathered significant modifications. Perceptions of a juvenile crime epidemic in the early 1990s fueled public scrutiny of the system's ability to effectively control violent juvenile offenders. As a result, states have adopted numerous legislative changes in an effort to crack down on juvenile crime.

This section describes the juvenile justice system, focusing on structure and process features that relate to delinquency and status offense matters. Topics covered in this section include a history of the juvenile court, significant Supreme Court decisions that have shaped the modern juvenile justice system, and comparisons between juvenile and criminal court processing. In addition, this section summarizes changes made by states with regard to the system's jurisdictional authority, sentencing, corrections programming, confidentiality of records and court hearings, and victim involvement in court hearings.

Much of the information presented in this section was drawn from the National Center for Juvenile Justice's analysis of juvenile codes in each state."

"Law Enforcement and Juvenile Justice"

This website (http://ojjdp.ncjrs.org/ojstatbb/crime/overview.html) does not contain all the same data as "Juveniles as Offenders" cited above even though there is much overlapping data. Here the policing view of its task in the system is presented. For a firm foundation, please consult the related reading *Law Enforcement and Juvenile Crime* by Howard N. Snyder.

Overview quoted from the website

"Juveniles enter the juvenile justice system most often through law enforcement (i.e., arrest). Often, law enforcement statistics are used as a proxy for examining trends in juvenile crime and offending. Law enforcement provides "input" for the rest of the juvenile justice system, and thus understanding these inputs is critical for examining how the system responds to juvenile crime.

This section provides access to detailed Uniform Crime Report (UCR) statistics on juvenile arrests. It presents the most current year of available data and historical trends. Statistics include juvenile arrest counts and rates, nationally and at the state and county levels. The statistics are broken down by basic demographics (age, race, and sex)."

"Juveniles in Court"

This website (http://ojjdp.ncjrs.org/ojstatbb/court/index.html) provides valuable data about the youth who go to juvenile court. Of course, many delinquents don't make it to court but are **diverted** elsewhere in the system, and some who enter the system are also diverted. Of special interest are the **differences among select demographic variables** such as income gender and race. Thwe website provides many opportunities for analysis and comparison of variables and trends. We refer you to the excellent article in the "related readings," *Juvenile Court Statistics: 1999,* by Puzzanchera et. al.

Overview quoted from the website:

Law enforcement agencies refer approximately two-thirds of all arrested youth to a court with juvenile jurisdiction for further processing. As with law enforcement agencies, the court may decide to divert some juveniles away from the formal justice system to other agencies for service. Prosecutors may file some juvenile cases directly in criminal (adult) court. The net result is that juvenile courts formally process nearly 1 million delinquency offense cases annually. Juvenile courts adjudicate these cases and may order probation or residential placement, or they may waive jurisdiction and transfer certain cases from juvenile court to criminal court. While their cases are being processed, juveniles may be held in secure detention.

This section quantifies the flow of cases through the juvenile court system. It documents the nature of, and trends in, cases received and the court's response, and examines race and gender differences. The case processing information is drawn from the National Juvenile Court Data Archive's primary publication *Juvenile Court Statistics,* which is funded by the Office of Juvenile Justice and Delinquency Prevention.

"Juveniles on Probation"

This section of the OJJDP site (http://ojjdp.ncjrs.org/ojstatbb/probation/index.html) is interesting because it is opening new and **sophisticated datasets** to criminology students and researchers. And this site will continue to add new data as the joint research effort with George Mason University moves forward. You can learn the current state of affairs from the "Frequently Asked Questions" and with some good fortune the *Census and Survey of Juvenile Probation* will be available.

Overview quoted from the website:

Juvenile probation has been termed the "workhorse of the juvenile justice system." Probation is a mechanism used by juvenile justice agencies at many different points in the system. It serves as a sanction for juveniles adjudicated in court, and in many cases as a way of diverting status offenders or first-time juvenile offenders from the court system. Some communities may even use probation as a way of informally monitoring at-risk youth and preventing their progression into more serious problem behavior. With such varied uses, there is no doubt that probation touches large numbers of juveniles. For example, probation was ordered in 58% of the more than 1.1 million delinquency cases that received a juvenile court sanction in 2000, compared with 14% that received placement in an out-of-home facility.

Our knowledge about the number of juveniles on probation and the nature of their offenses has been limited to information based on the juvenile court's use of probation. To broaden the knowledge base, OJJDP is currently funding a study that will collect data to create useful, valid, reliable estimates of the number of juveniles on probation at a specific point in time (much like the information we have on juveniles in corrections), as well as information about the types of services and programs offered by juvenile probation offices. The Census and Survey of Juvenile Probation is being conducted jointly by the U.S. Bureau of the Census and George Mason University. Results should be available in late 2004.

This section provides basic information about juveniles on probation, based on juvenile court dispositions. As results from OJJDP's new study become available, more information will be added.

"Juveniles in Corrections"

This site (http://www.ncjrs.org/html/ojjdp/202885/contents.html) is exceptionally comprehensive in nature and extent of data on the subject. The importance of corrections for the **protection of society** is noted. The history-making **Chil-**

dren in Custody Census is appropriately cited for its importance. A fine summary of current knowledge is found in Melissa Sickmund's *Juveniles in Corrections* in the "Related Publications."

Overview quoted from the website:

"The most severe sanction that a juvenile court can impose entails the restriction of a juvenile's freedom through placement in a residential facility. Most often, such placement occurs after a youth has been adjudicated delinquent for an offense; however, a youth may also be held in detention after arrest or during court proceedings. In a few cases, jurisdiction over the youth might be transferred to criminal court, which then carries out processing and sentencing.

Out-of-home placement results in a great burden both on the youth who receive this sanction and on the juvenile justice system itself. The youth experience a disruption in their normal routines, schooling, and family/social relationships. The juvenile justice system must bear the responsibility for mental health care, substance abuse treatment, and education, among other requirements.

In developing its data collection efforts in this area, OJJDP acknowledged the importance of corrections for both maintaining the safety of the community and providing essential services to the youth involved. OJJDP annually surveys facilities that house these youth. In odd-numbered years, OJJDP administers the Census of Juveniles in Residential Placement (CJRP). This census gathers critical information on each youth in custody, including age, race, sex, and offense. In even-numbered years, OJJDP administers the Juvenile Residential Facility Census (JRFC), which collects important information on facility services and characteristics.

This section draws on data from the CJRP and its predecessor, the Children in Custody (CIC) Census, to answer a wide range of questions about juveniles in custody. For example:

- How old are most juveniles in residential placement?
- What proportion of juvenile offenders in custody are being held for violent offenses?
- Do the same facilities house both violent juvenile offenders and nonviolent offenders?

The latest numbers and historical trends, counts and rates, and data for the United States as a whole and for individual states are available on this site. "

"Juvenile Reentry and Aftercare"

This site (http://ojjdp.ncjrs.org/ojstatbb/reentry_aftercare/index.html) describes an aspect of corrections that is often **under-utilized** in our system . The **financial priorities** today often dictate that reenty and aftercare are substantially **under-funded**. Moreover, the **same can be said about much of diversion.**

Overview quoted from the website:

Youth who are released from institutional confinement are more likely to succeed if they have access to services that can help them thrive in a noninstitutional environment. When high-quality reentry and aftercare services are available, youth need to spend less time in confinement, and the overall cost of juvenile corrections can be reduced.

Effective reentry/aftercare programs begin before a youth leaves the facility and involve the family and the community. Developing and testing new models of juvenile reentry/aftercare services is a major focus of OJJDP.

Statistical information on this aspect of the juvenile justice system, although currently limited, should increase substantially in the future. OJJDP is committed to building knowledge in the field to support the development of successful reentry strategies. This section of the Statistical Briefing Book will provide policymakers, juvenile justice professionals, and the public with the latest available statistics on the characteristics of youth leaving confinement and their experiences after release.

From *Office of Juvenile Justice and Delinquency Prevention* 2005.

Fighting Crime, One Kid at a Time

By Isabelle de Pommereau

Special to The Christian Science Monitor
JERSEY CITY, N.J.

Detective Calvin Hart's unmarked black Chevy screeches to a halt near a bleak 13-story building. The high-rise is one of six in Curries Woods, a massive public housing complex infested with crime and drugs.

It's stop No. 1 on the detective's night-long patrol in Jersey City, N.J., a multiethnic city of 230,000. Detective Hart is a full-time juvenile cop, and his job tonight—and every night—is to keep an eye on troubled youths.

"Get your behind home," Hart warns a teenager on the roam. There's a tinge of affection in his voice. Malik, the teenager, retorts with a cunning smile. He's no stranger to Hart. The boy's uncle was a childhood friend of the detective's who was killed in a drug-related dispute not long ago.

Hart represents an emerging breed of cop dedicated solely to what has long been considered the nation's most intractable urban crime problem: juvenile delinquency.

While the overall crime rate is falling across most of the United States, crimes committed by youths continue unabated. Now, in growing numbers, cities like Reno, Nev., Memphis, and New York are recognizing the important role youth-focused community cops can play in helping kids stay on the right track.

"There's an outreach effort by police departments to have police officers not just show up when there's a problem, but be an intricate part of the fabric of the community and be there at all times to participate," says Steve Riddell of the National Council of Juvenile and Family Court Judges, at the University of Nevada in Reno.

For Hart, this new role means serving as the first-ever juvenile-intervention officer for Jersey City's 10 public housing projects, coordinating the city's new curfew law, and, perhaps most significant, being a near-father figure to hundreds of streetwise youths.

'He's in the real world'

As Hart unlocks the door of Curries Woods' Building 3, he points to the peep holes in the plywood front—the glass was shattered long ago. Children drilled the holes, he says, so they could keep a lookout for the police.

The lobby is a world of decay. The floor is strewn with cigarette butts and half-eaten fried chicken legs. The air smells of urine. And every inch of the walls is covered with graffiti. But Hart's presence immediately warms this sordid setting.

"Uncle Calvin!" exclaims a young girl bundled head to toe in a yellow coat. Lacovia Huggins breaks away from a cluster of friends to hug the detective.

"Hey darlin', how are you doing?" asks Hart. The police officer knows the stories of the girls on his beat. Too often those stories include early pregnancy, absent fathers, domestic abuse, and drugs.

If Hart's mission seems personal, that's because in many ways it is. For him, Jersey City is more than a police beat, it's home.

Born and raised here, he grew up with the parents and grandparents of the young people he now supervises.

"He's not an outsider even though he's on the police force. He's in the real world," says Jeanette Drayton, guidance counselor at a Jersey City elementary school where Hart often lectures on drug prevention. "He was brought up here. He sees the problems kids face everyday—he has empathy."

His style is distinctive: He is a follow-through cop. He arrests drug users but gets them into drug treatment. He puts convicted youths in jail but visits them in their cells and helps find them jobs when they're released. He plays basketball with the older kids, picks up the smaller children at school, and calls their mothers and school principals if trouble looms.

Still, Hart says he has sent many to jail, and he's seen a few die violently.

A veteran narcotics and homicide detective, Hart has the skills experts say are crucial for fighting juvenile crime. These include knowing when and how to use force and, more important, knowing how to connect with the kids on his beat.

The teens here have dubbed him The Creeper, a term of grudging respect for his ability to be "everywhere at once."

"He's about the only cop that gets respect out here," says Carmen Strickland, a teenage resident of Curries Woods.

Changing role of youth officers

A consensus is emerging among police departments and law-enforcement experts that officers like Hart have a central role to play in interrupting young criminal careers, if they can successfully form partnerships not only with teens but also with the community's schools, churches, and parents.

The concept of youth-focused policing has become popular in the past few years, and versions of it are being attempted in cities and towns around the country.

In Reno, Deputy Police Chief Ondra Berry says his first priority is for officers to connect with young people. In the Bronx, Sgt. Ricardo Aguirre is enlisting the help of his fellow officers to work with troubled youths through a counseling program he created called "Keep Our Kids Alive."

At a conference in Reno this week, more than 1,300 judges, law-enforcement officials, and other juvenile-crime experts are meeting to discuss the importance of youth-beat officers

and the changing face of juvenile justice.

While many experts say they are encouraged by the successes they've observed, they also believe that police departments must learn better ways to recruit and train juvenile cops.

'I went through it all—sleeping in abandoned buildings, standing in the soup lines—and I wouldn't wish it to my worst enemy. That's why I do what I do. It's ... my way of giving back and making sure that the kids don't do the same.'

—Detective Calvin Hart

"We have turned the philosophy [of juvenile policing] around, but what we haven't turned around is who we bring to be police officers and how we train them," says John Firman of the International Association of Chiefs of Police in Alexandria, Va.

"We're still looking for guys who're driving cars and firing guns," Mr. Firman says. "But the involvement of the officer has to be a personal one, a commitment to understanding the kids' lives."

From alcoholic to role model

In Jersey City, Detective Hart doesn't just try to understand kids' lives, he's "here to save lives," he says. And he knows what saving lives means, because he saved his own. For years, he was an alcoholic, and the addiction cost him his home, jobs, and family.

"I went through it all—sleeping in abandoned buildings, standing in the soup lines, and I wouldn't wish it to my worst enemy," Hart remembers. As a result, his wife, Linda, divorced him and took their baby daughter with her when she left.

Several years after Linda left, Hart says he finally got tired of leading a

self-destructive life. With the encouragement and support of a close friend who was a Jersey City police officer, Hart conquered his alcoholism. The friend also inspired him to become a cop.

"That's why I do what I do," Hart says. "It's kind of my way of giving back and making sure that the kids don't do the same [things I did]."

"I became the oldest rookie in the Jersey City Police Department I know," he jokes.

To make things complete, Linda came back and they remarried. They have another daughter and are also raising his niece.

In the Jersey City Police Department, Hart rose fast. Within a year, he was promoted to narcotics detective, then to homicide detective. The housing authority recruited him to help rid the Curries Woods complex of its drug scourge. Major drug busts helped improve life for the 712 families living there, he says.

But Hart also achieved something deeper—he got residents to trust the police, at a time when distrust was running high. Last year, he became the housing authority's first juvenile-intervention officer.

"He's like a father to the projects," says Ms. Strickland.

Make no mistake about it, however. Calvin Hart can be just as tough as he is friendly, and the kids know it.

"If you do something wrong, [Uncle Calvin] takes you where you're supposed to go," says Monique Richburg.

She learned that firsthand when she was arrested for delivering drugs. "He'll come get you, knock at your door. [But] he won't be nasty [or] forceful—others will probably beat you up."

A friend for struggling parents

Stop No. 2 tonight is the Curries Woods weekly parenting session at 7:30 p.m. It's a haven of warmth and cleanliness in Building 6, which was renovated recently as part of a multimillion-dollar effort to make 40-year-old Curries Woods more hospitable.

When Hart arrives, he's greeted with laughter and hugs. Many of the mothers here know the detective both as their friend and as the only positive male role model their children have ever had.

"When it comes to him talking to the little ones, he can do it," says Maxine Warner, who went to school with Hart and now relies on him as a friend to her grandchildren, whose father isn't around.

Many parents and guardians here know that their children will listen to Hart, if to nobody else. Claretha Roach, for example, brings her young son, Jamal—who has been cursing at his mother—to the meeting so Hart can talk to him.

"I know how to whip him," Hart says grinning.

But Hart needs only words and his broad shoulders to impress Jamal. He invites the boy to sit near him on a big couch, and then begins firing questions at him: What does Jamal want to do when he grows up?

Be a basketball star, responds the boy.

How many points does he score? Hart asks. Does he know that out of 100,000 high school basketball players, only about 600 make it to the top? And what will happen if Jamal isn't one of them?

Jamal looks at the officer intently. Hart tells Jamal he'd better stick with school; in fact, he'll pick him up at school tomorrow. A smile creeps across Jamal's face.

Tough when he has to be

It's about 10:30 p.m. now, and stop No. 3 is Curries Woods' Building 4, a grim high-rise soon to be demolished. As Hart makes his way toward the door, the teenagers outside spot him coming. But rather than scatter at his approach, the kids flock to him.

"Colleer," Hart yells to a boy with a baby face and braided hair. "You back in school?"

Silence.

"If you don't know, who does know?"

Silence still.

In a voice filled with exasperation, Hart warns the teen that he'll have a word with him tomorrow. It was, after all, the detective who locked up Colleer's two older brothers, who were major drug pins. And now, Hart worries that Colleer is selling "wet"—a mixture of marijuana and PCP—to younger kids.

But Hart's cheerfulness quickly comes back when Elliott Smith shows up. Hart and Mr. Smith enjoy each other's company.

"He used to be slinging [selling drugs] out here," Hart says. Smith explains that, after he did jail time, it was the detective who recommended him for a temporary job as a warehouse worker. Now, Hart hopes to get Smith a permanent job at the city recycling plant. "It's minimum wage, but it's work history," says Hart.

At home on the streets

As midnight approaches, Hart is back in his Chevy and heading toward Martin Luther King Drive. Once bustling with shoppers, the street now teems with drug activity day and night. It went downhill when its middle class fled, along with its banks and stores.

Hart recognizes many of the young people clustered on the corners, some brazenly offering drugs. He knows who controls what.

One corner is powered by the brothers of a girl who was caught carrying drugs.

"She did a favor, and she got caught," Hart says. He ponders aloud: "How can you let your sister get trapped like this?"

As the car moves along, he points to another corner where a young girl is standing alone. "This girl is a hooker," Hart says. "I put her in drug rehab, but she came right back [to drugs and prostitution.]"

Cruising along this grim street, the detective reveals his dreams of restoring the neighborhood to the bustling center it was when he was a boy.

He points to where his grandfather's restaurant used to be; now it's part of a public-housing complex. On another corner stands a dilapidated building that used to be the Rainbow Shop, where Hart would buy stockings for his mother.

"This was the showplace at one time," he says with some excitement.

When Hart reaches a ramshackle building next to the St. Stephen Holiness Church, he stops the car.

The boarded-up house used to be his aunt's. Now, Hart owns it, and he plans to turn it into a computer learning center for kids and cops.

"We talk a lot about space for kids, things for them to do," Hart muses, "and we don't live up to our bargain."

Kids and Guns: From Playgrounds to Battlegrounds

Stuart Greenbaum

Late last year an 11-year-old boy was shot and killed. An 18-year-old allegedly killed the boy because he had shorted him on drug money (Thomas and Martin, 1996). The shooting should have rocked the Chicago neighborhood where it took place, except that this kind of thing happens all too often.

The lethal mix of children and guns has reached a crisis in the United States. Teenage boys are more likely to die of gunshot wounds than from all natural causes combined. The number of children dying from gunshot wounds and the number of children committing homicides continue to rise at alarming rates (McEnery, 1996).

Guns are now the weapon of choice for youth. As can be seen in the following box, "Juvenile Gun Homicides," gun homicides by juveniles have tripled since 1983, while homicides involving other weapons have declined. From 1983 through 1995, the proportion of homicides in which a juvenile used a gun increased from 55 percent to 80 percent (Snyder and Finnegan, 1997).

Disputes that would previously have ended in fist fights are now more likely to lead to shootings. A 1993 Louis Harris poll showed that 35 percent of children ages 6 to 12 fear their lives will be cut short by gun violence (Louis Harris and Associates, Inc., 1993). A 1990 Centers for Disease Control and Prevention study found that one in five 9th through 12th graders reported carrying a weapon in the past month; one in five of those carried a firearm (Centers for Disease Control and Prevention, 1991).

Buying guns illegally is relatively easy for juveniles.

"No corner of America is safe from increasing levels of criminal violence, including violence committed by and against juveniles," Attorney General Janet Reno has observed. "Parents are afraid to let their children walk to school alone. Children hesitate to play in neighborhood playgrounds. The elderly lock themselves in their homes, and innocent Americans of all ages find their lives changed by the fear of crime" (Coordinating Council on Juvenile Justice and Delinquency Prevention, 1996).

The number of murdered juveniles increased 47 percent between 1980 and 1994, according to figures from *Juvenile Offenders and Victims: 1996 Update on Violence* (Snyder et al., 1996). The Summary, which cites data from the Federal Bureau of Investigation's Uniform Crime Reporting Program, notes that from 1980 through 1994 an estimated 326,170 persons were murdered in the United States. Of these, 9 percent (30,200) were youth under age 18. While there was a 1-percent increase from 1980 through 1994 in the total number of murders, the rate of juveniles murdered increased from five per day to seven per day. Fifty-three percent of the juveniles killed in 1994 were teenagers ages 15 to 17, while 30 percent were younger than age 6. In 1994, one in five murdered juveniles was killed by a juvenile offender.

Programs to get guns out of the hands of young people are being put into place.

Recently, however, there has been good news. Between 1994 and 1995, juvenile arrests for murder declined 14 percent, resulting in the number of juvenile murder arrests in 1995 being 9 percent below the 1991 figure. Overall arrests for violent juvenile crime decreased 3 percent between

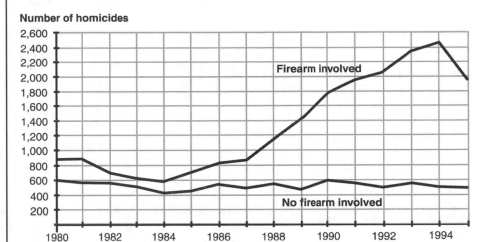

Juvenile Gun Homicides

Gun homicides by juveniles have tripled since 1983, while homicides involving other weapons have declined.

Number of homicides

Firearm involved

No firearm involved

◆ From 1983 through 1995, the proportion of homicides in which a juvenile used a gun increased from 55 to 80 percent.

Source: Snyder, H.N., and T.A. Finnegan. 1997. *Easy Access to the FBI's Supplementary Homicide Reports: 1980-1995* (data presentation and analysis package). Washington, DC: U.S. Department of Justice, Office of Justice Programs, Office of Juvenile Justice and Delinquency Prevention.

1994 and 1995—the first decline in 9 years. These efforts must continue, however, as even these reduced rates are substantially higher than 1986 levels (Snyder, 1997).

Often, teenagers turn guns on themselves. In 1991, 1,889 teens ages 15 to 19 committed suicide—a rate of 11 per 100,000 (Allen-Hagen et al., 1994). Between 1980 and 1994, the suicide rate for 15- to 19-year-olds rose 29 percent, with an increase in firearms-related suicides accounting for 96 percent of the rise (Centers for Disease Control and Prevention, 1996). The risk of suicide is five times greater for individuals living in households with guns than for those in households without guns (Kellerman et al., 1992).

What is causing this epidemic of violence and how can it be stopped? The deterioration of the traditional family and the impact of drugs, gangs, poverty, and violence in the media are among the factors cited as contributing to the violent behavior of today's teens. Many of these children—victims and perpetrators—come from one- or no-parent families (McEnery, 1996).

Guns are readily available to juveniles. Although Federal law mandates that a person must be at least 18 years old to purchase a shotgun or rifle, and at least 21 years old to buy a handgun, law enforcement officials and youth themselves report that buying guns illegally is relatively easy for juveniles. Increasingly, juveniles believe they need guns for protection or carry them as status symbols. As more guns appear in the community, a local arms race ensues.

This article describes some promising steps that have been taken to curb the violence endangering our youth and our communities. It also provides information about a number of initiatives that have focused on gun violence in particular.

U.S. Attorneys Join the Fight

Local, State, and national programs to get guns out of the hands of young people are being put in place. In a report to the Attorney General and the President, U.S. Attorneys outlined the following ways in which they are supporting State and local programs:

- Disrupting the markets that provide guns to youth.
- Taking guns out of the hands of young people through coordination with State and local law enforcement officials.
- Working with State and local prosecutors to enhance enforcement of their laws.
- Encouraging and providing financial support for State and local efforts to trace the sources of guns taken from juveniles.
- Launching targeted enforcement efforts in places where young people should feel safe, such as their homes, schools, and recreation centers.
- Participating in prevention efforts directed at juveniles in our communities through mentor-

ing, adopt-a-school (in which schools are "adopted" by civic groups or businesses), and Neighborhood Watch programs.

• Promoting increased personal responsibility and safety through public outreach and information on the consequences of juvenile handgun possession (Office of Juvenile Justice and Delinquency Prevention, 1996).

These approaches, also supported by other components of the U.S. Department of Justice (DOJ), are critical elements of a comprehensive youth gun violence reduction strategy.

To advance the U.S. Attorneys' violence prevention efforts and to help States and local jurisdictions respond to the problem of juvenile firearms violence, the Office of Juvenile Justice and Delinquency Prevention (OJJDP) published *Reducing Youth Gun Violence: An Overview of Programs and Initiatives* (Office of Juvenile Justice and Delinquency Prevention, 1996). This report provides information on a wide array of strategies—from school-based prevention to gun market interception. In addition to program descriptions, the report includes a directory of youth gun violence prevention organizations and a bibliography of research, evaluation, and publications on youth and guns.

Promising Programs

Many State and local programs designed to take guns out of the hands of teenagers have proven successful. In the Kansas City (Missouri) Gun Experiment, the U.S. Attorney's Office and the Kansas City Police Department worked with local agencies to focus law enforcement efforts on high-crime neighborhoods. Under this initiative, developed with Weed and Seed funding from the Bureau of Justice Assistance, traffic law violators were routinely stopped, as were youth violating curfews and individuals involved in other infractions of the law. During these stops, police looked for violations that established legal authority to search a car or pedestrian for illegal guns. These special gun-interception teams were 10 times more cost-effective than regular police patrols.

The experience of victimization by violence is far too common among children.

The success of the Kansas City Gun Experiment is striking. An evaluation funded by the National Institute of Justice (NIJ) found that crime in the 80-block target neighborhood, which had a homicide rate 20 times the national average, was cut in half in 6 months. Significantly, the program did not merely displace crime to other locations. Gun crimes did not increase in any of the

seven surrounding patrol beats. The active involvement of community and religious leaders in the development of the program resulted in broad support for the program in the community, which had objected to past police crackdowns on guns (Sherman et al., 1995).

In Boston, where juveniles in high-risk neighborhoods frequently carry guns, NIJ has launched a problem-solving project to devise, implement, and assess strategic interventions to disrupt illicit firearms markets and deter youth violence. Its initial focus was analyzing the supply and demand for guns. Strategic interventions by police, probation, and parole officers have presented gang members—prevalent among both victims and offenders—with a clear choice: Stop the flow of guns and stop the violence or face rapid, focused, and comprehensive law enforcement and corrections attention. Although it is too soon to evaluate the long-term effectiveness of this strategy, its immediate impact is encouraging; youth violence in Boston appears to have been substantially reduced (Kennedy, 1997).

Child abuse and neglect nearly doubled between 1986 and 1993.

NIJ's promising initiative in Boston was highlighted at OJJDP's August 1996 national satellite teleconference, Reducing Youth Gun Violence, which was viewed by more than 8,000 participants at 271 downlink sites. The teleconference, which is available on videotape from OJJDP's Juvenile Justice Clearinghouse, also featured the Detroit-based Handgun Intervention Program, carried out by volunteers in Michigan's 36th District Court, and the Shock Mentor Program, a collaborative effort among Prince George's County, Maryland, Public Schools, the Washington, D.C., chapter of Concerned Black Men, Inc., and Prince George's Hospital Center.

Partnerships To Reduce Juvenile Gun Violence

Based on a review of research and programs conducted by OJJDP and summarized in *Reducing Youth Gun Violence: An Overview of Programs and Initiatives,* OJJDP has started a new initiative, Partnerships To Reduce Juvenile Gun Violence. This effort is intended to increase the effectiveness of existing youth gun violence reduction strategies by enhancing and coordinating prevention, intervention, and suppression strategies and by strengthening linkages among the community, law enforcement, and the juvenile justice system. Its comprehensive approach addresses three critical factors: juveniles' access to guns, the reasons young people carry guns, and the reasons they choose to use guns to resolve conflicts. Partnerships have been forged through recent OJJDP grants to the Center for Community Alternatives in Syracuse, New

York; the City of East Baton Rouge, Louisiana; the Council on Alcoholism and Drug Abuse of Northwest Louisiana; and Youth ALIVE!, which services Oakland and Los Angeles, California.

OJJDP is funding an evaluation of Partnerships To Reduce Juvenile Gun Violence to document and analyze the process of community mobilization, planning, and collaboration needed to develop a comprehensive approach to combating youth gun violence.

The fundamental challenge in reducing juvenile firearm possession is to convince youth that they can survive in their neighborhoods without being armed. Community-based programs such as those listed above are working to dispel the perception by many juveniles that the authorities can neither protect them nor maintain order in their neighborhoods. A number of communities have implemented programs that address the risk of victimization, improve school safety, and foster a secure community environment.

Victimization and the Cycle of Violence

The experience of victimization by violence is far too common among children in America. A survey of inner-city high school students revealed that 45 percent had been threatened with a gun or shot at, and one in three had been beaten up on their way to school (Sheley and Wright, 1993). According to a survey released by the U.S. Department of Health and Human Services, child abuse and neglect nearly doubled between 1986 and 1993 (Sedlak and Broadhurst, 1996). Investigations by child protective services agencies in 49 States determined that more than 1 million children were victims of substantiated or indicated child abuse and neglect in 1995 (National Center on Child Abuse and Neglect, 1997).

OJJDP and NIJ have supported several studies focusing on this cycle of violence. The research indicates a relationship between experiences of childhood violence and subsequent delinquent behavior. OJJDP's Rochester (New York) Youth Development Study found that children who had been victims of violence were 24 percent more likely to report engaging in violent behavior as adolescents than those who had not been maltreated in childhood (Thornberry, 1994). An NIJ longitudinal study of childhood victimization found that child abuse increases the likelihood of future delinquency and adult criminality by nearly 40 percent (Widom, 1992).

With funding support from OJJDP, the New Haven (Connecticut) Department of Police Services and the Yale Child Study Center established the Child Development-Community Policing (CD-CP) program to address the adverse impact of continued exposure to violence on children and their families and to interrupt the cycle of violence affecting so many of our children. Reflecting New Haven's commendable commitment to community policing, the program brings law enforcement and mental health professionals together to help children who are victims, witnesses, and (in some instances) perpetrators of violent acts. The CD-CP program serves as a model for police-mental health partnerships across the Nation and is being replicated under the CD-CP grant in Buffalo, New York; Charlotte, North Carolina; Nashville, Tennessee; and Portland, Oregon (Marans and Berkman, 1997). In fiscal year 1997, OJJDP is enhancing the CD-CP program to provide training to school personnel, probation and parole officers, and prosecutors.

Public Information Campaigns

Researchers have found that long-term public education campaigns on violence prevention, family education, alcohol and drug prevention, and gun safety curriculums in schools are effective in helping to reduce delinquency (American Academy of Pediatrics, 1992; Centers for Disease Control and Prevention, 1991; Christoffel, 1991; DeJong, 1994). This may be especially true for education campaigns to prevent gun violence, because public awareness of positive activities can reduce fear, which is a powerful factor in juveniles choosing to carry guns. Involving teenagers in the development and operation of these programs is a critical ingredient to a program's success (Treanor and Bijlefeld, 1989). The public and private sectors, including the media, also can play significant roles in program design and implementation.

The goal of public information and education efforts should be threefold: to change public perceptions about youth violence and guns, to educate the community about the problem, and to convince youth and adults that their involvement is essential to the success of any program to curb possession and use of guns by youth. Public information campaigns can empower citizens to reach informed judgments about effective ways of preventing firearms violence by and against juveniles.

Public information campaigns can empower citizens to reach informed judgments.

Public information campaigns to reduce gun violence should:

- Provide accurate information to key policymakers about the causes, nature, and extent of juvenile delinquency and victimization, particularly gun-related violence.
- Communicate that juvenile gun violence and victimization are preventable.
- Publicize strategies and results of successful programs and encourage their replication.
- Motivate individuals, government agencies, and community service organizations to work

collaboratively to address the problem as a key to ensuring public safety.

A number of public information campaigns have been launched or are being developed. In California, the state-wide Campaign To Prevent Handgun Violence Against Kids has produced 30-second television public service announcements (PSA's) in English and Spanish; communicated critical information on youth gun violence to elected officials, media leaders, and public agencies; and received thousands of calls through its hotline and information service (Office of Juvenile Justice and Delinquency Prevention, 1996).

To assist communities in their public education efforts, the Center to Prevent Handgun Violence collaborated with Disney Educational Productions (1994) to produce *Under the Gun: A Story About Violence Prevention.] The video, intended for educational and law enforcement agencies, refutes the notion that guns are glamorous and that carrying guns makes communities safer.*

OJJDP and the Bureau of Justice Assistance are funding a public-private partnership to create and market PSA's with a three-part message designed to persuade young people to turn away from violence, educate parents and other community residents about solutions to youth violence, and show teens, parents, and youth-serving professionals how they can become part of the solution.

Conclusion

As disturbing as youth gun violence is, it need not be inevitable. It is preventable—Äas many programs throughout the United States are beginning to demonstrate. With the public alarmed about the problem, public servants and practitioners might bear in mind the Greek philosopher Solon's words, "There can be no justice until those of us who are unaffected by crime become as indignant as those who are."

References

Allen-Hagen, B., M. Sickmund, and H.N. Snyder. 1994 (November). *Juveniles and Violence: Juvenile Offending and Victimization.* Fact Sheet. Washington, DC: U.S. Department of Justice, Office of Justice Programs, Office of Juvenile Justice and Delinquency Prevention.

American Academy of Pediatrics, Committee on Adolescence. 1992. Firearms and adolescence. *Pediatrics] 89(4):784–787.*

Centers for Disease Control and Prevention. 1996 (November). *National Summary of Injury Mortality Data, 1987–1994.* Atlanta, GA: Centers for Disease Control and Prevention, National Center for Injury Prevention and Control.

Centers for Disease Control and Prevention. 1991. Weapon carrying among high school students: United States, 1990. *Morbidity and Mortality Weekly Report* 40(40):681–684.

Christoffel, K.K. 1991. Toward reducing pediatric injuries from firearms: Charting a legislative and regulatory course. *Pediatrics* 88(2):294–305.

Coordinating Council on Juvenile Justice and Delinquency Prevention. 1996 (March). *Combating Violence and Delinquency: The National Juvenile Justice Action Plan.* Report. Washing-ton, DC: U.S. Department of Justice, Office of Justice Programs, Office of Juvenile Justice and Delinquency Prevention.

DeJong, W. 1994 (November). *Preventing Interpersonal Violence Among Youth: An Introduction to School, Community and Mass Media Strategies.* NIJ Issues and Practices. Washington, DC: U.S. Department of Justice, Office of Justice Programs, National Institute of Justice.

Disney Educational Productions. 1994. *Under the Gun: A Story About Violence Prevention.* Burbank: The Walt Disney Company.

Kellermann, A.L., F.P. Rivara, G. Somes, D.T. Reay, J. Francisco, G. Banton, J. Prodzinski, C. Fligner, and B.B. Hackman. 1992. Suicide in the home in relation to gun ownership. *New England Journal of Medicine* 327:467–472.

Kennedy, D.M. 1997 (March). *Juvenile Gun Violence and Gun Markets in Boston.* Research Preview. Washington, DC: U.S. Department of Justice, Office of Justice Programs, National Institute of Justice.

Louis Harris and Associates, Inc. 1993. *A Survey of Experiences, Perceptions and Apprehensions About Guns Among Young People in America.* New York, NY: Louis Harris and Associates, Inc., and LH Research, Inc.

Marans, S., and M. Berkman. 1997 (March). *Child Development-Community Policing: Partnership in a Climate of Violence.* Bulletin. Washington, DC: U.S. Department of Justice, Office of Justice Programs, Office of Juvenile Justice and Delinquency Prevention.

McEnery, R. Today's schoolyard bully just might be armed. *Asbury Park Press.* Feb. 28, 1996.

National Center on Child Abuse and Neglect. 1997. *Child Maltreatment 1995: Reports from the States to the National Child Abuse and Neglect Data System.* Washington, DC: U.S. Department of Health and Human Services, National Center on Child Abuse and Neglect.

Office of Juvenile Justice and Delinquency Prevention. 1996 (May). *Reducing Youth Gun Violence: An Overview of Programs and Initiatives.* Program Report. Washington, DC: U.S. Department of Justice, Office of Justice Programs, Office of Juvenile Justice and Delinquency Prevention.

Sedlak, A.J., and D.D. Broadhurst. 1996 (September). *Third National Incidence Study of Child Abuse and Neglect.* Washington, DC: U.S. Department of Health and Human Services, National Center on Child Abuse and Neglect.

Sheley, J.F., and J.D. Wright. 1993 (December). *Gun Acquisition and Possession in Selected Juvenile Samples.* Research in Brief. Washington, DC: U.S. Department of Justice, Office of Justice Programs, National Institute of Justice and Office of Juvenile Justice and Delinquency Prevention.

Sherman, L.W., J.W. Shaw, and D.P. Rogan. 1995 (January). *The Kansas City Gun Experiment.* Research in Brief. Washington, DC: U.S. Department of Justice, Office of Justice Programs, National Institute of Justice.

Snyder, H.N. 1997 (February). *Juvenile Arrests 1995.* Bulletin. Washington, DC: U.S. Department of Justice, Office of Justice Programs, Office of Juvenile Justice and Delinquency Prevention.

Snyder, H.N., and M. Sickmund. 1995 (August). *Juvenile Offenders and Victims: A National Report.* Washington, DC: U.S. Department of Justice, Office of Justice Programs, Office of Juvenile Justice and Delinquency Prevention.

Snyder, H.N., M. Sickmund, and E. Poe-Yamagata. 1996 (February). *Juvenile Offenders and Victims: 1996 Update on Violence.* Statistics Summary. Washington, DC: U.S. Department of Justice, Office of Justice Programs, Office of Juvenile Justice and Delinquency Prevention.

Snyder, H.N., and T.A. Finnegan. 1997. *Easy Access to the FBI's Supplementary Homicide Reports: 1980–1995* (data presentation and analysis package). Washington, DC: U.S. Department of Justice, Office of Justice Programs, Office of Juvenile Justice and Delinquency Prevention.

Thomas, J., and A. Martin. Notorious block's deadly legacy, West Adams Street's world of fear, drugs, death. *Chicago Tribune.* Nov. 23, 1996.

Thornberry, T. 1994 (December). *Violent Families and Youth Violence.* Fact Sheet. Washington, DC: U.S. Department of Justice, Office of Justice Programs, Office of Juvenile Justice and Delinquency Prevention.

Treanor, W.W., and M. Bijlefeld. 1989. *Kids and Guns: A Child Safety Scandal.* Washington, DC: American Youth Work Center and Educational Fund to End Handgun Violence.

Widom, C.S. 1992 (October). *The Cycle of Violence.* Research in Brief. Washington, DC: U.S. Department of Justice, Office of Justice Programs, National Institute of Justice.

Stuart Greenbaum is president of Greenbaum Public Relations, a Sacramento, California, firm that specializes in public interest concerns, including high-risk youth services. A 20-year veteran of public safety communication, Mr. Greenbaum is a cofounder and past communications director of the National School Safety Center at Pepperdine University.

From *Juvenile Justice,* September 1997, pp. 3-10. Reprinted by permission of the U.S. Department of Justice, Office of Juvenile Justice and Delinquency Prevention.

**Bureau of Justice Statistics
Special Report**

State Court Processing Statistics, 1990–94

Juvenile Felony Defendants in Criminal Courts

BY
Kevin J. Strom and **Steven K. Smith**
BJS Statisticians
Howard N. Snyder
National Center for Juvenile Justice

In the Nation's 75 largest counties, juveniles handled as adults in criminal courts represented about 1% of all felony defendants. State statutes define which persons are under the original jurisdiction of the juvenile court system. In 1994, 39 States and the District of Columbia defined the upper age limit of juvenile court jurisdiction at age 17. The remaining 11 States set the upper age limit below age 17. Three States (Connecticut, New York, and North Carolina) defined 16- and 17-year-olds as adults. Eight States (Georgia, Illinois, Louisiana, Massachusetts, Michigan, Missouri, Texas, and South Carolina) defined 17-year-olds as adults.

Each State legislature, however, has put in place mechanisms that enable persons classified as juveniles in the State to be transferred to the adult justice system and handled in criminal court. These mechanisms include judicial waiver, concurrent jurisdiction, and statutorily excluding certain offenses from juvenile court jurisdiction. (See box, "Mechanisms by which juveniles can reach criminal court.")

Juveniles in criminal and juvenile courts

This report presents data on juveniles prosecuted as felony defendants in criminal courts within the Nation's 75 largest counties. Comparable data are also presented on juvenile defendants formally processed in the juvenile court system in a selected number of the Nation's 75 largest counties.

Every 2 years the Bureau of Justice Statistics (BJS) gathers information on a sample of felony defendants through the State Court Processing Statistics (SOPS) project. Data for this report were combined from the 1990, 1992, and 1994 data collections. An estimated 7,110 defendants under age 18 faced

charges in criminal court during May in the 3-year period— about a fourth (23%) of whom, based on age, would be considered juveniles by State law. Juvenile court data were provided by the National Center for Juvenile Justice (NCJJ).

Highlights

Juvenile defendants in criminal courts

• In the Nation's 75 largest counties, juveniles transferred to criminal courts represented about 1% of all felony defendants.

• Juveniles transferred to criminal court were generally violent felony offenders. Two-thirds were charged with a violent offense, including about 11% with murder, 34% with robbery, and 15% charged with felony assault.

• 63% of juveniles transferred to criminal courts were black males, 29% were white males, 3% were black females, and 2% were white females.

• 59% of juveniles transferred to criminal courts were convicted of a felony, and 52% of those convicted of a felony were sentenced to prison.

• About a third of juveniles in criminal courts sentenced to State prison received a sentence of 4 years or less. The average prison sentence for juveniles convicted in criminal courts was about 9 years; for those convicted of a violent offense, the average prison sentence was nearly 11 years.

Defendants in juvenile courts

• In the 75 largest counties, nearly 2% of juveniles handled in juvenile courts were transferred to criminal courts by judicial waiver. Among those referred to juvenile court for murder, 37% were judicially waived to criminal court.

• Of juveniles formally processed in juvenile courts, 48% were white males; 36%, black males; 7%, white females; and 5%, black females.

• 55% of juvenile defendants formally processed in juvenile courts were adjudicated delinquent.

• Among juvenile defendants adjudicated delinquent, 40% received a disposition of residential placement and 50% received formal probation.

Juvenile defendants in the 75 largest counties, 1990, 1992, and 1994

Characteristic	Criminal court	Juvenile court
Male	92%	88%
Female	8	12
White	31%	55%
Black	67	41
Other	2	4
Most serious arrest charge		
Violent	66%	24%
Property	17	46
Drug	14	13

Table 1. Characteristics of juvenile defendants in criminal and juvenile courts in the Nation's 75 largest counties, 1990, 1992, and 1994

Characteristic	Percent of juveniles in —	
	Criminal court	Juvenile court
Sex		
Male	92%	88%
Female	8	12
Race		
White	31%	55%
Black	67	41
Other	2	4
Age at arrest		
14 and under	8%	--
15	24	36
16	27	35
17	40	26
18 or over	--	3

Note: 1,638 juvenile defendants were prosecuted as adults in the Nation's 75 largest counties during May 1990, 1992, and 1994. 370,424 defendants were formally processed in juvenile courts in a selected number of the Nation's 75 largest counties in 1990, 1992, and 1994. Data on sex of defendants were available for 99% of the cases; on defendants' race, for 85%. General offense categories include offenses other than those displayed.
--Adult court sample includes only defendants under 18. Juvenile court sample includes only defendants age 15 or older.

Table 2. Most serious arrest charge for juvenile felony defendants in criminal courts, 1990, 1992, and 1994

Most serious arrest charge	Percent of juvenile defendants in the criminal courts of the Nation's 75 largest counties
All offenses	100%
Violent offenses	66%
Murder	11
Rape	3
Robbery	34
Assault	15
Property offenses	17%
Burglary	6
Theft	8
Drug offenses	14%
Public-order offenses	3%

Note: 1,638 juvenile defendants were prosecuted as adults in the Nation's 75 largest counties during May 1990, 1992, and 1994. Data for most serious arrest charge available for 100% of all cases. Detail may not add to total because of rounding. General offense categories include offenses other than those displayed.

The National Juvenile Court Data Archive provided data on more than 370,000 juvenile defendants formally processed in juvenile courts in a selected number of counties among the Nation's 75 largest. (See Methodology for description of sampled counties from the NCJJ.)

Most serious arrest charge

Criminal court

Among juveniles prosecuted in criminal courts in the Nation's 75 largest counties, two-thirds were charged with a violent felony offense—including robbery (34%), assault (15%), and murder (11%) (table 2). About a sixth were charged with a felony property offense. For the remainder of juveniles in criminal courts, the most serious arrest charge was a drug (14%) or a public-order offense (3%). Public-order offenses include weapons charges, driving-related charges, and other violations of social order.

Juvenile court

An estimated 24% of the defendants in juvenile courts in the Nation's 75 largest counties were referred for violent offenses, about 18% for public-order offenses, and 13% for drug-related offenses (table 3). Slightly less than half of the defendants in juvenile courts were referred for property offenses (46%)—including theft (22%) and burglary (13%).

Demographics

Criminal court

In the Nation's 75 largest counties, 92% of juveniles in criminal courts were male, with the proportion of male offenders varying slightly by offense type (table 4).

Table 3. Most serious referral offense for juvenile defendants age 15 or older in juvenile courts, 1990, 1992, and 1994

Most serious referral charge	Percent of defendants in juvenile courts of the Nation's 75 largest counties
All offenses	100%
Violent offenses	24%
Murder[a]	--
Rape[b]	1
Robbery	6
Assault	15
Property offenses	46%
Burglary	13
Theft	22
Drug offenses	13%
Public-order offenses	18%

Note: 370,424 defendants were formally processed in juvenile courts in a selected number of the Nation's 75 largest counties in 1990, 1992, and 1994. These defendants were not transferred to criminal court for prosecution. Data for most serious referral charge were available for 100% of all cases. Detail may not add to total because of rounding. The juvenile court sample represents counties from the National Juvenile Court Data Archive that were included in the Nation's 75 largest counties. General offense categories include offenses other than those displayed.
--Less than .05%.
[a]Murder includes manslaughter.
[b]Rape includes other violent sex offenses.

Table 4. Sex and race of juvenile felony defendants in criminal court, by most serious arrest charge: 1990, 1992, and 1994

Most serious arrest charge	Percent of juvenile felony defendants in the 75 largest counties						
	Sex			Race			
	Total	Male	Female	Total	White	Black	Other
All offenses	100%	92%	8%	100%	31%	67%	2%
Violent offenses	100%	92%	8%	100%	25%	73%	2%
Murder	100	96	4	100	25	69	6
Rape	100	89	11	100	28	72	0
Robbery	100	87	13	100	16	82	3
Assault	100	97	3	100	39	61	0
Property offenses	100%	95%	5%	100%	63%	31%	6%
Burglary	100	100	0	100	82	13	4
Theft	100	95	5	100	49	42	9
Drug offenses	100%	92%	8%	100%	19%	81%	0%
Public-order offenses	100%	89%	11%	100%	23%	77%	0%

Note: 1,638 juvenile defendants were prosecuted as adults in the Nation's 75 largest counties during May 1990, 1992, and 1994. Data on sex and race of defendants were available for 99% of all eligible cases. Detail may not add to total because of rounding. Zero indicates no cases in the sample. General offense categories include offenses other than those displayed.

Table 5. Sex and race of juvenile defendants in juvenile court, by most serious referral charge: 1990, 1992, and 1994

Most serious referral charge	Percent of defendants in juvenile courts of the Nation's 75 largest counties						
	Sex			Race			
	Total	Male	Female	Total	White	Black	Other
All offenses	100%	88%	12%	100%	55%	41%	4%
Violent offenses	100%	86%	14%	100%	48%	48%	4%
Murder[a]	100	94	5	100	59	36	5
Rape[b]	100	98	2	100	44	53	3
Robbery	100	92	8	100	37	60	3
Assault	100	82	18	100	51	45	4
Property offenses	100%	88%	12%	100%	61%	35%	4%
Burglary	100	94	6	100	69	26	5
Theft	100	83	17	100	56	40	4
Drug offenses	100%	92%	8%	100%	40%	59%	1%
Public-order offenses	100%	87%	13%	100%	59%	37%	4%

Note: 370,424 defendants were formally processed in juvenile courts of the Nation's 75 largest counties in 1990, 1992, and 1994. These defendants were not transferred to criminal court for prosecution. Data on sex of defendants were available for 100% of cases and for race of defendants, for 88% of all eligible cases. Detail may not add to total because of rounding. The juvenile court sample represents counties from the National Juvenile Court Data Archive that were included in the Nation's 75 largest counties. General offense categories include offenses other than those displayed.
[a] Murder includes manslaughter.
[b] Rape includes other violent sex offenses.

Females, who represented about 8% of all juvenile defendants in criminal courts, were charged with a violent offense in over 70% of cases (not shown in table). Over half of female defendants in criminal court were charged with robbery (55%).

Two-thirds of the juveniles in criminal courts were black, almost a third were white, and the remaining defendants were members of other racial groups.

Black males comprised 7 in 10 violent juvenile defendants in criminal courts (not shown in a table). About 65% of juvenile murder defendants in criminal court were black males, 72% of rape defendants, 78% of robbery defendants, 61% of assault defendants, and 65% of defendants charged with other types of violent crime.

Three-fourths of juvenile drug offenses in criminal court involved a black male defendant, as did two-thirds of public-order charges. White males comprised the majority of juveniles charged with burglary (82%).

Juvenile court

As in criminal court, juvenile defendants in juvenile courts were largely male (88%). By offense, males comprised the largest percentages among defendants referred to juvenile court for rape (98%), burglary (94%), and murder (94%) (table 5).

Fifty-five percent of defendants processed in juvenile courts were white, 41% were black, and 4% were members of other racial groups. Whites accounted for 59% of the murder defendants referred to juvenile court, 51% of assault defendants, 69% of burglary, 56% of theft, and 59% of public-order defendants. Black defendants comprised 53% of defendants referred to juvenile court for rape, 60% of robbery, and 59% of drug defendants.

Overall, black males accounted for about a third of defendants in juvenile courts (not shown in a table). About 40% of violent defendants in juvenile court were black males compared to 70% of violent juveniles in criminal courts. White males accounted for the majority of juvenile defendants referred to juvenile courts for murder (55%) and burglary (64%).

Pretrial release and detention

Criminal court

Overall, about half of juveniles prosecuted in criminal courts were released prior to the final disposition of their case (table 6). Public-or-

Table 6. Juvenile felony defendants in criminal court released before or detained until case disposition, by most serious arrest charge, 1990, 1992, and 1994

Most serious arrest charge	Juvenile defendants in the criminal courts of the Nation's 75 largest counties		
	Total	Detained until case disposition	Released before case disposition
All offenses	100%	49%	51%
Violent offenses	100%	56%	44%
Murder	100	87	13
Rape	100	53	47
Robbery	100	45	55
Assault	100	53	47
Property offenses	100%	26%	74%
Burglary	100	34	66
Theft	100	25	75
Drug offenses	100%	37%	63%
Public-order offenses	100%	81%	19%

Note: 1,638 juvenile defendants were prosecuted as adults in the Nation's 75 largest counties during May 1990, 1992, and 1994. Data on pretrial release were available for 93% of all eligible cases. Details may not add to total because of rounding. General offense categories include offenses other than those displayed.

der (19%) and violent (44%) juvenile defendants were the least likely to be released pretrial, while property (74%) and drug (63%) defendants were the most likely.

About half of juveniles in criminal courts charged with robbery (55%), assault (47%), or rape (47%) were released pretrial. Thirteen percent of juvenile murder defendants in criminal courts were released prior to case disposition.

Juvenile court

Over half of violent defendants in juvenile courts were released pretrial (57%), as were about two-thirds of those charged with property (71%), drug (60%), or public-order (65%) offenses (table 7). Among defendants referred to juvenile courts, 22% of murder defendants, 45% of robbery, and 56% of rape defendants were released pretrial.

Table 7. Juvenile defendants age 15 or older detained at any time prior to case disposition in juvenile court, by most serious referral charge, 1990, 1992, and 1994

Most serious referral charge	Defendants in juvenile courts of the Nation's 75 largest counties		
	Total	Detained[a]	Released
All offenses	100%	35%	65%
Violent offenses	100%	43%	57%
Murder[b]	100	78	22
Rape[c]	100	44	56
Robbery	100	55	45
Assault	100	38	62
Property offenses	100%	29%	71%
Burglary	100	35	65
Theft	100	28	72
Drug offenses	100%	40%	60%
Public-order offenses	100%	35%	65%

Note: 370,424 defendants were formally processed in juvenile courts of the Nation's 75 largest counties in 1990, 1992, and 1994. These defendants were not transferred to criminal court for prosecution. Data on pretrial release were available for 71% of all eligible cases. Details may not add to total because of rounding. The juvenile court sample represents counties from the National Juvenile Court Data Archive that were included in the Nation's 75 largest counties. General offense categories include offenses not shown.
[a]Includes those who did not post bail.
[b]Murder includes manslaughter.
[c]Rape includes other violent sex offenses.

Table 9. Adjudication outcome for defendants age 15 or above in juvenile courts, by most serious referral offense, 1990, 1992, and 1994

Most serious referral offense	Defendants in juvenile courts of the Nation's 75 largest counties		
		Adjudicated	
	Total	Delinquent	Not delinquent
All offenses	100%	55%	45%
Violent offenses	100%	51%	49%
Murder[a]	100	58	42
Rape[b]	100	55	45
Robbery	100	55	45
Assault	100	48	52
Property offenses	100%	55%	45%
Burglary	100	56	44
Theft	100	57	43
Drug offenses	100%	55%	45%
Public-order offenses	100%	59%	41%

Note: 370,424 defendants were formally processed in juvenile courts of the Nation's 75 largest counties in 1990, 1992, and 1994. These defendants were not transferred to criminal court for prosecution. Data on adjudication outcome were available for 100% of the eligible cases. The juvenile court sample represents counties from the National Juvenile Court Data Archive that were included in the Nation's 75 largest counties. General offense categories include offenses not shown.
[a]Murder includes manslaughter.
[b]Rape includes other violent sex offenses.

Table 8. Adjudication outcome for felony defendants defined as juveniles, by most serious arrest charge, 1990, 1992, and 1994

Most serious arrest charge	Percent of felony defendants defined as juveniles in the 75 largest counties							
		Convicted				Not convicted		
			Felony		Misde-		Dis-	Other
	Total	Total	Plea	Trial	meanor	Total[a]	missed	outcome[b]
All offenses	64%	59%	51%	8%	5%	27%	25%	9%
Violent offenses	59%	56%	47%	9%	4%	31%	29%	10%
Murder	50	56	37	19	3	31	24	10
Rape	54	54	54	0	0	38	39	8
Robbery	58	56	48	8	2	30	29	12
Assault	63	53	46	7	9	30	26	7
Property offenses	74%	61%	59%	3%	13%	19%	16%	7%
Burglary	77	64	64	0	13	19	9	4
Theft	76	59	54	6	16	16	16	8
Drug offenses	70%	68%	56%	12%	2%	24%	24%	6%
Public-order offenses	91%	91%	91%	0	0	9%	9%	0%

Note: 1,638 juvenile defendants were prosecuted as adults in the Nation's 75 largest counties during May 1990, 1992, and 1994. Eleven percent of all eligible cases were still pending adjudication at the end of the 1-year study period and are excluded from the table. Data on adjudication outcome were available for 85% of those cases that had been adjudicated. Detail may not add to subtotal because of rounding. General offense categories include offenses other than those displayed. Zero indicates no cases in the sample.
[a]Total not convicted includes acquittals.
[b]Includes other outcomes such as diversions and deferred adjudication.

Adjudication

Criminal court

Nearly two-thirds of juvenile defendants in criminal courts were convicted (table 8). About 9 in 10 of the convictions were for felonies. By general offense category, conviction rates in criminal court were 91% for public-order offenses and 59% for violent offenses. About 74% of juvenile property defendants in criminal court and 70% of defendants charged with drug offenses were convicted. Juvenile defendants in criminal court charged with public-order or drug charges were the most likely to have received a felony conviction.

In most cases where the juvenile was not convicted in criminal court, it was because the charges against the defendant were dismissed by the prosecutor or the court. Dismissal occurred in about a fourth of juvenile felony cases in criminal court. Nearly 40% of defendants charged with rape had their cases dismissed. Overall, about 2% of juvenile defendants in criminal court were acquitted, including 7% of murder defendants and 11% of burglary defendants. About 9% of juvenile cases in criminal court had other outcomes such as diversion or deferred adjudication.

Fifty-one percent of juvenile defendants in criminal court pleaded guilty to a felony, and an additional 5% pleaded guilty to a misdemeanor. About 10% of juvenile cases adjudicated within 1 year went to bench or jury trial. A fifth of the trials ended in an acquittal, while the remainder resulted in a guilty verdict.

Regardless of the method of adjudication, defendants who were convicted were usually convicted of the original arrest charge. This was most likely to be the case when the original offense was violent. Among those charged with murder and later convicted, 84% were convicted of the original arrest charge. The corresponding percentages were also high for robbery (87%) and assault (76%).

Juvenile court

Among juvenile defendants formally processed in the juvenile court system, 55% were adjudicated delinquent (table 9). Juvenile adjudication patterns differed little by offense type, as at least half or more in each major offense category were found delinquent. Among defendants referred to juvenile

Table 10. Juvenile felony defendants in criminal court, by conviction offense, 1990, 1992, and 1994

Most serious conviction offense	Juvenile defendants in the criminal courts of the Nation's 75 largest counties Percent
All offenses	100%
All felonies	92%
Violent offenses	51%
Murder	6
Rape	2
Robbery	25
Assault	14
Property offenses	21%
Burglary	7
Theft	10
Drug offenses	15%
Public-order offenses	5%
Misdemeanors	8%

Note: 1,638 juvenile defendants were prosecuted as adults in the Nations' 75 largest counties during May 1990, 1992, and 1994. Data on conviction offense type were available for 100% of cases involving defendants who had been convicted. Detail may not add to total because of rounding. General offense categories include offenses not shown.

Table 11. Defendants age 15 or older adjudicated delinquent in juvenile court, by most serious adjudication offense, 1990, 1992, and 1994

Most serious referral offense	Defendants in juvenile courts of the Nation's 75 largest counties Percent
All offenses	100%
Violent offenses	22%
Murder[a]	--
Rape[b]	1
Robbery	6
Assault	14
Property offenses	46%
Burglary	13
Theft	22
Drug offenses	13%
Public-order offenses	19%

Note: 370,424 defendants were formally processed in juvenile courts of the 75 largest counties in 1990, 1992, and 1994. These defendants were not transferred to criminal court. Data on adjudication charge available for 100% of all eligible cases. Details may not add to total because of rounding. General offense categories include offenses not shown. The juvenile court sample represents counties from the National Juvenile Court Data Archive that were included in the 75 largest counties.
--Less than .05%.
[a]Murder includes manslaughter.
[b]Rape includes other violent sex offenses.

court for public-order offenses, 59% were found delinquent, as were 51% of those referred for violent offenses.

Conviction and delinquent adjudication

Criminal court

Overall, about 9 in 10 juvenile convictions in criminal court were felonies, with over half representing violent convictions and a fifth property convictions (table 10). The remainder of juvenile defendants were convicted of drug-related offenses (15%), public-order offenses (5%) or misdemeanor offenses (8%). By conviction offense, 25% of juveniles in criminal court were convicted of robbery, 7% were convicted of burglary, 15% of drug offenses, 14% of felony assault, and 10% of theft.

Juvenile court

Nearly half of defendants in juvenile courts were adjudicated delinquent for a property offense, about a fifth for a violent offense, and a fifth for a public-order offense (table 11).

Sentencing

Criminal court

Overall, 68% of convicted juveniles in criminal court were sentenced to incarceration in a State prison or local jail (table 12). Over half of juvenile felony convictions resulted in a sentence to State prison, while over half of juvenile misdemeanor convictions resulted in a sentence to local jail.

Seventy-nine percent of juveniles convicted of violent offenses in criminal court were sentenced to incarceration, with nearly 7 in 10 violent convictions resulting in a sentence to State prison. Half of juveniles in criminal court convicted of offense type, three-fourths of juveniles in criminal court con-

Table 12. Most serious type of sentence received by convicted juvenile defendants in criminal court, by most serious conviction offense, 1990, 1992, and 1994

Most serious conviction offense	Percent of convicted juvenile defendants in the Nation's 75 largest counties sentenced to--						
	Total	Incarceration			Nonincarceration		
		Total	Prison	Jail	Total	Probation	Fine
All offenses	100%	68%	49%	19%	32%	31%	1%
All felonies	100%	69%	52%	16%	31%	30%	1%
Violent offenses	100%	79%	68%	11%	21%	21%	0%
Murder	100	100	100	0	0	0	0
Rape	100	100	25	75	0	0	0
Robbery	100	75	69	6	25	25	0
Assault	100	73	61	12	27	27	0
Property offenses	100%	57%	32%	25%	43%	40%	3%
Burglary	100	24	24	0	76	76	0
Theft	100	74	38	36	26	26	0
Drug offenses	100%	50%	34%	16%	50%	46%	3%
Public-order offenses	100%	60%	27%	33%	40%	40%	0%
Misdemeanor	100%	62%	5%	57%	38%	32%	6%

Note: 1,638 juvenile defendants were prosecuted as adults in the Nation's 75 largest counties during May 1990, 1992, and 1994. Data on type of sentence were available for 93% of cases involving juvenile defendants who had been convicted. Eight percent of prison sentences and 14% of jail sentences included a probation term. Fourteen percent of prison sentences, 19% of jail sentences, and 13% of probation sentences included a fine. Fines may have included restitution or community service. Total for all felonies includes cases that could not be classified into 1 of the 4 major offense categories. Detail may not add to subtotal because of rounding. General offense categories include offenses not shown. Zero indicates no cases in the sample.

drug offenses were sentenced to incarceration, with 34% sentenced to State prison.

Thirty-one percent of juveniles convicted in criminal court were sentenced to probation, and about 1% received other nonincarceration sentences. Forty-six percent of those convicted of drug offenses were sentenced to probation, while 21% of those convicted of violent offenses had a similar outcome. By specific victed of burglary were sentenced to probation.

Table 13. Disposition received by juveniles age 15 or older adjudicated delinquent, by most serious adjudicated offense, 1990, 1992, and 1994

Most serious adjudicated offense	Total	Placement	Probation	Other[a]
All offenses	100%	40%	50%	10%
Violent offenses	100%	44%	47%	9%
Murder[b]	100	77	21	2
Rape[c]	100	41	49	10
Robbery	100	57	37	6
Assault	100	38	51	11
Property offenses	100%	35%	54%	11%
Burglary	100	40	53	7
Theft	100	34	53	13
Drug offenses	100%	41%	48%	11%
Public-order offenses	100%	46%	45%	9%

Note: 370,424 defendants were formally processed in juvenile courts of the Nation's 75 largest counties in 1990, 1992, and 1994. These defendants were not transferred to criminal court for prosecution. Data on disposition available for 97% of all eligible cases. Detail may not add to subtotal because of rounding. The juvenile court sample represents counties from the National Juvenile Court Data Archive that were included in the Nation's largest 75 counties. General offense categories include offenses other than those displayed.
[a]Other outcomes includes such things as fines, restitution, and community service.
[b]Murder includes manslaughter.
[c]Rape includes other violent sex offenses.

Mechanisms by which juveniles can reach criminal court

All States allow juveniles to be proceeded against as adults in criminal court under certain circumstances. The following description of mechanisms that States use is summarized from *State Responses to Serious and Violent Juvenile Crime* by Patricia Torbet and others.

In all States except New Mexico, Nebraska, New York, and Connecticut, juvenile court judges may waive jurisdiction over the case and transfer it to criminal court. The waiver and transfer may be based on their own judgment, in response to the State prosecutor's request, or in some States at the request of juveniles or their parents.

In a related provision—called a *presumptive waiver*—juvenile offenders must be waived to criminal court unless they can prove that they are amenable to juvenile rehabilitation.

This type of provision shifts the burden of proof from the prosecutor to the juvenile. As of 1995, 12 States and the District of Columbia had enacted presumptive provisions.

Concurrent jurisdiction statutes, also called *prosecutorial discretion* or *direct-file*, give prosecutors the authority to file certain juvenile cases in either juvenile or criminal court. Ten States and the District of Columbia had concurrent jurisdiction statutes as of 1995.

Statutory exclusion of certain serious offenses from juvenile court jurisdiction is another mechanism in many States. This would also include mandatory waiver provisions. Thirty-six States and the District of Columbia exclude selected offenses from juvenile court jurisdiction. The most common offenses excluded are capital murder, murder of other types, and serious crimes against persons.

Several States exclude juveniles charged with felonies if they have prior adjudications or convictions.

Reverse waiver provisions have been enacted in 22 States that allow the criminal court, usually on a motion from the prosecutor, to transfer excluded or direct-file cases back to the juvenile court for adjudication and/or disposition.

"Once an adult, always an adult" provisions, enacted in 17 States and the District of Columbia, require that once the juvenile court jurisdiction is waived or the juvenile is sentenced in criminal court as a result of direct filing or exclusion, all subsequent cases involving the juvenile offender will be under criminal court jurisdiction. (For information about specific provisions of the various mechanisms listed above, see *Juvenile Offenders and Victims: A National Report*, 1995, pp. 85–89.)

Juvenile murder defendants and arrestees

In the 75 largest counties —

Juvenile murder defendant characteristic	In criminal court	In juvenile court
Sex		
Male	96%	94%
Female	4	6
Race		
White	25%	59%
Black	69	36
Other	6	5
Judicial processing		
Detained pretrial	87%	78%
Convicted/adjudicated delinquent	58%	58%
Sentence for murder convictions		
Prison/secured detainment	100%	77%
Probation	0	21
Maximum prison sentence for murder convictions		
Less than 2 years	8 %	--
2 to 10 years	16	--
10 or more years	76	--

Note: 174 juvenile defendants were prosecuted as adults for murder in the Nation's 75 largest counties during May 1990, 1992, and 1994. 1,343 murder defendants were formally processed in juvenile courts in the 75 largest counties during calendar years 1990, 1992, and 1994. Detail may not add to subtotal because of rounding. Zero indicates no cases in the sample.
--No data were available for length of detainment in juvenile facilities.

In the United States —

• 1,860 persons under age 18 were arrested for murder in 1980.

• The number of persons under 18 arrested for murder peaked in 1993 with 3,790 arrests.

• From 1993 to 1996 the number of murder arrests of those under 18 dropped nearly 25%.

Murder arrests of juveniles

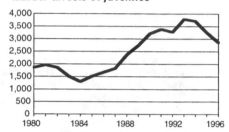

Note: Arrest estimates are based on data reported in the series *Crime in the United States* using an assumption that the annual proportion of juvenile arrests in the reporting sample is the same as in the U.S. population.

Source for Juvenile arrest data: Snyder, H. (1998). *Juvenile Murder Arrests: 1980-96.* Pittsburgh: National Center for Juvenile Justice.

Juvenile court

In juvenile court during this period, 40% of delinquent defendants were sentenced to residential placement, 50% were sentenced to probation, and 10% to other sanctions (table 13). Over half of defendants adjudicated delinquent for murder (77%) and robbery (57%) were sentenced to residential placement.

Among defendants adjudicated delinquent in juvenile court, half were sentenced to probation. Fifty-four percent of those adjudicated delinquent for property offenses and 47% of those adjudicated delinquent for violent offenses received probation.

Methodology

State Court Processing Statistics (SCPS)

The sample of juvenile defendants in criminal courts were selected from combined SCPS surveys from 1990, 1992, and 1994. Juvenile status was determined based on State statutes for maximum juvenile court jurisdiction. Age of defendant was age at arrest. In 1994 the maximum age for juvenile court jurisdiction was 17 or younger in 39 States and the District of Columbia (Alabama, Alaska, Arizona, Arkansas, California, Colorado, Delaware, District of Columbia, Florida, Hawaii, Idaho, Indiana, Iowa, Kansas, Kentucky, Maine, Maryland, Minnesota, Mississippi, Montana, Nebraska, Nevada, New Hampshire, New Jersey, New Mexico, North Dakota, Ohio, Oklahoma, Oregon, Pennsylvania, Rhode Island, South Dakota, Tennessee, Utah, Vermont, Virginia, Washington, West Virginia, and Wisconsin).

In eight States the maximum age for juvenile court jurisdiction was 16 (Georgia, Illinois, Louisiana, Massachusetts, Michigan, Missouri, South Carolina, and Texas). In an additional three states, the maximum age for juvenile court jurisdiction was 15 (Connecticut, New York, and North Carolina), For example, in New York all felony defendants 15 and younger in State court were considered to be juveniles by definition and reached criminal court by way of one or more juvenile transfer mechanisms. The mechanism by which these defendants reached criminal courts is unknown. Since 1994 New Hampshire and Wisconsin have lowered their juvenile age status from 17 to 16.

The SCPS sample was designed and selected by the U.S. Bureau of Census under BJS supervision. It is a 2-stage stratified sample, with 40 (or 39 in 1994) of the 75 most populous counties selected at the first stage and a systematic sample of State court felony filings (defendants) within each county selected at the second stage. The 40 (39 in 1994) counties were divided into 4 first-stage strata based on court filing information obtained through a telephone survey. In 1990 and 1992, 14 counties were included in the sample with certainty because

Appendix A. Judicial processing of felony defendants under 25, by State juvenile age definition, 1990, 1992, and 1994

The table shown compares the judicial processing of juvenile felony defendants in criminal courts with that of other young felony defendants. Data on persons younger than 25 years prosecuted in State courts are presented in three categories. The first column includes those defendants between ages 18 and 24 at the time of arrest. The second includes felony defendants under age 18 who, by definition, were considered adults by State age statute. For example, in New York all 16- and 17-year-old defendants were considered adults under 18. Finally, defendants defined by State age statutes as under the original jurisdiction of the juvenile courts were considered juveniles in criminal courts.

An estimated 57,129 felony cases were filed against defendants age 18 to 24 in the State courts of the Nation's 75 largest counties during May 1990, 1992, and 1994. By comparison, 7,110 felony defendants under age 18 were prosecuted in the State courts during a similar time frame. Of these defendants under age 18, 23% or 1,638 cases were defined as juveniles by State statutes and the remaining 77% (5,472 cases) were defined as adults under 18.

Juvenile defendants compared to adults 18 to 24

Defendants defined as juveniles in criminal courts were more than twice as likely to be charged with a violent offense than defendants 18 to 24. Among violent felony defendants, juveniles in criminal court were more likely than defendants 18 to 24 to be—

- detained pretrial prior to case disposition

- convicted of a felony offense

- sentenced to State prison.

Juvenile defendants compared to adults under 18

The average prison sentence for juveniles convicted of violent offenses in criminal courts was about 10½ years (a mean of 127 months and a median of 78 months). For adult defendants under 18 the average prison sentence for violent offenses was about 8 years (a mean of 97 months and a median of 72).

Of juveniles sentenced to prison for violent offenses—

- 7% were sentenced to 2 years or less

- 43% from 2+Plus+; years to 6 years

- 26% from 6+Plus+; years to 10 years

- 22% to over 10 years, and 2% to life imprisonment.

	Percent of felony defendants age 18 to 24	Percent of felony defendants under 18 defined as –	
		Adult	Juvenile
Most serious arrest charge			
Violent offenses	26%	36%	66%
Property offenses	35	36	17
Drug offenses	31	22	14
Public-order offenses	8	6	3
Pretrial release for violent felony charge	55%	71%	44%
Adjudication outcome for violent felony defendants			
Convicted			
Felony	45%	39%	56%
Misdemeanor	11	10	4
Not convicted	45	51	41
Most serious sentence for violent convictions			
Prison	57%	41%	68%
Jail	25	7	11
Probation	18	52	21
Mean prison sentence for violent convictions in months	98 mo	97 mo	127 mo

Note: Data for the specific arrest charge were available for 99% of the cases. Detail may not add to subtotal because of rounding.

of their large number of court filings. The remaining 26 counties were allocated to the 3 non-certainty strata based on the variance of felony court dispositions. In 1994, 12 counties were included in the sample with certainty because of their large number of court filings. The remaining counties were allocated to the three non-certainty strata based on the variance of felony court dispositions.

The second-stage sampling (filings) were designed to represent all defendants who had felony cases filed with the court during the month of May in 1990, 1992, and 1994. The participating jurisdictions provided data for every felony case filed on selected days during that month. In 1990, each jurisdiction provided data for the 5, 10, 15, or 31 days in May from which to sample all felony defendants who had felony charges filed. In 1992 and 1994, each jurisdiction provided data for 1, 2, or 4

weeks' filings in May. Data from jurisdictions that were not required to provide a full month of filings were weighted to represent the full month.

In 1990, data on 13,597 sample felony cases were collected from the 40 sampled jurisdictions, representing 512 weighted juvenile cases in criminal courts during the month of May in the 75 most populous counties. In 1992 data on 13,206 sample felony cases were collected from the 40 sampled jurisdictions, representing 480 weighted juvenile cases in criminal courts during May in the 75 most populous counties. In 1994, 14,691 sample felony cases were collected from the 39 sampled jurisdictions, representing 646 weighted juvenile cases in criminal courts during May in the 75 most populous counties. Cases that could not be classified into one of the four major crime categories (violent, property, drug, or public-order) because

Appendix B. Estimating the number of juveniles handled in adult courts

Sources for statistics on juveniles in adult courts

• The **National Judicial Reporting Program (NJRP)** is a biennial survey that compiles information on the sentences that felons receive in State courts nationwide and on characteristics of the felons. The 1994 survey estimated that 21,000 felons were younger than 18 at arrest, conviction, or sentencing in State courts nationwide. Of these felons, an estimated 12,000 were juveniles convicted of a felony in State courts.

• The **National Survey of State Prosecutors (NSP)** is a nationally representative sample drawn from a list of all prosecutors' offices that handle felony cases in State courts. The 1996 NSP estimated that 27,000 juveniles were proceeded against in criminal court by prosecutors' offices.

• The **National Juvenile Court Data Archive** which is supported by OJJDP grant number 95-JN-FX-0008, at the National Center for Juvenile Justice (NCJJ), contains the most detailed information available on youth involved in the juvenile justice system and on activities of U.S. juvenile courts. In 1990, 1992, and 1994, over 377,000 defendants age 15 or older were formally processed in juvenile courts in a selected number of the Nation's 75 largest counties. Of these defendants, approximately 1.9% were transferred to criminal court by way of *judicial waiver*.

• The **State Court Processing Statistics (SCPS)** program is a biennial data collection on the processing of felony defendants in the State courts of the Nation's 75 largest counties. During May of 1990, 1992, and 1994 an estimated 7,110 defendants under age 18 faced charges in criminal court--about a fourth of whom, based on age, would be considered juveniles by State law.

Difficulties in developing National estimates for the number of juveniles in adult courts:

• Lack of uniform reporting methods by States regarding juvenile transfer statistics, including the mechanisms by which juveniles reach adult courts

• Variation in the definition of *juvenile offenders* across States

• Frequent changes in State statutes defining juvenile court jurisdiction.

Appendix C. Juveniles adjudicated as adults in the Federal system

Juveniles may be adjudicated as adults in the Federal system if the offense charged was a violent felony or drug trafficking or importation and if the offense was committed after the juvenile's 15th birthday. Or, if the juvenile possessed a firearm during a violent offense, the juvenile may be adjudicated as an adult if the offense was committed after the juvenile's 13th birthday.

Before proceeding against a juvenile in Federal court, the U.S. attorney must certify to the court a substantial Federal interest in the case and at least one of the following:

• The State does not have jurisdiction.

• The State refuses to assume jurisdiction.

• The State with jurisdiction does not have adequate programs or services for juvenile offenders.

• The offense charged is a violent felony, a drug trafficking or importation offense, or a firearm offense (18 U.S.C. Section 5032).

While the U.S. Department of Justice does not systematically collect information on juvenile transfers to Federal courts, it is estimated that during the 12 months ending September 30, 1994, 65 juveniles were referred to the Attorney General for transfer to adult status.

Source: Juvenile Delinquents in the Federal Criminal Justice System, 1995, BJS Bulletin, NCJ-163066, 1997, pp. 1–2.

of incomplete information were omitted from the analysis. Data collection was supervised by the Pretrial Services Resource Center of Washington, D.C.

For counties found in the SCPS and NJCDA samples see Appendix D. Because the data came from a sample, a sampling error (standard error) is associated with each reported number. In general, if the difference between two SCPS-generated numbers is greater than twice the standard error for that difference, we can say that we are 95% confident of a real difference and that the apparent difference is not simply the result of using a sample rather than the entire population. All differences discussed in this report were statistically significant at or above the 95-percent confidence level.

Appendix D. Jurisdictions in the Nation's 75 largest counties used in the State Court Processing Statistics and National Juvenile Court Data Archive samples

State/county	Adult courts 1990	Adult courts 1992	Adult courts 1994	Juvenile courts 1990	Juvenile courts 1992	Juvenile courts 1994
Alabama						
Jefferson			■	■	■	■
Arizona						
Maricopa	■	■	■	■	■	■
Pima			■			
California						
Alameda			■	■	■	■
Contra Costa				■		
Fresno				■		
Los Angeles	■	■	■	■	■	■
Orange	■			■		
Riverside				■		
Sacramento	■	■	■	■	■	■
San Bernardino	■	■	■	■	■	■
San Diego	■	■		■	■	■
San Francisco		■	■	■	■	■
San Mateo				■		
Santa Clara	■	■	■	■	■	■
Ventura				■		
Connecticut						
Fairfield				■	■	■
Hartford				■	■	■
New Haven				■	■	■
Dist. of Columbia						
Washington	■	■				
Florida						
Broward	■	■	■			
Dade	■	■	■	■	■	■
Duval	■	■	■	■	■	■
Hillsborough	■	■	■	■	■	■
Orange			■			■
Palm Beach	■	■		■	■	■
Pinellas	■	■				
Georgia						
Fulton	■	■				
Hawaii						
Honolulu	■		■	■		
Illinois						
Cook	■	■	■	■	■	■
Du Page			■			
Kentucky						
Jefferson			■			
Maryland						
Baltimore				■	■	■
Baltimore City				■	■	■
Montgomery		■		■	■	■
Pr. George's				■	■	■
Massachusetts						
Essex	■	■				
Middlesex	■	■	■			
Suffolk	■	■				
Michigan						
Wayne	■	■	■			
Minnesota						
Hennepin				■	■	■
Missouri						
Jackson			■	■	■	■
St. Louis		■	■	■	■	■
New Jersey						
Bergen					■	■
Essex	■	■				■
Middlesex						
New York						
Bronx	■	■	■	■	■	■
Erie	■	■	■	■	■	■
Kings	■	■	■	■	■	■
Monroe	■	■	■	■	■	■
Nassau	■	■	■	■	■	■
New York	■	■	■	■	■	■
Queens	■	■	■	■	■	■
Suffolk	■	■	■	■	■	■
Westchester				■	■	■
Ohio						
Cuyahoga				■	■	■
Franklin						
Hamilton	■	■	■			
Oklahoma						
Oklahoma	■	■	■			
Pennsylvania						
Allegheny	■	■	■	■	■	■
Montgomery	■	■	■	■	■	■
Philadelphia	■	■	■	■	■	■
Tennessee						
Shelby	■					■
Texas						
Dallas	■	■	■			
Harris	■	■	■			
Tarrant	■	■				
Utah						
Salt Lake	■	■		■		■
Virginia						
Fairfax	■	■				
Washington						
King	■	■	■	■	■	■
Wisconsin						
Milwaukee		■	■			

National Juvenile Court Data Archive (NJCDA)

Data for juvenile defendants processed in the juvenile courts of the 75 largest counties in 1990, 1992, and 1994 were provided by Howard Snyder of the National Center for Juvenile Justice (NCJJ). The data were provided for counties matching those in the SCPS program for the respective years. The juvenile court sample includes only those youths age 15 or older in formally processed delinquency cases not transferred to criminal court. Defendants processed informally in the juvenile justice system were not included in this analysis. Due to the nature of the sample, standard errors cannot be calculated because the probability of selection was unknown.

In Florida, 67 counties are administered in 11 juvenile justice districts. These districts contain one or more counties, and each county is in only one district. In the juvenile court data, cases from different counties could not be distinguished within a specific district. As a result, this analysis includes data from any Florida district that contains at least one sampled county. The Florida districts included are the following: District 4 (Baker, Clay, Duval, Flagler, Nassau, St. Johns, and Volusia); District 5 (Pasco and Pinellas); District 6 (Hardee, Highlands, Hillsborough, Manatee, and Polk); District 7 (Brevard, Orange, Osceola, and Seminole); District 9 (Indian River, Martin, Okeechobee, Palm Beach, and St. Lucie); District 10 (Broward); and District 11 (Dade and Monroe).

From *Bureau of Justice Statistics Special Report,* September 1998, pp. 1-11. Reprinted by permission of the National Institute of Justice, National Criminal Justice Reference Service.

Juvenile Delinquents in the Federal Criminal Justice System

John Scalia
BJS Statistician

During 1995, U.S. attorneys filed cases against 240 persons for alleged acts of juvenile delinquency. Of these, 122 cases were adjudicated in Federal court, representing 0.2% of the 56,243 cases (both adult and juvenile) adjudicated during 1995. Almost half of juvenile delinquency cases involved a violent offense (32%) or a drug offense (15%). Federal prosecutors declined further action against 228 other juveniles referred to them.

Many of the juveniles adjudicated in the Federal system are Native Americans. When Native American tribal jurisdictions lack resources or jurisdiction or when there is a substantial Federal interest, a U.S. attorney may initiate juvenile delinquency proceedings. Further, the Federal Government has jurisdiction over certain offenses committed in Indian country (18 U.S.C. § 1152 and 1153).

In Federal courts, juveniles adjudicated delinquent were about half as likely as convicted adults to receive a sentence of confinement (*Federal Criminal Case Processing, 1982–93*, NCJ-160088, May 1996). The average length of confinement ordered was 34 months. During 1995 the majority

(59%) of juveniles adjudicated delinquent were placed on probation.

Federal Juvenile Delinquency Act

An act of *juvenile delinquency* is a violation of Federal law committed by a person prior to age 18 which would have been a crime if committed by an adult (18 U.S.C. § 5031). Under Federal law, a person accused of an act of *juvenile delinquency* may be processed as a *juvenile* provided the person has not attained age 21.

Federal juvenile delinquency proceedings

Adjudication of juveniles in the Federal system is limited. Federal law requires that prosecutors restrict proceedings against juveniles to those cases in which they certify to the court that there is a substantial Federal interest in the case and—

- the State does not have jurisdiction or refuses to assume jurisdiction;
- the State with jurisdiction does not have adequate programs or services for juvenile offenders; or
- the offense charged is a violent felony, a drug trafficking or importa-

Highlights

- During 1995, 468 juveniles were referred to Federal prosecutors for investigation—49% of these cases were declined for further action.
- During 1995, 122 juveniles were adjudicated as delinquent in the Federal courts—47% for either a violent or drug offense.
- During the 12 months ending September 1994, an additional 65 persons who allegedly committed acts of delinquency were referred for prosecution as an adult by a U.S. attorney.
- 37% of juveniles adjudicated delinquent were committed to a correctional facility. The average length of commitment was 34 months.
- 61% of juvenile delinquents confined by the Federal Bureau of Prisons were Native Americans.

tion offense, or a firearms offense (18 U.S.C. § 5032).

Unlike State-level criminal justice systems, the Federal system does not have a separate juvenile justice component. Juveniles are adjudicated by a U.S. district court judge or magistrate in a closed hearing without a jury. Af-

Juveniles in the State courts

In contrast to the Federal system, the State systems frequently charge juveniles with delinquency. During 1994 there were more than 1.5 million delinquency cases in courts with juvenile jurisdiction. Of these, almost 855,000 were formally processed in the juvenile justice system. Nearly half (49%) of those juveniles formally processed at the State level were charged with property offenses (table). Few (9%) were charged with drug offenses.

Approximately 58% of those juveniles formally charged at the State level were adjudicated delinquent (not shown in a table). Similar to those in the Federal system, approximately 29% of those juveniles adjudicated delinquent were committed to a correctional or other residential facility and 56% were placed on probation. Almost a third (31%) of those charged with a violent offense were committed.

During 1994 less than 2% of all juveniles charged with offenses in the State courts were waived to adult status. Similar to the Federal system, approximately 44% of juveniles transferred were charged with a violent offense. Drug offenders represented few (11%) of the transfers.

While 12,300 juveniles were judicially waived to adult status during 1994, others were statutorily excluded from juvenile court jurisdiction based on their age and offense or concurrent jurisdiction provisions. In 13 States the upper age of juvenile court jurisdiction is 15 or 16 years. Many States also exclude certain serious offenses—such as murder and other violent offenses—from juvenile court jurisdiction.

ter a juvenile has been adjudicated delinquent, a hearing concerning the disposition of the juvenile is held.

During the disposition hearing, a juvenile may be ordered to pay restitution, be placed on probation, or be committed to a correctional facility.

Juveniles under age 18 may be placed on probation or committed until they reach age 21. Juveniles between ages 18 and 21 may be placed

Delinquency cases in State courts, 1994		
Most serious offense	Number	Adult transfers
Total	855,200	12,300
Personal offenses	196,900	5,400
Property offenses	415,800	4,600
Drug offenses	73,400	1,300
Public-order offenses	169,100	1,000

Source: Jeffrey A. Butts, Howard N. Snyder, Terrence A. Finnegan *et al.*, *Juvenile Court Statistics 1994*, Office of Juvenile Justice and Delinquency Prevention (1996).

on probation for up to 3 years or confined for up to 5 years, depending on the severity of the offense.

Transfer to adult status

A person who committed an offense prior to age 18 may be adjudicated as an adult if—

- the offense charged was a violent felony or drug trafficking or importation offense *and* if the offense was committed *after* the person's 15th birthday.

- the person possessed a firearm during a violent offense and the offense was committed *after* the person's 13th birthday.

- the person had been previously adjudicated delinquent of a violent felony or drug offense (18 U.S.C. § 5032).

While the Department of Justice does not systematically collect information describing Federal juvenile transfers, it estimates that during the 12 months ending September 30, 1994, 65 persons accused of delinquency were referred to the Attorney General for transfer to adult status. It is not known how many were charged directly as adults based on their prior criminal records.

Juveniles investigated by U.S. attorneys

During 1995, 468 juveniles were referred to Federal prosecutors for investigation and prosecution. The U.S. attorneys declined to proceed against 49% of those juveniles referred to them—two-thirds of that number immediately and the remainder subsequently.

Juveniles adjudicated in U.S. district courts

Few cases involving juvenile delinquents are processed in U.S. district courts because of statutory restrictions. Between 1989 and 1994, the number of juveniles adjudicated for acts of delinquency in U.S. district courts ranged from 217 during 1990 to 122 during 1995 (table 1). The District of South Dakota (12.3%), the District of Arizona (10.7%), the District of Montana (10.7%), and the Eastern District of North Carolina (9.8%) accounted for approximately 44% of the total Federal juvenile caseload during 1995 (not shown in a table).

Offense committed

Consistent with the statutory directive, juveniles charged with acts of juvenile delinquency in U.S. district courts were most frequently charged with more serious offenses such as drug (15%) or violent (32%) offenses.

Adjudication

Of the 122 juveniles charged with delinquency whose cases were terminated in the U.S. district courts during 1995, approximately 81% were adjudicated delinquent. Of adjudicated delinquents 87% admitted to the facts alleged in the indictment (or information) and 13% were adjudicated delinquent after a hearing (not shown in a table). Of juveniles who were not adjudicated delinquent, 90% had the charges dismissed and 10% were found not delinquent.

Table 1. Juveniles in delinquency proceedings terminated in U.S. district courts, 1989-95

Most serious offense	Number of Federal delinquency proceedings terminated						
	1989	1990	1991	1992	1993	1994	1996
Total*	206	217	194	144	124	134	122
Violent offenses	49	66	62	43	41	56	34
Property offenses	65	40	37	53	30	18	27
Fraudulent	11	4	4	2	3	3	4
Other	54	36	33	51	27	15	23
Drug offenses	66	52	44	31	28	38	16
Public-order offenses	26	52	49	17	25	17	28
Regulatory	1	3	21	4	7	2	10
Other	25	49	28	13	18	15	18

*Total includes cases for which an offense category culd not be determined.

Data source: Administrative Office of the U.S. Courts, criminal docket data file, annual.

Table 2. Disposition of juveniles adjudicated delinquent in U.S. district courts, 1995

Type of disposition	Number	Percent
Total	99	100.0%
Confinement only	32	32.3
Confinement and probation	5	5.1
Probation only	58	58.6
No probation	4	4.0

Data source: Administrative Office of the U.S. Courts, criminal docket data file, annual.

Table 3. Juvenile delinquents confined by the Federal Bureau of Prisons, 1994

Most serious offense	Number	Percent
Total*	124	100.0%
Violent offenses	77	64.7
Property offenses	16	13.4
Drug offenses	17	14.3
Public-order offenses	9	7.6

*Includes cases for which an offense category could not be determined.

Data source: U.S. Department of Justice, Bureau of Prisons, SENTRY system data file, fiscal year ending September 30, 1994.

Disposition/sanction imposed

Of those juveniles adjudicated delinquent during 1995, 37% were committed to a correctional facility, 59% were placed on probation, and 4% received a sentence that did not include supervision or confinement (table 2).

Approximately 35% of those juveniles committed to a correctional facility were adjudicated delinquent of a violent offense. Of those 37 juveniles committed during 1995, the average length of commitment required was 34 months (not shown in a table).

Juvenile delinquents confined by the Federal Bureau of Prisons

As of September 30, 1994, 124 juvenile delinquents were confined in a State juvenile correctional facility under contract to the Federal Bureau of Prisons (table 3). (The Federal Bureau of Prisons does not have its own facilities for juvenile delinquents.) Most (64%) were adjudicated delinquent of a violent offense.

Sixty-one percent of the confined juvenile delinquents were Native Americans (table 4). The majority (81%) of the Native Americans confined were adjudicated delinquent of a violent offense—sex offenses (32%), assault (28%), negligent man-

Table 4. Demographic characteristics of juvenile delinquents confined by the Federal Bureau of Prisons, 1994

Characteristic	Number	Percent
Total*	124	100.0%
Race/ethnicity		
White	9	7.3
Black	15	12.1
Hispanic	19	15.3
Native American	75	60.5
Asian	6	4.8
Citizenship		
United States	109	87.9
Mexico	5	4.0
China	4	3.2
Other	6	4.9

Data source: U.S. Department of Justice, Bureau of Prisons, SENTRY system data file, fiscal year ending September 30, 1994.

The remainder were adjudicated delinquent of a property offense.

Almost all (88%) of the juveniles confined were U.S. citizens; 4% were Mexican citizens, and 3% were Chinese citizens.

During 1994, 102 juvenile delinquents were released by the Federal Bureau of Prisons from a juvenile correctional facility. The average time served was—

- 14 months for all those released
- 21 months for drug offenders
- 17 months for violent offenders.

133

Methodology

The primary source of data presented in this report is the BJS Federal Justice Statistics Program (FJSP) database. The FJSP database is presently constructed from the source files provided by the U.S. attorneys, the Federal courts, the U.S. Sentencing Commission, and the Federal Bureau of Prisons. Data tabulations, except where otherwise indicated, were prepared from BJS staff analysis of source agency datasets.

Juvenile delinquency proceedings were identified using a delinquency proceeding code included in the courts' database, the statute(s) charged (18 U.S.C. § 5031 *et seq.*), and a descriptive label in the name field—juvenile records in the data-

The Bureau of Justice Statistics is the statistical agency of the U.S. Department of Justice. Jan M. Chaiken, Ph.D., is director.

BJS Special Reports address a special topic in depth from one or more datasets that cover many topics.

John Scalia of the Bureau of Justice Statistics wrote this report. William J. Sabol of the Urban Institute provided statistical review. Gina Wood of the Office of Juvenile Justice and Delinquency Prevention and Steve Shandy of the Criminal Division, Department of Justice, provided assistance in the preparation of this report. Tom Hester and Tina Dorsey edited the report. Marilyn Marbrook, assisted by Yvonne Boston, administered production. February 1997, NCJ-163066

base typically do not include identifying information such as names. Juveniles under jurisdiction of the Bureau of Prisons are housed in facilities specifically for juveniles.

From *Bureau of Justice Statistics Special Report,* February 1997, pp. 1-4. Reprinted by permission of the National Institute of Justice, National Criminal Justice Reference Service.

With Juvenile Courts in Chaos, Critics Propose Their Demise

JUSTICE BESIEGED

FOX BUTTERFIELD

CHICAGO—The nation's juvenile courts, long a troubled backwater of the criminal justice system, have been so overwhelmed by the increase in violent teen-age crime and the breakdown of the family that judges and politicians are debating a solution that was once unthinkable: abolishing the system and trying most minors as adults.

The crisis began building a decade ago, when prosecutors responded to the growth in high-profile youth crime by pushing for the trials of greater numbers of children, dramatically raising caseloads.

But the courts have become so choked that by all accounts they are even less effective than before, with more juveniles prosecuted but fewer convicted and no evidence of a drop in rearrest rates for those who go to prison.

The resulting situation angers people across the political spectrum, from those who believe the juvenile court is too lenient, to those who feel it fails to prevent troubled children from becoming ensnared in a life of crime.

In interviews around the country, judges, probation officers, prosecutors and defense lawyers described a juvenile court system in perhaps the worst chaos of its history.

In Chicago, where the first juvenile court was created in 1899, judges today preside over assembly-line justice, hearing an average of 60 cases a day, about six minutes per case. In New Orleans, public defenders have to represent their poor clients with no office, no telephone, no court records and little chance to discuss the case before trial. In New York, where the recent case of Malcolm Shabazzwho—admitted setting the fire that killed his grandmother, Malcolm X's widow—focused new attention on Family Court, some officials say it is time to junk the system.

Almost everywhere, with juvenile courts starved for money, record-keeping is so primitive that often the judge, the prosecutor and the defense attorney have different records on the same defendant, making an accurate assessment of the case impossible. And because the courts cannot afford their own warrant squads, young defendants sometimes fail to show up for trial or simply skip out of the courtroom with virtual impunity.

Despite calls for tougher justice, the overcrowding and lack of resources mean that only a small percentage of the young people who move through the juvenile justice system are imprisoned, although there are other forms of punishment, the most common of which is probation.

Of the 1,555,200 delinquency cases referred by the police to prosecutors nationwide in 1994, 855,200, or just over half, resulted in what in adult criminal courts would be called indictments, said Jeffrey Butts, at the National Center for Juvenile Justice. Of these, Mr. Butts said, 495,000 defendants were found guilty.

In turn, 141,300 of these cases resulted in a juvenile's being incarcerated. That is 9 percent of those originally sent to prosecutors by the police.

By contrast, in adult criminal court, which is explicitly intended to be punitive, 90 percent to 95 percent of defendants who have been indicted plead guilty in a plea bargain, often as a way to win a lighter punishment. The philosophy of juvenile court traditionally was to rehabilitate rather than punish young offenders, a premise that has come under attack in recent years.

Congress is poised to pass legislation, backed by President Clinton, that would provide Federal grants to states that sharply increase the number of young people they try in adult court. The legislation, already passed by the House and likely to be adopted soon by the Senate, would further undermine the authority of the juvenile court at a time when many specialists predict there will be a new wave of youth crime, as the number of teen-agers increases by 15 percent in the next decade.

The Family Court is bankrupt, said Peter Reinharz, chief of New York City's juvenile prosecution unit. It's time to sell everything off and start over.

Mr. Reinharz is a longtime critic of the juvenile court, but even its staunchest defenders are now troubled by what they see.

It is no longer just the chronic problems that have long plagued the court, like overcrowding and making do with less, said Bart Lubow, a senior associate of the Annie E. Casey Foundation who has studied juvenile courts around the nation. Now there's a crisis of confidence, since the very notion that has been its cornerstone, that children are different from adults and therefore need to be treated differently, is in question.

Among the issues swirling in the nation's 3,000 juvenile courts are the following:

• As pressure to get tough on young criminals has increased, the number of juveniles arrested who are prosecuted in court has climbed to 55 percent in 1994 from 45 percent in 1985. But the percentage of young people convicted has not kept pace, rising to 33 percent in 1994 from 31 percent a decade earlier.

In Chicago, the figures show an even more dramatic effect of overloading the system. The Cook County State's Attorney has increased the number of juveniles he prosecutes to 85 percent of all those sent to him by the police, but about 70 percent of these cases are dismissed for lack of evidence or the failure of witnesses to appear, according to a new study by the Children and Family Justice Center of the Northwestern University School of Law.

"This is the dirty little secret of Cook County," said David Reed, the lead author of the report. "You have lots more cases but almost the same number of judges and prosecutors, and they can only do so much work and prove a certain number guilty.

So all these kids are brought in on criminal charges and then most are let go. It fosters cynicism about the court, makes the public and crime victims mad and teaches young people that justice is a joke."

• With an angry public demanding harsher punishments, it is becoming increasingly difficult for judges to differentiate between defendants who may have committed a youthful indiscretion and those who are on their way to a lifetime of crime. The distinction is critical. Almost 60 percent of those teen-agers sent to juvenile court for the first time never return. But every time a young person is sent back to court, his likelihood of being arrested again increases until recidivism rates reach 75 percent by a fifth appearance, said Howard Snyder, of the National Center for Juvenile Justice.

• Despite a rush by legislators in all 50 states over the past decade to pass laws trying young people in adult court, there is no evidence that being convicted in adult court or sentenced to adult prison is more effective in reducing youth crime than the juvenile justice route. A new study of 5,476 juvenile criminals in Florida, which followed them from their arrest in 1987 through 1994, concluded that those tried as adults committed new crimes sooner after their release from prison, and perpetrated more serious and violent crimes, than those tried as juveniles.

Charles Frazier, a sociology professor at the University of Florida and a co-author of the report, said that keeping young people in the juvenile justice system works better because juvenile institutions provide more education and psychological treatment for inmates, helping offenders rehabilitate themselves. By contrast, adult prisons now are more punitive and have largely abandoned trying to change criminals' behavior.

"Ultimately, you are going to release all these people back into the community, and the juvenile justice system does a better job of reclaiming them," Professor Frazier said.

19th-Century Origin
Firmly but Gently
Disciplining Youths

The criticism of the juvenile court misses a fundamental point, some specialists believe. With the breakdown of the family, can any court system, juvenile or adult, do the job society once did: instill discipline and values in children, punish them if they are bad and then help redeem them?

"The juvenile court was set up 100 years ago, in a very different America, to help cure kids of immigrant families with manageable problems, like truancy, petty thefts and fighting," said Jeffrey Fagan, the director of the Center for Violence Research and Prevention at Columbia University.

As envisioned by the pioneering social worker, Jane Addams, the juvenile court was to be a surrogate parent and the judge a kindly doctor, seeking to understand the social conditions that had led the child astray, the way a doctor would study a disease. This paternalism was reflected in the informality of the courtroom, with the judge sitting at an ordinary table, not behind a bench, and wearing only street clothes, not a robe.

The court's guiding principle was to do what was "in the best interest of the child," not to protect the community or insure the child's constitutional rights. So punishments were kept light, since children were thought to still be in the process of forming their personalities, and thus more amenable to reform than adults. And all proceedings and records were kept confidential.

An antiseptic nomenclature was even invented to avoid stigmatizing children. A boy was "taken into custody," not arrested. He had a "petition of delinquency" drawn against him, rather than being charged. And there were no convictions, only "adjudications," and no sentences, only "placements."

But today, poverty, joblessness and violent teen-age crime seem far worse than they were in the 1890's, often making the court's customs appear a quaint anachronism.

Also, as a result, Professor Fagan said, "The juvenile court can no longer do what it was set up to do. It certainly can't do what the public expects it to do, control juvenile crime."

Statistics only hint at the magnitude of the troubles the court is asked to resolve.

Since 1960, the number of delinquency cases handled by juvenile courts nationwide has risen almost four times, to 1.55 million in 1994. During the same period, the number of cases involving abused or neglected children, which are also handled by juvenile courts, has increased five times faster than even the delinquency cases, said Mr. Butts of the National Center for Juvenile Justice. And these abused and neglected children are often the very ones who become delinquents.

Among delinquency cases, violent crimes are rising the fastest. From 1985 to 1994, juvenile crimes involving weapons soared 156 percent, murders jumped 144 percent and aggravated assaults were up 134 percent. Property crimes were up 25 percent.

A Case in Point
In a Chicago Court, Beating the System

Perhaps the most revealing place to see the troubles is in Chicago, home to the nation's oldest and largest juvenile court. The Chicago court is not the best; that may be in Louisville, San Jose or Oakland, where the judges command wide respect. Nor is it the most beleaguered; that distinction may belong to Baltimore or New Orleans. Cook County is just a good example of what goes on in a high-volume juvenile court.

A tiny 13-year-old defendant, so short he could barely see Judge William Hibbler seated behind the bench, was on trial for murder.

The defendant—who will remain unidentified in accordance with the court's rules of confidentiality—was wearing an Atlanta Braves baseball jacket, and he looked more like a team mascot than a hardened criminal. But the teen-ager was charged with first-degree murder for shooting a man who was trying to buy crack cocaine.

At an even younger age, he was arrested for armed robbery and burglary, though without being sent to prison. This time, after his arrest for murder, he had been allowed to return home because the court had failed to give him a hearing within the 36-hour limit specified for juveniles.

While free awaiting trial for murder, he had stolen a car.

Neither his mother nor father was in court. His father had died of alcohol poisoning; his mother, a crack addict, was in a boot camp on a drug charge.

Judge Hibbler, the presiding judge of the delinquency division of the Cook County Juvenile Court, wore a black robe, a small sign of how the court has shifted from its original informality and evolved, in the judge's phrase, into more of a "mini criminal court."

The courtroom is inside the Cook County Juvenile Center, a modern structure a block long and eight stories high that from the outside looks more like an office building than a courthouse with a juvenile jail attached. The building was recently reconstructed as part of an effort to reverse the turmoil overtaking juvenile court.

Inside, however, the waiting rooms are still painted a dingy brown and are jammed with largely black and Hispanic families, many of them holding crying babies. In the men's rooms the toilets are broken and the metal mirrors are scrawled with graffiti.

These dilapidated conditions, said Mr. Lubow of the Casey Foundation, "basically say to the families and kids who come to juvenile court that we don't take them seriously, that we value them less as people."

Now, after talking with his lawyer, the youth begrudgingly confessed to murder as part of a plea bargain. Judge Hibbler then solemnly ordered that he "be committed to the Illinois Department of Corrections, Juvenile Division, till 21 years of age."

The boy smirked. He knew he had beaten the system again. He could be free in as little as five years. Without the plea bargain, he could have been transferred to adult court and faced a minimum sentence of 20 years.

It was the kind of case that infuriates conservatives and others, suggesting that juvenile court is little more than a revolving door.

But it was also the kind of case that makes children's rights advocates argue that juvenile court is failing to help young people from troubled families by intervening early enough to prevent them from becoming ensnared in a life of crime.

Even many judges themselves, who are often the only defenders of the juvenile court, concur that the court is foundering. But the judges tend to blame the politicians who have passed laws to try more teenagers in adult courts.

"There is a crisis," Judge Hibbler acknowledged. But, he contended, "Children don't stop being children just because they commit a crime, and calling for an end of the juvenile court is the same as saying we should do away with grammar schools and junior high schools and just put everyone in college."

Clogging the Courts
Convictions Flat As Caseload Soars

In the traditional juvenile court, probation officers played a key role.

They presided at what is still widely called "intake," or arraignment in adult terms. After the police decided which juveniles to send to court—usually about half were dismissed with the equivalent of a parking ticket—the probation officers would screen out children whose crimes were petty or who had no record. Nationwide, they filtered out about half the cases referred by the police.

But in Chicago in the late 1980's, in response to the epidemic of crack cocaine and the rise of teen-age gun violence, Richard M. Daley, then the Cook County State's Attorney, wrestled this power away from the court probation department. To appear tough on crime, he began prosecuting 97 percent of the cases forwarded to him by the police, according to an analysis by The Chicago Sun-Times.

Mr. Daley is now mayor of Chicago, and that figure is down to 85 percent, the State's Attorney's office says.

But Bernardine Dohrn, the director of the Children and Family Justice Center at Northwestern University, said that prosecuting such a high proportion of cases has overwhelmed the court, resulting in about 70 percent of the cases filed by the State's Attorney being dropped before trial.

A new study by Ms. Dohrn's center has found that while the number of delinquency cases heard each month has more than tripled in the last decade, the number of convictions has remained almost flat.

"They are clogging the system," Ms. Dohrn said, "and when you do this wholesale, you drive kids into the system who don't belong there and you don't find the kids who aren't in school and are getting into serious trouble. They are able to pass through for a long time without being stopped. So it's a double whammy, and dangerous."

Probation officers are also supposed to enforce the most commonly used punishment in juvenile court, probation—a court order requiring a young person to go to school or find a job and obey a home curfew the rest of the day.

But no one likes probation: not judges, who want more innovative alternatives; not the offenders, who chafe at the loss of freedom, and not the police or prosecutors, who regard probation as a farce. Worst of all, probation further undercuts the credibility of the court.

For judges, probation is part of a terrible dilemma. "I really have only two major choices," said Glenda Hatchett, the presiding judge of the Fulton County Juvenile Court in Atlanta.

"I can place these kids in incarceration, where they will learn to become better criminals, or I can send them home on probation, back to where they got in trouble in the first place," Judge Hatchett said.

Because governments have always regarded the juvenile court as a "poor stepchild" of the criminal justice system, Judge Hatchett said, there isn't money for the kinds of programs she believes would help, by reaching at-risk children and their parents when the children are 4, 5 or 6 years old, before it is too late.

Shifting Roles
Probation Officers Become Enforcers

Laura Donnelly is a Chicago probation officer with a master's degree in social work.

That makes her part of a vanishing breed, because today more and more probation officers have degrees in criminal justice. The change reflects the transition of the juvenile court from its origins in social welfare, treating the best interests of the child, to a criminal justice agency.

Ms. Donnelly has a caseload of 45 youths whom she visits a few times a month at home, school or work to make sure they are where they are supposed to be. Three of her clients have disappeared completely. She is confident she could find them, if she had enough time, which she does not.

She could also get a court-ordered arrest warrant, but the juvenile court cannot afford its own warrant squad, and police officers she knows are reluctant to spend time looking for children on warrants, unless the person is arrested on a new charge.

"A lot of officers don't want to waste their time on kiddie court when the judge is going to release the kid anyway," she said.

Ms. Donnelly stopped by a house on Chicago's South Side where one of her clients lived with his grandmother and 13 cousins, since his mother was a crack addict who couldn't be found. A husky 16-year-old, the boy was on probation for selling crack and was confined to his home 24 hours a day unless accompanied by his grandmother.

A charge of auto theft had been dropped when he repeatedly failed to appear for trial and the witnesses in the case tired of going to court without any result. That is a common way for young defendants to win.

Ms. Donnelly reminded the boy that he had another court date in two days, relating to a charge of theft and battery incurred while he was supposed to have been confined to home. He had forgotten about the appearance.

It was another day's work for Ms. Donnelly. "These kids have had nothing but chaos in their lives," she said. "That's what we have to overcome, to give them as much structure and consistency as we can."

"But how," she asked, "do you replace the absence of the family?" Sometimes she thinks the only answer is to move in herself. But she knows that would not work either.

A Move for Change
Young Suspects In Adult Courts

All these troubles have sparked a growing movement to drastically restructure and perhaps abolish the juvenile court.

Leading the charge are conservative politicians who have passed laws in all 50 states allowing juveniles to be tried in adult court and sent to adult prison.

In Illinois a person under 17 may be tried in adult court for crimes including murder, carjacking and armed robbery as well as possession of drugs or weapons within 1,000 feet of a school or housing project, a provision that disproportionately affects minorities. Illinois also has a version for juveniles of the "three strikes and you're out" law.

Congress is poised to pass the most Draconian law yet, with provisions for $1.5 billion in Federal grants to states that try larger number[s] of young people in adult court and making 14-year-olds subject to trial in Federal court if they commit certain felonies.

"It's the end of the juvenile court," said Ira Schwartz, dean of the School of Social Work at the University of Pennsylvania. "All you would have left is a court for larceny." Such a truncated court would not be financially viable and would probably be scrapped, he suggested.

At the same time, some left-wing legal scholars have also called for abolishing the juvenile court, though for very different reasons. Barry Feld, a professor of law at the University of Minnesota, believes that young people often fail to get adequate legal representation in juve-nile court and would fare better in adult court, where they would be more likely to be assigned decent lawyers.

Under his plan, as a further protective measure, juveniles in adult court would be given a "youth discount," or lighter sentences, depending on their age.

Some children's advocates who in the past championed the juvenile court have begun urging still another solution—that the court scale back its judicial role and transfer its functions to community groups or social service agencies that would provide better treatment for young people in trouble.

In the rush to try juveniles in adult courts, some critical questions go unasked. For example, are 13- and 14-year olds really competent to stand trial like adults?

Often such young defendants cannot tell a coherent story to help defend themselves, said Thomas Grisso, a psychiatry professor at the University of Massachusetts Medical Center. What then should the court do? Wait till they are more mature?

As a result of all this ferment, Mr. Schwartz said, "What we have right now in the juvenile court is chaos, with every state moving piecemeal on its own." A century after the creation of the juvenile court, he said, "Unless we take it more seriously, what we are headed for is its abolition by default."

Juvenile Justice Comes of Age

As younger and younger kids cmmit worse crimes, legislators are overcoming political and institutional obstacles in order to update juvenile justice systems.

Donna Lyons

Youngsters under 18 who rob, rape and murder have forced an examination of outdated juvenile justice systems designed for another time. Violent juvenile crime rates have soared 67 percent in the last 10 years. And although the percentage of youth doing these things is low (one out of 200), juveniles are still disproportionally represented among violent criminals.

Today's young offenders turn as easily toward crime and violence as young men of past generations took up smoking in the boys' room, says New York Senator Steve Saland, who has become the Senate's expert on juvenile crime and delinquency. He says that many aspects of family courts and the juvenile justice system have become archaic. "We need to face the fact that the existing system is incapable of dealing with the most serious, violent kids out there."

Fixing the system isn't easy. Optimistic congressional leaders have placed juvenile justice among their top 10 priorities this year, but state experience shows that the politics of the problem are messy, and that planning for reform is a tedious and long-term undertaking. Advocacy groups and the public tend to think that changing the system to take care of serious juvenile crime should be easy enough. Researchers point out that we know more today than ever about "what works" and what does not to control juvenile crime. Make punishment for offenders swift and sure. Provide services that prevent young lives from spiraling into crime and violence. But legislators find numerous political and institutional hurdles to a quick fix.

LEGISLATIVE STRUGGLES

An agreement to reform New York's juvenile justice system was announced in February by Senate Republican leaders and Republican Governor George Pataki. The proposal includes longer sentences for violent juveniles and lock-down and limited privileges for the most serious offenders. It would significantly alter family courts to promote juvenile accountability and parental involvement, and would allow those courts to issue search and arrest warrants and to hear from victims in sentencing young offenders.

"This has been a long, laborious process—but one that is certainly well worth the fight," says Saland, who is Republican chairman of the Senate Committee on Children and Families. Indeed, the Senate's pact with the governor follows three years' work on juvenile justice reform, which still must earn the approval of the Democratic Assembly. Public fear of juvenile crime has been particularly acute in New York where rates of juvenile violence, especially homicides, have been well above the national average.

Lawmakers elsewhere wrestle with the same issues of how to update systems, created primarily for young thieves and vandals, to deal as effectively with juvenile rapists and armed robbers. Consensus for change can be difficult to come by when the policy issues involved are so ideologically divisive. Members split on issues like whether you should spend money to prevent crime or to punish young offenders. And it is an arduous task for legislatures to get a handle on juvenile justice, which reaches into courts, corrections, education and children's services. Trying to make comprehensive changes is complicated by the differing perspectives of all the committees. To manage the issue, many states have formed task forces, interim study committees or other special work groups to deliberate and make recommendations on juvenile justice reform.

Recent crime statistics show downturns in overall rates of violent crime. This might have eased political pressure on legislatures to act, but now Congress and the Clinton administration want to have a say. Federal measures could change guiding philosophies on detention of juveniles and put new "get tough" requirements on states. Proposals include things like graduated sanctions for young offenders and other programs that various states have done already—and often done well. More than a

"LAST CHANCE" PROGRAMS DIVERT SOME YOUNG OFFENDERS

States are transforming juvenile justice, and among their innovations are "third systems" that lie between traditional juvenile justice and adult corrections. To date, at least a dozen states have created systems that blend juvenile and adult system jurisdiction when juveniles commit serious crimes. Designed to rehabilitate criminal youths, third systems often apply strict discipline, education and behavior modification.

"We can't just write off 14-year-olds," says Regis Groff, director of the Colorado Youthful Offender System, which was created by the General Assembly in 1993. "Kids who are convicted of certain felonies and sentenced to adult prisons can be better served in special programs that might be harsh, but are designed for them," says Groff, a former state senator.

Designed primarily for gun- and gang-related offenders and operated in the adult corrections department, the YOS program is a precondition for a suspended sentence for some juveniles 14 to 18 years old who are sent, under state law, directly to district court. These youths are then committed to YOS for up to six years. The military-type program couples positive peer culture with education. Its focus on self-control and physical activity helps break down a violent mentality so youths begin to develop positive self-concepts and learn the value of service to others, according to Groff.

What sets YOS apart from the adult system is the opportunity for youths who successfully complete the program to phase into supervised community release for six to 12 months. But YOS is a one-time shot—if they of fend again they will go into the adult system. So far, Groff said, of 18 kids who have gone through the program only two have committed new offenses.

Other states are following Colorado's lead with "last chance" systems for tough, young offenders. North Carolina created a labor intensive community service program for 16- to 25-year-olds sentenced as adults. As in Colorado, discipline is combined with education and rehabilitation. Connecticut, Minnesota, Missouri and Wisconsin have created third, or dual jurisdiction, systems for serious offenders. In 1996 alone, six states applied the concept of blended juvenile and adult system jurisdiction. Kansas, Utah and Virginia included third systems in major reform acts, while Massachusetts, Michigan and New Mexico incorporated similar sentencing options for some serious offenders.

While the popularity of intermediate systems is on the rise, some experts contend that early intervention, not middle-tier programs like YOS, is key to keeping young people out of juvenile and criminal justice systems.

"It's just another rearrangement of boxes and kids, but not a solution," says former House Majority Leader Bill Purcell, who now directs the Child and Family Policy Center at Vanderbilt Institute for Public Policy Studies in Nashville, Tenn. Purcell said that while states may benefit from changing procedures to allow dual sentencing, they first must develop thoughtful, broad policy on how they are going to deal with all aspects of juvenile crime and justice.

—Julie Featherstone, NCSL

dozen states have significantly reformed their juvenile systems in recent years. And in a manner that might be instructive to Capitol Hill, state legislatures are substantially changing juvenile justice despite what sometimes are partisan differences, and often as a result of spade work that has developed consensus among the "stakeholders" in state and local criminal justice and child welfare systems.

IT CAN BE DONE

"It's doable politically if you are willing and patient enough to take it one bite at a time," says Representative Jeanne Adkins, chair of the House Judiciary Committee in Colorado, where both chambers are controlled by Republicans. Perseverance has paid off in Colorado, where reforms started four years ago when Adkins got together with a like-minded Republican attorney general to deal with gangs and other juveniles who commit crimes with guns. Several high-profile crimes had fueled public alarm about juvenile violence, including news of two young

sters in Adkins' suburban Denver district accused in the shooting death of a sheriff's deputy. A bill Adkins carried in 1993 to impose tougher sanctions for juveniles who commit gun crimes made it out of the House, but was killed in the Senate. Later that year, popular Democratic Governor Roy Romer stole some thunder when he called a special legislative session in which lawmakers approved juvenile gun restrictions and sentencing measures. Included in the package was legislation creating the Youthful Offender System, an intermediate system for juveniles who otherwise would have been sentenced as adults. At least a dozen states have since emulated Colorado's "third system."

The special session may have been the most climactic point in juvenile justice reform in Colorado, but it did not divert the legislature's attention from the issues. An Interim Committee on Youth Violence, a task force on the recodification of the children's code and the Legislative Oversight Committee followed with more than three years of work to retool many aspects of the system.

> *"We all say we want what is best for kids and the public, but these things can fall apart once you get into fighting over money."*
>
> —Representative Michael Lawlor, Connecticut

"The push and pull of prevention versus punishment was always there," says Adkins, who was instrumental in the study efforts along with chairing the Legislative Oversight Committee, "but we ended up with a cohesive, bipartisan effort." Her 1996 legislation approved by the General Assembly addresses detention, transfer to adult court and parental responsibility, and places limits on a juvenile's right to a jury trial. Other legislation last year ensures that no less than 20 percent of crime prevention grants focus on early childhood.

Recent Colorado law also established performance-based audits of certain programs so that future policy and funding can be based on more than just anecdotal evidence. This helps reduce interagency politics, which can be as difficult as the partisan issues, according to Adkins. She compliments the governor for involving key department heads in the work of the legislature. "People who could truly make changes were at the table suggesting them," she says.

AVERTING AGENCY POLITICS

Lawmakers often must coordinate the many arms of state and local government involved in juvenile justice, since agency responsibilities may overlap in some areas and leave cracks elsewhere. In Connecticut, legislation in 1995 to transform juvenile justice policy incorporated a second stage of planning for the agency reorganization necessary to successfully carry out the law.

"We all say we want what is best for kids and the public, but these things can fall apart once you get into fighting over money," says Connecticut Representative Michael Lawlor, who co-chairs the Joint Judiciary Committee for House Democrats. He also worked to build consensus for the reform package in the Senate. "The policy decisions that changed laws ultimately would affect budgets and missions of a number of agencies," he says. The General Assembly dealt with this by requiring that the agencies meet and make recommendations on bureaucratic and budget changes necessary under the new law. A plan presented to the Legislature last year resulted in reallocation of about $62 million and authorization of another $16 million to expand existing programs. A contract study reviewed and documented what dispositions were being given juveniles in various courts and created an offender profile for the state. This information provided a factual basis for the reorganization plan and helped to extinguish turf battles.

Lawlor says the reform act represented a fusion of punitive measures for tough kids and shifting of resources to allow for early intervention and alternative sanctions for others. A number of factors aided bipartisan agreement. A joint committee structure in Connecticut, in which the chambers and parties are used to working together, proved practical. Further, new rules implemented in 1994 by House Speaker Thomas Ritter were intended to get bills out of committees quicker and avoid bogging down policy in partisan politics. And observers say that on issues like youth policy, the culture of the legislature traditionally has been one of rolling up its sleeves and finding workable solutions. Connecticut also has a fairly centralized justice system and a recent, decent track record in adult sentencing. The reform legislation charged the judiciary's Office of Alternative Sanctions with creating a range of options to deal with juvenile offenders, akin to a successful overhaul of its adult system.

Lawlor says that a key to lasting, bipartisan satisfaction with the reforms has been the reported average savings of $125,000 per year for each youth diverted from juvenile corrections facilities to alternative programs or the adult system. Also a selling point: Expansion of pretrial alternatives for lower risk offenders helped the state address litigation it faced over crowding of detention facilities.

Although the judiciary in Connecticut was given a freer hand in creating a range of sanctions for young offenders, lawmakers invested much discretion with prosecutors for transferring kids to adult court. "All kids selling drugs are not alike," Lawlor says. "Many can be handled in the juvenile system, but a few are up-and-coming Al Capones. The prosecutors know who the really bad kids are."

PARTISAN STRIPES

Significant juvenile justice reform has in recent years happened more often in states where the same political party controls both chambers of the legislature, with little difference as to which party happens to have leadership. In 1994, Democratic-controlled legislatures in Arkansas, Florida, Minnesota and Oklahoma made substantial changes to youth policy, as did Missouri and Texas in 1995, and Kentucky and Virginia in 1996. In addition to Republican-led Colorado reforms that began in 1993, GOP-controlled legislatures in Oregon, Pennsylvania and Wisconsin in 1995, and Kansas and Utah in 1996 passed important reforms. Some of these legislatures had the possible advantage of working with a governor of the same political stripe, but six states significantly revised juvenile justice policy with a governor of a different party from one or both chambers in the statehouse.

The ease with which lawmakers in Connecticut and elsewhere have prevailed over partisanship may be harder to come by elsewhere. Although New York may be primed for juvenile justice reform in 1997, it also has a history of partisan gridlock over criminal justice issues.

FEDERAL PLANS FOR JUVENILE JUSTICE

The 105th Congress opened with no shortage of proposals to modify the federal approach to juvenile justice. Two separate bills (S 3 and S 10) are offered by the Senate majority, along with a minority measure (S 15). The House, similarly, has a majority bill (HR 3) and a minority proposal (HR 278). What these bills have in common are provisions to prosecute juveniles as adults in federal courts, to allow preconviction detention, to open juvenile records and to provide more money to reduce juvenile gun crime. While part of these plans would place conditions on states to receive grants, others are actions aimed at federal prosecution of certain juvenile offenders.

In late February, the president offered his strategy for dealing with gangs and youth violence. The administration's proposal (HR 810, S 362) contains provisions similar to the others. But the bill also proposes funds to be used by prosecutors, courts, probation, parole, public defenders, victims' offices, and others in state and local criminal justice systems to develop better ways to respond to violent, serious juvenile crime. Other funds are earmarked for initiatives that will help children who are most likely to be led into crime, including antitruancy and other school and community-based programs.

The administration's juvenile crime bill continues mandates on states that receive federal money for juvenile justice. Most of these mandates have been in place since the Juvenile Justice and Delinquency Prevention Act of 1974. Those include keeping juvenile offenders separate from adults, removing young status offenders (youth arrested for offenses such as truancy that wouldn't be crimes if they were adults) from adult lockups and taking measures to correct disproportionate minority confinement. At the same time, the bill would give greater authority to the federal agency to waive requirements where states can justify a need for flexibility. Today, Congress is more interested in guaranteeing punishment for youthful offenders. S 10 would eliminate the stringent mandates of the 1974 act and replace them with a requirement that juveniles who are detained are not in institutions where they would have "regular sustained physical contact" with adult prisoners.

While the federal approach to juvenile crime appears to have toughened since the 1974 act, the motivations seem surprisingly similar. In findings of the 1974 act, Congress noted that juveniles accounted for almost half of the serious crimes in the United States and concluded that state and local communities do not have sufficient expertise or resources to deal comprehensively with juvenile delinquency. The federal Office of Juvenile Justice and Delinquency Prevention (OJJDP) created at that time would now, under various proposals before Congress, evolve into a renamed "crime control" agency.

Last year's pre-election season renewed partisan sparring about Washington's appropriate role in juvenile crime. Passed during the waning days of the 104th Congress, the omnibus appropriations bill included an incentive grant pushing states toward graduated punishments for juveniles, beginning with sanctions for first-time nonviolent offenders. While that move may have whetted the appetite of members who are anxious to do more, the slow start of this Congress adds to uncertainty about what direction it will steer on juvenile justice.

—*Jon Felde, NCSL*

But despite what often have been troubled relations between Republican Governor Pataki and the Legislature, especially the Assembly, major adult sentencing reforms were achieved in 1995. Some lawmakers are optimistic that the same bipartisan agreement can be forged on juvenile justice.

At press time, Assembly Democrats said they were still working on a set of juvenile crime initiatives but had not yet unveiled legislation. Speaker Sheldon Silver has said his interests include longer sentences for violent juveniles, arrest powers for family courts, sanctions like restitution and community service, and parental responsibility—proposals similar to those agreed to by Saland and the governor. Observers say the pact between the Senate and the governor puts political pressure on Assembly leaders to act, and speculate that the Democrats are developing proposals to balance tougher sentencing with certain preventive approaches and service components absent from the Republicans' package. Last year under Saland's leadership, the Senate passed a sweeping Juvenile Justice Reform and Delinquency Prevention Act that failed to get Assembly attention.

PREVENTION IN CALIFORNIA

This will be a cutting-teeth year for committee leadership in California. In part because of term limits, brand new legislators chair the committees that must deal with recommendations issued last fall by a task force on juvenile crime. Created by the Legislature, the task force was composed of an Assembly Republican and a Senate Democrat, along with district attorneys, corrections and social service officials, judges, and other representatives of law enforcement and child welfare systems. Concern was

STATES ACTIVE IN JUVENILE JUSTICE REFORM

More than a dozen states in recent years have passed major juvenile justice system reforms. They include: Arkansas, Colorado, Connecticut, Florida, Kansas, Kentucky, Missouri, Oklahoma, Oregon, Pennsylvania, Texas, Utah, Virginia and Wisconsin. Some of the reform acts broadly address early intervention and prevention, graduated sanctions for juvenile offenders, parental responsibility, and treating serious offenders like adult criminals, including opening of certain juvenile records and proceedings.

Nearly all states have passed laws addressing various components of juvenile justice reform. Significant, selected state laws have included:

Authorizing photographs, fingerprints of certain young offenders: Alabama, Arizona, Hawaii, Idaho, New Hampshire, North Dakota, Ohio.

Opening certain juvenile records, proceedings: Georgia, Indiana, Louisiana, Pennsylvania, South Carolina, South Dakota.

Creating juvenile criminal history that can follow one to adult court: Georgia, Oklahoma, Virginia.

Providing mandatory adult handling of certain serious crimes, offenders: Alabama, Arizona, Delaware, Georgia, Indiana, Kansas, Massachusetts, Michigan, Minnesota, Mississippi, Nevada, North Dakota, Utah, South Carolina.

Lowering the age of allowable transfer to adult court of certain young offenders: Colorado, Idaho, Michigan, New Mexico, North Carolina, West Virginia, Wisconsin, Wyoming.

Defining, setting penalties for gang-related crime: Arkansas, Arizona, California, Florida, Georgia, Kansas, Illinois, Indiana, Michigan, Nevada, North Dakota, Tennessee, Wisconsin.

Establishing, funding juvenile crime prevention: Arkansas, Arizona, California, Colorado, Connecticut, Florida, Georgia, Illinois, Oklahoma, Ohio, Oregon, Mississippi, Missouri, North Carolina, Tennessee, Texas, Utah, Virginia, Washington, Wisconsin, Wyoming.

Holding parents responsible: Alaska, Arizona, California, Colorado, Idaho, Illinois, Indiana, New Hampshire, Michigan, New Mexico, Oregon, Rhode Island, Vermont, Virginia, Washington.

raised early on that the group, heavy with gubernatorial appointments, might serve as a rubber stamp for Republican Governor Pete Wilson's policies. This resulted in an understanding that 14 of the 17 members had to agree on each of the final recommendations. Ultimately, it meant that the task force was silent on lightning-rod issues like transfer of juveniles to adult courts.

The task force recommended that prevention of juvenile crime should be a priority—policy already embraced by the Legislature. Earlier in 1996, California lawmakers created two programs for prevention and early intervention grants when Senate President Pro Tem Bill Lockyer wangled $50 million for the prevention efforts during final budget negotiations. The legislation already is getting good reviews for bringing together local agencies and service providers that previously had not worked together. There remains sentiment in the Senate that local funding for juvenile crime prevention can have more impact than anything else the Legislature might do. Bills introduced by Senator Lockyer early this year would support the commitment to prevention by creating a Youth Violence Prevention Authority in state government, as well as renew grant programs and establish early intervention strategies in schools.

The governor has reportedly been shopping the Legislature for interest in proposals for direct, legislative transfer of certain serious juvenile offenders to adult court.

California's current "fitness law" relies entirely on judicial discretion for waiver to adult court, while the governor, prosecutors and victims' groups have suggested giving district attorneys more transfer authority or providing statutory certainty that certain juvenile offenders will be treated as adult criminals.

Legislation introduced by Senator Adam Schiff, the new chair of the Senate's subcommittee on juvenile justice, could significantly change the state's approach to transfer of juveniles to criminal courts. One bill would procedurally combine the separate "fitness hearing" to send a juvenile case to adult court and the preliminary hearing that takes place in district court. Another would create blended juvenile and adult jurisdiction for some serious offenders [reviving the "third system" concept floated unsuccessfully last year], and for the first time under California law allow direct file in adult court cases of juveniles who commit murder or rape. Noticeably absent from the California task force recommendations was comment on the transfer issue, reportedly because the panel found this to be a touchy subject on which they could not agree.

VOTERS DECIDE

Perhaps the most difficult of all for legislatures is when frustrated citizens decide to take matters into their own hands. Ballot initiatives in two Western states gave voters the say in setting policy for trial and sentencing of violent juveniles.

In Oregon, voters approved a 1994 citizen initiated "get tough" juvenile crime measure that requires certain violent 15-, 16- and 17-year olds to be tried as adults and receive mandatory sentences. The measure prohibits judges from treating first-time young offenders differently from repeat offenders. Lawmakers, while sympathetic to judges' concerns, have limited options for amending voter-initiated policy.

In Arizona, the Legislature is working to implement juvenile justice reforms approved by 63 percent of the voters last fall as an amendment to the state's Constitution. The measure, championed by the governor, mandates transfer of certain juvenile offenders to adult court. It requires that juveniles 15 and older be tried as adults when accused of certain violent offenses or if they are chronic offenders. Less definitive than the Oregon initiative, Arizona's voter-approved reforms left it to the Legislature to define violent and chronic juvenile offenders. New judiciary chair Senator John Kaites is garnering support for the implementation legislation by rounding it out with prevention and early intervention.

From *State Legislatures*, May 1997, pp. 12-18. 1997 by the National Conference of State Legislatures. Reprinted by permission.

The Bastard Stepchild of *Parens Patriae:* The American Juvenile Incarceration Structure

The right of the State, as parens patriae, to deny to the child procedural rights available to his elders was elaborated by the assertions that a child, unlike an adult, has a right not to liberty but to custody. He can be made to attorn to his parents, go to school, etc. If his parents default in effectively perform-ing their custodial functions—that is, if the child is "delinquent"—the state may intervene. In doing so, it does not deprive the child of any rights, because he has none.

—In re Gault
Supreme Court of the United States, 1967

by KENNETH WOODEN

The practice of incarcerating children and the conditions ex-isting therein have legal roots dating back to England during the late fourteenth and early fifteenth centuries. There, under the doctrine of *parens patriae,* the King's Court of Chancery held power of guardianship over children who were abandoned or willfully neglected by their parents.

In 1636, *parens patriae* was introduced in America when young Benjamen Eaton of Plymouth Colony, indentured by the state, was given to Bridget Fuller, a widow, and ordered by the governor "to kelp him at schoole two years and to imploy him after in shuch service as she saw good and that he should be fit for; but not to turne him over to any other, without ye gov'n consente."

Still another legal concept that derived from the Common Law of England was that of *mens rea*—guilty mind. A child of seven or younger could not be found guilty of a crime because he had not reached the age of reason. From age eight on, how-ever, the law forced the child to stand trial and endure the se-verity of full criminal prosecution. For example, in the early 1800's a child of eight who was accused of "malice revenge and cunning" for setting fire to some barns was convicted and hanged. In 1828 a New Jersey boy of thirteen was hanged for a crime he committed when he was twelve.

In 1727 the city of New Orleans built the first institution in America for neglected or homeless children. Up to that time and well into the nineteenth century, neglected and delinquent youths were placed in jails, prisons and almshouses with adults. Even today the same practice persists in many areas of the United StAtes: the laws of forty-six states still approve placing juveniles in county jails, and thirty-four of these states don't even require a special court order.

It wasn't until 1825 that New York City set up the House of Refuge, the first separate institution whose sole purpose was to aid juvenile offenders. Within a few years other cities—Phila-delphia and Boston, for example—followed suit and estab-lished similar accommodations. Although these facilities were set up to deal with juvenile offenders, unfortunately they were eventually obliged to admit neglected children because there was no place else for them to go once they became wards of the state. This practice is still common in all but three states.

These "houses of refuge" proved to be a historical milestone in the American family culture. For the first time family-cen-tered discipline was replaced by institutional discipline admin-istered by city, county or state governments. Parents, grandparents, older sisters and brothers were replaced by guards and superintendents.

Progressive in its philosophy, the New York House of Refuge early initiated the practice of "binding out" or placing delinquent children in foster homes. In his daily journal the su-perintendent of the Manhattan House of Refuge recorded the following entry on May 10, 1828:

> We saw the eight boys for Ohio start in good spirits.... It excited considerable warm good feeling to see so many little fellows bound for such a good and suitable place from the House of Refuge, among the passengers on board the steamboat.

Sixty-five years later, in 1893, foster home advocate Homer Folks vigorously promoted the practice of binding out delin-quent children. Folks believed that of all the children incarcer-ated within institutions, "only a very small number show lack of moral sense and are dangerous to the community." The genuine human concern of this nineteenth-century progressive has been echoed by each new generation of reformers for the last eight decades. As children's justice becomes an increasingly popular issue in the 1970's, more and more groups are quoting the National Council for Crime and Delinquency, which has said that only 10 percent of all juvenile offenders require incarceration.

However, the rhetoric of reformers and progressive organizations did little to prevent the powerful growth of the state-supported and state-operated training school complex. Massachusetts created the first such penal facility for children in 1847. Called the Lyman School for Boys, it became one of the worst institutions in America and one of the first training schools to be closed down in 1972 for massive failure and child brutality. By 1960 there were two hundred training schools in fifty states, the District of Columbia, Puerto Rico and the Virgin Islands. The daily population numbered 40,000, with close to 100,000 children a year being processed through their gates. By 1974 the national network of these schools had a combined operating budget of close to $300 million and a recidivism* rate of eight out of ten children.

The early juvenile penal facilities were located on the outskirts of urban areas, but as the cities grew in size and encompassed the old "reform schools" and "houses of refuge," there was a movement to relocate on large acreages in rural areas. Thus began what is known in youth corrections as "the colony system." Whole institutions became self-sufficient entities. The economics of the small towns where they located have become tightly interwoven with the institutions because a majority of the local townspeople have become dependent on them for their livelihood.

World War I imposed its military mentality on the youth correctional system, when, according to one historian, "Living units became barracks; cottage groups, companies; housefathers, captains; superintendents, majors or more often colonels; and the kids wore uniforms." That influence is still alive in Texas and Arizona State training schools; I personally witnessed boys in the atmosphere of a military stockade, forced to march and take orders in a military fashion from guards in military-style uniforms.

One of the most distressing social phenomena in juvenile justice is that earlier liberal reforms designed to help children ended up hurting them. In 1890 the first juvenile courts were organized and they quickly spread throughout the country after the turn of the century. Compulsory educational laws were also passed, making it mandatory for children to attend school. Yet another reform was the progressive Social Security Act of 1935, a section of which permitted governmental agencies, using tax monies, to provide for the neglected child. What has happened, though, is that the well-meaning intent of reform has turned into the tyranny of reform: the state now has gained greater social control over the dependent youngster. Children who fail to attend school for any of an assortment of reasons are hauled into juvenile court and incarcerated in state training schools for years. State welfare agencies, with vast sums of money, arbi-

trarily take children from blood relatives and ship them to institutions in and out of state.

In 1967 the United States Supreme Court concluded that "the Latin phrase (*parens patriae*) proved to be great help to those who sought to rationalize the exclusion of juveniles from the constitutional scheme; but its meaning is murky and its historical credentials are of dubious relevance." Regardless of such legal rhetoric, America's youth are still being incarcerated in every state of the union. Because of old legal procedures and laws, because of our national tradition of juvenile institutionalization and because numerous "social reforms," neglected and delinquent juveniles find themselves caught in the destructive net of incarceration behind locked doors in one of four different institutions: juvenile detention center, county or municipal jail, state training school or private facility approved by the presiding juvenile system.

First offenders are usually sent to one of the 300 detention centers, where approximately 13,000 kids* sit for an average of twelve days with nothing to do, awaiting the court's decision on their fate. Because the police and most juvenile workers fear they'll run away, they are detained behind locked doors. Most detention centers I have visited throughout the country are situated in or near the same building that houses the juvenile court. To the casual observer or group on tour given by the personnel, these facilities look rather harmless and almost like college dorms. But behind the public relations veneer, a penitentiary atmosphere prevails; guards, heavy iron doors, countless keys and closed circuit TV give paramount security and control. Solitary confinement is readily employed for the slightest infraction.

According to the National Council on Crime and Delinquency, 50 percent of the youngsters in detention centers have committed no crime and 40 percent will be released from custody after court appearance. Still in increasing numbers, children are filling up our detention centers, and the politicians are calling for new multimillion-dollar facilities that will be operated by county governments. The politics of jobs are very real.

Where no juvenile detention center exists, the child is held in a county or municipal jail until he appears before a juvenile judge. United States Senator Birch Bayh, chairman of the Senate Subcommittee on Delinquency, commented during hearings on the subject in September of 1973: "On any given day, there are close to 8,000 juveniles held in jails in the United States. It is estimated that more than 100,000 youths spend one or more days each year in adult jails or police lockups."

These local penal accommodations, the oldest facilities in the United States for both youthful and adult offenders, are, in the words of Daniel P. Starnes, a leading expert in the field of

---

*Recidivism rate is really a failure rate; it refers to the number of children who return to the institution.

*A shocking report entitled "Hidden Closets" by George Saleebey, former Deputy Director of the California Youth Authority, reveals that in January, 1975, California was locking away noncriminal youngsters at such a rate that, based on national figures, the Golden State would account for one third of all children so incarcerated throughout the country. Prior to this controversial report, California was listed as having a moderate amount of children in detention. If the report is accurate, the ramifications are ominous as to how little we really know concerning the actual numbers of children locked away.

corrections, "notorious as a constant source of verified filth, perversion, sadism and corruption." More than a million town drunk and men and women of violence, most with criminal records, enjoy the company of nearly 100,000 youngsters annually, 75 percent of whom are locked in the same rooms with adults. In 1970, 66.1 percent of these were later released, free of any charges.

In 1970, a statewide breakdown of a national survey by the University of Chicago showed that in Illinois ten thousand children made up 6 percent of the total city, county-jail population for that year. Out of 160 jails in the state, 142 detained juveniles and only 9 of them segregated the children from adults. A mere 15 percent of the 142 jails had supervisory personnel to keep the children from the harm of molestation and rape.

Training schools, which operate in every state except Massachusetts, represent the nadir in a class filter system for juvenile malefactors who are picked up by police, arrested, detained in a juvenile hall and eventually sentenced by a judge for rehabilitation. Almost all are state-operated and controlled. The laws that govern their legal functions specify that training schools are to provide custody and to rehabilitate the child so that his confinement will build toward a more useful life for himself and his community.

I found basically two types of training schools. The first is a miniature penitentiary with high walls surrounding the grounds. All the buildings and cell block wings therein are interlocked by long corridors. Not only are individual cell doors secured, but each wing is also locked at all times. There is almost always a self-sufficient industrial complex on the grounds—laundry, hospital, maintenance shop and any other facility needed to keep strangers out and the children in. Dubious educational and religious services are available to the children, along with the standbys of solitary confinement and of bloodhounds to locate any who run away.

The second and more common type of training school is the cottage system. Its concept was introduced in 1856 to give children the closest thing to some form of home life. Those in charge are "house parents" rather than "guards." The outside area is usually quiet and pleasant and bears little semblance to a penal facility. The cottages are usually small, esthetically pleasing, dormlike structures. Unfortunately, those I have seen have no back or side doors, or if they do, the doors are always chained and locked. The windows are also secured with heavy wire and in the event of emergencies such as fire, escape would be impossible except through the front door.

Such a situation occurred in Arizona sometime during the 1960's, according to several state employees I interviewed. After a fire the charred remains of seventeen youngsters were found piled in front of a chained exit door, but the full circumstances of their needless deaths have been kept from the general public to this day.

The cottage system always reserves one building for secure treatment, solitary confinement. Any child who acts up in a solitary cottage is further isolated in a special single room for indefinite periods of time.

Still another facility for the incarceration of wayward youths is the private institution. Few people know much about these private institutions and very little has been written about them. Generally these facilities are for children of well-to-do parents or parents who have special benefits because of their job or station in life. They are usually located in isolated, wooded, rural areas. Their geographic setting and private nature adds greatly to the public's lack of information about their performance. These private "hospitals," "ranches," "homes," etc., run the gamut—from exceedingly good to exceedingly poor; from state-approved and -licensed to unsupervised and unevaluated. Some have established excellent reputations; others have recently sprung up in response to newly available state and federal monies. Some, like the Menninger Foundation in Topeka, Kansas, have the noble purpose of truly helping to relieve and direct the troubled; others are designed to help themselves by warehousing and administratively exploiting both disturbed and normal children while the owners amass sizable fortunes.

In many cases the only difference between the private institution and public state training schools is the cost. The control philosophy is the same. The children are usually there by court order. They are locked in the buildings during the day and in their rooms at night. The view from the windows is obscured by steel and thick wire mesh. Solitary confinement is used consistently as punishment for breaking minor rules. Most frightening of all is the unsupervised environment that allows for a new agent of control—chemical restraints—to be used with little thought to their ultimate effects on the child's body or mind. And all the while the American taxpayer is paying, directly or indirectly, financially and socially.

What we have today, then, is a juvenile justice system that originated as a small community concern, by people of good will but whose reform programs and laws created a national industry. Without public awareness a system that was designed to help children in trouble has become a tyrannical monster, destroying the very children it was mandated to save.

From *Weeping in the Playtime of Others,* Ohio State University Press, 1999, pp. 23-30. © 1999 by Ohio State University. Reprinted by permission.

Quick Fix

Pushing a medical cure for youth violence

Annette Fuentes

Several prestigious New York City medical centers have been experimenting on 6- to 11-year-old boys in an effort to prove that violence, aggression and even criminal behavior are caused by biological factors. One of these studies, first launched in 1992, was still underway in April when patient advocacy groups charged the researchers with violating federal ethics rules, unleashing a torrent of media scrutiny and outrage.

Critics are asking why peer review panels at the New York State Psychiatric Institute (NYSPI), Mount Sinai Medical Center and the National Institute of Mental Health (NIMH), approved the experiments. Serious ethical considerations are raised by the age of the boys, the fact that many were poor minorities, and that the experiments were not designed to provide treatment for an existing illness. Investigators are looking at the researchers' use of fenfluramine, a drug banned last fall by the Food and Drug Administration (FDA) when the agency discovered that it had caused heart damage as part of the popular diet drug fen-phen. And legal advocates are examining the role of New York City's chief juvenile justice prosecutor in helping one team of researchers gather young subjects. Responding to the outcry, Congress held hearings in April on the FDA's role in approving the drug for experiments on children.

But the studies also raise larger questions about the social and political implications of research into the roots of violence that focuses on disenfranchised, inner-city communities. NIMH, the federal agency that funded much of the research, has granted millions of dollars to studies investigating serotonin, the chemical that transmits signals between cells in the brain, and how it is connected to violent behavior. If they discover biological factors that lead to violence in minority boys, the research could inaugurate wholesale drug intervention for youngsters identified as "at-risk" for anti-social behavior. In an era when the government trades its previous commitment to battling poverty for a strategy of battling the impoverished, research that seeks the causes of violence in individuals and their body chemistry has an obvious appeal. If biology, not sociology, can be the predictor of crime, then that could justify clamping down on suspect populations.

The New York City experiments involved one team of psychiatric researchers at NYSPI, part of Columbia University, and another team doing similar research at Queens College and Mount Sinai Medical Center in Manhattan. Several of the researchers had been laboring since 1990 to find a link between behavior and genetics in their sample of urban youth. "The proliferation of violence by youth in our society is reaching epidemic proportions," the NYSPI researchers told reporters in a prepared statement. "Each day we see instances of children committing violent acts against other children and adults, most recently [the schoolyard murders in] Jonesboro, [Ark.].... The correlation between serotonin and aggression in children needs to be studied in order to identify children at highest risk for impulsive, aggressive behavior."

The NYSPI researchers, led by Daniel Pine and Gail Wasserman, were trying to prove that their subjects— young brothers of jailed delinquents—were predisposed to criminal behavior because of familial histories of aggressive behavior. In an article published last September in the *Archives of General Psychiatry*, Pine and Wasserman conclude: "In young boys, aggressive behavior and social circumstances that are conducive to the development of aggressive behavior are positively correlated with a marker of central serotonergic activity." In other words, kids who grow up around aggression are likely to be aggressive *and* have low levels of serotonin.

The Queens College/Mount Sinai team was led by Jeffrey Halperin, whose findings were published last October in the *Journal of the American Academy of Child Adolescent Psychiatry*. Halperin's study also sought to correlate behaviors with serotonin levels in children. Based on a study of boys with aggressive pasts and Attention Deficit Hyperactivity Disorder (ADHD), he points to a correlation in his data between aggressive behavior in parents and lower serotonin levels in aggressive boys with ADHD, a psychiatric diagnosis that some researchers believe is a predictor of aggressive behavior in adults. But Halperin says he couldn't determine "the extent to which this association is environmentally and/or genetically transmitted."

In both studies, researchers gave boys one-time doses of fenfluramine to help measure the amount of serotonin in their brains. All the boys had restricted diets for a month and were required to fast for 12 hours prior to the test. They were attached to IVs for up to six hours as blood samples were taken and only allowed to drink water. Halperin's group consisted of 41 boys with ADHD. Twelve of Halperin's subjects on medication for ADHD were required to stop taking it for a month before the test—a procedure known as "a wash-out." Pine and Wasserman followed virtually the same protocols in their two studies, which involved 34 boys in one and 100 in the other.

Many aspects of these experiments raise red flags for those who monitor the ethical implications of medical research on human subjects, but it was the use of fenfluramine that captured media attention. Though one dose of fenfluramine is unlikely to cause permanent heart damage, there is no research on the drug's effects in children. One study on adults showed that 90 percent of healthy subjects who were given doses of the drug experienced fatigue, headaches, lightheadedness and lack of concentration.

The FDA's director, Dr. Michael Friedman, acknowledges that his agency approved researchers' continued use of fenfluramine on the boys even after the drug had been pulled from the market because it caused heart valve damage in some dieters. But he defended that decision at hearings before the House Committee on Government Reform and Oversight in April, saying that in February NYSPI revised the parental consent form to provide warnings about possible harmful side effects. But that was five months after fenfluramine was pulled from the market, and the FDA allowed NYSPI to enroll two more youths in the study before publicity halted it in April.

Researchers at NYSPI also received cooperation from other governmental agencies. Wasserman began assembling subjects in 1991, at first using the New York City Department of Probation to find 6- to 10-year-old boys whose older brothers were incarcerated delinquents. After one month, probation officials balked, deciding that families of the youth might feel coerced into participating.

Wasserman and her colleagues ultimately were aided by Peter Reinharz, head of the family court unit of the city's law department. Reinharz reportedly gave the researchers access to family court records, which are supposed to be confidential. His actions are being investigated by the Legal Aid Society. "We've filed a Freedom of Information request to find out which youth were identified," says Jane Spinak, the head of Legal Aid's juvenile rights division. "We think many of them

were our clients. We believe their civil rights may have been violated."

Attorneys at Disability Advocates and New York Lawyers in the Public Interest get credit for exposing the experiments. They came across the two studies while doing their own research for an ongoing case against the state Office of Mental Health. That suit challenges the state's practice of permitting research on incapacitated patients—children and adults—at psychiatric facilities, arguing that it violates the patient's right to informed consent. "There are so many angles that are problematic," says Ruth Lowenkron of New York Lawyers in the Public Interest. "To see this kind of non-therapeutic research raises questions about what was told to the parents. How was consent obtained? In the Mount Sinai experiments, kids were taken off their medication. What happened to them?"

When the lawyers found out about the violence research studies in December, they filed a complaint with the Office of Protection from Research Risks (OPRR) at the Department of Health and Human Services. OPRR is the government agency charged with monitoring all medical research involving human and animal subjects to insure that it conforms with federal guidelines on informed consent and safety. Gary Ellis, OPRR head, says his office is investigating four complaints related to the studies, the most recent of which was filed in April. The complaints question whether the children in the studies and their families were adequately informed of the risks of the experiments and were therefore able to give real informed consent to participate. Ellis says his office will also investigate whether the studies violated government rules against exposing healthy children to potential harm in experiments that offer no therapeutic benefit. For its part, NYSPI asserts that the children in one group were at risk for suicide, so the experiments did offer some promise of helping them. Ellis says his investigation will take up to six months to complete.

A racial component of the research also raises disturbing questions. In one of Pine and Wasserman's experiments, 60 percent of the 34 boys who participated were black, and the other 40 percent Latino. NYSPI insists that the racial/ethnic mix of the boys Pine and Wasserman studied simply reflects the population living around the institute. But for Ronald Walters, a political scientist at the University of Maryland, the New York studies are just a continuation of what started at NIMH in the early '90s. Walters served on a panel appointed by then Health and Human Services secretary Louis Sullivan in 1992 that reviewed government-funded research into violence for potential race bias. Then, as now, Walters and other critics believed such research reflects a widespread view among many whites that black and Latino people are predisposed by biology to commit crimes and violent acts. "Why haven't members of the Black and Hispanic Congressional Caucuses been more concerned with this?"

asks Walters. "Black and brown children will be the obvious target in the inner city. This research is a shortcut way to deal with violence."

The experiments in New York were conducted in the shadow of a long-running controversy over the very nature of the research: looking for biological causes for violence in individuals instead of examining social and economic factors. Six years ago, the federal National Institutes of Health was embroiled in a debate over the legitimacy of a five-year plan to study the causes of violence that including looking at genetic and biological factors. Dubbed "the violence initiative," the plan was scuttled after Dr. Frederick Goodwin, then head of the Alcohol, Drug Abuse and Mental Health Administration of NIMH, gave a speech in 1992 in which he compared inner-city males to Rhesus monkeys. A coalition of psychologists and sociologist from predominantly African-American organizations attacked Goodwin's pronouncements and his research agenda. Plans for a national conference on genetics and crime were jettisoned, discussions of the violence initiative became muted and Goodwin was forced to resign his post.

Although Goodwin no longer heads the NIMH agency, research into the genetic and biological roots of aggression has continued. According to a 1993 article in *Science* magazine, NIMH was then funding close to 300 research projects into aggression and violence, many with multiyear grants. Since 1990, Pine, Wasserman and their colleagues have received three grants from NIMH totaling more than $7 million. Wasserman launched her initial work with a $1.25 million grant from the private Leon Lowenstein Foundation. Halperin has received nearly $1 million from NIMH since 1990 for his research. None of the researchers responded to interview requests, but senior researchers at NYSPI defended the studies in an interview published in the April 23 issue of *Nature*. Pine told *Nature* that his studies obeyed all federal ethics rules. He called violence "a major public health problem" and criticized his critics for opposing any study of "the relationship between aggression and biology."

The search for a link between ethnicity and violence is not new. The phrenology movement of the late 1800s claimed criminal behavior could be predicted by examining the contours of the human head. Early criminologists and psychologists studied the skulls of juvenile delinquents—mostly Irish immigrant youth back then—in their search for the causes of aggression and anti-social behaviors.

So how real is the link between serotonin levels in the brain and aggressive or violent behavior? In the past decade, psychiatric researchers have developed a fascination with serotonin. Serotonin deficits have been linked to depression and alcoholism, and drugs such as Prozac are designed to raise serotonin levels to inhibit depression. Today, some researchers believe that low levels of serotonin also are responsible for impulsive, even violent behavior. But there is no proof that genetics determine serotonin levels or even that serotonin levels alone are the cause of anything.

Neurobiologist Evan Balaban of the Neurosciences Institute in San Diego is critical of serotonin research like that conducted in New York. He and two colleagues published an article in the October 1996 *Journal of Neurogenetics* that reviewed the findings in 100 studies claiming violent people have very low serotonin levels. They found the studies methodologically suspect and the results inconclusive. While they concurred that biology is important, it is not the sole causative factor. They concluded: "Geneticists and other biologists who are interested in understanding aggressive behavior should take a second look at whether the human and animal literature justifies linking the words 'serotonin' and 'aggression' with the words 'specific relationship.'"

Dr. David Shore, director for clinical research at NIMH, says research into the biological causes of violence and aggression represents a small slice of the work funded by his agency. But Shore says that this kind of research is legitimate. "I don't think data linking violence and serotonin are strange," he says. "There have been studies that have shown all sorts of behavioral problems." Shore defends NIMH's funding of both studies: The researchers not only had to pass the peer review process at their own institutions but survive scrutiny of a panel of NIMH experts. He noted that the panel met in May and that the controversial New York studies were part of its agenda. Halperin's grant, now in its seventh year, is up for renewal, but Shore would not comment on whether the council voted to continue his funding.

Sadly, it has become easier and easier to convince a frightened public that the goal of combating youth crime justifies any means. It has come to the point where NYSPI can boldly declare that the Jonesboro shootings in Arkansas are a justification for violating the integrity of six-year-old boys from Harlem and the Bronx.

Annette Fuentes *is a 1997–98 Prudential Fellow at Columbia Graduate School of Journalism, researching issues on children and the news.*

HARD TIME
A special report.

Profits at a Juvenile Prison Come With a Chilling Cost

FOX BUTTERFIELD

TALLULAH, La.—Here in the middle of the impoverished Mississippi Delta is a juvenile prison so rife with brutality, cronyism and neglect that many legal experts say it is the worst in the nation.

The prison, the Tallulah Correctional Center for Youth, opened just four years ago where a sawmill and cotton fields once stood. Behind rows of razor wire, it houses 620 boys and young men, age 11 to 20, in stifling corrugated-iron barracks jammed with bunks.

From the run-down homes and bars on the road that runs by it, Tallulah appears unexceptional, one new cookie-cutter prison among scores built in the United States this decade. But inside, inmates of the privately run prison regularly appear at the infirmary with black eyes, broken noses or jaws or perforated eardrums from beatings by the poorly paid, poorly trained guards or from fights with other boys.

Meals are so meager that many boys lose weight. Clothing is so scarce that boys fight over shirts and shoes. Almost all the teachers are uncertified, instruction amounts to as little as an hour a day, and until recently there were no books.

Up to a fourth of the inmates are mentally ill or retarded, but a psychiatrist visits only one day a week. There is no therapy. Emotionally disturbed boys who cannot follow guards' orders are locked in isolation cells for weeks at a time or have their sentences arbitrarily extended.

These conditions, which are described in public documents and were recounted by inmates and prison officials during a reporter's visit to Tallulah, are extreme, a testament to Louisiana's well-documented violent history and notoriously brutal prison system.

But what has happened at Tallulah is more than just the story of one bad prison. Corrections officials say the forces that converged to create Tallulah—the incarceration of more and more mentally ill adolescents, a rush by politicians to build new prisons while neglecting education and psychiatric services, and states' handing responsibility for juvenile offenders to private companies—have caused the deterioration of juvenile prisons across the country.

Earl Dunlap, president of the National Juvenile Detention Association, which represents the heads of the nation's juvenile jails, said, "The issues of violence against offenders, lack of adequate education and mental health, of crowding and of poorly paid and poorly trained staff are the norm rather than the exception."

Recognizing the problem, the United States Justice Department has begun a series of investigations into state juvenile systems, including not only Louisiana's but also those of Kentucky, Puerto Rico and Georgia. At the same time, private juvenile prisons in Colorado, Texas and South Carolina have been successfully sued by individuals and groups or forced to give up their licenses.

On Thursday, the Juvenile Justice Project of Louisiana, an offshoot of the Southern Poverty Law Center, filed a Federal lawsuit against Tallulah to stop the brutality and neglect.

In the investigations by the Justice Department, some of the harshest criticism has been leveled at Georgia. The department threatened to take over the state's juvenile system, charging a "pattern of egregious conditions violating the Federal rights of youth," including the use of pepper spray to restrain mentally ill youths, a lack of textbooks, and guards who routinely stripped young inmates and locked them in their cells for days.

A surge in the inmate population forced Georgia's juvenile prison budget up to $220 million from $80 million in just four years, but the money went to building new prisons, with little left for education and psychiatric care. "As we went through a period of rapid increase in juvenile crime and record numbers of juvenile offenders," said Sherman Day, chairman of the Georgia Department of Juvenile Justice, it was "much easier to get new facilities from the Legislature than to get more programs."

After reacting defensively at first, Gov. Zell Miller moved quickly to avert a takeover by agreeing to spend $10 million more this year to hire teachers and medical workers and to increase guard salaries.

Louisiana, whose juvenile system is made up of Tallulah and three prisons operated by the state, is the Justice Department's latest target. In hundreds of pages of reports to a Federal judge who oversees the state's entire prison system under a 1971 consent decree, Justice Department experts have depicted guards who routinely resort to beatings or pepper spray as their only way to discipline inmates, and who pit inmates against one another for sport.

In June, two years after the Justice Department began its investigation and a year after it warned in its first public findings that Tallulah was "an institution out of control," consultants for the department filed new reports with the Federal judge, Frank J. Polozola of Federal District Court in Baton Rouge, warning that despite some improvements, conditions had deteriorated to "a particularly dangerous level."

Even a former warden at Louisiana's maximum-security prison, acting as a consultant to Judge Polozola, found conditions at Tallulah so serious that he urged the judge to reject its request to add inmates.

"I do not make these recommendations because of any sympathy for these offenders," wrote the former warden, John Whitley. "It shocks me to think" that "these offenders and their problems are simply getting worse, and these problems will be unleashed on the public when they are discharged from the system."

The Private Prison
When the Profits Are the Priority

Some of the worst conditions in juvenile prisons can be found among the growing number of privately op-

erated prisons, whether those built specifically for one state, like Tallulah, or ones that take juveniles from across the country, like boot camps that have come under criticism in Colorado and Arizona.

Only 5 percent of the nation's juvenile prisons are operated by private, for-profit companies, Mr. Dunlap of the National Juvenile Detention Association estimates. But as their numbers grow along with privately operated prisons for adults, their regulation is becoming one of the most significant issues in corrections. State corrections departments find themselves having to police contractors who perform functions once the province of government, from psychiatric care to discipline.

In April, Colorado officials shut down a juvenile prison operated by the Rebound Corporation after a mentally ill 13-year-old's suicide led to an investigation that uncovered repeated instances of physical and sexual abuse. The for-profit prison housed offenders from six states.

Both Arizona and California authorities are investigating a privately operated boot camp in Arizona that California paid to take hundreds of offenders. A 16-year-old boy died there, and authorities suspect the cause was abuse by guards and poor medical care. California announced last Wednesday that it was removing its juveniles from the camp.

And recently Arkansas canceled the contract of Associated Marine Institutes, a company based in Florida, to run one juvenile institution, following questions of financial control and accusations of abuse.

A series of United States Supreme Court decisions and state laws have long mandated a higher standard for juvenile prisons than for adult prisons. There is supposed to be more schooling, medical care and security because the young inmates have been adjudged delinquent, rather than convicted of crimes as adults are, and so are held for rehabilitation instead of punishment.

But what has made problems worse here is that Tallulah, to earn a

profit, has scrimped on money for education and mental health treatment in a state that already spends very little in those areas.

"It's incredibly perverse," said David Utter, director of the Juvenile Justice Project of Louisiana. "They have this place that creates all these injuries and they have all these kids with mental disorders, and then they save money by not treating them."

Bill Roberts, the lawyer for Tallulah's owner, Trans-American Development Associates, said that some of the Justice Department's demands, like hiring more psychiatrists, are "unrealistic." The state is to blame for the problems, he said, because "our place was not designed to take that kind of inmate."

Still, Mr. Roberts said, "There has been a drastic improvement" in reducing brutality by guards. As for fights between the inmates, he said, "Juveniles are a little bit different from adults. You are never going to stop all fights between boys."

In papers filed with Judge Polozola on July 7 responding to the Justice experts and Mr. Whitley, the State Attorney General's office disputed accusations of brutality and of high numbers of retarded and mentally ill inmates at Tallulah.

In a recent interview, Cheney Joseph, executive counsel to Gov. Mike Foster, warned there were limits to what Louisiana was willing to do. "There are certain situations the Department of Justice would like us to take care of," he said, "that may not be financially feasible and may not be required by Federal law."

The Entrepreneurs
A Idea Born Of Patronage

The idea for a prison here was put forward in 1992 by James R. Brown, a Tallulah businessman whose father was an influential state senator.

One of the poorest areas in a poor state, Tallulah wanted jobs, and like other struggling cities across the country it saw the nation's prison-building spree as its best hope.

Louisiana needed a new juvenile prison because the number of youths being incarcerated was rising steeply; within a few years it more than doubled. Adding to that, mental health experts say, were hundreds of juveniles who had no place else to go because of cuts in psychiatric services outside of jail. Mental health authorities estimate that 20 percent of juveniles incarcerated nationally have serious mental illnesses.

To help win a no-bid contract to operate a prison, the company Mr. Brown formed included two close friends of Gov. Edwin W. Edwards—George Fischer and Verdi Adam—said a businessman involved in the venture's early stages, who spoke on the condition of anonymity.

None of the men had any particular qualification to run a prison. Mr. Verdi was a former chief engineer of the state highway department. Mr. Fischer had been the Governor's campaign manager, Cabinet officer and occasional business partner.

Tallulah opened in 1994, and the town of 10,000 got what it hoped for. The prison became its largest employer and taxpayer. From the beginning, the company formed by Mr. Brown, Trans-American, pursued a strategy of maximizing its profit from the fixed amount it received from the state for each inmate (in 1997, $24,448). The plan was to keep wages and services at a minimum while taking in as many inmates as possible, said the businessman involved in the early stages.

For-profit prisons often try to economize. But the best-run companies have come to recognize that operating with too small or poorly trained a staff can spell trouble, and experts say state officials must pay close attention to the level of services being provided.

"Ultimately, the responsibility belongs to the state," said Charles Thomas, director of the Private Corrections Project at the University of Florida.

Louisiana officials say they monitored conditions at Tallulah and first reported many of the problems

there. But in fiscal year 1996–97, according to the State Department of Public Safety and Corrections, Tallulah still listed no money for recreation, treatment or planning inmates' return to society. Twenty-nine percent of the budget went to construction loans.

By comparison, 45 percent of the $32,200 a year that California spends on each juvenile goes to programs and caseworkers, and none to construction. Nationally, construction costs average 7 percent of juvenile prison budgets, Mr. Dunlap said.

"That means either that Tallulah's construction costs are terribly inflated, or the services they are providing are extraordinarily low," he said.

The Inside
Hot, Crowded, Spartan, Neglectful

Part of Tallulah is a boot camp, with boys crammed so tightly in barracks that there is room only for double bunks, a television set and a few steel tables. Showers and urinals are open to the room, allowing boys who have been incarcerated for sexual assault to attack other inmates, according to a report in June by a Justice Department consultant, Dr. Bernard Hudson.

The only space for the few books that have recently been imported to try to improve education is a makeshift self on top of the urinals. Among the aging volumes that a reporter saw were "Inside the Third Reich," "The Short Stories of Henry James" and "Heidi."

From their wakeup call at 5:30 A.M., the inmates, in white T-shirts and loose green pants, spend almost all their time confined to the barracks. They leave the barracks only for marching drills, one to three hours a day of class and an occasional game of basketball. There is little ventilation, and temperatures in Louisiana's long summers hover permanently in the 90's.

The result, several boys told a visitor, is that some of them deliberately start trouble in order to be disci-

plined and sent to the other section of Tallulah, maximum-security cells that are air-conditioned.

Guards put inmates in solitary confinement so commonly that in one week in May more than a quarter of all the boys spent at least a day in "lockdown," said Nancy Ray, another Justice Department expert. The average stay in solitary is five to six weeks; some boys are kept indefinitely. While in the tiny cells, the boys are stripped of all possessions and lie on worn, thin mattresses resting on concrete blocks.

The crowding, heat and isolation are hardest on the 25 percent of the boys who are mentally ill or retarded, said Dr. Hudson, a psychiatrist, tending to increase their depression or psychosis.

Although Tallulah has made some improvements in its treatment of the emotionally disturbed over the last year, Dr. Hudson said, it remains "grossly inadequate."

The prison still does not properly screen new arrivals for mental illness or retardation, he reported. The part-time doctor and psychiatrist are there so infrequently that they have never met, Dr. Hudson said. Powerful anti-psychotic medications are not monitored. Medical charts often cannot be found.

And the infirmary is often closed because of a shortage of guards, whose pay is so low—$5.77 an hour—that there has been 100 percent turnover in the staff in the last year, the Justice Department experts said.

Other juvenile prisons that have come under investigation have also been criticized for poor psychiatric treatment. But at Tallulah this neglect has been compounded by everyday violence.

All these troubles are illustrated in the case of one former inmate, Travis M., a slight 16-year-old who is mentally retarded and has been treated with drugs for hallucinations.

Sometimes, Travis said in an interview after his release, guards hit him because his medication made him sleepy and he did not stand to attention when ordered. Sometimes they "snuck" him at night as he slept in his bunk, knocking him to the cement floor. Sometimes they kicked him while he was naked in the shower telling him simply, "You owe me some licks."

Travis was originally sentenced by a judge to 90 days for shoplifting and stealing a bicycle. But every time he failed to stand for a guard or even called his grandmother to complain, officials at Tallulah put him in solitary and added to his sentence.

After 15 months, a judge finally ordered him released so he could get medical treatment. His eardrum had been perforated in a beating by a guard, he had large scars on his arms, legs and face, and his nose had been so badly broken that he speaks in a wheeze. A lawyer is scheduled to file suit against Tallulah on behalf of Travis this week.

One reason these abuses have continued, Mr. Utter said, is that juveniles in Louisiana, as in a number of states, often get poor legal representation. One mentally ill boy from Eunice was sentenced without a lawyer, or even a trial. Poorly paid public defenders seldom visit their clients after sentencing, Mr. Utter said, and so are unaware of conditions at places like Tallulah.

Another reason is that almost all Tallulah's inmates are from poor families and 82 percent are black,

Mr. Utter noted, an imbalance that afflicts prisons nationwide to one degree or another. "They are disenfranchised and no one cares about them," he said.

The New Guard
A Retreat From Brutality

In September, Tallulah hired as its new warden David Bonnette, a 25-year veteran of Angola State Penitentiary who started there as a guard and rose to assistant superintendent. A muscular, tobacco-chewing man with his initials tattooed on a forearm, Mr. Bonnette brought several Angola colleagues with him to impose better discipline.

"When I got here, there were a lot of perforated eardrums," he said. "Actually, it seemed like everybody had a perforated eardrum, or a broken nose." When boys wrote complaints, he said guards put the forms in a box and pulled out ones to investigate at random. Some were labeled, "Never to be investigated."

But allegations of abuse by guards dropped to 52 a month this spring, from more than 100 a month last summer, Mr. Bonnette said, as he has tried to carry out a new state policy of zero tolerance for brutality. Fights between boys have declined to 33 a month, from 129, he said.

In June, however, Ms. Ray, the Justice Department consultant, re-

ported that there had been a recent increase in "youth defiance and disobedience," with the boys angry about Tallulah's "exceptionally high" use of isolation cells.

Many guards have also become restive, the Justice Department experts found, a result of poor pay and new restrictions on the use of force.

One guard who said he had quit for those reasons said in an interview: "The inmates are running the asylum now. You're not supposed to touch the kids, but how are we supposed to control them without force?" He has relatives working at Tallulah and so insisted on not being identified.

The frustration boiled over on July 1, during a tour by Senator Paul Wellstone, the Minnesota Democrat who is drafting legislation that would require psychiatric care for all incarcerated juveniles who need it. Despite intense security, a group of inmates climbed on a roof and shouted their complaints at Senator Wellstone, who was accompanied by Richard Stalder, the secretary of Louisiana's Department of Public Safety and Corrections.

Mr. Stalder said he planned to create a special unit for mentally ill juvenile offenders. One likely candidate to run it, he said, is Trans-American, the company that operates Tallulah.

Juvenile Boot Camps:

Lessons Learned

Eric Peterson

In response to a significant increase in juvenile arrests and repeat offenses over the past decade, several States and many localities have established juvenile boot camps. The first juvenile boot camp programs, modeled after boot camps for adult offenders, emphasized military-style discipline and physical conditioning. OJJDP has supported the development of three juvenile boot camp demonstration sites. This Fact Sheet describes those demonstration projects, their evaluations, and lessons learned that will benefit future boot camp programs.

Pilot Programs

In 1992 OJJDP funded three juvenile boot camps designed to address the special needs and circumstances of adolescent offenders. The programs were conducted in Cleveland, Ohio; Denver, Colorado; and Mobile, Alabama.

Focusing on a target population of adjudicated, nonviolent offenders under the age of 18, the boot camp programs were designed as highly structured, 3-month residential programs followed by 6 to 9 months of community-based aftercare. During the aftercare period, youth were to pursue academic and vocational training or employment while under intensive, but progressively diminishing, supervision.

Evaluations

OJJDP undertook impact evaluations for all three sites that compared the recidivism rates for juveniles who participated in the pilot programs with those of control groups. The evaluations also compared the cost-effectiveness of juvenile boot camps with other dispositional alternatives.

Reports of the three impact evaluations are available. The evaluations of the Mobile and Cleveland programs are interim reports that present data from the earliest cohorts. As neither program had stabilized when the data were collected, OJJDP is considering expanding the evaluation to include the remaining cohorts. The Denver program is no longer active.

Findings

Most juvenile boot camp participants completed the residential program and graduated to aftercare. Program completion rates were 96 percent in Cleveland, 87 percent in Mobile, and 76 percent in Denver.

At the two sites where educational gains were measured, substantial improvements in academic skills were noted. In Mobile approximately three-quarters of the participants improved their performance in reading, spelling, language, and math by one grade level or more. In Cleveland the average juvenile boot camp participant improved reading, spelling, and math skills by approximately one grade level.

In addition, where employment records were available, a significant number of participants found jobs while in aftercare.

The pilot programs, however, did not demonstrate a reduction in recidivism. In Denver and Mobile, no statistically significant difference could be found between the recidivism rates of juvenile boot camp participants and those of the control groups (youth confined in State or county institutions, or released on probation). In Cleveland pilot program participants evidenced a higher recidivism rate than juvenile offenders confined in traditional juvenile correctional facilities. It should be noted that none of the sites fully implemented OJJDP's model juvenile boot camp guidelines, and that some critical aftercare support services were not provided.

Lessons Learned

Several significant lessons have emerged from the pilot programs:

The appropriate population should be targeted. Boot camps should be designed as an intermediate intervention. At one site, youth who had been previously confined were significantly more likely to recidivate, while youth with the least serious offenses were also more likely to recidivate.

Facility location is important. Cost issues and community resistance were major obstacles to securing residential and aftercare facilities. To increase attendance and reduce problems, aftercare facilities should be located in gang-neutral areas accessible by public transportation.

Staff selection and training needs are critical. To reduce staff turnover, fill gaps in critical services, and ensure consistent programming, the screening, selection, and training of juvenile boot camp and aftercare staff must be sensitive to the programmatic and operational features of a juvenile boot camp. This is particularly important with regard to youth development issues. Moreover, continuous treatment between the residential and aftercare phases should be integrated philosophically and programmatically, particularly through staffing.

Aftercare programs are challenging to implement. Successful aftercare programs require attention at the outset to develop a comprehensive model with the flexibility to respond to local needs and concerns. Aftercare programs are unlikely to succeed if their participants fail to receive the full range of services prescribed for them. Aftercare programs must be broad-based and flexible enough to meet the particular educational, employment, counseling, and support needs of each participant. The aftercare component should form dynamic linkages with other community services, especially youth service agencies, schools, and employers.

Coordination among agencies must be maintained. All three sites experienced difficulties in maintaining coordination among the participating agencies. Considerable attention should be paid to building and maintaining a consensus among participating organizations concerning the program's philosophy and procedures.

Effective evaluation begins with planning. To assess the program's successes and failures, quantifiable data should be collected about participation in treatment by juveniles in the boot camp and in the control group. Measures of program success should include a broad spectrum of outcomes. Recidivism measures should capture all subsequent delinquent activity, not simply the first new adjudication, and data on new offenses should include information on the origin and circumstances of the complaint to determine whether there is a monitoring effect, in which the intensity of the supervision causes an increase in recorded offending.

When boot camps are used as an alternative to confinement, savings can be achieved. Communities often implement juvenile boot camps, in part, to reduce costs. The experience of the pilot sites indicates that when boot camps are used as an alternative to traditional confinement, costs can be reduced considerably because of the significantly shorter residential stay. However, if boot camps are used as an alternative to probation, savings will not be realized.

Conclusion

Juvenile boot camps embrace a variety of objectives: reducing recidivism, improving academic performance, cutting the cost of treating juvenile offenders, and inculcating the values of self-discipline and hard work. In attempting to reach these objectives, OJJDP is collaborating with the Office of Justice Programs (OJP) to enhance program models, policies, and practices of juvenile boot camps. As a result, many of the lessons learned from OJJDP's three demonstration sites have been incorporated in the OJP Boot Camp Corrections Program.

For Further Information

Jurisdictions considering or operating a juvenile boot camp may receive technical assistance from the National Institute of Corrections. This assistance is available without regard to whether the jurisdiction is receiving, or contemplating applying for, Federal funding.

Eric Peterson is a Program Specialist in OJJDP's Research and Program Development Division.

From *Office of Juvenile Justice and Delinquency Prevention Fact Sheet No. 36*, June 1996. Reprinted by permission of the National Institute of Justice, National Criminal Justice Reference Service.

A Spotty Record of Health Care at Juvenile Sites in New York

By PAUL von ZIELBAUER

It was early February 2000, and Judge Paula J. Hepner said she could hardly believe what a doctor in the city's juvenile justice system had done to the girl standing before her in Brooklyn Family Court.

The girl, Tiffany S., was 14, with a history of suicide threats and a set of serious psychological problems well documented by doctors at a psychiatric hospital for children. They had treated her bipolar disorder with powerful medicines and, knowing that she was facing detention, had recommended that she keep receiving them when the Department of Juvenile Justice took her into custody.

But soon after Tiffany entered the system, Dr. Ralph L. Williams—an employee of Prison Health Services and the only full-time doctor for 19 juvenile centers across the city—stopped her medications. Instead, he placed her on Ritalin, a drug meant to treat attention deficit hyperactivity disorder.

It took only days for Tiffany to deteriorate. Soon, she said in an interview, she was hallucinating, fighting with other girls and spending hours staring at a wall. As an additional measure, she said, a Prison Health employee asked her to sign a pledge not to kill herself.

Judge Hepner ordered Tiffany back to the hospital, records show, and moved to hold Dr. Williams in criminal contempt. In doing so, Judge Hepner joined at least five other judges who would order more vigorous treatment by Prison Health, a company that cares for hundreds of thousands of inmates in New York State and across the country.

That May, for instance, Judge Philip C. Segal of Brooklyn Family Court held the juvenile justice commissioner—whose agency represented Prison Health in court—in contempt after the company staff neglected to give a 13-year-old boy his H.I.V. medication. Later that month, Harold J. Lynch, a judge in the Bronx, ordered a 13-year-old girl in the agency's custody returned to the Bronx Children's Psychiatric Center. The girl, court records show, had tried to kill herself after a Prison Health doctor discarded her psychiatric medications and gave her Ritalin instead.

"This is not just a single case," Judge Lynch told city lawyers. "It's many cases."

But those cases are only one distressing facet of what would be a four-year effort by Prison Health to provide care to young people in the city's network of juvenile detention centers and group homes—a job that made the company about $15 million in revenue before it was replaced in 2003. Independent investigations have criticized the quality of that care. Questions have also been raised by some city officials about whether the company was forthright with various other city agencies about its work at Juvenile Justice.

Of the roughly 500 youngsters, ages 7 through 16, who were in custody on any given day, some had committed serious crimes. Others had been turned over by parents who could not or would not care for them. Still others were there simply because there was nowhere else to go. One thing is clear about most of them: they were sick and in need of help.

Prison Health, a profit-making corporation with a troubling record in many states, appears to have poorly served many of those youngsters, according to a review of its work, based on court records and audits, as well as interviews with children, judges, Legal Aid Society lawyers and current and former Juvenile Justice employees. The results, those documents and interviews make clear, were often confusion and mistreatment throughout the company's time in the juvenile justice system, from January 1999 to April 2003.

For the 5,000 youngsters who passed through each year, the one full-time doctor Prison Health employed oversaw a staff composed mostly of part-time physician assistants, social workers and nurses. Sometimes, current and former counselors who worked at Juvenile Justice said, the medical staff mistakenly gave children medication that had not been prescribed to them. One counselor said that to avoid further errors, Polaroid photos were stapled to medical files to help nurses match names with faces.

The only independent audit of the company's medical care, commissioned by the Juvenile Justice Department in 2003, six months after Prison Health had already left, found that patient records had been in disarray, and that no doctor had appeared to consult them anyway. Many children with serious illnesses received no follow-up care, the audit said, and most teenagers were not tested for sexually transmitted diseases. The audit was never made public.

"The work was poor and put young people at risk," the city comptroller, William C. Thompson Jr., said in an interview. "I'd almost say deplorable."

Juvenile Justice officials have said they were "generally satisfied" with the company. The agency declined interview requests for this article for five months, until aides to Mayor Michael R. Bloomberg ordered the department's spokesman to answer questions about Prison Health's tenure. Even then, in two interviews, department officials would not discuss the company's record.

Richard D. Wright, the president and chief executive of Prison Health, defended its work and the services it offered youngsters in custody. "There were a lot of professional people dedicated to that contract," he said in an interview. "We thought that they were sufficient to deal with the workload."

Prison Health's performance at Juvenile Justice is the least known aspect of its long and lucrative work in New York. The care the company provided in upstate county jails in recent years has been assailed by state investigators. And its work at the jail complex on Rikers Island has been consistently, if not always diligently monitored by New York City, which awarded the company a new $300 million contract in January.

But the care Prison Health provided children in the juvenile system, the city comptroller now says, should have been examined by the city when the company was seeking the Rikers contract in 2000.

Prison Health took over care at Juvenile Justice in 1999 when it bought EMSA Correctional Care, a smaller competitor that had been doing the job for three years. When it was vying for the Rikers contract, though, Prison Health listed EMSA in disclosure statements as an affiliate and indicated that EMSA was still working at Juvenile Justice.

The city comptroller now says that Prison Health was in charge of providing juvenile care from the time it bought EMSA, and that EMSA existed only on paper. The comptroller says that the company misled the city, and that as a result, the city missed an opportunity to get a hard look at Prison Health's work in its own backyard before it hired the company for its adult jails.

Prison Health says that its filings properly listed EMSA as a separate concern in 2000. The city agencies in charge of awarding the Rikers contract, the Health and Hospitals Corporation and the Mayor's Office of Contract Services, say they found no problem with Prison Health's disclosures.

Over the years, as Prison Health has expanded nationally, followed by accusations of flawed care by regulators, many of its critics have wondered how it kept winning new contracts, sometimes in a county or state next to one it had left under a cloud. In New York City, anger among judges and lawyers in the juvenile justice system did not prevent the company from landing a huge jail contract across town.

Of course, caring for youngsters inside the city's three jail-like detention centers and 16 less restrictive group homes can be as dangerous and frustrating as caring for adult inmates. Few young people entering the system have received consistent health care and, as a result, lack any medical record to guide doctors. Often, there are not even family members to question.

For many of them, as a result, detention offers the only opportunity to get a physical or dental examination, or even talk to an adult willing to listen. Proper medical and mental health care, say experts and the department's own employees, is vital in helping them become productive adults.

That care has improved under the two companies hired to replace Prison Health, say city officials and lawyers working in the Family Court system. It could hardly have gotten worse, said Jennifer Baum, a Legal Aid lawyer who represented many youngsters during Prison Health's tenure.

"I saw troubled and needy children being mistreated by shabby medical care," she said.

Checkups and Warnings

By the time Prison Health Services acquired it, EMSA had been treating the city's incarcerated children since 1996. EMSA had more experience with children than Prison Health, but it had problems, too.

In Westchester County, EMSA had paid $750,000 to settle a lawsuit by the parents of a 17-year-old girl who hanged herself at the jail there in 1996, after a psychiatrist stopped her antidepressant medication. The doctor, Harvey N. Lothringer, had pleaded guilty to second-degree manslaughter three decades before, admitting that he dismembered the body of a young woman who had died during an illegal abortion he performed, and then flushed her remains down a toilet. He spent four years in prison, but in 1973, the State Board of Regents declared the doctor "rehabilitated" and restored his medical license. He began working for EMSA in 1996.

At Juvenile Justice, counselors and Legal Aid lawyers said they had found EMSA's medical staff too small to properly treat all the children who needed help. But a little less than a year after Prison Health arrived, taking responsibility for the care, that private grumbling turned public.

Prompted by complaints from Ms. Baum, a half-dozen Family Court judges filed at least 12 court orders or contempt motions in 2000 to force Juvenile Justice to fix mistakes in care. In one instance, Dr. Joseph K. Youngerman of the Bronx Children's Psychiatric Center pleaded with Judge Lynch to help the suicidal 13-year-old girl who had been taken off her medication; if he could not, the doctor wrote, the center would take her back—"to spare her (and us all) any repeat" of her breakdown.

For nearly two years, though, those concerns remained buried in court files. Then, in 2002, the city comptroller, during a routine review, uncovered several problems.

He urged Prison Health to re-examine its staffing, which provided only one full-time psychiatrist and one part-time physician for all medical services. The company, the comptroller's office found, did not provide the group counseling required in its contract. There was no system, the comptroller said, to ensure that children taking psychiatric drugs received them on days they were sent to court; unmedicated, they sometimes broke down in front of a judge.

Indeed, several employees said that they sometimes were told that drugs for some of the children were unavailable or simply unnecessary, leaving them to handle the untreated patients.

"If they get disruptive," said one longtime counselor at a group home, "the staff has to put them in a restraining position, and then you end up with a child-abuse charge."

For reasons that its spokesman declined to disclose, the Department of Juvenile Justice commissioned its own review in 2003. It was a rare move, and it came only after Prison Health had left.

This would be the only outside medical audit. Done by IPRO, a well-known nonprofit health-care auditing firm, it found serious deficiencies, showing that things had been even worse than the comptroller's office had thought.

Medical charts had been badly disorganized, the audit said, and "there was little evidence of an oversight physician" reviewing them. Young people who developed medical problems were "almost never" seen by a doctor, but typically examined instead by a nurse, the audit said.

About one in six youngsters with chronic health problems like epilepsy, sickle cell anemia and kidney disease never received follow-up treatment while in custody. Tests critical to running an institution full of troubled young people were so haphazardly administered that fewer than one-third of the eligible girls received a Pap test, and only about 1 in 5 eligible youngsters were tested for gonorrhea, chlamydia and syphilis.

But Prison Health was by now largely beyond accountability. It had left the previous April, when the Department of Juvenile Justice replaced it with two other companies: Health Star Plus, which now provides medical care, and Forensic Health Services, which handles mental health services. Department officials, who had given Prison Health mostly satisfactory evaluations during its four years, would not discuss the problems raised by the audit.

"At this point, we have new providers," said Scott Trent, a department spokesman. "It's a new contract. It's entirely irrelevant."

One Girl's Tale

Tiffany grew up in Brownsville, Brooklyn, and her early life was a painful one. She was put in her grandmother's care by city child-welfare workers when she was 3 to escape the abuse of two drug-addicted parents. But that did not last long. After her brother sexually abused her sister, Tiffany was moved yet again. When she was 13, she ran away.

On the streets, she was beaten, and she began to hear voices. She found herself telling people, "I'm not crazy!"

Tiffany ended up in the custody of the juvenile justice system after she was accused of a minor nonviolent crime in 1999; she agreed to be interviewed on the condition that the charge not be disclosed. But before she got there, she spent a month in the adolescent psychiatry unit at Kings County Hospital Center in Brooklyn.

The conclusion of doctors there was precise: Tiffany suffered from bipolar disorder and behavioral problems and required psychiatric medication and individual psychotherapy. Without them, her doctors wrote, "Tiffany is at risk for harming herself."

Once in custody, Tiffany was placed in a holding center in Manhattan on Jan. 5, 2000. She was taking Depakote to control her mood swings, and Risperidone, an antipsychotic. The next day, records show, she was examined by Dr. Williams.

Prison Health had hired the doctor several weeks earlier. But Dr. Williams had already made a mostly negative impression on some lawyers working with the youngsters in custody. In interviews, the lawyers said he replaced psychiatric medication with cheaper, less appropriate drugs.

Mr. Wright, the president of Prison Health, said Dr. Williams felt that black children were too frequently put on psychiatric medications they did not need. But Mr. Wright said that the doctor's decisions to withdraw those medications were inappropriate, and that Prison Health forced the doctor to resign in August 2001. Dr. Williams did not return messages left with his lawyer seeking comment for this article.

Records show that Dr. Williams, after one 80-minute exam, concluded that Tiffany suffered from attention deficit hyperactivity disorder, and despite three court orders discontinued her psychiatric medications in late January. Soon the hallucinations started again, she said in an interview, and her antisocial behavior came roaring back.

"I'd see stuff, shadows, people's faces," Tiffany recalled. "I'll be scared. I'll be crying. I always think people are out to get me."

She eventually threatened to kill herself, she said, setting in motion her return to Judge Hepner's courtroom, and ultimately the psychiatric hospital, where doctors put her back on her previous medication.

"When you have medicine that is working, it seems really irresponsible to alter it," Judge Hepner, in an interview, recalled saying in court. She ordered Dr. Williams to pay a $1,000 fine.

The kind of treatment Tiffany received, records and interviews show, began before Prison Health took over EMSA, but judges and lawyers said the pattern grew increasingly familiar afterward.

In July 2000, a suicidal 15-year-old girl was taken off Depakote prescribed by doctors at Craig House, an upstate psychiatric clinic—and placed on Ritalin, according to court filings and lawyers and judges involved in her case. It would take five weeks to have her medication restored.

In March of that year, a 15-year-old boy at Bridges Juvenile Center, a secure center in the Bronx, went days without his psychiatric medications because Dr. Williams visited the center only twice a week. Prison Health's policy, according to court transcripts and interviews, was to discontinue youngsters' medications until a company doctor could complete his own evaluation.

But rather than wait for Dr. Williams to show up days later at Bridges, a Manhattan Family Court judge, alerted by the boy's lawyer, ordered the boy sent to Bellevue Hospital Center. "They can't say there's no psychiatrist on staff at the hospital," the judge, Sheldon M. Rand, said in a hearing.

The company's strategy for treatment, when it went beyond drugs, included the unusual approach of asking a youngster to write up and sign a pledge not to commit suicide. Such pledges, experts in mental health treatment say, accomplish little.

"It's an awful tool," said a former Prison Health mental health supervisor in the juvenile system. "It's designed to make the clinician go home and sleep better at night."

Tiffany said the whole exercise was stupid. "I just wrote it so they would stop following me," she said.

Article 40

LIFE SENTENCES WITHOUT PAROLE INCREASINGLY IMPOSED ON JUVENILES

Because of a 1990s trend toward trying serious juvenile offenders in the adult justice system, 41 states now allow a sentence of life without parole to be imposed on juveniles, according to a study by the American Civil Liberties Union of Michigan (ACLU). In 14 of those states, there is no minimum age for such a punishment.

There are no complete national statistics on the number of juvenile offenders who have been "sentenced to die in prison," the ACLU said, but the number is estimated to be in the thousands, according to the group's research. In Michigan alone, 307 offenders were found serving life without parole (LWOP) for crimes committed before their 18th birthday.

The civil rights group, calling such sentences "cruel and disproportionate," recommended a nationwide reconsideration of the laws authorizing them. "This report illustrates the need to re-examine the laws that allow children to be sentenced to life in adult prisons when they can't even legally use alcohol, serve on juries, or be drafted for military service because they are presumed to lack the capacity to be able to handle adult responsibilities," said Kary Moss, executive director of the organization.

In fact, some of the youths sentenced to LWOP were not even old enough to drive a car, live away from their parents, make decisions about their education or medical treatment, or sign a contract, the ACLU noted. "Despite their young age, these juveniles are expected to negotiate the legal system and understand the consequences of decisions that could result in a life-without-parole sentence, even though research suggests they are not capable of understanding what 'forever' means," the ACLU said in a report on its findings.

The reports cites case histories of Michigan inmates serving LWOP terms for crimes committed as juveniles, in part to illustrate that youths often are ineffective in managing their own legal defenses. For example, the report says, Amy Black began to suffer sexual abuse at age seven, and as a teenager began using drugs and running away from home. When she was 16, her older boyfriend got into a fight with another man and stabbed him to death. Amy "helped clean up the mess." When she and her boyfriend were arrested a few days later, the boyfriend told Amy to take the blame because she was only 16. She confessed, and was convicted in 1991 of aiding and abetting first-degree murder. She has now served 13 years of a LWOP sentence in adult prison.

"Dramatic and rapid changes occur in the development of adolescents' physical, intellectual, emotional, and social capabilities from ages 12 to 17," the report said. "Cognitive and psychological features of adolescence, such as immaturity, inability to calculate consequences, and inability to understand how their actions affect others, can reduce adolescents' ability to anticipate the effects of their actions."

Yet in the early 1990s, the justice system expanded the circumstances under which juveniles can be tried in adult court, based on "the fiction of juveniles being the same as adults," the ACLU said.

In other areas of criminal law, punishment is based not only on the severity of the offense but also on the perceived culpability of the offender, the report noted. For example, murder committed with premeditation is punished more severely than murder committed impulsively. "Yet the current scheme of automatic adult treatment and mandatory life sentences for juveniles fails to take into account this lesser culpability and competency of children," the report said.

Many juveniles are not competent to stand trial or assist in their own defense, the report said. "A study of adolescents found that at least one-third of 15- and 16-year-olds do not have an accurate conception of what a 'right' is. ... Adolescents have greater difficulty understanding the roles and motives of different actors in our complex adversarial system. ... Because of their vulnerability, juvenile defendants are especially dependent on their legal counsel. The vast majority of juvenile lifers in Michigan (78 percent) relied on appointed counsel, as they lacked the resources to hire private defense counsel. The problems inherent in indigent defense systems have been well documented."

One juvenile offender sentenced to LWOP in Michigan never saw his attorney except briefly inside the courtroom, the report said. "He never asked me if I even did the crime," the offender said. "I called his office and no one accepted the calls. He never visited me; I never had any kind of interview about the crime." The youth saw the lawyer moments before his sentencing, "and he told me that I'd be getting natural life. I asked him how long that was and he told me, but I couldn't understand the whole thing, and I kept asking him when I'd be going home."

Later, "another inmate explained it all to me," the youth said.

"Since the 1980s, the number of children given life sentences without hope of release has increased dramatically, and the cost of warehousing them for life is staggering to our communities and to our humanity," the report said. "Each one of these lifers will cost the state at least one million dollars. Rather than keep these juveniles in prison until they die, individual assessments and proportional punishment would allow these individuals the opportunity to rejoin and contribute to society."

Report: *Juvenile Life Without Parole* is available online a www.aclumich.org/pubs/juvenilelifers.pdf.

Crime and Punishment, Juvenile Division

PATRICK T. MURPHY

CHICAGO—After a tragedy like the one in Jonesboro, Ark., this week, Americans cry out for vengeance, for justice, for change! We want quick solutions, whether it is to a Mississippi flood, teen-age pregnancy, or children throwing children out of windows or blasting them with shotguns in schoolyards.

There is outrage that 11- and 13-year-olds cannot be tried as adults, cannot be sent to the penitentiary and may be released from a juvenile prison as early as their 18th birthdays. (In most states, a juvenile delinquent can be held until he is 21. That is apparently not the case in Arkansas.) Any child old enough to kill is old enough to be tried as an adult, the argument goes.

But before the mob descends on our legislatures demanding Draconian laws, it may be prudent to consider a few points. First, child murderers are exceedingly rare, in rural America and in inner-city America. And when these crimes occur and the children go off to juvenile institutions, other 11- and 13-year-olds do not repeat their crimes. In Chicago a few years ago, a 10- and 11-year-old threw a 5-year-old to his death from a housing project window. It did not set off an epidemic of little boys killing each other.

Eleven- and 13-year-olds are not short adults. They are children. Their sense of time is a universe apart.

Their judgment is skewed because they have no real point of reference or life experiences other than what their parents have given them or what they have seen on television. In my experience, even the toughest-talking among them are fragile and often terrified.

We can send children off to jail, as we did 100 years ago, or execute them, as we did 200 years ago. But we will be admitting defeat. A hundred years ago, Jane Addams and others created the first juvenile courts. The bold premise was that children should not be treated like adults. Because their characters are not formed, we have a chance to influence them, to divert them from becoming hardened criminals. In most cases, the system still works. We manage to get most children through a rocky adolescence without resorting to harsh penalties.

But it is time to do some tinkering with the juvenile court premise. Older predator children should be treated more harshly and, in some cases, tried and punished as adults. Very young children convicted of particularly heinous crimes could be compelled to take part in mandatory reporting programs for an indeterminate part of their adulthood once they are released from a juvenile prison.

In addition, the entire juvenile court system, including court

records, should be opened to the public through the press. Right now, for the most part, the public is in the dark about what motivates children to commit their crimes. We cannot begin to reform the system when the public does not know what goes on inside it.

There is another reason to get the records of these youngsters. We cannot pass judgment in the Jonesboro case in particular, but it has been my experience, having represented hundreds of children who have gotten in various degrees of trouble, that in virtually every case their parents shared at least some of the blame. Sometimes, parents are so involved in their own lives that they forget their responsibility to direct, discipline and nurture their children. Other times, the circumstances are more dire. I will never forget the parents of one of the boys who threw the 5-year-old out of the window here. The father, when he was out of prison, taught his son gang signs. The mother slept through most of her child's trial.

Senator Richard Durbin of Illinois has introduced Federal legislation that would impose criminal sanctions on parents who even unintentionally make their weapons available to young children. A good idea. But much worse than making a gun available to a child is walking away from parental responsibilities.

In extreme cases, like the one in Chicago, we must begin to analyze the responsibility of parents and to consider imposing criminal and civil liability if the evidence shows that their abuse or neglect has led to their children's heinous acts.

Children today are a lot less innocent than they were 30 years ago when I first began representing them. Why are they growing up so fast? The proliferation of guns did not cause it, and sending children to the penitentiary will not prevent it. Turn on the television any night, and you and your children will be bombarded with violence and sex that would have been unthinkable even a decade ago.

But let's not turn the clock back to the harsh justice of the 19th century. Let's treat juveniles who commit crimes like the children they are. If we as a society are saying that it is already too late for an 11- and 13-year-old, we have a lot of soul-searching to do.

Patrick T. Murphy, the Public Guardian for Cook County, is the author of "Wasted: The Plight of America's Unwanted Children."

UNIT 4
Future Prospects

Unit Selections

Key Points to Consider

- What are the main U.S. cultural values?

- What values exist in our nation in addition to the mainstream ones? What are they?

- Do you think the mainstream of U.S. culture is positive and productive for our nation?

- Where and how does the community fit into the creation of juvenile justice policy and practice?

- Should what you would want for your own children and teens in the future be provided for every child and teen? If so, how should it be done?

Student Website
www.mhcls.com/online

Internet References
Further information regarding these websites may be found in this book's preface or online.

An Examination of Three Model Interventions and Intensive Aftercare Initiatives
http://www.ncjrs.org/txtfiles/effectiv.txt

Children's Defense Fund
http://www.childrensdefense.org

Combatting Violence and Delinquency: The National Juvenile Justice Action Plan
http://www.ncjrs.org/txtfiles/jjplanfr.txt

Girl Power!
http://www.health.org/gpower/

Implementing the Balanced and Restorative Justice Model
http://www.ojjdp.ncjrs.org/pubs/implementing/contents.html

A Legislator's Guide to Comprehensive Juvenile Justice
http://www.ncsl.org/programs/cyf/jjguide.htm

Long-Term Effects of Early Childhood Programs on Social Outcomes and Delinquency
http://www.futureofchildren.org/information2826/information_show.htm?doc_id=77676

No Child Left Behind
http://www.nochildleftbehind.gov

What Works Clearinghouse
http://www.w-w-c.org

Ours is a shrinking world, while the masses of data we can access expand exponentially—is this a self-destructive Hegelian synthesis? I think not. To me it is an exciting time to be observing and studying. As much as I enjoy looking forward, my experiences in diagnosing behavior and dealing with people and organizations is that one of the best predictors of the future is the past. For example, in the past, the series of decisions made around *in re Gault*, 387 U.S. 1 (1967) transformed a rehabilitation-oriented juvenile court system into an adversarial adult court. Moreover, the process essentially moved the system from informal/traditional to formal/bureaucratic. More recently, the justice model has demanded both revenge and time served. This has been followed by a trend toward mediation and restorative justice that may swing the pendulum back. The nature of society and of the juvenile environment and culture in the United States has changed radically, fueled by technology and an ability to share in the culture that has never before existed in our history.

When we consider technology and cultural exposure as trends of the future, we must begin to seriously consider writers who have discussed these phenomena deeply and then we must try to apply these trends to the future of juveniles and the juvenile justice system. In *The Third Wave*, Alvin Toffler predicts that we will live and function in a free-flowing style of organization as opposed to traditional hierarchies. In the future we will have to be even more adaptable than we are today. Trends will deemphasize representative democracy and promote participatory democracy. Our society and organizations will rapidly synthesize vast amounts of information and expand opportunities for human intelligence, intuition, and imagination to make a more significant contribution to culture and society. At the very surface level this future would encourage values that would better incorporate juveniles into society and push the juvenile justice system more toward emerging concepts of restorative justice.

While Toffler is fascinating, I prefer the work of John Naisbitt for understanding what is coming for adult and juvenile criminal justice. In his nationwide best seller, *Megatrends*, and its successor books, Naisbitt has discussed "ten new directions transforming our lives." These 10 trends show us moving into a very different version of human and organizational life than we enjoy today. We will move from an industrial society to an information-based society, from short-term thinking to long-term perception, from centralization to decentralization, from institutional help to self-help hierarchies, from networking and either/or thinking to multiple-option thinking.

Among these, the trends that will most affect juveniles and juvenile justice are the change from (1) institutional help to self-help; (2) an industrial to an information-based society; (3) centralization to decentralization; (4) hierarchies to networking, and (5) getting out of the either/or mentality. While it is problematic, given the past behavior of some of our policymakers, we must hope that we change from short-term thinking to long-term thinking. All of Naisbitt's predictions assume a technology that continues to become more complex, to become more sophisticated, more available, more expensive and, despite its problems, more essential for full functioning in the current world. This scenario will be played out in a population that has continuing fluctuations in the size of the at-risk populations.

If Naisbitt is accurate, these futures will enable a world in which the community will have a stake in the life of each juvenile. This was precisely the thinking that created the concept of delinquency and the mechanism of the juvenile court 100 years ago. It is already agreed—although scorned by cynics when it was restated—that "it takes a community to raise a child." The articles in this section certainly seem to augur that future.

References
Naisbitt, John, *Megatrends,* New York: Warner, 1982.
Toffler, Alvin, *The Third Wave*, New York: Bantam Books, 1980.

COMPARATIVE CRIMINOLOGY AND CRIMINAL JUSTICE RESEARCH: THE STATE OF OUR KNOWLEDGE*

RICHARD R. BENNETT**
American University

The events of September 11, 2001 fueled interest in cross-national and especially transnational crime. What had been relegated to isolated interest sections in scholarly organizations suddenly became front page copy in the news media. Is this heightened interest in comparative research only a fleeting reaction to the immediacy of the terrorist attacks or will interest and research continue to grow and expand the comparative field in criminology and criminal justice? This presidential address attempts to help formalize the field of cross- and multinational research by presenting a typology of comparative studies. The benefits of comparative research as well as the impediments to the comparative approach are then explored. Finally, the future of comparative criminology and criminal justice is addressed through an examination of the role of professional organizations, university curricula, funding agencies and individual scholars in advancing the field.

The events of September 11, 2001 certainly focused our attention and interest in better understanding terrorism, but they also fueled an increased interest in comparative crime/criminal justice and especially transnational crime. What was once the province of relatively small interest sections at annual meetings of scholarly organizations became front page copy in the news media.[1] In addition to increased public interest in terrorism and international crime, academically oriented research on these subjects has also expanded since September 11th. As an example, the

*The author thanks Sandra Baxter, Applied Research Analysts, James P. Lynch, American University, Jay S. Albanese, National Institute of Justice, and Gary LaFree, University of Maryland, for their critical comments on an earlier draft of this address. The author also thanks Editor Donna Bishop for agreeing to publish this article in the March 2004 issue of *Justice Quarterly*. Address correspondence to Richard R. Bennett, Professor of Justice, Department of Justice, Law and Society, American University, Washington, D.C. 20016; e-mail:bennett@american.edu.

** Richard R. Bennett is a Professor of Justice at the American University, Washington, D.C. He has published extensively in the area of cross-national correlates of crime, police cognitions and behaviors, and is currently researching crime and police issues in developing nations. He has served as a police officer, a criminal investigator, and criminal justice consultant to both national and international government commissions, universities, and contract research organizations. He is currently completing a book on policing in the Caribbean.

proportion of panel sessions devoted to comparative research at the scholarly meetings of the Academy of Criminal Justice Sciences (ACJS) and the American Society of Criminology (ASC) has increased substantially each year since then.[2] And this year for the first time, 28 societies of criminology from around the world have joined together to sponsor an international crime conference in Paris, France with the theme *What Works in Reducing Crime*.

Such increased attention to terrorism and comparative studies is not a surprise, really. The attacks awakened the American public's interest and attention to something that has been a major concern of many nations for many years. Since the demise of the Soviet Union and the decline in state-sponsored terrorism worldwide, terrorist groups have found new funding sources in organized and transnational crime involving smuggling and trafficking in humans, drugs, and stolen property. Although a small band of comparative researchers was aware of the increases in international/transnational crime and the need to understand its causes and possible control, the attacks on America gave a sense of urgency to their research agendas. The important question for our discipline now is whether the current interest will level out, decline, or become the seed-crystal for the institutionalization of comparative research as a mainstream field in criminology and criminal justice.

The comparative approach is not new to social science; E. B. Taylor originally identified the benefits of comparative research in his presentation to the Royal Anthropological Institute of Great Britain in 1889. However, with a few notable exceptions, his call for comparative studies went unheeded by nonanthropological researchers until the mid-1950s. Then researchers in sociology, psychology, and political science began using comparative methods to construct and test their disciplines' theories. It was not until the late 60s and early 70s that criminologists began exploring crime comparatively (DeFleur, 1969; Friday, 1971; Clifford, 1978). Since these early efforts, there has been a slow but expanding body of criminological literature that employs comparative techniques (e.g., LaFree, 1999). Similarly, comparative studies of justice systems have emerged relatively recently in the scientific literature (Miller, 1977; Bayley, 1969, 1976).

The field has grown as researchers have used comparative methods to study an ever-expanding array of topics.[3] The scholarly publishing industry has responded by creating more outlets for researchers. In the last five years, the number of journals devoted to international and comparative criminology and criminal justice research has almost doubled from 6 to 13 (see Appendix A).

This address has several objectives. First, I present a typology that categorizes the recent literature in an effort to clarify the nature and methods of comparative criminology and criminal justice research. Second, I discuss the benefits of doing comparative research. Although all good research is inherently comparative (comparing various levels of one or more independent variables with various levels of one or more dependent variables), I focus exclusively on comparisons among nations. Third, I identify and discuss the impediments to conducting and publishing comparative research. Fourth, I discuss what actions can be taken by organizations and individuals to overcome the barriers to conducting comparative research. Finally, I comment on the future of the field and prognosticate as to whether the current flurry of comparative activity is simply a reaction to a traumatic event or the emergence of a mainstream field in criminology and criminal justice.

A TYPOLOGY OF COMPARATIVE STUDIES

In his 1987 presidential address to the American Sociological Association, Melvin Kohn identified four types of comparative studies: where nation is treated as an object, where nation is treated as context, where nation is treated as a unit of analysis, and transnational studies that treat two or more nations as components in a larger international system. His typology was based on the explanatory purpose of a study. Although the typology was a useful analytic tool to categorize sociological literature at that time, it does not adequately differentiate among the types of research now being conducted in criminology and criminal justice.

I propose that the research-based knowledge in our field can best be understood by grouping studies on an-

Figure 1. A Typology of Studies of Crime and Justice

Column A	Column B	Column C	Column D
Approach	*Scope*	*Data*	*Design*
❑ Descriptive	❑ National	❑ Qualitative	❑ Cross-sectional
❑ Analytic	❑ Multinational	❑ Quantitative	❑ Longitudinal
	❑ Transnational		

other set of four dimensions. These dimensions are based on the approach of the study, the scope of comparisons drawn, the type of data employed, and the study's research design.[4] Under each dimension is a further set of alternative types of studies. A given research effort can then be described, like a meal ordered from a stereotypical Chinese restaurant menu, as falling into one category under column A, one under column B, etc. (see Figure 1).

The first dimension is the approach of the research. If the intent is to increase understanding of the structure, nature, or scope of one or more nations' criminal justice systems or crime problems, then the study is descriptive. These studies contribute to the comparative literature by documenting how different nations conduct the business of justice. In many but not all instances, these studies are published as textbooks for comparative criminal justice courses. Prime examples of this type of work include Reichel's (2002) multinational treatment of criminal justice systems, Terrill's (1999) description of five nations' justice systems, Fairchild and Dammer's (2001) discussion of six model nations, Skolnick and Bayley's (1988) description of community police practices around the world, Findlay and Zvekic's (1993) collection of essays on selected nations' policing styles, and Ebbe's (2000) edited work covering more than a dozen nations. However, studies also exist that describe in detail a single nation's system (e.g., Jones, 1995; Miyazawa, 1992; Shelley, 1996). All these studies closely parallel what Kohn (1987) would label comparative research where nations are objects.

If the intent of the research is to understand how national systems work and what factors cause them to operate as they do, then the study can be categorized as analytic.[5] David Bayley's (1985) work on the structure, role, and functioning of police in a sample of nations is a prime example of this type of study. Comparative criminology also has many examples of this type of approach (e.g., Bennett, 1991b; LaFree & Kick, 1986).

The second dimension of the typology is scope. By scope I mean the number of nations sampled or the transnational nature of the study. Ivkovic, Klockars, Cajner-Mraovic, and Ivanusec (2002), Harriott (2001), Wiegand and Bennett (1992), Fairchild (1988), Punch (1985, 1979), Shelley (1984), Clinard and Abbott (1973), Clinard (1978), and Defleur (1969) investigated the operations of a segment of the justice system or extent of crime in one nation. Finckenauer (1995), LaFree and Birkbeck (1991), Bennett and Flavin (1994), and Frase (2001) used data from two nations to explain the function of the Russian juvenile system, situational characteristics of crime in the United

States and Venezuela, the relationship between culture and fear of crime in the United States and Belize (Central America), and sentencing in Germany and the United States, respectively. Bennett (1997a, 1997b) used data from three nations to analyze the effects of various factors on police use of force and job satisfaction. Similarly, Farrington, Langan, and Wikstrom (1994) investigated crime trends in the United States, England, and Sweden; Lynch (1993, 1988) studied prison use and custodial sentences in the United States, England and Wales, West Germany, and Canada; and MacCoun and Reuter (2001) studied drug policies in selected European nations. These types of studies are categorized as national because they rely upon data from only one or a few countries.

In contrast, studies such as those conducted by LaFree and Kick (1986), Messner (1982) and Anderson and Bennett (1996) are examples of multinational comparative studies. They are so categorized because they employ a large set of nations in their analyses (N = 47, N = 50, and N = 33 nations, respectively). These studies focus on how system or national level constructs influence criminal behavior. Similar in nature but employing a different analytic approach is Adler's (1983) work that compares nations to understand why some are not obsessed with crime. Only recently have similar studies in the field of criminal justice emerged (e.g., Bennett 2003). This category closely parallels Kohn's (1987) set of studies where nation serves as the unit of analysis.

The third alternative under the scope dimension is transnational. These studies explore how various cultures and nations deal with crime that transcends their borders and justice systems rather than a comparison of the nations themselves. It is an important emerging body of research that deserves mention in a typology of comparative studies. Most of these studies tend to employ a descriptive approach rather than an analytic one. Examples include the research by Naylor (2002), Friman and Andreas (1999), Passas (2000), and Kyle and Koslowski (2001). The close relationship between transnational crime and terrorism will only increase the future importance of this type of research which is similar to Kohn's (1987) fourth category of studies, also called transnational.

The third dimension of the typology is data and is determined by the form of empirical evidence used in a study. Empirical studies rely upon either qualitative or quantitative data. Qualitative methods have been used successfully in studying criminal justice systems and crime. As examples, Danns (1982) and Harriott (2001) used observation and interviews to study police in the Caribbean,[6] interviews were used by Huggins, Haritos-Fatouros, and Zimbardo (2002) in their research on police torture and murder in Brazil, by Chevigny (1995) in research on police abuse of human rights in several nations, and by Gunst (1995) to investigate criminal gang activity in both the United States and Jamaica. Although no descriptive studies employ quantitative methods, analytic

studies especially those that are multinational—almost always do (cf. Anderson and Bennett, 1996; Gartner, 1990; Avison and Loring, 1986; Fiala and LaFree 1988).

The final dimension of the typology concerns the design of the data collection activity and the type of analyses performed. There are two categories here: longitudinal and cross-sectional. Longitudinal studies can be either national or multinational in scope. An example of a longitudinal design with national scope is Stack's (1982) time series analysis of crime data in Sweden. Examples of a multinational, longitudinal design include Archer and Gartner's (1984) study of violence, Anderson and Bennett's (1996) study of routine activities, Gartner's (1996) study of homicide, and Bennett and Basiotis' (1991) study of juvenile delinquency. Examples of multinational studies employing a cross-sectional design include Krahn, Hartnegel, and Gartrell's (1986) study of inequality and homicide; Krohn's (1976) study of inequality, unemployment, and crime; Messner's (1989) study of economic deprivation and homicide; Avris and Lorning's (1986) study of population density and homicide; studies of criminal victimization by van Dijk, Mayhew, and Killias (1990), van Kesteren, Mayhew, and Nieuwbeerta (2000), and Lee and Earnest (2003); and Schaefer and Lynch's (2001) study of crime seriousness.

Given this typology of comparative/transnational research and the work that fits into its various categories, what do we know about the origins of crime, the correlates of transnational crime, and the operations of the many justice systems? Of these three areas, we currently know most about the correlates of common property and violent crimes. This knowledge comes to us through the studies that are analytic, multinational, quantitative and both cross-sectional and longitudinal in design. This category of research not only has the longest tradition in comparative work but "has amassed the largest body of literature. Nevertheless, we still know relatively little about the effects of culture, family, religion, and other social institutions on criminality. Future research should include these explanatory constructs in comparative research models.

We are just beginning to understand the nature and correlates of transnational crime. For the longest time researchers ignored this form of criminality in favor of common crime. When its predecessor, organized crime, was studied, the focus was usually limited to the national boundaries of the researcher's nation. These studies still tend to be descriptive in approach, qualitative in analysis, and longitudinal in design. However, if global terrorism is to be reduced and stability brought to the developed and especially the developing nations of the world, we must know more about how terrorists are funded by transnational organized criminal enterprises. This can only be accomplished by devoting more resources to fund transnational crime research.

Similarly, our knowledge of the world's criminal justice systems is minimal. There is a paucity of studies and the vast majority of them are descriptive, national, qualitative and quantitative and cross-sectional. Thus, we know very little about the factors associated with variations in police, court, and correctional systems. We need to foster research projects that are analytic, multinational, quantitative, and longitudinal, i.e., research that investigates the variations in structure, function, and operations that affect the systems' effectiveness.

BENEFITS OF COMPARATIVE RESEARCH

There are four broad benefits of conducting comparative or transnational research. All relate to the approach's ability to expand our intellectual horizons and to deepen our understanding of how systems of crime and justice operate. The first two benefits have direct and immediate implications for policymakers and practitioners. The remaining two benefits focus more on theory development about crime and justice, also having policy implications although they may not be immediately evident.

One of the outcomes of the terrorist attacks in 2001 was a shocking awareness that terrorism is international and inextricably tied to transnational criminal activity. The more we know about transnational crime, the more prepared we are to fight international terrorism. We need to understand how criminal and terrorist organizations fund themselves and exploit our inability to link and analyze criminal activity that transcends national borders. We need to organize our justice systems to better identify, investigate, and apprehend those who threaten global security. National intelligence organizations have been engaged in these activities for some time, but academic researchers have just begun to study the issues. The benefit of academic research over national intelligence assessments is that scholars look for the cultural foundations, organizational structures, and social processes that underlie any specific criminal or terrorist group so we gain an in-depth understanding of their behavior and perhaps generalize our findings to similar groups. National intelligence allows us to react to likely and known threats whereas scholarly knowledge allows us to understand and thus control or at least reduce the threatening behavior.

Second, comparative research provides an in-depth understanding of how justice systems throughout the world operate. This knowledge has immediate and direct policy implications on a number of fronts. First, by understanding how various systems work (e.g., common law vs. civil code vs. religious) one can propose effective linkages among those systems for more effective control of global crime and terrorism. Second, understanding how justice systems work and develop gives us the basis for helping developing nations advance their justice systems to better cope with internal and transnational crime problems (as the United States is now doing in countries of the former Soviet Union). Finally, by studying justice systems worldwide, we can begin to collect an inventory of "best

practices" in criminal justice. Although nationalism and national pride tend to blind Americans to the benefits of other systems and processes not "Made in America," the globalization of crime damns those who do not search out best practices and then implement them as appropriate.

Third, as Melvin Kohn (1987) argued in his presidential address, one of the greatest benefits of comparative research is the testing of the generalizability of theories, especially if our theories are evaluative rather than generative (Bennett, 1980). In almost all cases, theory is developed to explain an observed phenomenon. What is implicit in most theory generation is that the phenomenon is bound by time, space and culture, and the ensuing theoretical model is limited (if not idiosyncratic) to the social, political, and economic environment in which the phenomenon occurred. Theory development benefits from comparative research because a theory can be readily tested in varying environments and then modified or adapted to explain similar phenomena occurring globally, or a theory can be revealed as a limited *ad hoc* explanation of a culture bound phenomenon. For example, my work in the Caribbean indicated that theoretical models developed in the United States and the United Kingdom concerning police use of force and job satisfaction fared well when applied to developing nations (Bennett 1997a, 1997b). Bayley (1985), on the other hand, used comparative research not to test a theory of policing but to develop one. By looking at the development and operation of various policing systems throughout the world and abstracting what was similar across them, he developed a comprehensive theory of policing.

In the criminological literature, LaFree and Kick (1986) and Bennett (1991a) have shown that level of development affects rates and types of crime cross-nationally. Bennett (1991b) and Anderson and Bennett (1996) found that some relationships theorized to be linear within nations were in fact curvilinear. In short, the comparative method affords researchers the opportunity to assess the power of a theory either by determining its generalizability or, more importantly, by using comparison groups on the social-system level to show what factors influence the strength of the key hypothesized relationships.

Finally, comparative research allows for the examination of variables that have limited range within a single nation. As an example, social welfare spending varies across states in the United States but the variance is only at the margins. Due to the restricted variance, the statistical relationship between spending and crime is weak at best and unstable and unreliable at worst. By employing a cross-national sample where variance in spending is greater, a researcher can better ascertain the correlation and the role of related variables (Savage, Bennett, & Danner 2004). Such research, if properly designed and conducted, can generate unbiased knowledge for policy discussions within and across nations.

These benefits cannot be realized through single-nation research: This is especially true for transnational crime that, by its very nature, involves more than one nation. The first two benefits have immediate and obvious policy implications: a better understanding of the nature of transnational crime and terrorism and a better understanding of ways to harness the energies of the world's criminal justice systems to combat them. The policy relevance of the second two benefits is less readily apparent although equally important: If we are to ameliorate the conditions that cause violence and crime, we must have a better understanding of the causal factors and their respective roles. The policy implications of this research may not be acted upon for political reasons, but we are nevertheless obligated to deduce and state them.

IMPEDIMENTS TO COMPARATIVE RESEARCH

One of the major impediments to comparative research is lack of adequate funding. Any study that involves more than one nation will be costly whether it employs archival data, observations, interviews or the administration of surveys. U.S. governmental funding for comparative and transnational research first emerged on the scene as a result of our War on Drugs. This funding was targeted for transnational studies of drugs and money laundering as well as studies that aided in the investigatory and apprehension capabilities of specific nations. The National Institute of Justice later created the International Center in 1998 with a modest research budget but a lofty mission (as articulated by its first director, James Finckenauer). In the first few years of the Center's operation, only three Challenge Grants were awarded. Grant activity has expanded recently and the Center now funds projects in eight broad categories. The current director, Jay Albanese, is continuing to develop and implement the Center's ambitious goals, which include stimulating awareness of transnational crime and its effect on local communities, forging global research partnerships among researchers and practitioners, assessing the national and global consequences of transnational crime and the effectiveness of alternative prevention and control strategies, and disseminating information on best practices for crime control.

Also in the late 1990s, the Ford Foundation funded the U.S. based Police Assessment Resource Center as part of a worldwide program on human rights and democratic policing. In 2002, the center hosted a global meeting on civilian oversight of the police that was attended by Ford grantees and government officials from eight nations. Starting in 2004, nongovernmental organizations (NGOs) in those nations will create a new global alliance, Altus, whose function will be to encourage more NGOs around the world to work on reform issues such as police accountability and oversight. Hopefully, this effort will include opportunities for research to be funded by the Ford Foundation and other Altus donors.

The European Council and the United Nations are also sources of funding for comparative and transnational crime and criminal justice research. For example, the Council is currently funding a four-year project (based at the University of Utrecht, The Netherlands) concerning human rights practices of the police in four nations: Brazil, Mexico, Costa Rica and Jamaica. The Soros Foundation has also funded comparative research in criminal justice, including a study of democratic policing and human rights in postcommunist societies (Uildriks and van Reenen 2003).

Although these funding sources are important, their research budgets represent a tiny fraction of the funds allocated for general crime and justice research within the U.S. and abroad. The competition for grants and contracts supporting comparative research is fierce and the researchable topics are limited because each organization has its own funding priorities. As an example, the Ford Foundation (www.fordfound.org) is interested in human rights, especially as they are honored or not by the police. The International Center funds research that falls within its eight categories (www.ojp.usdoj.gov/nij/international. If a comparative researcher is not interested in pursuing any of the targeted topics, funding options decrease precipitously.[7]

The researcher's background and networks are also influential in securing research funds. To produce a competitive research proposal, the researcher must be able to demonstrate to the funding agency in advance that he or she has access to the information to be analyzed. This requires the researcher to have previously established international relationships that would facilitate access. Unless the researcher has established these relationships through such avenues as a Fulbright award, presentations at international conferences, or networking with international scholars at professional meetings in the United States (e.g., ACJS or ASC), the research proposal is unlikely to be competitive.

There are four other major impediments to conducting comparative research. First, access to the subject of the research is often problematic. Access can take the form of securing sensitive and confidential governmental data (not necessarily classified data), interviewing members of sensitive institutions, observing clandestine activities, or gaining access to illegal organizations and/or activities. Although problems of access are not limited to comparative research (the same limiting factors are encountered in criminal justice research within the U.S.), they are usually more pronounced in comparative settings, especially in the developing world.

Governments do not like to be embarrassed. Crime data as well as information regarding the misfeasance and malfeasance of government employees or agencies can be sources of international embarrassment. What does a government have to gain by granting access to sensitive areas of operations to an outsider over whom it probably has little control? Access stems from trust in the researcher and trust takes time and effort to develop and maintain. My access to the police forces in the Caribbean required finding an intermediary in each nation who was trusted by the police and who would begin to negotiate access on my behalf. Once conditional access was granted, it fell upon me to demonstrate my trustworthiness to both the command staff and the individual constables I observed and interviewed.

Studying transnational crime also presents a myriad of access problems. On the governmental side, officials who might be implicated in the illegal activities do not want to be discovered. Even when governmental officials are not directly involved, they equate crime within their borders to failure in their administration. Thus they are reticent to cooperate with researchers and tend to punish those who do.[8] Additionally, the people who run illegal enterprises frequently do not want the notoriety that goes along with such research (although this is not always the case; see Gunst, 1995). Finally, conducting research—especially field research—on transnational crime can be personally dangerous for the researcher and should be undertaken with caution.

The second impediment to comparative research is language. Although most non-U.S. researchers are proficient in English, proficiency in foreign languages is uncommon among researchers from the United States. The inability to read the literature of a country in which one wishes to conduct research is a distinct liability even if one is employing data that are archived. For example, INTERPOL reports crime data for a sample of nations. The data are numeric and are categorized by the nation that voluntarily submits them. The general categories supplied by INTERPOL do not always adequately cover the unlawful behavior found in each nation's penal code. More important, by not being able to read and understand the penal procedural code of the nation, the researcher is unaware of what the data actually represent. For example, can an officer arrest on probable cause alone or does the officer need an arrest warrant prior to apprehension? The answer could dramatically influence the arrest data submitted to INTERPOL.

The problem becomes even more complex when one is conducting field research that requires interviews and interaction with field subjects. Lack of proficiency in the language or dialects of the subjects (especially their idioms) either precludes the research or forces one to collect data through the filter of a translator/informer. The latter can be successfully accomplished, as seen in Bayley's (1976) work with the Japanese police. However, the use of translators is costly and unless the researcher is intimately familiar with the culture, the researcher will not always know the correct questions to ask or how to interpret the subjects' translated responses. These language barriers force researchers to select national samples based upon the language spoken or to partner with other researchers who are proficient in the languages of the nations sampled. For examples of the latter, see the body of work by LaFree and Birkbeck (e.g., LaFree & Birkbeck, 1991) and the collaborative efforts of Layne and researchers from the Ukraine concerning heroin transiting in that nation (Layne, Khruppa, & Musyka, 2002).[9]

The third impediment involves the reliability and validity of comparative data on crime and justice. Kalish (1988) discusses issues of data reliability and concludes that official crime data should only be used with the greatest of caution and that comparisons across nations or rankings of nations cannot be validly done. Bennett and Lynch (1990) agree that direct comparisons or rankings produce varying results based upon the data source, yet they demonstrate that when such data are used for explanatory purposes, with statistical techniques such a regression analysis, the results will be very similar regardless of the data source chosen.

The reliability and validity of comparative victimization data are also problematic. Although van Dijk et al. (1990) and van Kesteren et al. (2000) have done a commendable job in orchestrating the collection of victimization data worldwide, the comparability of data is still suspect due to differences across nations in sampling and survey procedures. Even when the same survey instrument is used in two or more nations, the comparability of the resulting data is questionable (Bennett & Flavin, 1994).

Finally, even if one is successful in securing adequate funding, gaining access to research subjects or data, conquering the language barrier, and collecting reliable and valid data, one still has to find an acceptable outlet in which to publish. The number of journals dedicated to comparative research has almost doubled in the past five years, but publishing comparative articles in mainstream criminological, criminal justice, sociological, or political science journals remains difficult. One of the major reasons is that most mainstream journals have a very strong quantitative orientation. This bias is not as great an impediment for cross-national criminological studies as it is for comparative criminal justice and transnational studies. Many cross-national criminological studies employ sophisticated quantitative analyses because data amenable to such analyses are readily available (see, e.g., Bennett & Lynch, 1990). Comparative criminal justice researchers, however, have easy access to quantifiable data only on the most developed nations of the world. Most studies of the developing world's justice systems are nonquantitative. In addition, since most transnational crime links developed to developing nations, quantifiable data to analyze this form of criminality does not exist in a readily available form.

The use of qualitative approaches in most criminal justice (especially if the research involves a single nation) and transnational research studies relegates the resulting manuscripts to dedicated comparative journals with limited circulation, to book publishers, or to the dusty shelves of a report depository.[10] And unless the manuscript is designed as a textbook, it is likely to be of interest only to university presses (e.g., Bayley 1969, 1976, 1985; Harriot 2001; Huggins et al., 2002;

Kyle & Koslowski 2001; Naylor 2002) with limited marketing budgets and small printings.

Although these impediments to comparative and transnational research are real and pervasive, motivated researchers have obtained funding, gained access, dealt with language barriers and issues of reliability and validity, and found suitable publishing outlets. What remains to be seen, however, is whether the increased interest in comparative and transnational research post-September 11th will build to the point where it constitutes a mainstream field in criminology and criminal justice.

PROMOTING THE GROWTH OF COMPARATIVE RESEARCH

If the comparative crime and criminal justice area is to grow into a recognized field of study similar to comparative politics in the discipline of political science, then action must be taken on four fronts simultaneously. First, professional organizations such as the ACJS and ASC must do more to develop, support, and recognize comparative research as a true field of study within the discipline. Both organizations have established interest sections devoted to comparative study. Approximately 9% of ACJS members belong to its International Section and ASC has an active International Division that claims to be the largest division in the organization. However, more can and should be done. Mentoring, funding and publication opportunities for members (especially younger ones) should be created not only to aid their professional careers but also to show symbolically that the comparative field is a viable area of study and that those who work in it will be rewarded similarly to those who pursue traditional criminology and criminal justice research (through tenure and promotion in academia, and promotion and recognition in the research and practitioner communities). The discipline's leading organizations should also promote the development of theory and conceptual models to explain and predict phenomena across nations and cultures, as well as the development of methodologies to better research comparative issues. The organizations should collaboratively support the creation of a specialized journal for comparative studies and commit to making its stature the same as their premier journals, *Criminology* and *Justice Quarterly*. Finally, the organizations should support the development of comparative and transnational pedagogy by identifying best practices in curriculum development and program delivery and disseminating the results widely.

Second, academic institutions should encourage development of a comparative curriculum that is more than an odd course presented now and then. This means integrating substantive comparative courses into the main curriculum and including comparative elements in each traditional course taught. These changes will sensitize students and faculty to the importance of this area of study and will increase the likelihood that students will incorporate a comparative focus into whatever career field they pursue. Equally important, these changes will increase the use of a comparative perspective in public discourse about crime and justice problems and policies. In order for this realistically to take place, premiums should be paid to faculty who make the effort to retool their old classes and develop new ones. In addition, personnel decisions on junior faculty should be based, in part, on their ability to integrate the comparative approach into their classrooms and perhaps into their research agendas.

No discussion of the advancement of an area of study would be complete or realistic if it did not include a discussion of financial rewards and support. Not only should individual career advancement be tied to promoting the field, but governmental and nongovernmental agencies should supply the funding to promote the comparative approach and studies that use it. Governmental funding is inescapably tied to politics, so lobbying/advocacy should be undertaken to convince those in power that comparative and transnational research is both necessary and important. They should be convinced that funding of these areas will result in a large return on investment and will be in the best interest of the country (and their own political careers). This is another role for our professional organizations to play. Nongovernmental organizations should also be lobbied to better support comparative and transnational research because the findings will help in accomplishing their missions. Of course, stating that these initiatives to garner financial support should be undertaken is easy; determining the strategies that will be successful in accomplishing this goal is another matter.

There is much that individual researchers, academics, and practitioners can do to promote the growth of the comparative and transnational field. After all, it is individuals who are members of the professional organizations, who are members of the faculty that will develop curriculum and teach the students, and who are the voices to convince our political and public leaders that funding of the comparative field is necessary. These individuals will need leadership and skill development to accomplish these tasks, and this too should be a top priority of the professional societies.

CONCLUSIONS

Every type of comparative research has added immensely to our understanding of crime and justice. Descriptive studies have alerted us to differences in the field of justice and helped focus our search for crime patterns throughout the world. Analytic studies have increased our understanding of the causes of crime and the correlates of criminal justice functioning and have produced empirically informed policy alternatives. Finally, transnational studies have shown us that crime is not bounded by national borders and how national social systems collectively inhibit or enhance criminal activity.

If the comparative and transnational area of study is to become a mainstream field in criminology and criminal justice and not just a temporary fad, then concerted effort must be devoted to fostering increased involvement of professional organizations, the development of a new generation of researchers and research consumers, and a coordinated strategy to increase governmental, foundation, and other funding. We must fulfill the promises of comparative research by showing that our understanding of the effects of culture, family, religion and other social institutions on criminality is deepened by studies that use comparative research designs. We must overcome the impediments to transnational research and explore how transnational criminal enterprises such as terrorism operate across national borders. Finally, we must hasten the use of comparative methods in criminal justice research by showing that police, court and correctional systems vary widely because they reflect their national context but also share striking similarities. Without these efforts, comparative and transnational research will remain a specialized interest area of study.

I predict that the continued globalization of business, economics, politics, and cultures will create a demand for global criminology and criminal justice research. As the demand grows, comparative research will also grow in popularity and prestige in all categories of the typology. The tragedy of the September 11th terrorist attacks created an opportunity for comparative and transnational research to demonstrate its relevance and potential in today's world. With the support of academics, practitioners and funding agencies, this area of study will assume its rightful place as a mainstream field in criminology and criminal justice.

REFERENCES

Adler, F. (1983). *Nations not obsessed with crime.* Littleton, CO: F.B. Rothman.

Anderson, T., & Bennett, R. R. (1996). Development, gender and crime: The scope of the routine activity approach. *Justice Quarterly, 13,* 31-56.

Archer, D., & Gartner, R (1984). *Violence and crime in cross-national perspective.* New Haven: Yale University Press.

Avison, W. R., & Loring, P. L. (1986). Population diversity and cross-national homicide: The effects of inequality and heterogeneity. *Criminology, 24,* 733-749.

Bayley, D. H. (1969). *The police and political development in India.* Princeton: Princeton University Press.

Bayley, D. H. (1976). *Forces of order: Police behavior in Japan and the United States.* Berkeley: University of California Press.

Bayley, D. H. (1985). *Patterns of policing: A comparative international analysis.* New Brunswick, NJ: Rutgers University Press.

Bennett, R. R. (1980). Constructing cross-cultural theories in criminology and criminal justice: Application of the generative approach. *Criminology, 18,* 252-268.

Bennett, R. R. (1982). The effect of police personnel levels on crime clearance rates: A cross-national analysis. *International Journal of Comparative and Applied Criminal Justice, 6,* 177-193.

Bennett, R. R. (1991a). Development and crime: A cross-national, time-series analysis of competing models. *Sociological Quarterly, 32,* 343-363.

Bennett, R. R (1991b). Routine activities: A cross-national assessment of a criminological perspective. *Social Forces, 70,* 147-163.

Bennett, R. R. (1997a). Excessive force: A comparative study of police in the Caribbean. *Justice Quarterly, 14,* 651-686.

Bennett, R. R. (1997b). The determinants of job satisfaction among police constables: A comparative study in three developing nations. *Justice Quarterly, 14,* 295-323.

Bennett, R. R. (2003, August). Governmental legitimacy and policing styles: The effect of corruption on citizen-police behavior. Paper presented at the XIII World Congress of Criminology of the International Society of Criminology, Rio De Janeiro, Brazil.

Bennett, R. R., & Basiotis, P. (1991). Structural correlates of juvenile property crime: A cross-national time-series analysis. *Journal of Research in Crime and Delinquency, 28,* 262-287.

Bennett, R. R., & Flavin, J. (1994). Determinants of fear of crime: The effect of cultural setting. *Justice Quarterly, 11,* 357-381.

Bennett, R. R., & Lynch, J. P. (1990). Does a difference make a difference? Comparing cross-national crime indicators. *Criminology, 28,* 153-181.

Bennett, R .R., & Wiegand, B. (1994). Observations on crime reporting in a developing nation. *Criminology, 32,* 135-148.

Chevigny, P. (1995). *Edge of the knife: Police violence in the Americas.* New York: The Free Press.

Clifford, W. (1978). Culture and crime in global perspective. *International Journal of Criminology and Penology. 6,* 61-80.

Clinard, M. B. (1978). *Cities with little crime.* Cambridge: Cambridge University Press.

Clinard, M. B., & Abbott, D. J. (1973). *Crime in developing nations: A comparative perspective.* New York: John Wiley.

Danns, G. K. (1982). *Domination and power in Guyana.* New Brunswick, NJ: Transaction Books.

DeFleur, L. B. (1969). Alternative strategies for the development of delinquency theories applicable to other cultures. *Social Problems, 17,* 30-39

Ebbe, O. N. I. (2000). *Comparative and international criminal justice systems.* Boston: Butterworth-Heineman.

Edie, C. J. (1994). *Democracy in the Caribbean.* Westport, CT: Praeger

Fairchild, E. (1988). *German police.* Springfield, IL: Charles C. Thomas.

Fairchild, E., & Dammer, H. R. (2001). *Comparative criminal justice systems.* Belmont, CA: Wadsworth.

Farrington, D. P., Langan, P., & Wikstrom, P. (1994). Changes in crime and punishment in America, England and Sweden between the 1980s and the 1990s. *Studies on Crime and Crime Prevention, 3,* 104-130.

Fiala, R., & LaFree, G. (1988). Cross-national determinants of child homicide. *American Sociological Review, 53,* 432-445.

Finckenauer, J. O. (1995). *Russian youth: Law, deviance, and the pursuit of freedom.* New Brunswick, NJ: Transaction Publishers.

Findlay, M., & Zvekic, U. (1993). *Alternative policing styles: Cross-cultural perspectives.* Deventer, The Netherlands: Kluwer Law and Taxation Publishers.

Frase, R. S. (2001). *Sentencing in Germany and the United States: Comparing aap-fel with apples.* Freiburg, Germany: Max Planck Institute.

Friday, P. C. (1971). Problems in comparative criminology: Comments on the feasibility and implications of research. *International Journal of Criminology and Penology, 1,* 151-160.

Friman, R., & Andreas, P. (1999). *The illicit global economy and state power.* Lanham, MD: Rowman and Littlefield.

Gartner, R. (1990). The victims of homicide: A temporal and cross-national comparison. *American Sociological Review, 55,* 92-106.

Gunst, L. (1995). *Born fi' dead.* New York: Henry Holt and Company.

Hansmann, H. B., & Quigley, J. M. (1982). Population heterogeneity and the sociogenesis of homicide. *Social Forces, 61,* 206-224.

Harriott, A. (2001). *Police and crime control in Jamaica: Problems in reforming ex-colonial constabularies.* Kingston, Jamaica: The University of West Indies Press.

Horton, C. (1995). *Policing in France.* London: Policy Studies Institute.

Huggins, M. K., Haritos-Fatouros, M., & Zimbardo, P. G. (2002). *Violence workers: Police torturers and murderers reconstruct Brazilian atrocities.* Berkeley, CA: University of California Press.

Ivkovic, S. K., Klockars, C., Cajner-Mraovic, I., & Ivanusec, D. (2002). Controlling police corruption: The Croatian perspective. *Police Practice and Research, 3,* 55-72.

Jones, T. (1995). *Policing democracy in the Netherlands.* London: Policy Studies Institute.

Kalish, C. B. (1988). *International crime rates: Special report.* Washington, DC: Bureau of Justice Statistics.

Kohn, M. (1987). Cross-national research as an analytic strategy. *American Sociological Review, 52,* 713-731.

Krahn, H., Hartnagel, T. F., & Gartrell, J. W. (1986). Income inequality and homicide rates: Cross-national data and criminological theories. *Criminology, 24,* 269-295.

Krohn, M. D. (1976). Inequality, unemployment, and crime: A cross-national analysis. *Sociological Quarterly, 17,* 303-313.

Kyle, D., & Koslowski, R. (2001). *Global human smuggling: Comparative perspectives.* Baltimore, MD: Johns Hopkins University Press.

LaFree, G. D., & Birkbeck, C. (1991). The neglected situation: A cross-national study of the situational characteristics of crime. *Criminology, 29,* 73-98.

LaFree, G. D., & Kick, E. L. (1986). Cross-national effects of development, distributional and demographic variables on crime: A review and analysis. *International Annals of Criminology, 24,* 213-236.

Layne, M., Khruppa, M. S., & Musyka, A. A. (2002). *The growing importance of Ukraine as a transit country for heroin trafficking: Final report.* Washington, DC: Abt Associates.

Lynch, J. P. (1988). A comparison of prison use in England and Wales, Canada, the United States, and West Germany: A limited test of the punitiveness hypothesis. *Journal of Criminal Law and Criminology, 79,* 180-217.

Lynch, J. P. (1993). A cross-national comparison of the length of custodial sentences for serious crimes. *Justice Quarterly, 10,* 639-660.

Lee, M. R, & Earnest, T. (2003). Perceived community cohesion and perceived risk of victimization: A cross-national study. *Justice Quarterly, 20,*131-157.

MacCoun, R. J., & Reuter, P. (2001). *Drug war heresies: Learning from other vices, times and places.* Cambridge, UK: Cambridge University Press.

Mawby, R. I. (1999). *Policing across the world: Issues for the twenty-first century.* London: UCL Press.

Messner, S. F. (1982). Societal development, social equality and homicide: A cross-national test of a Durkheimian model. *Social Forces, 61,* 225-240.

Messner, S. F. (1989). Economic discrimination and societal homicide rates: Further evidence on the cost of inequality. *American Sociological Review, 54,* 597-611.

Miller, W. R (1977). *Cops and bobbies: Police authority in New York and London 1830-1870.* Chicago: University of Chicago Press.

Miyazawa, S. (1992). *Policing in Japan: A study on making crime.* Albany, NY: State University of New York Press.

Naylor, RT. (2002). *Wages of crime: Black markets, illegal finance, and the underworld economy.* Ithaca: Cornell University Press.

Parker, L. C. (2001). *The Japanese police system today.* Armonk, NY: M. E. Sharp.

Passas, N. (2000). Global anomie, dysanomie, and economic crime: Hidden consequences of neoliberalism and globalization in Russia and around the world. *Social Justice, 27,* 16-44.

Punch, M. (1979). *Policing the inner city: A study of Amsterdam's Warmoesstraat.* London: MacMillan Press.

Punch, M. (1985). *Conduct unbecoming: The social construction of police deviance and control.* London: Tavistock Publications.

Reichel, P. L. (2002). *Comparative criminal justice systems: A topical approach.* Upper Saddle River, NJ: Prentice Hall.

Savage, J., Bennett, R. R., & Danner, M. (2004). Social welfare spending and crime rates: The effect of economic assistance on crime. Manuscript submitted for publication.

Schaefer, M., & Lynch, J. P. (2001). The seriousness of crime: A cross-national comparison. In H. Kury (Ed.), *International Comparison of Crime and Victimization: The ICVS* (pp. 90-102). Ontario, Canada: de Sitter Publications.

Shelley, L. I. (1996). *Policing Soviet society.* London: Routledge.

Shelley, L. I. (1984). *Lawyers in Soviet work life.* New Brunswick, NJ: Rutgers University Press.

Skolnick, J. H., & Bayley, D. H. (1988). *Community policing: Issues and practices around the world.* Washington, DC: National Institute of Justice.

Stack, S. (1982). Social structure and Swedish crime rates. *Criminology, 20,* 499-513.

Terrill, R J. (1999). *World criminal justice systems: A survey.* Cincinnati, OH: Anderson Publishing.

Uldriks, N., & van Reenen, P. (2001). *Policing post-communist societies.* Antwerp, Belgium: Intersentia.

van Dijk, J. J. M., Mayhew, P., & Killias, M. (1990). *Experiences of crime across the world.* Deventer, The Netherlands: Kluwer Law and Taxation Publishers.

van Kesteren, J., Mayhew, P., & Nieuwbeerta, P. (2000). *Criminal victimisation in seventeen industrialized countries.* Den Haag, The Netherlands: WDOC.

Wiegand, B., & Bennett, R. R. (1992). The will to win: Determinants of public support for the drug war in Belize. *Crime, Law, and Social Change, 19,* 203-220.

Zhang, S. X., & Chin, K. (2002). *The social organization of Chinese human smuggling: A cross national study.* San Diego, CA: San Diego State University press.

Notes

1. Major newspapers increased their coverage of the subjects exponentially. As an example, during the 3 years preceding the attacks on U.S. soil, there were 732 articles in major papers with the word terrorism in the headline. Most of these stories were found in the international section of the papers. For the month following the attacks there were over 1,000 articles and they were no longer relegated to the back pages of the paper. These data were secured from a Lexus-Nexus search where "terrorism" was found in the headline and "international" found in the text. The phrase, "over 1,000," refers to the display limit set by a Lexus-Nexus search. A more restricted search including the first 15 days of October, 2001 yielded the same conclusion: Over 1,000 articles were printed in major newspapers during that period.

2. At the March 2001 ACJS meeting, 7.1% of the panel sessions addressed comparative issues (18 of the 253 sessions). At the 2003 meetings in Boston, 9.5% of the sessions were so oriented (29 of 306 sessions). At the ASC meetings in November 2001, 2.6% of the sessions dealt with comparative issues (11 of the 422 sessions) while 6.7% of the sessions in Denver in 2003 were comparative (28 of the 415 sessions). These data were collected from

Appendix A.   A Partial list of Comparative Journals and the Number of Years in Publication

Journal Name	Years in Publication
Journal of International Criminal Justice	1
International Journal of Comparative Criminology	3
Criminal Justice: The International Journal of Policy & Practice	3
Crime Prevention & Community Safety: An International Journal	5
International Journal of Police Science & Management	5
Police Practice & Research: An International Journal	5
International Review of Victimology	10
International Criminal Justice Review	13
International Journal of Drug Policy	15
International Journal of Police Strategies and Management	26
International Journal of Comparative and Applied Criminal Justice	26
International Journal of the Sociology of Law	32
International Journal of Offender Therapy and Comparative Criminology	47

the programs of both organizations. The preliminary program for the 2004 meeting of ACJS indicates there will be 17 sessions including over 50 papers on terrorism alone.

3. I became interested in comparative research during graduate school at Washington State University while working with Lois DeFleur, but it wasn't until 1978 that I first became active in the area. My first comparative publication concerned the advantage of the comparative technique in the development of theory (Bennett, 1980). This led me to begin collecting comparative data and resulted in a couple of cross-sectionally designed analyses on crime patterns and police effectiveness (e.g., Bennett, 1982). On my first sabbatical, I began developing the Correlates of Crime (COC) data archive to address what I believed was a pressing need for longitudinal data to test comparative criminological theories adequately. I had considerable difficulty finding journal editors willing to publish these studies. Reviewers constantly questioned the validity of my dependent variable: crime. Jim Lynch and I embarked on a study to develop an error profile for comparative crime data and published "Does a Difference Make a Difference?" (Bennett & Lynch, 1990). Once the relative reliability of comparative crime data was demonstrated, my comparative pieces began to be published in the leading journals in the field.

My interest in comparative work then shifted from the use of archival data to the use of original data. I traveled to Belize, Central America to conduct a victimization study and used those data to investigate fear of crime, crime reporting, and other topics. My next sabbatical, with funding from a Fulbright Senior Research Award, allowed me to spend a year in the Caribbean researching various issues of policing in the developing world. I am continuing this work by investigating justice systems in developing nations.

As President of the ACJS, I selected *The Globalization of Crime and Justice* as the theme for the 2003 annual meeting. Academics and practitioners from 17 nations attended the meeting which was one of the largest in the organization's history.

4. Although my typology differs from that of Kohn (1987), it draws heavily upon his conceptualization. My typology differs in that it not only considers the explanatory purpose of the study but also the research design and analytic methods employed. I have noted in the text where the two typologies intersect.

5. The line between a descriptive and analytic study is sometimes very fine. Most descriptive studies attempt to explain why a system works the way it does or why crime occurs as it does, but these explanations are mainly post hoc and not part of an analytic approach that involves the testing of hypotheses, either stated or implied.

6. Although they also used survey data in their studies, the primary data collection tools were interviews and observations.

7. Some funding organizations like the NIJ have a non-solicited or "investigator-initiated" research program which allows the researcher to propose his or her own research issue and methodology. However, such programs are usually very limited in terms of the funds available.

8. In the acknowledgment section of their research report on human trafficking, Zhang and Chin (2002) demonstrate the value of collaboration and the threats such aid creates for those who give it. They state:

"In particular, we want to thank all of our subjects who were brave enough to trust us with their most confidential information, and our fellow researchers in China whose familiarity with local cultural nuances greatly enhanced our understanding of the social context of illegal human migration. Without these individuals for whom we are not at liberty to reveal their identities, this study would not have been possible (pg. iii)."

9. This partnership began in 1999 through a collaboration between the National Institute of Justice and the Ukrainian Academy of Law Sciences. Five U.S.-Ukrainian research teams were created with a total of 22 Ukrainian and five U.S. members. Prior to the initiation of this or any of the other projects, the teams met to overcome communication barriers and to resolve divergences in methodological approaches, of which there were many.

10. Many of the current comparative criminal justice studies investigate one or just a few justice systems (usually selected because of research access to them). In many cases, the study uses the case study approach which generates findings not easily captured in the 20 pages or less normally allocated to an article in most social sciences journals.

From *Justice Quarterly*, Vol. 21, No. 1, March 2004, pp. 1-21. Copyright © 2004 by Taylor & Francis Journals. Reprinted by permission. www.tandf.co.uk/journals

CRIMINAL NEGLECT

" … A top-to-bottom overhaul of the nation's juvenile justice systems is mandatory if these [troubled youngsters] ever are to avoid becoming adult crime statistics."

Joseph A. Califano, Jr. and Charles W. Colson

Thirty years ago, Charles W. Colson and Joseph A. Califano, Jr., were at each other's throats. Colson, the White House "hatchet man," was busy defending Pres. Richard Nixon during the Watergate scandal. Califano, meanwhile, was going after Nixon, filing the lawsuit against the Committee to Reelect the President and representing The Washington Post *during Watergate. Today, these men are brothers-in-arms in their concern for youngsters caught up in American juvenile justice systems.*

ONE OF US has seen prison from the inside out, serving time for a Watergate-related crime—and has visited 600 correction facilities over the past 30 years. The other has spent many years studying the link between crime and substance abuse. Although we come from opposite ends of the political spectrum and have vastly different life experiences, on one issue, at least, we have arrived at the same bleak conclusion: The U.S. is criminally negligent when it comes to children caught up in the nation's juvenile justice systems.

In October, 2003, The National Center on Addiction and Substance Abuse (CASA) at New York's Columbia University released a report based on a five-year study. "Criminal Neglect: Substance Abuse, Juvenile Justice and the Children Left Behind" is the most comprehensive analysis ever undertaken of substance abuse and juvenile justice. Among its most significant findings: The road to juvenile crime and incar-

ceration is paved with drugs and alcohol. Four out of every five children and teen arrestees are under the influence of alcohol or drugs while committing their crimes, test positive for drugs, are arrested for an alcohol or drug offense, admit to having substance abuse and addiction problems, or share some combination of these characteristics. While the most commonly used drugs are alcohol and marijuana, a significant number of kids test positive for cocaine, amphetamines, and opiates.

Drug and alcohol abuse is implicated in all types of juvenile crime, including almost 70% of violent offenses, 72% of property offenses, and more than 80% of other offenses, such as vandalism and disorderly conduct.

The problem is, virtually nothing is being done to stem this disturbing tide. CASA found that some 1,900,000 of the 2,400,000 juvenile arrestees are drug and alcohol abusers or addicts. Yet, only 68,600 of them—

a mere 3.6%—receive any treatment. Moreover, substance abuse is not the sole problem that goes unaddressed in these kids' lives. Many come from broken and troubled families, have been abused or neglected, live in crime-infested neighborhoods, and struggle with learning disabilities and mental health problems such as depression and schizophrenia.

State juvenile justice systems were created more than 100 years ago to protect and reform young people who commit crimes—to provide care, custody, and discipline in a way that closely would approximate that which should be given by parents. This is the goal, but the reality is a grim, modern version of Charles Dickens' *Oliver Twist*. Instead of providing care and rehabilitation, many facilities are nothing more than colleges of criminality for these kids.

Just look at the sorry state of affairs:

Alcohol and drug abuse and addiction go untreated. While 44% of the 10- to 17-year-olds arrested in the past year already meet the clinical definition of substance abuse or dependence (while 28% meet the clinical test of hard-core addiction), less than four percent receive treatment. These arrested juveniles are six times more likely to be substance abusers and eight times more likely to be hooked on drugs and alcohol than their contemporaries.

Mental health problems go unheeded. Three out of four of all incarcerated juveniles are likely to suffer a mental illness such as depression, anxiety, or schizophrenia, yet mental health services are scarce. Kids in the "system" are almost five times as likely to have a mental health problem than their peers. Thousands of children are held in juvenile detention simply because no mental health treatment is available.

Learning disabilities and special education needs are not addressed. As many as 80% of jailed juveniles have learning disabilities. They need special education classes, yet most programs do not meet even the lowest state criteria in this area.

Lack of spiritual grounding. Almost half of arrested kids never attend religious services. Such teens are more likely to smoke, consume alcohol, binge drink, and use marijuana and other illicit drugs compared to those who consider religion an important part of their lives. Research has found that religious commitment and spiritual practice can help prevent substance abuse and addiction while aiding in recovery. Yet, CASA found no program that provides for the spiritual enrichment of incarcerated youngsters, such as the Prison Fellowship Ministries initiative, which has proven so successful with adult inmates.

More girls are entering the system. Although most juvenile arrests involve males, the number of females entering detention jumped 50% between 1990-99, compared with a four percent rise for males. Females are more likely to be charged with crimes such as prostitution,

running away from home, truancy, and curfew violations.

Cases referred to juvenile court are twice as likely to involve blacks as whites. Black juveniles are more likely to be arrested for committing violent or drug crimes, while white juveniles are more likely to be arrested for committing alcohol-related offenses.

Facilities are overcrowded and conditions inhumane. Forty percent of juvenile facilities are severely overcrowded, and children often are mistreated and abused. States across the nation—including Arizona, California, Connecticut, Florida, Maine, Maryland, Mississippi, Nevada, and New York—have come under fire for mistreating juvenile detainees.

- At a facility in Mississippi, girls have been stripped naked and placed in the "dark room," a locked, windowless, isolation cell with a drain in the floor that serves as a toilet; youth report being hog-tied, pole-shackled, and pepper-sprayed.
- In Nevada, corrections officials punched youths in the chest, shoved them against lockers and walls, threw them to the floor, and smashed their heads in doors.
- In a Connecticut facility, juveniles have been pulled by the hair, jerked by the ears, and kicked in the ribs by corrections officials.

One of us (Colson) has walked the cellblocks and looked at the vacant, hopeless expressions of kids staring through the bars. Instead of attending to the needs of our most desperate children, we are writing them off, warehousing them in detention centers, or sending them back to their troubled families and neighborhoods—only to register them later as crime statistics.

We ignore the needs of juvenile arrestees at our own peril. At least 30% of adult inmates serving time for felony crimes were first locked up as juveniles. Like substance abuse itself, substance-related crime can run in the family, creating a vicious spiral descending into deeper addiction and more serious illegal activity.

Incarcerated adults are likely to be children of parents who were in prison; these adults are themselves the fathers and mothers of 2,500,000 offspring. Kids of jailed parents are likelier than children whose parents have not been locked up to end up in prison.

Eighty percent of the adult men and women behind bars in the U.S. were high at the time they committed their crimes, stole property to buy drugs, have a history of drug and alcohol abuse, or share some combination of these characteristics. Most began their life of substance abuse and addiction as children and teens.

If Congress, the president, and state governors are serious that "no child be left behind," we must end the neglect for these children who are left the furthest behind.

Here is what we propose:

- The Federal government should create a model juvenile justice code to set a standard of practices and accountability for states in handling juvenile offenders.
- All those connected with the juvenile justice system—judges, law enforcement officers, various court personnel, etc.—should be trained to recognize and deal with substance-involved offenders.
- Diversion programs—such as drug courts—should be extended to juveniles.
- An initiative similar to Prison Fellowship Ministries should be used as a prototype to provide troubled youth with the spiritual support that can make a difference in their lives.
- Proper healthcare, education, and job training programs are a must for those in the juvenile justice system.
- Federal grant programs for juvenile justice and delinquency prevention need to be expanded and such grants have to be conditioned on reform of state systems.
- State and national data need to be compiled to judge the progress in meeting the needs of these children.

In short, a top-to-bottom overhaul of the nation's juvenile justice systems is mandatory if these unfortunate youths ever are to avoid becoming adult crime statistics.

If we are not motivated by concern for our most troubled kids, we should at least consider the high cost of ignoring their plight. The CASA report finds that, were society to invest $5,000 for treatment and securing comprehensive services and programs for each of the 123,000 substance-involved juveniles who otherwise would be incarcerated, we would break even on our investment in the first year if just 12% of them stayed in school and remained drug- and crime-free. If we could pre-

vent the crimes and imprisonment of just 12% of adults with juvenile records, there would be 60,000 fewer adult inmates. This would save $18,000,000,000 in criminal justice and health care costs—and do not forget the added economic benefits of employment or the 6,000,000 fewer crimes that would be committed.

Of course, even with all the help in the world, some juveniles still will embark on a life of crime. Yet, the overwhelming proportion of youngsters currently ensnared in juvenile justice systems can grow up to be productive, tax-paying, law-abiding

citizens and responsible parents. This, however, only can happen if we stop looking the other way. Here is a problem we can fix; not to do so would be a crime.

Joseph A. Califano, Jr., is president of the National Center on Addiction and Substance Abuse at Columbia University, New York. He was Pres. Lyndon Johnson's assistant for domestic affairs and Pres. Jimmy Carter's Secretary of Health, Education and Welfare.

Charles W. Colson is chairman and founder of Prison Fellowship Ministries. He served as Pres. Richard Nixon's White House counsel, and is the author of several books.

Tokyo's Teen Tribes

The Sydney Morning Herald

It's past midnight in Shibuya, a funky entertainment district popular with Tokyo's younger generation. Three high-school boys are lying unconscious outside a busy bar. Two teenage girls in party gear are throwing up. A third, who looks about 16, is striking erotic poses in the middle of the street while three boys grope her breasts and buttocks. Ten yards away, a uniformed officer studiously ignores the scenes of drunken teenage debauchery that have become an almost nightly event in this part of town.

Welcome to the world of the *kogyaru*, the *femio kun*, the *boso zoku*—the new tribes of Japan's younger generation who are worrying the wits out of their parents with their wild behavior.

International surveys show that Japanese youngsters are more discontented with their materialistic society than kids in other countries. They also tend to be more apathetic and less ambitious. The latest poll, conducted by the government's Management and Coordination Agency, found that only 44 percent of Japanese under 20 were happy with their lives—a far lower percentage than in the United States, Europe, and even Russia.

Rebelling against what psychiatrist Masao Miyamoto calls the "straitjacket society" where kids have their whole lives predetermined for them by the time they reach junior high school at 13—Japanese youth are shocking the authorities with their sex, drugs, and rock 'n' roll. Particularly the sex.

A national survey of 3,600 14- and 15-year-olds by the National Congress of Parents' and Teachers' Associations confirmed every parent's worst fears. One quarter of the girls admitted that they had frequented *terekura* ("telephone clubs"), the 500-odd dating agencies in Tokyo, where frustrated men pay for introductions to schoolgirls. The girls boast they can earn $700 or more in cash and gifts for a date.

Two thirds of the students said they regularly drank alcohol (the drinking age in Japan is 20), one in six said they had shoplifted, and 7 percent said they used drugs—an extraordinarily high figure in a country where possession of even one marijuana joint almost invariably brings a stiff jail sentence.

Hiroshi Itakura, a professor of criminal law at Tokyo's Nihon University, says the survey showed Japanese youngsters had "an undeveloped sense of right and wrong and a general attitude of permissiveness." He asserts: "Someday this will lead to Japan's ruin."

The schoolgirl date-club phenomenon sprang into the headlines last year when three 15-year-olds confessed that they had picked up a 43-year-old office worker through a club and gone with him to a love hotel—one of thousands of specialized hotels in Tokyo that rent rooms with video cameras by the hour. There

the girls squirted him in the eyes with a tear-gas canister and fled with his wallet containing $1,500. The man told police he thought the girls were treating him to some kinky S&M and didn't realize he was being robbed until too late.

In the uproar that followed, police were ordered to crack down on the clubs. Teachers and police rounded up no fewer than 526 schoolgirls—some as young as 13—and charged more than 100 of them with prostitution. The clubs, however, soon resumed business.

Not far from the Shibuya bar, two casually dressed 16-year-olds named Yuko and Akiko are primping at a street corner, waiting for someone to pick them up. They are typical *kogyaru* (literally "child/girls"), attending school by day, partying by night.

Yuko denies selling her body but cheerfully admits she sleeps with strangers who sometimes leave her money. She sold her school knickers, along with a photo of herself wearing them, to one of the *buru sera* sex shops in Tokyo for $95. *Buru sera* means "sailor's bloomers," and the stores are the latest craze among Tokyo's dirty old men, who are also willing to pay liberally for schoolgirls' fingernails, vials of saliva, and used tampons.

Both girls say they use drugs—amphetamines, marijuana, hash, and LSD. The latest craze is inhaling capsules of a liquid used to clean video-recorder heads.

Although Japan still has an enviably low rate of drug use, police figures show a dramatic increase among the young. Last year, police arrested more than 10,000 juveniles for drug use or dealing; most of the arrests involved paint-thinner abuse. Inhalation of thinners has been blamed for a rash of deaths among teenagers and for last New Year's Eve's suicide attempt by five junior-high-school girls who leapt from an apartment building. Three were killed and two terribly injured.

The *boso zoku* ("reckless tribe") have been around Tokyo since the early 1970s. Now, however, bikers and their rivals in hotted-up cars are giving police and law-abiding drivers a bigger headache than ever. Wearing black leather and chains, and sporting tattoos and rings through their ears, noses, tongues, belly buttons, nipples, and genitals, the reckless riders turn sections of Tokyo's Shuto expressway into a raceway. More than a third of the 1,000-odd motorcycle deaths last year involved teenagers, and

police are now pushing for tougher laws to try to cut down on the mayhem.

Then there are the *femio kun* ("feminine lads"). Although they deny they are gay, anywhere else in the world they would be regarded as having a severe case of gender confusion. Wearing berets over their short "monkey-hair" cuts and carrying dainty backpacks, these kids parade around the streets wearing necklaces and makeup and dressed in tight skivvies over lacy blouses, miniskirts or billowing bell-bottom trousers, and platform shoes.

A whole new industry has sprung up to cater to this latest subculture, and social commentators are falling over themselves to explain the appeal of the androgynous look. "They [the feminine lads] are very popular with the girls," says one young woman. "They are not macho or threatening—it's like having a pet to play with."

No one has yet come up with a snappy name like Generation X to describe the kaleidoscope of subcultures. The term most commonly used by tut-tutting TV com-

mentators is *shiji machi sedai*, which translates clumsily as "a generation awaiting instruction." Nor can any two sociologists agree on the causes, or consequences, of Japan's youth rebellion.

Author Hideo Kato, 65, blames frustration over the Japanese education system, under which a child's education and hence career has already been mapped out by the time he or she—particularly she—leaves primary school. Teenage suicide is common—almost 3,000 deaths in the past decade—under the relentless pressure to succeed at school.

Hideo Kato says: "When their future is decided for them in this way, there is often a gap between their parents' expectations and what their teachers say is possible. They develop an inferiority complex and a shaky sense of identity. The future is not worth thinking about, so they pursue the pleasures of the moment—that's why they sell their bodies or their underwear. They don't care any more what society thinks."
—Ben Hills (with research by Mayu Kanamori), "Sydney Morning Herald" (centrist), Oct. 7, 1995.

From *World Press Review*, January 1996, oo. 39 40. Originally published in the *Sydney Morning Herald*, Sydney Australia © 1996 by Ben Hills. Reprinted with permission.

The National Juvenile Justice Action Plan: A Comprehensive Response to a Critical Challenge

Sarah Ingersoll

"More and more of our Nation's children are killing and dying. The only way we can break the cycle of violence is through a truly national effort implemented one community at a time. Everyone has a role—businesses, schools, universities, and especially parents. Every community and every citizen can find practical steps in the Action Plan *to do something now about youth violence."*

Attorney General Janet Reno

On the heels of the crack epidemic, the Nation has witnessed the drive-by murder of a 3-year-old girl playing in the wrong place at the wrong time, a 12-year-old boy caught in a deadly feud over drug turf, and a homeless man set on fire in the subway by boys who should have been in school. Lurid headlines have captured the public's attention as youth violence takes center stage in the domestic debate.

Responses to these events have been as swift as they have been varied, but often they are reactions to a crisis rather than solutions based on analysis.

A Comprehensive Plan

In 1994, Attorney General Janet Reno convened the first meeting of the restructured Coordinating Council on Juvenile Justice and Delinquency Prevention, which comprises nine juvenile justice practitioners and representatives from the U.S. Departments of Justice (DOJ), Health and Human Services (HHS), Housing and Urban Development, Labor, Treasury, and Education (ED); the Office of National Drug Control Policy; and the Corporation for National Service. The Attorney General charged the Council to create an agenda to reduce youth violence. *Combating Violence and Delinquency: The National Juvenile Justice Action Plan* (Coordinating Council on Juvenile Justice and Delinquency Prevention, 1996) is the Council's call to action. Drawing on decades of research, previously summarized in the Office of Juvenile Justice and Delinquency Prevention's (OJJDP's) *Comprehensive Strategy for Serious, Violent, and Chronic Juvenile Offenders* (Wilson and Howell, 1993), the *Action Plan* encourages

helping youth throughout their development while responding to juvenile crime in a way that ensures public safety. The Coordinating Council calls on citizens to work together to advance the *Action Plan*'s eight key objectives to combat youth violence:

- Provide immediate intervention and appropriate sanctions and treatment for delinquent juveniles.
- Prosecute certain serious, violent, and chronic juvenile offenders in criminal court.
- Reduce youth involvement with guns, drugs, and gangs.
- Provide opportunities for children and youth.
- Break the cycle of violence by addressing youth victimization, abuse, and neglect.
- Strengthen and mobilize communities.
- Support the development of innovative approaches to research and evaluation.
- Implement an aggressive public outreach campaign on effective strategies to combat juvenile violence.

OJJDP is working to implement the *Action Plan* through a coordinated initiative of demonstration grants, training and technical assistance, research and evaluation programs, and information dissemination activities. The following examples demonstrate the scope of these initiatives.

Strengthening the Juvenile Justice System

Attaining the first objective of the *Action Plan* requires strengthening the Nation's juvenile justice system.

Through Formula Grants, Title V Community Prevention Grants, and State Challenge Grants, OJJDP provides States with funds to plan and implement comprehensive State and local programs to prevent and control delinquency and enhance the effective operation of the juvenile justice system.

In five program sites, OJJDP is demonstrating the graduated sanctions approach that is part of the Comprehensive Strategy for Serious, Violent, and Chronic Juvenile Offenders. OJJDP is also supporting development of a stronger juvenile justice system through the SafeFutures Program; developing, testing, and expanding model juvenile community assessment centers; and promoting statewide adoption of the Comprehensive Strategy through intensive technical assistance and training in Florida, Iowa, Maryland, Rhode Island, and Texas.

In addition, OJJDP is training juvenile justice system personnel to implement the balanced and restorative justice model. Restorative justice holds the offender responsible for making restitution to the victim and restoring the state of well-being that existed in the community before the offense. The balanced approach also suggests that the juvenile justice system improve the ability of offenders to pursue legitimate endeavors after their release. Training and technical assistance are also being provided to probation officers and juvenile justice practitioners to enable them to establish restitution and community service programs. States interested in juvenile code reforms that reflect the balanced and restorative justice model are also receiving training and technical assistance. By the end of 1995, at least 24 States had adopted, or were examining, codes or procedures incorporating the concepts of balanced and restorative justice.

Prosecuting Serious, Violent, and Chronic Offenders

The second objective of the *Action Plan* addresses how to deal with juvenile offenders whose offenses, or offense history and failure to respond to treatment, merit criminal prosecution. In recent years, no other juvenile justice policy has received more legislative attention or yielded such a multitude of different approaches for dealing with serious, violent, and chronic juvenile offenders.

OJJDP has published a research summary of legislative changes taking place across the country between 1992 and 1995. *State Responses to Serious and Violent Juvenile Crime* (Torbet et al., 1996) covers such topics as juvenile court jurisdictional authority, including waiver and transfer mechanisms; sentencing options, including blended sentencing practices; corrections options for juveniles; confidentiality and information sharing; victim rights in the juvenile justice system; and comprehensive State system reforms to respond to serious, violent, and chronic delinquency. In addition, OJJDP is funding the

National Conference of State Legislatures to help improve State juvenile justice systems by providing State legislators and staff with the latest research, effective State policies, and model responses to youth violence through both publications and intensive training.

With each new legislative debate regarding new provisions, State legislators and criminal justice officials are faced with a lack of reliable current information on the effectiveness of newly adopted laws and policies. To address this information gap, OJJDP is currently funding three studies in Arizona, Florida, New Jersey, New York, Pennsylvania, South Carolina, and Utah to determine the outcome and impact of waiver and transfer provisions on juvenile offenders under varying legal and administrative configurations. The research will control for the presenting offense, offense history, and offender's age and will include the kind of case attribute information that is often missing from studies in this subject area.

OJJDP is funding studies to determine the impact of waiver and transfer provisions on juvenile offenders.

The studies are being done collaboratively. Universities and research organizations are teaming up with key State and local criminal justice agencies to answer critical questions about the process, impact, and comparative effectiveness of new strategies. Two of the current studies involve replication and expansion of prior research and will provide information on differences in processing and outcome in the strategies of the 1980's compared with those of the 1990's; another looks at long-term trends.

All of the studies have gone beyond the limited data routinely available in automated record systems to study in greater detail critical aspects related to offenses, such as the offender's role in the commission of the crime, harm to the victim, and involvement of drugs or guns in the offense. It is hoped that more indepth characterization of cases will reveal patterns in the determinations made by prosecutors and judges to transfer a juvenile to criminal court for prosecution.

One of the goals of the research program is to explore the possibility of developing a system to collect routine information from a broader range of sources on the processing, outcomes, and impacts of criminal prosecution nationally. Researchers from all sites will collaborate to produce a cross-jurisdictional comparison of critical dimensions of the process.

In addition to these studies, OJJDP and the Bureau of Justice Statistics will be funding State-initiated studies of juvenile transfers through the State Justice Statistics Program for Statistical Analysis Centers in fiscal year 1997.

Targeting Guns, Drugs, and Gangs

Objective three of the *Action Plan* also identifies programmatic and strategic prevention, intervention, and suppression activities that target three critical areas affecting juvenile violence—guns, drugs, and gangs.

Guns. From 1985 to 1992, the number of homicides committed by juveniles with firearms more than doubled. Under Partnerships To Reduce Juvenile Gun Violence, OJJDP is funding four initiatives—one in California, two in Louisiana, and one in New York—that are linking community mobilization efforts with law enforcement to address this problem. An evaluation of the Partnerships effort is also being sponsored by OJJDP. In addition, OJJDP has held a national satellite teleconference on programs designed to reduce youth gun violence. The teleconference, which is available on videotape from OJJDP's Juvenile Justice Clearinghouse, was viewed by approximately 8,130 people at 271 downlink sites.

The Youth Substance Use Prevention Grant Program will support 10 community-based, youth-led prevention initiatives.

Drugs. In response to an increase in drug use by young people, OJJDP is administering the $1 million Youth Substance Use Prevention Grant Program of the President's Crime Prevention Council, which will support 10 community-based, youth-led prevention initiatives. OJJDP is also funding an evaluation of the program that will build local program grantees' capacity for designing, implementing, and interpreting evaluations; determine whether youth-led delinquency and substance use prevention activities have a greater impact on youth than adult-led prevention activities; and define the elements critical to implementing a successful youth-led prevention activity. OJJDP is also continuing to fund the Community Anti-Drug Abuse Technical Assistance Voucher project and the Congress of National Black Churches' National Anti-Drug/Violence Campaign—programs that help grassroots organizations and churches address juvenile drug abuse. The Race Against Drugs Program is a unique drug awareness, education, and prevention campaign implemented with the help and assistance of 23 motor sports organizations, the Federal Bureau of Investigation, Drug Enforcement Administration, U.S. Navy, and others. OJJDP is also working with the American Probation and Parole Association to train and help juvenile justice practitioners identify and treat drug-involved youth. OJJDP held a national satellite teleconference on preventing drug abuse among youth that was viewed by approximately 10,000 people at 300 downlink sites.

Gangs. OJJDP is implementing and testing a research-driven, community-based approach to suppressing, intervening in, and preventing gang violence through its Comprehensive Response to America's Youth Gang Problem Initiative. Five jurisdictions experiencing an emerging or chronic gang problem (Mesa and Tucson,

© Getty Images/PhotoLink/S. Meltzer

Arizona; Riverside, California; Bloomington, Illinois; and San Antonio, Texas) have been funded under this initiative to implement the comprehensive model for 3 years. OJJDP has established the National Youth Gang Center to promote effective and innovative strategies, collect and analyze statistical data on gangs, analyze gang legislation, and review gang literature. OJJDP also funded Boys & Girls Clubs of America gang-prevention programs that have reached 6,000 youth at risk for gang involvement, OJJDP has also established the interagency, public/private Gang Consortium as part of the Comprehensive Response initiative. The Consortium seeks to facilitate and expand ongoing coordination activities and enhance youth gang prevention, intervention, and suppression policies and activities, including information exchange and technical assistance services provided by the many Federal agencies with program emphasis on youth gangs and related problems. OJJDP's national satellite teleconference on strategies to prevent, intervene in, and suppress juvenile gang violence was viewed by approximately 17,000 people at 635 downlink sites.

OJJDP is testing a research-driven, community-based response to youth gangs.

Enhancing Opportunities for Youth

Objective four of the *Action Plan* calls for the Nation to provide positive opportunities for youth. Research dem-

© Getty Images/PhotoLink/Tomi

onstrates that mentoring, afterschool activities, conflict resolution programs, remedial education, and vocational training can prevent young people from becoming delinquents. OJJDP is actively disseminating a variety of research-based documents. *Delinquency Prevention Works* (Office of Juvenile Justice and Delinquency Prevention, 1995a) and the *Guide for Implementing the Comprehensive Strategy for Serious, Violent, and Chronic Juvenile Offenders* (Howell, 1995) both offer many examples of effective prevention and intervention programs. Other helpful publications are the OJJDP Bulletins in the Youth Development Series, which OJJDP created this year to present findings from the Program of Research on the Causes and Correlates of Delinquency, a longitudinal research program studying 4,000 young people in Denver, Colorado; Pittsburgh, Pennsylvania; and Rochester, New York. Series titles developed thus far are *Epidemiology of Serious Violence* (Kelley et al., 1997), *Gang Members and Delinquent Behavior* (Thornberry and Burch, 1997), and *In the Wake of Childhood Maltreatment* (Kelley et al., 1997). In addition, OJJDP has published a number of individual Bulletins on specific promising programs, including *Allegheny County, PA: Mobilizing To Reduce Juvenile Crime* (Hsia, 1997), *Treating Serious Anti-Social Behavior in Youth: The MST Approach* (Henggeler, 1997), and *Mentoring—A Proven Delinquency Prevention Strategy* (Grossman and Garry, 1997).

Conflict resolution education reduces juvenile violence and improves school atttendance.

DOJ is also funding expanded opportunities for youth and training for youth service professionals. Boys & Girls Clubs have provided afterschool activities that have increased school attendance, improved academic performance, and reduced the juvenile crime rate in high-risk neighborhoods. In addition to funding the Law-Related Education Program and the Teens, Crime, and the Community Initiative, which involves young people in community safety efforts, OJJDP has provided professional development training for youth workers and programmatic support to 93 mentoring programs funded under the Juvenile Mentoring Program (JUMP). A recent national evaluation of the Big Brothers Big Sisters of America mentoring program found that the young people involved in this program were 46 percent less likely to start using drugs, 33 percent less likely to exhibit aggressive behavior, and 27 percent less likely to start using alcohol than their peers. Mentoring is a component of OJJDP's SafeFutures initiative, which assists communities in combating delinquency by developing a full range of coordinated services. In addition to JUMP and SafeFutures, OJJDP supports more than 90 mentoring efforts in individual States through its Formula Grants Program (Grossman and Garry, 1997). OJJDP recently held a national satellite teleconference on mentoring.

Addressing conflict resolution programming in schools, the community, and juvenile justice settings, a 1995 OJJDP satellite teleconference provided more than 10,000 participants with information on conflict resolution programs that have reduced the number of violent juvenile acts, decreased the number of chronic school absences, reduced the number of disciplinary referrals and suspensions, and expanded classroom instruction. These conflict resolution programs and approaches are described in *Conflict Resolution Education: A Guide to Implementing Programs in Schools, Youth-Serving Organizations, and Community and Juvenile Justice Settings* (Crawford and Bodine, 1996), published by OJJDP and ED's Safe and Drug-Free Schools Program. OJJDP has funded a training and technical assistance program that supports the implementation of conflict resolution efforts at the local level.

Supported by OJJDP in collaboration with the U.S. Departments of Health and Human Services, Commerce, and Defense, the Communities In Schools dropout-prevention program has reached more than 97,000 youth and their families, increased students' likelihood of attending and staying in school, and improved their academic performance. OJJDP and ED have also funded the National School Safety Center to focus attention on the problems of youth who do not attend school regularly because they are truants or dropouts, are afraid to attend school, have been suspended or expelled, or are in need of help to be reintegrated into mainstream schools after spending time in juvenile detention and correctional settings. Four forums on Youth Out of the Education Mainstream were held in summer 1996 to highlight effective and promising programs. Intensive training and technical assistance are being delivered to 10 sites to implement comprehensive approaches to this problem.

Breaking the Cycle of Violence

In 1995, child protective service agencies investigated an estimated 2 million reports alleging the mistreatment of almost 3 million children (National Center on Child Abuse and Neglect, 1997). Studies show that childhood abuse and neglect increase a child's odds of future delinquency and adult criminality. Data from the Rochester Youth Development Study (RYDS) show that self-reports of youth violence increased with exposure to more types of family violence. RYDS is one of three coordinated, longitudinal research projects of OJJDP's Causes and Correlates Program, the largest shared-measurement approach ever achieved in delinquency research.

The fifth objective of the *Action Plan*, therefore, challenges us to eliminate the disturbing cycle of domestic violence, child abuse and neglect, and youth violence. OJJDP is collaborating with other bureaus in the Office of Justice Programs to support Safe Kids/Safe Streets: Community Approaches to Reducing Abuse and Neglect and Preventing Delinquency. This initiative is designed to help youth at risk for abuse and neglect and their families, to encourage communities to strengthen the response of their criminal and juvenile justice systems to child abuse and neglect, and to enhance system coordination with child and family service agencies. Five communities (Huntsville, Alabama; the Sault Sainte Marie Tribe of Chippewa Indians in Michigan; Kansas City, Missouri; Toledo, Ohio; and Chittenden County, Vermont) have been selected for funding under the Safe Kids/Safe Streets Program. The funding agencies are also sponsoring an evaluation of the program.

The CD–CP program serves as a national model for police-mental health partnerships.

In addition, OJJDP is working with the Executive Office for Weed and Seed and HHS to implement the David Olds Nurse Home Visitation Program in six sites. Six hundred low-income, first-time mothers (some of whom are drug addicts) and their babies will be served through this prenatal and early childhood home-visitation program. Through home visits in the first 2 years of a child's life, program nurses work intensively with new mothers to improve key aspects of health and early child development and strengthen the mother's parenting and vocational skills.

Studies show that childhood abuse and neglect increase a child's odds of future delinquency.

In October 1995, OJJDP entered into a 3-year cooperative agreement for a project called Training and Technical Assistance for Family Strengthening, which is being implemented by the University of Utah, Department of Health Education, in Salt Lake City. This project allows the university to continue work it has been conducting since 1990 to identify the most effective family programs for the prevention of delinquency. This project is designed to help close the gap between the state of research and the state of practice in family-focused prevention. The university will synthesize and disseminate information about model family strengthening programs through training and technical assistance and the development of written materials.

OJJDP is also funding the Yale/New Haven Child Development–Community Policing (CD–CP) Program to engage community police and mental health professionals in addressing the psychological burdens of increasing levels of community violence on children, families, and communities. The CD–CP Program, a collaborative effort of the New Haven (Connecticut) Department of Police Services and the Child Study Center at the Yale University School of Medicine, serves as a national model for police-mental health partnerships (Marans and Berkman, 1997).

Deterring delinquency requires a substantial investment of financial and human resources.

In addition, OJJDP is sponsoring four regional children's advocacy centers to coordinate the response of judicial and social service systems to child abuse. The regional centers act as clearinghouses, distributing resource materials and other tools, providing training and technical assistance, and facilitating information sharing. OJJDP supports the National Network of Children's Advocacy Centers, which provides funding, training, and technical support to local children's advocacy centers. Thanks to such efforts, nearly 300 communities now have children's advocacy centers. Moreover, through OJJDP's support of the National Court Appointed Special Advocates Association, some 700 communities have established court appointed special advocate (CASA) programs providing volunteers to serve as advocates in court proceedings for victims of child abuse (Office of Juvenile Justice and Delinquency Prevention, 1997).

Putting the *Plan* Into Action

The remaining objectives of the *Action Plan* focus on mobilizing communities, engaging a variety of disciplines to ensure that research serves as the foundation of program activities, and conducting an outreach campaign on effective strategies to combat juvenile violence.

OJJDP is helping communities mobilize to prevent juvenile delinquency and transferring the research base on the causes and correlates of delinquency through the Title V Community Prevention Grants. These grants have been distributed to 49 States, 5 territories, and the District of Columbia. Nearly 4,000 participants have been trained in risk- and protective-factor-focused delinquency prevention, and 3-year Community Prevention Grants have been awarded to approximately 400 communities. OJJDP's *Title V Delinquency Prevention Program Community Self-Evaluation Workbook* (Office of Juvenile Justice and Delinquency Prevention, 1995b) is helping communities evaluate their progress and results under this program.

In partnership with the Bureau of Justice Assistance, OJJDP will be providing additional information on strategies that work through a public information campaign. Using the Comprehensive Strategy and *Action Plan* as guides, community leaders and other concerned citizens will have access to information on effective delinquency prevention; gang, gun, and drug violence reduction; and juvenile justice reform strategies and programs.

Through its Juvenile Justice Clearinghouse, OJJDP annually distributes more than 2 million copies of Reports, Summaries, Bulletins, Fact Sheets, and other publications providing research findings and program information. OJJDP publications are available through a toll-free telephone line, and by mail, fax, and the Internet. OJJDP also continues to present national satellite teleconferences on key juvenile justice issues and is currently completing production of an interactive CD-ROM on effective prevention and intervention programs. Information about these services and activities can be obtained by calling the Juvenile Justice Clearinghouse, toll free, at 800-638-8736.

Conclusion

Deterring delinquency and reducing youth violence require a substantial, sustained investment of financial and human resources by both the public and private sectors. If this Nation truly intends to ensure public safety and reduce youth violence and victimization, it must make a greater commitment to a juvenile justice system that holds juvenile offenders immediately accountable (before they become hardened criminals) and responds appropriately to the issues that bring young people to the courtroom in the first place. All young people should be guaranteed the opportunity to be healthy, safe, and able to learn in school and to engage in positive, productive activities. This requires the targeted and coordinated use of new and existing resources. The research-based goals and objectives of the *Action Plan* and the model established by OJJDP's Comprehensive Strategy can be successfully implemented, but only if a long-term commitment is made to work together to achieve them.

REFERENCES

Coordinating Council on Juvenile Justice and Delinquency Prevention. 1996 (March). *Combating Violence and Delinquency: The National Juvenile Justice Action Plan* Report. Washington, DC: U.S. Department of Justice, Office of Justice Programs, Office of Juvenile Justice and Delinquency Prevention.

Crawford, D., and R. Bodine. 1996 (October). *Conflict Resolution Education: A Guide to Implementing Programs in Schools, Youth-Serving Organizations, and Community and Juvenile Justice Settings.* Washington, DC: U.S. Department of Justice, Office of Justice Programs, Office of Juvenile Justice and Delinquency Prevention, and U.S. Department of Education, Safe and Drug-Free Schools Program.

Grossman, J.B., and E.M. Garry. 1997 (April). *Mentoring—A Proven Delinquency Prevention Strategy.* Bulletin. Washington, DC: U.S. Department of Justice, Office of Justice Programs, Office of Juvenile Justice and Delinquency Prevention.

Henggeler, S.W. 1997 (May). *Treating Serious Anti-Social Behavior in Youth: The MST Approach.* Bulletin. Washington, DC: U.S. Department of Justice, Office of Justice Programs, Office of Juvenile Justice and Delinquency Prevention.

Howell, J.C., ed. 1995 (June). *Guide for Implementing the Comprehensive Strategy for Serious, Violent, and Chronic Juvenile Offenders.* Washington, DC: U.S. Department of Justice, Office of Justice Programs, Office of Juvenile Justice and Delinquency Prevention.

IIsia, H.M. 1997 (June). *Allegheny County, PA: Mobilizing To Reduce Juvenile Crime.* Bulletin. Washington, DC: U.S. Department of Justice, Office of Justice Programs, Office of Juvenile Justice and Delinquency Prevention.

Kelley, B.T., D. Huizinga, T.P. Thornberry, and R. Loeber. 1997 (June). *Epidemiology of Serious Violence.* Bulletin. Washington, DC: U.S. Department of Justice, Office of Justice Programs, Office of Juvenile Justice and Delinquency Prevention.

Kelley, B.T., T.P. Thornberry, and C.A. Smith. 1997 (August). *In the Wake of Childhood Maltreatment.* Bulletin. Washington, DC: U.S. Department of Justice, Office of Justice Programs, Office of Juvenile Justice and Delinquency Prevention.

Marans, S., and M. Berkman. 1997 (March). *Child Development—Community Policing: Partnership in a Climate of Violence.* Bulletin. Washington, DC: U.S. Department of Justice, Office of Justice Programs, Office of Juvenile Justice and Delinquency Prevention.

National Center on Child Abuse and Neglect. 1997. *Child Maltreatment 1995: Reports Prom the States to the National Child Abuse and Neglect Data System.* Washington, DC: U.S. Department of Health and Human Services, National Center on Child Abuse and Neglect.

Office of Juvenile Justice and Delinquency Prevention. 1995a (June). *Delinquency Prevention Works.* Program Summary. Washington, DC: U.S. Department of Justice, Office of Justice Programs, Office of Juvenile Justice and Delinquency Prevention.

Office of Juvenile Justice and Delinquency Prevention. 1995b. *Title V Delinquency Prevention Program Community Self-Evaluation Workbook.* Washington, DC: U.S. Department of Justice, Office of Justice Programs, Office of Juvenile Justice and Delinquency Prevention.

Office of Juvenile Justice and Delinquency Prevention, 1997 (March), *Court Appointed Special Advocates: A Voice for Abused and Neglected Children in Court*, Bulletin. Washington, DC: U.S. Department of Justice, Office of Justice Programs, Office of Juvenile Justice and Delinquency Prevention.

Thornberry, T.P., and J.H. Burch II. 1997 (June). *Gang Members and Delinquent Behavior*. Bulletin. Washington, DC: U.S. Department of Justice, Office of Justice Programs, Office of Juvenile Justice and Delinquency Prevention.

Torbet, P., R. Gable, H. Hurst IV, I. Montgomery, L. Syzmanski, and D. Thomas. 1996 (July). *State Responses to Serious and Violent Crime*. Washington, DC: U.S. Department of Justice, Office of Justice Programs, Office of Juvenile Justice and Delinquency Prevention,

Wilson, J.J., and J.C. Howell. 1993 (December). *Comprehensive Strategy for Serious, Violent, and Chronic Juvenile Offenders*. Program Summary. Washington, DC: U.S. Department of Justice, Office of Justice Programs, Office of Juvenile Justice and Delinquency Prevention,

Sarah Ingersoll is a Special Assistant to the Administrator of the Office of Juvenile Justice and Delinquency Prevention.

From *Journal of the Office of Juvenile and Delinquency Prevention*, September 1997. Reprinted by permission of the National Institute of Justice, National Criminal Justice Reference Service.

BREAKING THE CYCLE OF JUVENILE VIOLENCE

Roger Przybylski

Juvenile crime continues to be the focus of much attention in Illinois and across the country. At the national level, Congress has introduced legislation to extend federal jurisdiction to selected crimes committed by juveniles, and several states are currently debating juvenile justice system reforms. In Illinois, the Juvenile Justice Reform Act, which would significantly change the way juvenile offenders are handled, will likely be reintroduced in the legislative session in November.

The mounting concern about juvenile crime and the need for juvenile justice reform are due, at least in part, to the surge in juvenile violence that began nearly a decade ago. This surge stands in sharp contrast to the falling violent crime rates that most of the country has experienced in recent years.

Contradictory trends

Professor James Alan Fox of Northeastern University suggests that the nation is experiencing two crime trends—one for the young and one for the mature—that are moving in opposite directions. From 1990 to 1994, the overall rate of murder in America declined about 4 percent. For this same period, the rate of killing at the hands of adults aged 25 and older declined 18 percent, and that for young adults, aged 18 to 24, rose only 2 percent. However, the rate of murders committed by teenagers aged 14 to 17 jumped 22 percent.

The escalation in youth crime during the past 10 years actually occurred while the population of teenagers was on the decline. But this demographic trend is about to change. By the year 2005, the number of teens between the ages of 14 and 17 will increase by 20 percent nationwide. (In Illinois, the teenage population is expected to grow more modestly, rising by 20 percent by the year 2010.) As a result, Fox argues, we will likely face a future wave of youth violence that will be even worse than that of the past decade.

> ## "Demographics do not have to be our destiny."
>
> —*Attorney General Janet Reno*

Although these demographic projections are cause for concern, the future is far from predetermined. As Attorney General Janet Reno recently stated, "Demographics do not have to be our destiny." More young people will not mean more violence if the rate of offending can be reduced.

Precursors of violence

Several studies on juvenile crime and victimization provide valuable new knowledge about the precursors of violence and the steps that must be taken to interrupt the trajectory toward a criminal career. These studies offer new insights about the pathways to delinquency and the cycle of violence that often begins in the home. Taken together, they offer compelling evidence that the best way to influence the rate of offending and reduce juvenile violence is through a multidisciplinary approach that incorporates both prevention and early intervention.

The National Youth Survey, conducted by the University of Colorado, Center for Violence Prevention, has been studying a nationally representative sample of about 1,700 youths since 1976. The most recent wave of interviews occurred in 1993, when many of the youths were already in their thirties. One of the major findings from the survey is that there is a considerable time lag between the peak age of offending and the peak age for arrest, suggesting that the justice system is intervening too late. The peak age of serious violent offending in the NYS sample was 17, while the age of onset was even younger. In contrast, arrests peaked around the ages of 18 and 19, and arrest rates remained high until age 25.

Risk factors

The National Research Program on the Causes and Correlates of Delinquency, sponsored by the U.S. Department of Justice, Office of Juvenile Justice and Delinquency Prevention, has studied large samples of high-risk, inner-city youth in Denver, Pittsburgh, and Rochester, N.Y. The OJJDP-sponsored research found that chronic violent offenders exhibited co-occurring problem behaviors and multiple risk factors, such as dropping out of school and gang membership.

Dropping out of school can have a profound impact on a young person's life. While high-school dropouts experience lower earnings and more unemployment during their work careers, they also are more likely to end up on welfare or in prison than students who complete high school or college.

> **Suffering abuse and neglect as a child increases the likelihood of engaging in violent crime by 38 percent.**
>
> —*Researcher Cathy Spatz Widom*

More states seeing benefits of early intervention and prevention programs

SUBSTANTIAL RESEARCH INDICATES that the best programs and policies to prevent juvenile crime are based on a continuum of care that starts early in the child's life and continues through the teens. Studies show that quality early education and care in preschool and beyond help children get better grades and reduce dropout rates. Better education provides access to more employment opportunities, which in turn helps reduce crime.

Prevention in early childhood

State legislatures are increasingly seeing the advantages of supporting strong early childhood programs. As of 1995, 27 states funded preschools, 14 states supported Head Start programs, and eight states supported both.

For the last several years, **Colorado** has heavily funded early childhood education and care. In 1996, the General Assembly increased funding for at-risk preschools by $4.2 million to accommodate 1,850 more preschoolers. Increased legislative support means that Colorado serves 8,500 at-risk children across the state. In addition, the legislature allocated $7 million for violence prevention programs and approved third-year funding for a pilot program for family centers in at-risk communities.

Child abuse and neglect prevention

Because much research connects child abuse and neglect with juvenile crime, lawmakers are increasingly funding programs aimed at reducing abuse and neglect. The Healthy Start

Program, started in **Hawaii** in 1985, focuses on families at risk of child abuse and neglect. Social workers visit new parents at home and provide child care education, as well as health-related services for infants. Evaluations show substantial decreases in abuse and neglect; only 0.5 percent of program participants reported child abuse or neglect, compared with confirmed abuse and neglect in 2.7 percent of nonparticipating families. Due to Healthy Start's success, the National Committee to Prevent Child Abuse launched a national initiative called Healthy Families America to help all states and the District of Columbia develop similar programs.

In 1994, **Tennessee** created a Healthy Start program along with an initiative to provide early child care and education for at-risk 3- and 4-year-olds, and double the number of school-related family centers, among other resources.

Family preservation programs

At least 21 other states have started comprehensive family preservation programs, including **Michigan**. Its Families First program, started in 1988, provides at-home counseling to families in danger of losing their child to foster care due to abuse and neglect. The program provides four to six weeks of counseling and communication education. Michigan's program reportedly has saved $55 million in its first three years, and the program costs $6,000 to $8,000 less per family than the cost of a year in foster care.

Sharing information

While youth who commit first-time, less serious offenses have contact with social services and schools, research shows that few of these resources are equipped to handle troubled children and their families. The Hennepin County Attorney's Office in **Minnesota** conducted a study on the extent of communication between child welfare agencies and the juvenile justice system. The study found that most delinquent children younger than age 10 who were referred to social services did not get the help they needed. In addition, most of these children had contact with other public agencies—91 percent of the children's families had received Aid to Families with Dependent Children, and 81 percent had a history of child abuse or neglect. Therefore, the researchers decided that the child welfare system could best identify and help these youth, and in 1995, the Minnesota legislature initiated an early intervention program for delinquents younger than 10. The program combines the services of the County Attorney's Office and Children and Family Services, among others.

Experts agree that effective prevention and intervention require that agencies outside the juvenile justice system get involved, and information sharing is a key component. In more than 30 states, laws allow the release of juvenile offenders' names under certain circumstances. For example, **Connecticut, Maryland, Texas, and Virginia** require law enforcement to notify school officials of students' delinquency.

—*Kristi Turnbaugh*

(Source: National Conference of State Legislatures (1996), "A legislator's guide to comprehensive juvenile justice.")

Another important finding from the OJJDP research was that children who were neglected or abused, or who witnessed violence in the home, were more likely to commit violent acts themselves later in life.

This cycle of violence also has been documented in a series of studies sponsored by the National Institute of Justice, the National Institute of Alcohol Abuse and Alcoholism, and the National Institute of Mental Health. The research is examining the lives of 1,575 child victims identified in court cases of abuse and neglect dating from 1967 to 1971. By 1994, almost one-half of the victims—most of whom were then in their late twenties and early thirties—had been arrested for some type of offense. Eighteen percent had been arrested for a violent crime.

Cathy Spatz Widom, a researcher from the State University of New York at Albany who has studied extensively the impact of abuse and neglect, has reported that suffering abuse and neglect as a child increases the likelihood of engaging in violent crime by 38 percent. And while the likelihood of later violence is greater for children who experience violence firsthand, neglected children also display an elevated level of violence later in life.

Prevention and early intervention

It is apparent from each of these studies that reducing juvenile violence requires a multidisciplinary prevention and early intervention effort involving a variety of institutions. Risk-focused approaches to prevention have been successfully used to reduce cardiovascular disease and traffic fatalities, and they hold considerable promise for reducing juvenile violence. Risk factors can be found not only in the family, but in school, the community, and the individual and his or her peers. Protective factors that can mediate the impact of risk factors have also been identified. The interaction of risk factors and protective factors explain why some youth succumb to delinquency and others do not. As risk factors are decreased and protective factors enhanced, the likelihood of delinquency and violent offending can be reduced.

Recent research by the Rand Corporation provides compelling evidence that prevention and early intervention efforts not only work, they also can be cost-effective. In its recent study, "Diverting Children from a Life of Crime, Measuring Costs and Benefits," Rand assessed the cost-effectiveness of several prevention strategies, and found that they compared favorably with a high-profile incarceration alternative (California's three strikes law guaranteeing extended sentences for repeat offenders) in terms of serious crime averted per dollar expended. While the estimated crime reductions that were achievable through the additional incarceration of the three strikes law were considerable—about 20 percent—the monetary cost of implementing "three strikes" was approximately $5.5 billion per year. For less than $1 billion more per year, Rand reports, parent training and graduation incentives could roughly double the amount of crime reduction.

In light of what we know about the precursors of violent offending, prevention and early intervention programs are critical. The juvenile justice system cannot solve the complex problem of juvenile violence unilaterally; it cannot make up for the failures of families and the shortcomings of other institutions.

Breaking the cycle

In Illinois, more than 1.3 million cases of child abuse or neglect were reported to the Department of Children and Family Services between fiscal years 1983 and 1995; the number of cases reported annually has skyrocketed. And although we know that three out of every four state prison inmates did not complete high school, an intolerably high number of children—more than 35,000—drop out of school in Illinois each year. If we are to have an appreciable impact on violent juvenile offending, the number of children exposed to these risk factors must be reduced. Until we break the cycle of violence that starts in the home, and find ways to keep young people in school, there will always be a pool of individuals predisposed to delinquent behavior.

Reducing juvenile violence requires the coordinated efforts of social service agencies, juvenile justice agencies, schools, and other institutions in both the public and private sectors. Improving public safety requires breaking the cycle of violence and preventing juvenile violence before it occurs.

Roger Przybylski was director of the Authority's Research and Analysis Unit from 1994 through September 1997.

Understanding the Roots of Crime: The Project on Human Development in Chicago Neighborhoods

Christy A. Visher

Why do some communities and not others become the settings for high rates of delinquency, crime, substance abuse, and drug marketing? Why do some people and not others become habituated to a life of criminal behavior? What is the relationship among community structure, family functioning, and a person's own individual development as factors in influencing criminal behavior? If answers to these questions could be found, they would contribute greatly to our understanding of criminal behavior and could serve as the basis for prevention strategies. In a major National Institute of Justice (NIJ)-sponsored study now under way, researchers are seeking these answers, and others, in an attempt to achieve that understanding.

The cornerstone of NIJ's health and justice initiative, the Project on Human Development in Chicago Neighborhoods, is an unprecedented, long-range program of research designed to study a broad range of factors at the level of the community, the family, and the individual believed to be important in explaining early aggression and delinquency, substance abuse, and criminal behavior, including violence.

The Project is directed by Felton Earls of the Harvard School of Public Health and Albert J. Reiss Jr., of Yale University. A group of distinguished scientists (see exhibit 1) has been involved in the planning and design of the study from its inception.

The project's rationale

A critical premise of the Project is that an individual's behavioral development is deeply rooted in multiple contexts. Moreover, the complex interactions among them—the relationships of individual traits, community characteristics, the school and family setting, and peer group relations (friends and acquaintances)—also affect that development.

The program of research is also based on the theory that patterns of criminal behavior have a long gestation period. Because they develop over time, knowledge about what evokes, sustains, or alters this long-term development can be put to good use in devising means of prevention and intervention.

It is difficult to know how much influence to assign to any one of these factors in contrast to the others; that is, to find out the extent to which someone is the product of neighborhood influences and the extent to which her or his behavior results from individual development. Previous research has been unable to disentangle these factors to help distinguish the effects of one from the others. The Project on Human Development in Chicago Neighborhoods will attempt to do this and will give equal attention to influences at the individual level and the community level that may affect development throughout the course of a person's life.

Exhibit 1. Scientific Directors and Advisory Group

Robert Cairns, Ph.D.
Professor of Psychology
University of North Carolina

Felton Earls, M.D.
Professor of Human Behavior and Development
Harvard School of Public Health

David Huizinga, Ph.D.
Research Associate
University of Colorado

Terrie Moffitt, Ph.D.
Associate Professor of Clinical Psychology
University of Wisconsin

Stephen Raudenbush, Ed.D.
Associate Professor of Education
Michigan State University

Albert J. Reiss, Jr., Ph.D.
Professor of Sociology
Yale University

Robert Sampson, Ph.D.
Professor of Sociology
University of Chicago

Elizabeth Susman, Ph.D.
Professor of Behavioral Health
Pennsylvania State University

Findings of the Pilot Studies

Studying the development of the individual in the social context

Before the study began, the research design, measurement strategies, and method of data analysis were examined and then refined. Sample sizes were set for the age cohorts and the neighborhoods. The researchers showed that continuity and change over time in behavior—aggression, delinquency, and criminal activity—could be revealed by linking the information, even when information from different age cohorts was used. They also developed a detailed analytic plan to study how the social context (family, school, or neighborhood) can affect individuals' behavior.

Does testosterone affect aggression in children?

The link between the male hormone testosterone and aggression has been demonstrated in animal studies and in some studies of adult men. Other research has shown that aggressive children continue to display this type of behavior into adulthood. But the results of the pilot study conducted for this project cast strong doubts on the possibility that testosterone levels explain aggression in young children or can be used as a marker for later aggression in adolescence or adulthood. In a study of a small group of highly aggressive prepubertal boys, no significant difference was found between their testosterone levels and those of nonaggressive children.

The father's role in child/adolescent development

The involvement of fathers in their children's development was found to have positive effects, according to the findings of another pilot study. This study of fathers' interaction with high-risk infants revealed that three-fourths played with their children on a daily basis (although for one-third of these children the paternal figure changed during the 3-year period covered by the study).

Another study involved interviews with fathers (both those who live with their children and those who do not). Researchers found that fathers furnished unique information about family processes, including child behavior.

Effects of neighborhood characteristics on drug use and sales

A large city in the Northeast was studied to examine the extent of neighboring, local personal ties, income level, participation in community organizations, and extent of deviant-criminal subculture. Researchers wanted to find out if the type of neighborhood affects the amount of criminal behavior that takes place in it.

They found that differences by neighborhood in these community characteristics could account for the differences among certain neighborhoods in the amount of substance abuse and explained differences in substance abuse by individuals within a given neighborhood. This study is being expanded in Chicago.

Peer social networks

Conventional wisdom and previous research hold that friends and acquaintances exert strong influences on young people's behavior. The primary focus of pilot studies was the availability of reliable information about peer social networks. Researchers found that the peer associates of highly deviant adolescents could be interviewed, that information about gang activity can be obtained through studies of peer social networks, and that large numbers of students in a classroom can be sources of information about social status and social networks of their friends and acquaintances.

Is delinquency related to child caretaking arrangements?

Children in high-risk neighborhoods were found to have different caretaking provided for them than the caretaking arrangements for children in the overall sample: there were more single mothers and single fathers in the high-risk sample. However, the arrangements did @i[not] affect delinquency among high-risk children. By contrast, in the general, citywide sample, child caretaking arrangements were related to delinquency. For example, children in the larger, citywide sample who lived with single mothers were much more delinquent than those living with two parents. In the high-risk sample, children with single mothers were no more delinquent than those in two-parent families. This illustrates complex interactions between family structure, neighborhood characteristics, and behavior.

Focus on prevention

Because the Project was conceptualized with an eye to interventions that may deter criminal behavior, preventable conditions will receive particular emphasis. Thus, special attention will be given to conditions that develop before birth (during the mother's pregnancy), as well as in infancy and early childhood. The objective is to ascertain which elements of a child's development influence the pathways from behavioral problems in the early years to aggression and crime—particularly violent crime—later in life.

If interventions are to be used to the best effect in preventing criminal behavior, it is essential to know at what points in a person's development they should be applied. Accordingly, the program of research will identify opportunities during childhood and adolescence when interventions are most likely to produce the greatest benefit. Testing various strategies that promise effective intervention will also be part of the Project.

Such knowledge can promote the development of informed public policies and programs geared to prevention.

How the study was designed

Taken together, the elements of the study design constitute a unique approach:

- Investigation of behavioral problems, by age, including early aggression, delinquency, substance abuse, and criminal behavior among both males and females.

- Examination of how influences generated in the neighborhood, school, and family contexts interact with the strengths and vulnerabilities of individuals to affect the onset of antisocial behavior and its patterns from preadolescence to adulthood.
- Comparison of these contexts and individual differences by group (African-Americans, Hispanics, and Caucasians) and further distinguishing the groups by social class and gender.
- Use of an accelerated longitudinal approach, involving nine age cohorts spaced from birth to age 32, permits information-gathering in a relatively brief period of time that would otherwise take several decades.

The startup phase

Over the past 5 years, NIJ, in conjunction with the John D. and Catherine T. MacArthur Foundation, has supported the planning and design of the study. It is a major component of NIJ's research program and addresses NIJ's statutory mandate to study "the causes and correlates of crime and juvenile delinquency." NIJ and its funding partner, the MacArthur Foundation, have jointly invested $10 million in the development and design phase. More than 100 scientists with numerous theoretical perspectives, who represent several disciplines—among them pediatrics, biology, psychology, sociology, and criminology—have been involved thus far.

Laying the groundwork. The early phases, under way since 1989, included exploring particular study topics and finding out which study methods would work best. Pilot studies were carried out to answer specific questions, and two volumes on the method used to conduct a study with an accelerated longitudinal design were produced. A series of reports presented in outlines the design of a comprehensive study of the roots of crime. These reports included exhaustive reviews of previous studies in relevant topic areas: early childhood development and conduct disorder, adolescent development and juvenile delinquency, the influence of family and community factors on crime and criminal behavior, and the development of criminal careers.

The pilot studies, whose findings are summarized in a box (*Findings of the Pilot Studies*) explored several specific issues, some of which will be studied in greater depth over the course of the project, including:

- The amount of interaction fathers have with their infants and preschool children and the impact of that interaction.
- The effect of endocrine influences on aggression (for example, the accuracy of measures of the hormone testosterone in saliva in aggressive and nonaggressive boys).
- The influence of peer groups (friends and acquaintances) on delinquency.
- The use of social services such as counseling by adolescents and their parents.

The researchers also conducted pilots to find measurement tools that would be useful for the study. Thus, they developed and tested various psychological measures appropriate to the different age groups in the study. For example, they wanted to find out how best to measure stress and family interaction. They also wanted to make certain the measures they chose were appropriate to the various cultural groups being studied.

How the information will be gathered

Information will be collected over a period of 8 years on 11,000 people, male and female, and at three points during the project on approximately 40,000 additional individuals who live in the same community areas. An innovative study design, which essentially accelerates the pace of a long-term study, permits tracing in just 8 years how criminal behavior develops from birth to age 32. The acceleration occurs through the study of the nine groups of people (cohorts) whose ages overlap.

From the *National Institute of Justice Journal*, November 1994, pp. 9-12. Reprinted by permission of the National Institute of Justice, National Criminal Justice Reference Service.

Saving the Nation's Most Precious Resources:

OUR CHILDREN

The role of parents is critical since studies have shown that youngsters' basic intellectual capacity and their emotional and character formation are established by the age of three.

Gene Stephens

TOO MANY of America's children have been neglected, abused, and ignored. Without change, the dark spectre of generational warfare predicted by some could become all too real. If that deadly conflict occurs, it will be because no one pays attention to the all-too-evident trends and there is failure to pursue diligently new directions that can lead to a safe, sane, productive 21st-century society.

The concept of youth at risk has been defined in many ways and under many names (*e.g.*, children at risk, children in trouble, at-risk teens, even at-risk families). A decade ago, the Domestic Policy Association in Dayton, Ohio, teamed with the Kettering Foundation in Washington, D.C., to work with communities across the U.S. to identify and save the nation's "at-risk" youth. In its literature, the movement suggested that up to 15% of the 16- to 19-year-old population was "at risk for never reaching their potential, at risk of being lost in society." Others

would add children of any age if they are at risk of failing to become self-supporting adults; if indicators are that they are headed for a life in institutions (for delinquency, crime, mental illness, addiction); might become dependent on taxpayer or charity support programs; and may face life on the streets, homeless and unemployed. Expanding the category well beyond 15% of the population are those who add teens and preteens who take on child-rearing themselves and/or drop out of elementary or secondary school—most of whom, according to statistical probability, will face a life of underemployment, diminished expectations and opportunities, and failure to become productive, contributing citizens.

The task of "saving" these youngsters has become even more formidable, made more difficult by the expanding gap between rich and poor; the larger number of single-parent households and homes

where both parents work; the growing gun culture with increasingly higher-tech weapons reaching the street level; and the increasing negativity about children manifested by curfews, treating younger and younger youths as adult criminals, and declaring kids "undesirable" in gated communities. Possibly most alarming is that only one of three American households today includes a child under 18. Increasing numbers of lower- and middle-income children are growing up with little or no adult supervision, often without adequate resources for nurturing (and sometimes insufficient necessities for survival), and with a clear message from society that they are not wanted.

Without hope for the future and a stake in society, they often turn to peers for attention and guidance; to easily obtainable guns for protection, security, and status; and to sex and drugs for comfort, relief of boredom, and sometimes for subsistence. The gang often becomes their "family"—the only place they get attention and approval—and anti-social values fill the void left by family and society.

Their lack of faith in a future leaves them present-oriented and oblivious to society's laws. Living for today makes sense to them, especially when every day they are bombarded by media messages of enormous material wealth on the one hand and ever-prevalent violence and death on the other. Is it any wonder many of these youth seemingly without emotion steal and even attack others to obtain what they need and/or desire or just for momentary thrills or release of anger?

Criminologist James Fox of Northeastern University has extrapolated from social/demographic trends that a juvenile crime wave such as the U.S. never has seen will occur over the next decade. Citing statistics indicating 30% of children grow up in single-parent homes, most without fathers, with 20% raised in poverty, Fox predicts the 4,000 murders by teenagers in 1995 will skyrocket as the 39,000,000 kids under age 10 grow and increase by 20% the portion of the population in the teen years in the first decade of the 21st century.

Of course, having youth at risk is not a problem unique to the U.S. Wars, social upheaval, rapidly changing economic systems, political instability, and cultural animosity have placed millions of youngsters at risk across the planet. Thousands die of starvation, while others wander aimlessly in search of home and family. Many atrophy in sweatshops; others are sold into prostitution to support their families. Even more horrifying are those who are sacrificed for their body parts to satisfy a graying world population and those who are killed simply because they were born the wrong sex to satisfy their parent(s).

Nevertheless, catastrophe is *not* inevitable. There are some signs of hope—a slightly decreased birth rate among American teenagers in the mid 1990s; a bipartisan concern raised in Washington for "saving the children"; many community-based experiments to try to meet the needs of youth; and a movement to consider insufficient prenatal care, poor parenting skills, child abuse, and child neglect as public health as well as social problems.

Beyond this, whereas data is sketchy, a striking change in the rearing of children in many families is taking place. Countering the trend to ignore or even abuse children is a movement to cherish and nurture youngsters by thousands of parents who are taking turns working while the other stays at home and makes childcare almost a full-time vocation. Whatever is lost in job advancement and professional development seems to have been gained tenfold in the joy and satisfaction they find in watching their offspring blossom. These parents express the belief they have not given up anything valuable compared to what they have received. There is an unrecognized renaissance in parenting that is progressing quietly in neighborhoods across the nation.

Psychoanalyst Sigmund Freud postulated decades ago that an adult's behavior best could be explained by examining the significant events of the first six years of his or her life. These childhood experiences were seen by Freud as the subconscious motivator of actions taken later in life. Recent scientific advances have indicated he was on the right track, but might have given too much latitude to the time period. Now, it appears that basic intellectual capacity and emotional and character formation are established by the age of three, and, increasingly, evidence points to the prenatal period and first year of life as most important.

The implication of these findings is enormous. Focus must be changed from reactive, remedial attention when the problems begin to show up in misbehavior or delinquency in the teen or preteen years to a proactive, preventive approach in the formative period—prebirth to one year old. Prenatal care-unavailable to many unwed and/or poor mothers to be—becomes a critical element in reducing youth at risk, as does effective nurturing in the days and weeks immediately following birth.

Children crave attention more than anything else, especially positive attention. Researchers find a baby who is cuddled, talked to, and stimulated in the first six weeks of life is much more likely to be intelligent and well-adjusted than one who is ignored and simply fed and cleaned up in silence. Later, the youngster who is rewarded with praise for accomplishments is much more likely than others to become optimistic and achievement-oriented.

Since studies indicate any attention is a reward, as any attention is better than none, even spankings or harsh words in effect serve as rewards, thus reinforcing rather than extinguishing the behavior given attention. Many scholars feel this helps explain why kids who are abused grow up to be child abusers themselves. At-risk children, often starved for attention, are particularly susceptible to accept abuse as a reinforcer. Beyond this, the only time they get attention seems to be for anti-social behavior, including by the juvenile and criminal justice systems. The first time they get positive reinforcement often is from a gang or from the inmate subculture in a juvenile institution or prison.

How does one extinguish unacceptable behavior? One way is by ignoring it, usually accomplished by a "time-out"—removing the child from the "playing field" and eliminating his or her ability to seek and gain attention. This can be done in a number of ways, ranging from having youngsters sit in a corner for a few minutes to placing them in a closed room alone for a few minutes. Later, they can be praised for learning to become toilet-trained, walk, talk, master new words, read, excel in classes, play with friends without hitting, do things for others, accomplish new tasks, etc.

To be successful in shaping socially acceptable, law-abiding behavior, positive reinforcement must become a way of life for parents, teachers, and others. It is a philosophy of rearing children—your own and others as well—that must be taught and reinforced by parents and all members of the community to be most effective. Pats on the back, awards, and ceremonies to celebrate accomplishments are particularly effective in fostering pro-social behavior and giving the at-risk youth a stake in society, thus helping overcome lack of hope and lack of faith in the future.

EFFECTIVE PROGRAMS

Parent education. Teaching positive reinforcement and other skills to prospective parents has proven effective in reducing the at-risk population. In *Licensing Parents*, author Jack C. Westman wonders why it is "you need a license to drive a car or own a dog, but not to raise a child." Clearly, there are many concepts and skills that are necessary to nurture a child successfully from total dependence to independent living. Short of requiring a license, parent education can provide information and skills to evaluate clearly whether to have a child and, if so, how to learn and use good child-rearing practices. Such classes are offered in many school districts and, in some cases, through community centers and churches.

To be effective in reducing teenage parenting, these classes must reach children early—sixth grade or shortly thereafter. Many teenagers enrolled in programs that force them to carry a computerized crying and wetting doll around for a couple of weeks decide to postpone parenthood.

Healthy Start. Both the U.S. Department of Health and Human Services (DHHS) and the U.S. Department of Justice (DOJ) have Healthy Start programs. The DHHS's was designed to strengthen the maternal and infant care systems at the community level, while the DOJ's is part of the National Institute of Justice's research focus on family violence through investigation of interdisciplinary approaches involving children, their families, and their communities. Caseworkers in these programs aid families before the child's birth, striving to reduce stress and improve family functioning, foster parenting skills, enhance child health and development, and, ultimately, prevent abuse and neglect. A similar initiative, Healthy Families America, was launched in 1992 by the National Committee to Prevent Child Abuse to help establish home visitation programs, service networks, and funding opportunities so all new parents can receive necessary education and support.

Mentoring. A large majority of at-risk children have no stable male role model, as they are being raised by their mothers and/or other female relatives. Some have no available family and are bounced around among foster homes and institutions. The stable father figure is important both to male and female children, but particularly to young boys. Because of the macho culture where respect is gained by toughness and fearlessness, young males without family and material resources are particularly at risk of being "disrespected" by peers. Without guidance from mature males they respect, their response often is to adopt violent reaction to disrespectful and/or challenging rhetoric or actions by peers and others.

Positive male role models have proven to be possibly the most effective remedy to this at-risk situation. So convinced are the leaders in Kansas City, Mo., that they are on a quest to recruit, train, and assign 30,000 mentors—one for every at-risk child in the city. Other communities greatly have expanded existing mentoring programs, such as Big Brothers and Big Sisters.

Mentoring appears to be one of the few remedial programs that work and thus is a cornerstone in any at-risk project. To be successful, it takes thorough understanding and commitment from mentors, who must be willing to spend considerable time with youngsters and become involved—at least to the level of listening to and advising them concerning all aspects of life; encouraging and assisting them in social, moral, and intellectual development; and attending and applauding significant events in their lives. In return, patient mentors see the youth blossom, cast off pessimism, and flourish.

A word of warning: A disinterested or uncommitted mentor can do much harm to an at-risk young male, since inattention and/or broken promises can reaffirm his negative image of himself and the world, deepen his despair and hopelessness, and add to his frustration and anger.

Nonviolent conflict resolution. Handling disrespect or physical attack without violent retaliation has proven to be a difficult task for at-risk youth. Already burdened by anxiety and feelings of inferiority, the conditioning often is to react violently to "prove" his manhood (or her self-worth). Few at-risk youth have been exposed to views/skills to cope with adversity via rational dialogue and problem-solving behavior. Now, though, programs are appearing in schools and community centers in many locales to provide attitudes and skills necessary to resolve conflict nonviolently.

Models have been developed by the American Bar Association, the U.S. Department of Justice, and the Public Broadcasting System, as well as by educators. One of the best involves training school staff (from teachers to administrators, from custodians to bus drivers and cafeteria workers) in creative nonviolent conflict resolution methods. Older students are taught the methods in required classes, and they then teach younger students, taking advantage of peer pressure. For the very youngest—kindergarten and the lowest primary grade students—the nonviolent approach is integrated into all activities in all classes. For example, preschool and kindergarten children are taught, and the approach is followed, that there is to be "no hitting, no spanking, no slapping, no pushing" by children or adults. Seeing adults spank or shake children reinforces the legitimacy of violence to resolve conflict.

Community schools programs. Not all communities use their schools effectively in breaking the cycle of violence and frustration among at-risk youth. A Federal initiative—the Community Schools Program—has been effective in rallying the community around the school. Other examples of successful partnerships include:

- In Missouri, 6,000 volunteers keep 675 schools open for extra hours.
- Boys & Girls Clubs offer mentoring in New Jersey schools.
- In New York City, Safe Haven programs provide secure environments and positive after-school tutoring and enrichment programs.
- Year-round schools in many communities facilitate better learning—since students no longer have the entire summer to forget—and foster more opportunities for extracurricular programs, from tutoring and mentoring to family activities and counseling.

Character education in schools generally revolves around universally accepted values (e.g., love, truthfulness, fairness, tolerance, responsibility) that find little opposition based on differing political, social, and religious beliefs. Schools with large numbers of at-risk youth have reported pregnancy and dropout rates cut in half, along with reduced fights and suspensions, after character education took hold.

Youth service. Surveys by the Gallup Poll, Wirthlin Group, and others consistently find that 95% of teenagers believe it is important for adults and teens to get involved in local civic, charitable, cultural, environmental, and political activities. More than 75% of teens say they already are participating in some volunteer programs, such as working at soup kitchens for the poor, nursing homes for the elderly, or shelters for the homeless.

Programs such as Americorps, Job Corps, and Peace Corps provide young people with a chance to learn the joy of giving to others. At the same time, it gives them a stake in society by developing skills, discipline, and grants and loans to go to trade school or college. Many communities and even some states (Georgia, for instance) are developing youth-oriented community service programs of their own.

Community policing. Law enforcement programs increasingly are working in partnership with the community to identify crime-breeding problems and implement solutions. Many of the at-risk youths' difficulties thus become community issues and lend themselves to community solutions. Homelessness, poverty, lack of positive adult role models, and poor health care may lead to safe shelters, community assistance, mentors, and in-school or community clinics.

One of the best examples of this approach took place in Milton Keynes, England, which faced a rash of shoplifting, burglary, and store robberies. Rather than seek out, arrest, and prosecute the young offenders, Police Commander Caroline Nicholl instituted a series of conferences wherein police, merchants, and neighbors met with offenders and suspects to identify reasons for the youth crimes. As a result, Nicholl says, "We learned about child abuse, bullying, alcoholism, and many other problems, and the community set to work on these."

Restorative justice. Most at-risk youth encounter the justice system early in life. Where juvenile justice once focused on their *needs*, it now focuses on their *deeds* and a belief that someone—adult or child—has to pay for the offense.

Countering this trend is a restorative justice movement, which holds that the purpose of justice is to bring peace and harmony back to the community by restoring victim, community, and the offender to a symbiotic relationship. Often, restoring includes restitution, service, and reclamation. In the case of juvenile offenders, the youth usually makes restitution to the victim either by his or her own earnings or through closely monitored personal service (cutting the lawn, raking leaves, chopping wood, or making home repairs); several hours of service to the community; an apology to the victim; counseling; and preparing essays and/or school talks on the harm the offense does to society. Once the restitution is completed, the child's record is purged.

There are literally hundreds of these programs being tried in small and large communities across the nation and, indeed, worldwide.

A COMPREHENSIVE PLAN

The following plan represents a consensus from groups to whom I have given the same assignment over the past decade: "Develop a program to turn your community's youth into productive, happy, law-abiding adults." These groups have included students from high school to graduate school, practitioners from police to social service workers, and community leaders, all participating in brainstorming and planning sessions to alleviate the youth-at-risk problem. Here is a comprehensive 10-point plan based on my years of experience with these exercises:

1. Commit to positive reinforcement through community- and school-based parenting classes (mandatory in schools), ongoing media campaigns, and positive attention and recognition in all schools (preschool through high school) and community-based programs.

2. Promote nonviolent conflict resolution among peers through mandatory educational programs for students, parents, teachers, counselors, and administrators, as well as through media and community campaigns.

3. Encourage mentoring for all children. Civic, business, and community campaigns should recruit and train mentors, matching them by needs and temperament. Programs such as Big Brothers and Big Sisters should be expanded.

4. Establish community-school partnerships to offer before- and after-school tutoring. Enlist youths to perform services to the community to enhance their stake in society. Year-round programs are particularly important to provide children with safe havens and enrichment and remedial initiatives before and after school, as well as during vacation periods.

5. Develop community-oriented proactive policing programs that begin with a philosophy of prevention. Examples include midnight basketball leagues, police-youth athletic leagues, neighborhood housing project substations, and foot patrols. These all involve partnerships of police, parents, church, business, civic, and community organizations.

6. Initiate ethical and cultural awareness programs that build on partnerships among family, church, school, media, civic, business, and other community groups. These should emphasize finding common ground on basic values, such as respect, responsibility, and restraint.

7. Design youth opportunity programs to provide all youngsters with the chance to reach their potential, regardless of circumstances. They could be run through school, business, and community partnerships that provide in-school jobs and child care, career counseling and training, opportunity scholarships, and recognition for achievement.

8. Set up peer counseling hotlines to help youths to aid each other through the trying times of adolescence.

9. End child neglect and abuse via guaranteed health and child care through parent/school/church/business/government/community partnerships to provide an array of services—e.g., community and school health clinics for all; a home for every child; capable parent(s), whether biological or adoptive, for all

kids; nurturing child care; and mandatory parenting classes for all parents-to-be.

10. Establish proactive focus throughout the community, with all public and private organizations joining parents and neighbors in seeking to prevent social problems via early identification, appraisal, and remedy. When delinquency or crime does occur, youthful offenders should be handled under a restorative approach, recognizing that the offense touched victim, offender, families of each, and the community. Harm is to be ameliorated and restoration of the community is to be achieved via mediation-arbitration, restitution, service to victim and community, reclamation, and/or reconciliation.

Every community, state, and nation can develop programs guided by this model. The more comprehensive the program and the more dedicated the participants, the more likely it significantly will reduce or even eliminate the youth-

at-risk problem in the community (at whatever level). All plans, though, have to adopt certain guiding principles that must permeate the approach to have any real expectations of success.

First, remember all children want attention above everything. Thus, attention is a reinforcer of behavior and no attention is an extinguisher of it. Praising reinforces good behavior, and punishing bad behavior often reinforces it.

Second, instill optimism and faith in the future in all children, as that is a key to success. Pessimism and hopelessness not only will lead to more at-risk youth, but eventually to inability to sustain society itself.

Third, try to remember your own adolescence. The very nature of this traumatic period of every person's life is to challenge authority (including legal authority). Most youngsters drift through this troubled period and become basi-

cally law-abiding, mature adults *unless* they become labeled as delinquents/criminals/losers/incapable/etc. and then seek solace and acceptance with other social outcasts. No child successfully negotiates adolescence without firm, but tender, loving care and concern from attentive adults. Even then, many carry scars well into adulthood.

Fourth, consider how much harder this whole process of developing intellectually, socially, and morally and obtaining the adult mentoring and self-esteem necessary to move from childhood to adulthood is for the at-risk child. We must reach out and lend a hand to help this bundle of possibilities to have an opportunity to meet all the promise that lies in the world's most precious resource—its children.

Dr. Stephens, Associate Law and Justice Editor of USA Today, *is professor of criminal justice, University of South Carolina, Columbia.*

Index

Index

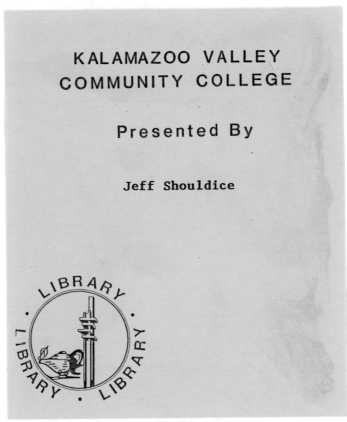

Test Your Knowledge Form

We encourage you to photocopy and use this page as a tool to assess how the articles in *Annual Editions* expand on the information in your textbook. By reflecting on the articles you will gain enhanced text information. You can also access this useful form on a product's book support Web site at *http://www.mhcls.com/online/*.

NAME:

DATE:

_____

TITLE AND NUMBER OF ARTICLE:

_____

BRIEFLY STATE THE MAIN IDEA OF THIS ARTICLE:

_____

LIST THREE IMPORTANT FACTS THAT THE AUTHOR USES TO SUPPORT THE MAIN IDEA:

_____

WHAT INFORMATION OR IDEAS DISCUSSED IN THIS ARTICLE ARE ALSO DISCUSSED IN YOUR TEXTBOOK OR OTHER READINGS THAT YOU HAVE DONE? LIST THE TEXTBOOK CHAPTERS AND PAGE NUMBERS:

_____

LIST ANY EXAMPLES OF BIAS OR FAULTY REASONING THAT YOU FOUND IN THE ARTICLE:

_____

LIST ANY NEW TERMS/CONCEPTS THAT WERE DISCUSSED IN THE ARTICLE, AND WRITE A SHORT DEFINITION:

We Want Your Advice

ANNUAL EDITIONS revisions depend on two major opinion sources: one is our Advisory Board, listed in the front of this volume, which works with us in scanning the thousands of articles published in the public press each year; the other is you—the person actually using the book. Please help us and the users of the next edition by completing the prepaid article rating form on this page and returning it to us. Thank you for your help!

ANNUAL EDITIONS: Juvenile Delinquency and Justice 06/07

ARTICLE RATING FORM

Here is an opportunity for you to have direct input into the next revision of this volume.
We would like you to rate each of the articles listed below, using the following scale:

1. **Excellent: should definitely be retained**
2. **Above average: should probably be retained**
3. **Below average: should probably be deleted**
4. **Poor: should definitely be deleted**

Your ratings will play a vital part in the next revision.
Please mail this prepaid form to us as soon as possible.
Thanks for your help!

RATING	ARTICLE
	1. Too Young to Die
	2. Juvenile Population Characteristics
	3. The Crackdown on Kids: The New Mood of Meanness toward Children—To Be Young Is to Be Suspect
	4. Juvenile Offenders: Should They Be Tried in Adult Courts?
	5. Juveniles as Victims
	6. The Coming Crime Wave Is Washed Up
	7. Kids Who Kill: A Conversation with John Dilulio
	8. Does Kindergarten Need Cops?
	9. Frustrated Officials Find Standard Answers Don't Suffice
	10. Early Violence Leaves Its Mark on the Brain
	11. What Makes Teens Tick
	12. Why the Young Kill
	13. From Adolescent Angst to Shooting Up Schools
	14. The Culture of Youth
	15. Preventing Crime, Saving Children: Sticking to the Basics
	16. Boys Will Be Boys
	17. Crimes by Girls Flying Off the Charts
	18. Girls Study Group Launches Web Site
	19. The Real Root Cause of Violent Crime: The Breakdown of the Family
	20. When Our Children Commit Violence
	21. The Children's Crusade
	22. The Victims of Victims
	23. An Epoch of Cheating
	24. The Trouble With Ecstasy
	25. A Sad Fact of Life: Gangs and Their Activities are Spreading into Small-Town America
	26. Criminal Behavior of Gang Members and At-Risk Youths
	27. Gang World
	28. Statistical Briefing Book
	29. Fighting Crime, One Kid at a Time
	30. Kids and Guns: From Playgrounds to Battlegrounds
	31. Juvenile Felony Defendants in Criminal Courts

RATING	ARTICLE
	32. Juvenile Delinquents in the Federal Criminal Justice System
	33. With Juvenile Courts in Chaos, Critics Propose Their Demise
	34. Juvenile Justice Comes of Age
	35. The Bastard Stepchild of *Parens Patriae*: The American Juvenile Incarceration Structure
	36. Quick Fix: Pushing a Medical Cure for Youth Violence
	37. Profits at a Juvenile Prison Come with a Chilling Cost
	38. Juvenile Boot Camps: Lessons Learned
	39. A Spotty Record of Health Care at Juvenile Sites in New York
	40. Life Sentences Without Parole Increasingly Imposed on Juveniles
	41. Crime and Punishment, Juvenile Division
	42. Comparative Criminology and Criminal Justice Research: The State of Our Knowledge
	43. Criminal Neglect
	44. Tokyo's Teen Tribes
	45. The National Juvenile Justice Action Plan: A Comprehensive Response to a Critical Challenge
	46. Breaking the Cycle of Juvenile Violence
	47. Understanding the Roots of Crime: The Project on Human Development in Chicago Neighborhoods
	48. Saving the Nation's Most Precious Resources: Our Children

(Continued on next page)

BUSINESS REPLY MAIL
FIRST CLASS MAIL PERMIT NO. 551 DUBUQUE IA

POSTAGE WILL BE PAID BY ADDRESEE

McGraw-Hill Contemporary Learning Series
2460 KERPER BLVD
DUBUQUE, IA 52001-9902

Iıludılılldlıdlıııılllldılılılulldıdıll

ABOUT YOU

Name

Date

Are you a teacher? ❐   A student? ❐
Your school's name

Department

Address   City   State   Zip

School telephone #

YOUR COMMENTS ARE IMPORTANT TO US!

Please fill in the following information:
For which course did you use this book?

Did you use a text with this ANNUAL EDITION? ❐ yes ❐ no
What was the title of the text?

What are your general reactions to the *Annual Editions* concept?

Have you read any pertinent articles recently that you think should be included in the next edition? Explain.

Are there any articles that you feel should be replaced in the next edition? Why?

Are there any World Wide Web sites that you feel should be included in the next edition? Please annotate.

May we contact you for editorial input? ❐ yes ❐ no
May we quote your comments? ❐ yes ❐ no